P.C.P. SERIES IN ACCOUNTING AN

Consulting Editor: Michael J. Sherer

The aim of this series is to publish lively and readable textbooks for university, polytechnic and professional students, and important, up-to-date reference books for researchers, managers and practising accountants. All the authors have been commissioned because of their specialist knowledge of their subjects and their established reputations as lecturers and researchers. All the major topics in accounting and finance will be included, and the series will give special emphasis to recent developments in the field and to issues of continuing debate and controversy.

COST AND MANAGEMENT ACCOUNTING

Alan Pizzey graduated from the London School of Economics as a B.Sc. (Econ.) and subsequently qualified as a certified accountant and as a chartered secretary. He is a member of the British Institute of Management. After experience as an industrial accountant, he became a teacher of accounting, first in the private sector with Foulks Lynch and then in the public sector at Middlesex Polytechnic. He was appointed a principal lecturer in accounting at Trent Polytechnic in 1972, and has taught a mixture of degree and professional students there, and also as a visiting lecturer at the University of Nottingham and Loughborough University of Technology.

Alan Pizzey has always maintained an interest in the professional accounting examinations. From 1969 to 1980 he was Scrutineer to the Association of Certified Accountants' examinations, and served on the Council of the Association from 1980-1983. From 1975 to 1985 he was an examiner for the Association of Accounting Technicians. Since 1986 he has acted as Vertical Moderator to the Chartered Institute of Management Accountants. This experience has enabled him to advise a number of colleges as chief external examiner, and to write articles for both accountants and students. He is the author of *Accounting and Finance–A Firm Foundation* (1979), *Financial Accounting Techniques – A Practical Approach* (1982), *Principles of Cost Accounting – A Managerial Perspective* (1986) and *The Regulatory Framework of Accounting* (1988).

COST AND MANAGEMENT ACCOUNTING

AN INTRODUCTION FOR STUDENTS

THIRD EDITION

ALAN PIZZEY

Nottingham Polytechnic

P·C·P
Paul Chapman
Publishing Ltd

This edition first published 1989
Paul Chapman Publishing Ltd
144 Liverpool Road
London
N1 1LA

British Library Cataloguing in Publication Data
Pizzey, Alan
    Cost & management accounting. – Rev. ed
    1. Cost accounting
    I. Title II. Pizzey, Alan. Costing
    657′ .42

ISBN 1—85396—049—7

Typeset by Burns & Smith, Derby
Printed in Great Britain by Athenaeum Press, Newcastle upon Tyne.

B C D E F 7 6 5 4

To all students starting their studies in management accounting

Contents

PART II   COST DETERMINATION

Series Editor's Foreword

Alan Pizzey's *Cost and Management Accounting* is the companion volume to the introductory financial accounting textbook written by Dick Edwards and Howard Mellett and published in the Accounting and Finance Series in 1989.

Alan Pizzey has brought his very considerable experience as a lecturer and writer to this introductory text on cost and management accounting. As a consequence, *Cost and Management Accounting* is a highly readable book which is suitable both for students on the first year of an accounting or business studies degree course and for students studying for professional accountancy and management examinations.

Cost and Management Accounting successfully combines a clear exposition of the different methods which are used for cost determination with a critical evaluation of the usefulness of cost allocations for managerial decisions.

Many of the conventions and assumptions of traditional cost accounting, for example the absorption of fixed overheads into product cost and the alternative ways of valuing work-in-process inventory in a process costing system, seem very strange to non-accountants. Alan Pizzey unravels the mysteries of cost accounting by discussing the rationale for these techniques and providing clear, step-by-step, illustrations of the methodology and calculations required.

In contrast, recent developments in management accounting have recognized the increasing importance of the appropriate cost and revenue information for effective managerial decision making. For example, the management accounting system needs to generate relevant costs, based on the economists's concept of opportunity costs, to evaluate which products or services should be provided and whether or not to sub-contract work currently undertaken by the organisation. Alan Pizzey demonstrates how different costs can be useful for different decisions and draws upon his industrial experience to provide helpful illustrations of how relevant costs can be used in practice.

Cost and Management Accounting has been designed as a complete textbook for students. Each chapter deals with a discrete topic, is clearly written and illustrated, and is accompanied by a set of multiple choice questions and practice exercises, the solutions to which can be found at the end of the book. For these reasons *Cost and Management Accounting* will prove very popular with students who want a thorough, and entertaining, introduction to the subject.

Michael Sherer

Preface

The purpose of the first edition of this book in 1979 was to introduce the subject of cost accounting to students. This purpose remains in the third edition, but has been refined in that a greater emphasis has been placed on the use of cost information by managers, and on the needs of students to pass the professional and other examinations. My intention is to help students to understand the principles of cost accounting and their application to management accounting, and to appreciate the significance of cost information. I hope that this book will enable students to develop their ability to focus on what is relevant, which will raise the standard of management information they produce in practice, and to improve their chances of success in the examination room.

The book is not designed just to cover the minimum requirements of one professional syllabus or another, but is intended for use on any course where cost accounting is introduced and developed into management accounting. The emphasis is on explanation, the development of arguments for and against certain methods, ample illustration and plenty of question and answer practice. Although there is no real substitute for the discussion produced by contact with a teacher, it is intended that students who do not have access to oral tuition will be able to use this book to advantage. At the same time I hope that teachers will feel able to guide their students through these exercises when practice in examination technique is required.

I am indebted to the Chartered Association of Certified Accountants and the Chartered Institute of Management Accountants for permission to use some of their recent examination questions as exercises. These appear at the end of most chapters. My solutions to these and other questions are set out at the end of the book. Students are urged to make a serious attempt to work through the exercises before studying the solutions, so that they reap the full benefits to be derived from question and answer practice. I am indebted to Norman Ellis, Bryan Abraham, and to Mike Sherer, for their helpful comments on the text at the production stage. Finally, my thanks are due to Barbara Pizzey, without whose encouragement and significant practical assistance this third edition might not have been produced.

PART 1

INTRODUCTION TO COST AND MANAGEMENT ACCOUNTING

1 Costs in the Management Accounting System

OBJECTIVE

The purpose of this chapter is to introduce management accounting by showing how cost information can be used by managers. Definitions of management accounting agree that it concerns the provision of information for management, but vary in the scope attributed to the subject. The Chartered Institute of Management Accountants definition cites financial accounting as a subsidiary activity of management accounting. The purpose of management information under this definition is to:
(a) assist in policy formulation;
(b) facilitate planning and control within the organization;
(c) improve decision-making between alternative courses of action;
(d) enable disclosure of financial details to shareholders, employees and others; and
(e) ensure the safeguarding of the assets of the organization.

Clearly (d) and (e) above might be construed as financial accounting and auditing. Note the use of the term 'organization' instead of business, because managers use these techniques, even though they work for non-profit-making bodies such as health authorities, local government and other organizations.

THE FUNCTIONS OF COST AND MANAGEMENT ACCOUNTING

The management accountant is a member of the team of executives who organize the operations of a business or a non-profit-making body. It is the accountant's responsibility to provide the team members with information which will help them in this task. The managers must plan future operations; communicate their plans to others; organize action; maintain control as the plan unfolds; analyse and evaluate the results; and act to remedy mistakes – all in order to maximize the profits made or the service supplied by the organization. At all these stages in management the accountant's expertise will help to improve performance. Management accountants do not take business decisions but the cost accounting statements they produce, and the advice they give based on these statements, assist decision-making, with benefit to the quality of the decisions made by the management team.

Cost accounting is the set of techniques whereby transactions are recorded, and costs are ascertained, classified and allocated to products or activities within the business. Thus the cost of various activities can be disclosed and set against revenue to measure profitability in detail. Costing is an analysis the management accountant uses to derive meaningful figures, which can be presented in a statement or report to managers. There is no clear dividing line between costing and management accounting, except that the term 'costing' tends to describe the systematic recording and ascertainment of amounts, whereas management accounting is taken to mean the use of the data for interpretation, or other management purposes. Cost is a measure of the resources used up to achieve a certain aim, and can be expressed as so much per unit of production or as the cost of operating a section of the business.

HOW COST INFORMATION IS USED BY MANAGERS

Cost information can be used in a variety of ways.

Planning or budgeting future operations

Before action can take place, managers must decide what they intend to do, and ensure that their intentions will benefit the organization and achieve its objectives. The business plan (corporate strategy) sets long-term objectives and suggests the means by which they are to be achieved in the light of available resources and expected market conditions. The long-term strategy is regularly reviewed. A short-term plan, a budget, decides in detail how the business will move towards its long-term goal during the forthcoming period, say a year. Profit is no longer the result of a happy accident or lucky circumstances, but is derived from carefully planned and executed activities. Management information is vital to the successful formulation of plans in the long and short term. Without accurate cost estimates a budget cannot be computed with any degree of confidence.

Controlling operations

Timely costing statements, at appropriate intervals as the budget plan unfolds, will inform management about the success or otherwise of their operations. A good manager will be able to see what is taking place in his or her part of the organization, but a costing statement confirms his or her observations and provides a monetary or quantitative measure of success or failure. Cost statements which compare cost incurred against planned cost expressed in the budget can reveal departments which are overspending or inefficient, and can quickly check on wastage of materials or labour. The manager will therefore feel more in control of the cost centre or department. Budgetary control provides a detailed plan for managers to follow, and checks their progress periodically by means of a variance statement. The provision of accurate cost data summarized as a cost per product will disclose the profitability of various products in the range. This facilitates the control of investment by indicating the return on capital employed of various activities, and suggesting areas for future investment.

A basis for estimating

If costs are analysed to show the expected cost of making a product, e.g. material used, labour time expended, and a proportion of the overhead expenses of the factory, the selling operation and the administrative departments, the information will form the basis for tendering and pricing. Accurate knowledge of likely costs combined with trustworthy records of the costs of past operations enable a company to decide with confidence on a quotation that will cover cost and lead to a profit. Conditions beyond the seller's control, e.g. supply and demand, often regulate prices, but a reliable estimate of cost will be helpful to show an amount below which price cannot be set.

Decision-making

All decisions have an effect on costs, and the management accountant must explain the cost effect of alternatives to managers charged with the duty of selecting the best course of action. Such decisions may be 'one-off', or part of the overall planning of the business. The cost accountant may need to produce data concerning a decision to make or buy out a component, to close a cost centre or extend a service. In such cases it is good practice to follow up the decision with a statement setting actual cost against estimate to check on the validity of the decision-making process.

THE PROPERTIES OF A GOOD COST STATEMENT

To be of use to management a cost statement must conform to certain principles.

Relevance

Only data which an executive needs to assist his or her function is really useful. All other managerial information supplied to that executive may be ignored and thus wasted. Irrelevant information may complicate the issues on which a decision is to be made, and lead to an incorrect decision. Some accountants believe that a cost statement submitted to a manager should concern only items controllable by that manager, and for which he or she is responsible.

Timeliness

Information supplied soon after the event will be of great assistance to a manager. As the time-lag increases between the end of a costing period, so the utility of that information is decreased. If there is delay between the time at which losses are made and organizing remedial action, costs will become out of control. Managers are by nature forward looking, thinking of the next set of transactions to be organized, so it is difficult for them to cast their minds back to a previous period if cost information is delayed.

Brevity

A good cost statement should be brief, and edited in such a way as to highlight significant factors, allowing busy managers to assimilate its contents as easily as possible. A page of complicated figures, which leaves a manager to draw his or her own conclusions, is not very helpful.

Simplicity

Complications in the system increase the cost of gathering information. There are bound to be complex matters in any organization, but they should be clearly explained in the statement.

Perspective

Cost data alone can be confusing unless set in perspective by the inclusion of other figures against which it can be compared. Such figures are called 'comparators'. If costs for this month are compared with costs for the same month last year, or costs expected when the activity was planned, the statement is better able to comment on the current situation. A cost stated as so much per unit of output, or as a percentage of the total cost, will often add dimension to otherwise lifeless figures. The management accountant can use statistical devices such as pie charts, graphs, means and standard deviation to drive home the message contained in the statement.

MANAGEMENT ACCOUNTING AND FINANCIAL ACCOUNTING – DIFFERENCES OF APPROACH

The financial accountant and the management accountant adopt different attitudes to their task. These attitudes are partly derived from the situation in which they work. Major differences concern the following matters.

Users

The management accountant produces statements tailored to fit the needs of particular managers within the business. The financial accountant produces accounts for publication outside the business and these are read by several groups of users from shareholders to creditors and from bankers to the Inland Revenue. In all but small businesses the owners and the managers will be different.

Statutory requirements

Financial accounts are drafted according to the disclosure regulations of the Companies Act 1985, and the rules of best accounting practice as set out in Statements of Standard Accounting Practice. This legal and regulatory framework states the minimum information which must be disclosed to the public, and the form in which disclosure is to be made. There is no set format for management accounts, the statement being drafted in a form designed to be most helpful to the recipient. Management information is not for public disclosure and is often confidential. However, accurate costs are needed to find the amount for materials, labour and overhead to be carried forward in the financial accounts as stock.

Period

Financial accounts usually report on past events; they look back on the previous financial year and are produced several months after the year-end. Management accounts must be produced promptly after the end of the period to be relevant, and often look forward as a forecast or budget to show what is planned to happen rather than what has happened. Financial accounts are tied to reporting the results of a year or half-year, but the period covered by a management statement is governed by the circumstances, e.g. a week or month etc.

Analysis

The management accountant analyses the performance of the business to show the contribution made by its constituent parts to the overall profit figure; reports are made in terms of departments or products. The financial accounts give an overview of the whole business – whether a single entity or a group of companies – which, although there are rules for segmental reporting and the disaggregation of total figures, fails to give an insight into the current performance of individual departments. A report of stewardship devised for the shareholders to show the profit and financial position does not help managers at all.

Techniques

The management accountant is not bound to use only financial accounting techniques when drafting statements. The logic of the economist, the method of the mathematician, the expertise of the marketing specialist and the theories of the behavioural scientist are all brought into play, when they can improve the information provided for management.

Audit

Because of the statutory requirements, the financial accounts must be audited, to ensure that they conform to the law and best accounting practice. There is no audit for management accounts, other than the checks and balances which the accountant builds into the system, and the professional appraisal made before statements are submitted to managers.

THE ADVANTAGES DERIVED FROM A MANAGEMENT ACCOUNTING SYSTEM

Once the costs incurred by an organization have been analysed, it is possible to demonstrate the relative profitability of various activities, so that the loss-making parts of the business are revealed and can be abandoned or improved. A formal analysis of costs and revenues will produce reliable figures, rather than estimates or suspicions, which are not a sure foundation on which to base decisions. If managers are able to see where funds are being spent, those areas within the organization where costs are excessive will be identified, so that appropriate action can be taken to control costs. If profit fluctuates up or down, a cost analysis will provide figures which a management accountant can use to show the reasons for the fluctuation. Once elements causing such fluctuations are isolated, action can be taken to mitigate the effects of loss-making items, and promote the effects of those factors which have improved profitability.

A costing system brings other benefits. If the costs of materials and wages are carefully recorded they will be easier to control, so that waste can be avoided. Early knowledge of an escalating cost will provoke speedy control action, but if management are ignorant of the fact that one particular cost is increasing, it may be months before remedial action is organized. A further benefit from a costing system is that the management accountant can use the figures for *ad hoc* cost statements which help the choice between alternative courses of action. In some industries there is an attempt at uniform costing, which is the classification of costs and their recording under common agreed cost headings. If many firms in an industry cost uniformly, an inter-firm comparison can be organized. Many companies operate what is called a standard costing system, where standards of performance are laid down, sometimes within the budgeting procedure, before the start of an accounting period and the actual costs are then compared with the standards to see whether a department has performed according to plan.

A cost analysis will break down the expenditure of the business into main and subheadings, so that management can be told exactly how the company's funds have been spent, and can also ascertain the ratio of each cost to total costs or to sales. A detailed knowledge of the costs involved to make a product, to provide a service or to undertake some operation within the firm's sphere of activity, can be used when standards are set. Standard costs are used to estimate a price for a job in answer to business inquiries, to plan out the costs of alternative courses of action when decisions are made, or to compare with actual costs to see if performance is up to standard. Cost information can be used to show the extent of the profit made in various sectors of the business, those parts of the business which are inefficient and wasteful, and the cost or profit consequences of certain planned actions. The very fact that overhead expenses are allocated to operations will highlight the amount of overhead not absorbed by activity because certain parts of the business are operating below planned capacity levels. Overhead expenses are charged out to production on the basis of rates computed at the bginning of the accounting year and based on expected levels of activity. If the actual level of activity is less than that planned, the overheads incurred will not all be charged out.

On a long-term contract adjustments may be agreed to allow for inflationary price levels. Accurate costing records will facilitate the formulation of a claim for such costs.

DISADVANTAGES OF MANAGEMENT ACCOUNTING

It is expensive to analyse accounting data, so cost statements should be regularly reviewed to see whether they are used by the executives who receive them, whether they can be improved, and whether their usefulness is worth the expense of their production. Some costing systems become far too complex, so that eventually executives in the business cannot understand the implications of the statements produced. In that case costing has defeated its own object, and tends to become a weapon used by those few managers who understand the system. Misuse of cost analysis in this way will lead other managers to be suspicious of cost statements, so that the task of the management accountant is made immeasurably more difficult as trust is diminished. A further disadvantage of costing is that the complication of the basic data often requires forms to be filled in and returns made. Employees producing the basic data may not fully appreciate how useful the information can be. The arbitrary nature of rules used in some costing systems reduces their usefulness when conditions change.

DESIGNING A COSTING SYSTEM

When a costing system is designed it must be made to fit the company concerned. The answers to certain basic questions will influence the system proposed.
1. *What information does management require, and at what level of detail is it needed?* Costing is expensive, and it would be wasteful to provide data which would not be used. Executives must be asked to identify information which they would find helpful rather than being presented with data which an outsider thinks they should have. A discussion may broaden their requirements, but it will also appraise the management accountant of their true needs. A regular check will establish that the information produced is being used. Unused cost statements should be discontinued if a process of redesign or management education fails to increase their utility.
2. *How often is the information required?* Cost statements may be needed daily, weekly, monthly, etc. according to the situation. The provision of

information costs money, so make sure the interval between statements is correct.

3. *How soon after the event is the information required?* If cost statements are delayed, the forward-thinking managers in a company will be less interested in them, but speed is expensive.

4. *How accurate should the information be?* Accuracy takes time, so tolerances must be agreed with users of costing information when the question of timing is discussed.

5. *Who needs the information?* Care must be taken not to spread confidential information to those who do not require it, and also not to supply more information to an executive than he or she needs since this will only waste time. Selecting relevant data and accentuating significant items are important.

A good costing system is simple to understand and cheap to operate. It should be designed to produce information in good time, so that it is of interest to the executive who receives it, and relevant to the operations within his or her span of control. The system should be capable of adaptation to meet changing circumstances. Systems analysts have been known to attempt to change the organization to fit the system that they have in mind.

MULTIPLE CHOICE QUESTIONS

1.1   Which of the following attributes are significant features for the design of a good cost statement?
   (a)   Relevance.
   (b)   Timeliness.
   (c)   Perspective.
   (d)   Monetary measurement.

(a)   (a + b)   (a + b + c)   (all)

1.2   Which of the following items does not cause a difference of approach between management accounting and financial accounting?
   (a)   Statutory requirements.
   (b)   Turnover.
   (c)   Audit.
   (d)   Period.

(a)   (b)   (c)   (d)

1.3   Which of the following statements is untrue?
   (a)   Cost accounting can be used to help managers to control business activity.
   (b)   Good tendering relies on accurate cost figures.
   (c)   Decisions are best made without the use of cost information.

    (d) A budget expresses what future costs are intended to be.

(a)   (b)   (c)   (d)

1.4 Cost accounting is a set of techniques whereby:
    (a) Transactions are recorded.
    (b) Costs are classified.
    (c) Capital expenditure is recognized.
    (d) Costs are allocated to products.
    Which statement is untrue?

(a)   (b)   (c)   (d)

EXERCISES

1A You have been appointed management accountant to a medium-sized company in the road transport business. The company operates from its depot in Nottingham, and owns thirty vehicles, twenty of which are large articulated general goods carriers. All maintenance work is undertaken at the depot, which also includes a sales and administrative office.

    How could your expertise as an accountant help to improve the efficiency of the business?

1B Contrast the accounting requirements for external and internal reporting, and outline the role of cost accounting in meeting these requirements.

                          (Association of Certified Accountants)

1C A manufacturing company has automated certain operations in its factory to replace expensive skilled labour. As a cost accountant what data would you analyse to control:
(a) operating costs;
(b) machine utilization; and
(c) to provide costs to assist in decision-making?

1D The Clifton Laundry uses a coal-fired boiler to generate steam used in the washing process. Last year the boiler house metered 60 million pounds of steam into the factory; 120 tonnes of coal were delivered each month at a cost of £60 per tonne. The boiler attendant is paid £130 per week, including three weeks' paid holiday per year when the plant is closed down. He is assisted by two casual labourers who each work twenty-five hours per week at an hourly rate of £3. Their job is to carry coal and ashes to and from the boiler house. The boiler is now five years old and is depreciated at 10 per cent a year on the straight line basis.

    The laundry manager is considering the suggestion that he should convert the boiler to an oil-fired operation. The coal staithes would be removed at a cost of £475, and in their place a storage tank would be installed at a cost of £3,500.

Modification and conversion work to the boiler would cost a further £3,825. The oil company representative has suggested a price of 50p per litre for oil, and has produced statistics of similar installations to show that a litre of oil can produce 10,000 British Thermal Units (BTUs), and that 1,000 pounds of steam is equivalent to 26,000 BTUs. He claims that the oil-fired system is automatic and needs no supervision.

Required

(a) Prepare a cost statement to assist the manager in making his decision.
(b) Comment on the maximum price that could be paid for oil so that it remained competitive with coal.
(c) Comment briefly on other matters that should be considered before the decision is taken.

This problem demonstrates that there is more to simple decision-making than just a comparison of costs.

2 The Elements of Cost Accounting

OBJECTIVE

The objective of this chapter is to explain how elemental costs are combined to compute prime and total costs. These elemental costs can be classified in several ways. This classification shows how cost data can be rearranged and used to focus attention on different aspects of the business, and leads to a discussion of the various bases and methods used in cost accounting.

Analysis to classes of cost is facilitated by cost coding.

COST UNITS AND COST CENTRES

A cost unit is that unit of output, service, or time, to which costs can be allocated and for which it is convenient to express a cost per unit, e.g. cost per kg, job, litre, kilowatt hour, per 1,000 bricks, per 1,000 lb of steam produced by a power house, per car assembled, per shirt laundered, or per kg/km operated in a transport business. The selection of the cost unit depends on what is appropriate to the business concerned.

A cost centre is any part of a firm to which it is convenient to group certain costs. It can be a location, function or item of equipment. Cost centre costs can then be charged or related to cost units as they pass through the cost centre. In a factory some cost centres will be directly concerned with production while others provide a service to production departments. Examples of cost centres in a factory are the assembly department, the painting department, the finishing department, the power house, the canteen, the toolroom. the stores, the cost office and the maintenance department. A cost centre is a focus of activity and as such it is convenient to ascertain costs for that activity and to allocate responsibility to an executive to operate it successfully.

PROFIT CENTRES

A profit centre represents a segment of the business to which separate activities can be analysed. It generates revenues and incurs costs and is a convenient business unit for the analysis of profit to various activities, with the responsibility for that profit assigned to a particular manager. A complex of machines may act as a cost centre, and in turn the factory departments in which the machines operate can also be cost centres, but the factory itself may be a profit centre, its manager being responsible for sales as well as production. Circumstances will determine whether the factory production is sold on the open market, or within the company at prices fixed by a central authority. Alternatively, a profit centre may be a single product or marketing area, rather than a factory, but the activity of the business can be divided up between profit centres, and the expected profit planned and controlled on that basis with the centre managers.

A further concept is that of the investment centre, where revenue and expense are analysed to profit centres and then related to the funds invested in the centre. The idea is that if a manager is in charge of a machine complex in which several million pounds have been invested, he or she should be responsible for the return on capital employed under his or her control.

THE BUILD-UP TO TOTAL COST

The major costs of manufacturing a product are those costs of the raw materials and the direct labour used in production. The total of these costs is termed 'prime cost', the amount of direct cost incurred. There are also very significant indirect costs, or overheads. Production (or factory) overhead costs include all the expenses of running the factory (rent, heat, light, insurance, depreciation etc.) and the cost of providing the services without which production could not take place (buying, storing, maintenance, and power if the company generates its own). Indirect labour is usually an important production overhead expense.

Other indirect expenses relate to selling and distribution, research and development, and administration.

The prime cost of each unit produced, plus an appropriate share of the factory overheads, gives total unit cost of production. This is called the 'fully absorbed cost' because the factory overheads have been absorbed into the total cost of production. The other indirect expenses are usually charged to the profit and loss account for the year.

Example 2.1: Cost statement

An example of a cost statement showing the result of the operations of Cimmico Compounds plc, a manufacturer of an industrial scaling compound, is set out in Figure 2.1. The cost unit is a litre drum of the finished product.

If more than one material is used in the process, or if the manufacture can be divided into several operations, further analysis might be worthwhile. A

Cimmico Compounds plc		Operating statement period .... (4 weeks ending ....)				
Standard cost	% to total	Current Period Production – Budget: 6,000 litres – Actual: 7,000 litres			% to total	Cumulative this year Budget: 30,000 litres Actual: 37,000 litres
Per unit £			Total £	Per unit £		Total Per unit £ £
		Production costs				
2.60	31.9	Direct material	18,900	2.70	31.9	
1.70	20.8	Direct labour	12,600	1.80	21.3	
4.30	52.7	Prime cost	31,500	4.50	53.2	
2.10	25.7	Factory overhead	15,400	2.20	25.9	
6.40	78.4		46,900	6.70	79.1	
		Non-production costs				
0.48	5.9	Selling	2,800	0.40	4.7	
0.18	2.2	Distribution	1,190	0.17	2.0	
1.10	13.5	Administration	8,400	1.20	14.2	
8.16 9.50	100.00	Total cost Sales revenue	59,290 70,000	8.47 10.00	100.00	
1.34		Net profit	10,710	1.53		
Circulation				Date prepared		

Notes
1. Alternatively, cost classifications can be percentaged to sales.
2. Cumulative figures for the same five months last year would provide a useful comparator.

Figure 2.1   Cost statement

reconciliation of actual profit to budgeted profit would lead to an investigation of important differences.

Note that the statement in Figure 2.1 shows budgeted or standard figures and permits a comparison of actual current and cumulative performance with the plan in terms of both cost and quantity. Costs are also expressed in total and per unit. Costs have been classified according to the purpose for which they are incurred, e.g. producing, selling, distributing etc. If Cimmico Compounds plc made more than one product, the cost analysis would separate the costs of those products to enable a separate statement to be computed for each.

Example 2.2: Costs used in estimating

Jobbing Engineering plc has been asked to quote for three different jobs, using bought-in components and raw materials which are manufactured in the machining assembly and finishing departments of the factory. Each factory department has its own overhead cost absorption system.

The form in which the quotation is compiled from costing data might be as shown in Figure 2.2. The quotation reflects the cost structure of the jobs (materials, labour and overheads) and analyses these costs to the departments which contribute to the jobs. A quoted price should cover unit cost, but cost is only one factor in the complicated pricing decision.

Job number	158		159		160	
	£	£	£	£	£	£
Materials ex stores	51.00		175.00		275.00	
Bought-in components	47.00	98.00	61.00	236.00	26.00	301.00
Direct labour:						
Machining	38.00		–		41.00	
Assembly	29.00		107.50		13.90	
Finishing	17.00	84.00	51.80	159.30	6.20	61.10
Prime cost		182.00		395.30		362.10
Factory overhead:						
Machine shop	19.10		–		8.40	
Assembly dept	26.30		46.80		11.20	
Finishing dept	8.60	54.00	21.90	68.70	5.30	24.90
Factory cost per unit		236.00		464.00		387.00
Selling and administration						
costs		59.00		116.00		96.75
Total cost		295.00		580.00		483.75
Profit margin						
(12.5% on price)		42.14		82.86		69.11
Price		337.14		662.86		552.86
Price to be quoted		£338.00		£663.00		£553.00

Notes
1. An amount of 25% of factory cost is added to cover selling and administration costs.
2. A profit margin of 12.5% of selling price (one-eighth) is added to total cost to complete the quotation. Therefore total cost is 87.5% of selling price, and once cost is computed the selling price can be calculated as:

$$\frac{100}{87.5} \times \text{Cost} = \text{Selling price}$$

$$\frac{100}{87.5} \times £295 = £337.14$$

Figure 2.2   Example of a quotation

COST CLASSIFICATION

The first step in analysing cost information is to group costs into similar classifications. There are, however, several different ways of classifying costs, which enable analysis to proceed in various directions. Costs can be classified having regard to their nature or the purpose for which the analysis is being undertaken: as to period; function; product; behaviour (fixed or variable); relation to the product (direct or indirect); controllability; or normality.

Function

Costs can be classified as production costs (further classified as materials, labour, factory overheads), or selling costs, distribution costs, or costs derived from the research and development or the administration of the business. The Cimmico Compounds cost statement in Figure 2.1 is an example of this classification.

Such an analysis can reveal the relationship of each function to total cost, perhaps expressed as a percentage. A variation of function analysis is to classify costs to a particular department, either within the factory, as in the quotation example in Figure 2.2, or within other functions such as administration. Thus a cost can be identified for certain activities such as buying, group property administration, pension fund organization, and cost accounting itself.

Behaviour

Costs can be classified as fixed or variable according to how they behave when circumstances change. Some costs are fixed by their very nature and do not fluctuate as the level of activity changes within the business. Such costs are fixed only in the short run, and will be expected to change eventually, e.g. rent is fixed for a year or more by the terms of the lease but may increase when the lease is reviewed, and if an expanding business acquires additional premises, then again rent will increase.

Other costs are variable by nature, changing in proportion to changes in activity. Take direct materials, for example; if no products are made the cost will be nil, if 10,000 are made the cost will be 10,000 times the unit cost. Some costs are by their nature partly fixed and partly variable, and are called 'semi-variable costs', e.g. a telephone expense will include a fixed standing charge (say £200 per quarter) and a variable cost per call unit made (say two pence per minute). Some semi-variable costs increase by a stepped progression, e.g. supervision where one supervisor (costing say £16,000 p.a.) can organize, say, up to twelve operatives but, beyond that number, a second supervisor will be needed. Cost will therefore step up to £32,000 at this point, but will remain at £32,000 until further expansion necessitates the employment of a third supervisor.

Variable costs per unit may not change but the total variable cost fluctuates with activity. Fixed costs may not change but as production volume increases the cost per unit will fall as overheads are spread over more production.

In Example 2.1 above, direct materials cost £2.70 per unit so 7,000 units will cost £18,900, but 10,000 units will cost £27,000. If the administration costs of £8,400 are fixed, the unit cost is £1,20 if 7,000 units are made, but falls to 84p if 10,000 units are made. It is often difficult to recognize or identify fixed, variable, and semi-variable costs, especially since the behaviour of costs is not stable, and a fixed cost in one situation may behave as a variable cost in other circumstances.

Period and product

It is appropriate to write off some costs to the costing period during which they are incurred, e.g. the month of May, whereas under the matching or accrual concept, some costs are carried forward to a later period. Costs included in the valuation of stock or work-in-progress are transferred from one period to another. The concept of depreciation spreads the capital cost of an asset over the period of its useful economic life. Period costs usually include the costs of administration, selling, distribution and research undertaken during the period, and are charged accordingly.

In Example 2.1 above, the administration overheads of £8,400 are charged against sales for period 5 (Figure 2.1). In that example all production is sold, but if 1,000 units produced during period 5 had not been sold, the manufacturing cost of those units (direct material plus labour plus factory overhead at £6.70 per unit), £6,700, would be carried forward to period 6 when they would be sold.

Product costs such as labour, materials and factory overheads can be classified to items produced showing cost per unit, and where necessary carried forward in the volume of stocks. Such a classification is also useful in profit measurement where cost can be set against revenue.

Relation to the product

This classification divides cost into direct and indirect groups. A direct cost is directly related to a product; in Example 2.1 direct materials of £2.70 per unit and direct labour, which is the cost of paying the employees who work on the manufacturing process, of £1.80 per unit. Indirect costs are not directly related to production units, although without such expenditure the production processes would not function, e.g. factory overhead expenses such as indirect labour, which classification covers all factory workers not employed on the production processes, such as storekeepers, cost clerks, chargehands, labourers etc.

Indirect labour often costs more in total than direct labour, because so many workers are in this classification. In the example the factory overhead costs averages £2.20 per unit. In some businesses certain departments, e.g. assembly, painting, finishing, are seen as direct cost departments because units of production flow through them, whereas other departments, e.g. maintenance, power house, canteen etc., are seen as indirect cost centres because they provide 'back-up' service to production processes.

Controllability

Some costs are controlled by managers, in that the cost can be influenced by the person in control of the cost centre. Other costs are said to be non-controllable, because they can be made to fluctuate by factors outside the business. A manager's span of control may limit his or her ability to influence a cost which is nevertheless significant for the department. An executive should not be held responsible for costs which are beyond his or her control. The rent of a factory workshop may be a proportion of total factory rent under a lease negotiated by the company secretary five years previously: the workshop manager cannot influence the total rent, or the share apportioned to him or her, and cannot therefore be held responsible for it. The manager must of course be informed of the amount of rent; it forms part of the departmental overhead and must be covered by revenue-earning activities if a profit is to be made.

It is not always possible to determine which manager is in control of a certain cost; for example, if poor quality material is purchased the responsiblity rests with the buyer, but the material may cause excessive scrap in the factory, for which the production manager is held to account. The term 'controllable' or 'managed' cost is sometimes used. 'Discretionary costs' or 'policy costs' are directly linked to a management decision, to spend a certain amount on one activity within the business, e.g. advertising or research.

Normality

Costs may be classified as to what is expected (a normal cost level) and abnormal costs, which differ from the costs planned for in the budget. The chapters on budgetary control and standard costing will show how variances from expected cost levels are highlighted, to identify abnormal costs and trigger an investigation which may lead to remedial action. In Example 2.1 the costs which were estimated to be incurred are shown for comparison with the actual costs incurred.

Relevance

When a decision is taken it is necessary to consider that decision in the light of 'relevant costs', i.e. those costs which will change as a result of the decision. Non-relevant costs are fixed in the context of the decision, and are sometimes called 'sunk' or 'committed' costs because expenditure has taken place before the decision point and cannot be changed as the result of the decision. Thus variable costs are significant for decision-making, but it is also important to realize that costs may behave abnormally as circumstances change. The rent of a shop is a fixed cost of say, £25,000 per annum under the lease, until closure of the shop is considered. If the lease is sold the cost is no longer incurred. This is sometimes called an 'avoidable cost' because it would be avoided if that activity or sector of the business did not exist.

'Opportunity cost' is relevant in decision-making. When selecting the most profitable alternative, a manager must bear in mind the benefits forgone by not pursuing rejected alternative courses. A certain path is chosen because it will lead to greater benefits than those to be derived from alternative opportunities; the benefit of opportunities forgone is opportunity cost.

For example, if a manager decides to process scrap material at a cost of £5 per kg, to sell it later for £10 per kg, part of the cost of this operation would be the revenue lost because the scrap material is no longer sold at £1 per kg.

COSTING BASES – ABSORPTION, DIRECT AND STANDARD

The basis on which costs are computed and expressed is a matter of concept. The full absorption costing method holds that the cost accounts should show the full cost of producing the cost units, i.e. direct costs such as material and direct labour, known as prime cost, should be combined with a share of the indirect cost or production overhead. These indirect costs are charged to cost units by various methods which absorb the costs to production. Part of the production overhead is thus carried forward into the next period, in the cost of work-in-progress and finished goods stock. On this basis cost is related to production and the principal of accrual and matching is significant in the measurement of profit, i.e. the full absorbed cost of units sold is set against sales revenue.

In Example 2.1 above, direct material at £2.70 and direct labour at £1.80 per unit comprise the prime cost of £4.50, and 7,000 units (litres) cost £31,500 to make. The indirect cost of factory fixed overheads of £15,400 is divided by the 7,000 units produced, to give a unit cost of £2.20; therefore the full absorbed cost of production would amount to £6.70 for each unit. If sales amount to 6,000 units, but 7,000 units are produced, the 1,000 units of closing stock would be carried forward into the next period at a cost of £6.70 each. This figure includes £2.20 of production overhead for each unit so 1,000 × £2.20, or £2,200, of this overhead is carried forward to the next period to charge against sales revenue when the 1,000 units are sold. It would be wrong to include the costs of selling and distribution as part of the cost of unsold units, therefore these costs are treated as period costs and charged against sales revenue for the period in which they are incurred. The administration costs are also treated as period costs.

The alternative concept is that of marginal or direct costing, which holds that unit costs should be computed only for direct costs. Marginal or direct cost should be used for stock valuation purposes, and fixed costs (overheads) should be written off against profit for the period in which they are incurred. In the Cimmico example above, the marginal cost of production is prime cost of £4.50, and unsold stocks are carried forward at this unit cost. 1,000 units of stock at £4.50 would be £4,500, as opposed to £6,700 under the full absorption system. The difference is the £2,200 of production overhead.

A third basis of cost accounting is standard costing, which holds that preset standards should be used to cost resources used up when profit is measured, and that any variances between actual cost and standard should be identified for management and then charged against profit for the period. Standard costing can be used on a full absorption or marginal basis.

In Example 2.1 the fully absorbed standard cost of production is £6.40 per unit, so the standard cost of producing 7,000 units (£44,800) would be set against the actual cost of £46,900, and the difference, or variance, of £2,100 would be charged to period 5. Any unsold units would be carried forward as stock at a standard cost of £6.40 each.

Standard marginal costing would use £4.30 (£2.60 + £1.70) as the standard to set against the actual direct cost of £4.50 (£2.70 + £1.80). The factory overhead costs of £15,400 would be charged against profit in period 5.

COSTING METHODS - HOMOGENEOUS UNITS OR SPECIFIC ORDERS

Once cost data has been gathered and recorded, it must be expressed in a cost statement. The method used depends upon the circumstances of the business. If the product is mass produced and of an homogeneous nature, some form of unit costing would seem appropriate. Cost could be expressed per 1,000 units of output (say, bricks) or production could be divided into batches to facilitate cost accounting. If many similar units go through a series of processes, process costs can be expressed for the throughput of each process cost centre. In a jam factory fruit is heated, mixed with sugar, cooled, mixed with pectin, packed into jars, then labelled – six processes in all. Batch costing can be applied for jams of different flavours. When the product is not a physical unit but a unit of service, the method can be adjusted to measure costs in this way.

Not all production concerns large volumes of similar items. In some businesses each job is seen as an individual item, and thus costs are accumulated to the job, e.g. large pieces of machinery or switchgear built in a workshop or a casting forged to individual requirements. Job costing (or specific order costing) maintains a cost statement for each job, and can even be used to treat a batch of similar jobs as a cost centre. A particular form of job costing is found in the civil engineering or construction industry, where each contract or building site is treated as a separate cost centre.

Figure 2.3 shows the various costing bases and methods described above in diagrammatic form.

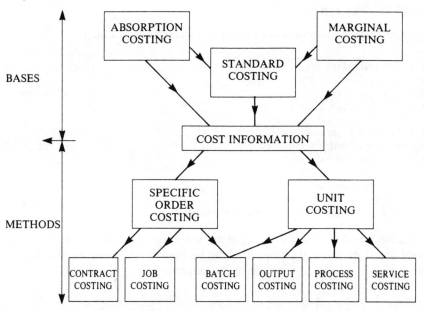

Bases are the principles or concepts which guide the treatment of cost data. *Methods* are the techniques whereby the data is used.

Note: Cost data can be produced by the full absorption costing assumption or by the adoption of the marginal costing concept. Both bases can be with or without standard costing. A batch can be produced as part of a continuous operation to provide a batch of units or in response to an order for a batch of products.

Figure 2.3   Cost data: bases and methods

COST CODING

A cost code is a set of symbols designed to be applied to classified costs, thus making it easier to identify and group them, enter them into the cost accounting system, and then to analyse them. A code avoids the ambiguity which can arise from using descriptions; it is a fast and easy means to recognize like items, and reduces the cost of entering and storing data in a computer system, by minimizing the digits to be stored in the system.

A good code should be brief, but understandable, unambiguous and comprehensive in that it covers the full range of cost data while leaving room for the introduction of new cost headings. A code which is numeric only may be difficult for personnel to assimilate, thus a letter code is often used in conjunction with numbers in order to remind personnel of the name of the item.

Example 2.3: Cost coding in the contracting industry

This is the cost code of the UK companies of a large civil engineering group. It gives a realistic impression of the extent to which costs need to be analysed in a complex business situation.

Financial coding UK companies

This is a four-digit code indicating classes of expenditure as under:

```
1000 = Job cost–Materials
2000 = Job cost–Subcontract
3000 = Job cost–Wages                                    Direct costs
4000 = Job cost–Plant running costs

5000 = Job cost–Plant overheads
6000 = Job cost–NMP (Non-mechanical plant)               Indirect costs
7000 = Job cost–Site overheads

8000 = Trading Expenses
9000 = HO Expenses–Revenue accounts                      Nominal ledger
       Assets and liabilities in alphabetical order
```

On main codes 8 and 9 the last three digits are sub-codes. On main codes 1–7 only the second and third digits are sub-codes with the fourth digit reserved to indicate that additional processing is required by the computer.

```
0 = Normal and insignificant
3 = Required for insurance returns (wages and salaries etc.)
```

Materials alone are analysed under 50 subheadings, as is shown by the coding sheets below. Note the gaps in the progression of the second and third digits to allow for the insertion of new materials. In this company each site or contract is also coded to facilitate contract cost analysis. The contract code is numeric and alphabetic to assist staff in their use of the code, e.g. 3592/Dorking.

Cost coding instruction sheet

Computer code	Short title	Unit of quantity	Examples and remarks
Class 1 Material			
1010	Cement	Tonnes	All Portland and Rapid Hardening Cement
1020	Cement SR	Tonnes	Sulphate Resisting, Aluminous and other special cements
1030	Fine Aggte	cu m/tonnes or yds/tons	Sharp sand, washed sand chippings 5 mm (3/16″) down to dust
1040	Coarse Aggte	cu m/tonnes or yds/tons	All in ballast, stone 5 mm (3/16″) up to 40 mm (1½″)
1060	R.M. Concrete	cu m	Ready Mixed Concrete
1070	Precast Concrete	–	Kerbs, paving slabs, lintels, cills, floor beams, Portland and special stone for masons, granite set, walling stone, Finlock gutters, Mono supplies, concrete sleepers and slate cills (*except pipes Code 1160 and concrete blocks – Code 1250*)
1080	Concrete Sundries	–	Concreting paper, hessian, straw, hardeners, water proofers, anti-freeze compounds, Evoset, Tricosal, Febspeed, Tretol and other additives, mould oil foamed slag, vermiculite, bolt boxes. Plastering material if cost code applicable, see also 1210
1090	Expansion Joint	–	Expansion jointing, Flexcell, water stops etc.
1100	Hardfill	cu m/tonnes	Hardcore, rubble and large stone 50 mm (2″) up. Clinker Fly ash, ashes slag etc.- Code 1240 for special fillings.
1110	Mild Steel Rod	Tons/tonnes	All M.S. rod, bars etc. 6 mm (¼″) up including binding wire, binding and cutting cost.
1120	Reinforce Fab.	Sq metres	BRC fabric, welded rod and wire expamet weldmesh, Hyrib etc.
1130	Prestress Matl.	–	H.T. wire, anchors, jacks, tubes, sheaths and prestress materials generally.
1140	Steel Piles	Tons/tonnes	Steel piling forming part of the permanent works—see 6140 for temporary piling.
1160	Non Metal Pipes and fittings	–	Plastics, salt glazed pipes and conduit, asbestos, land drains, pipes and channels.

Cost coding instruction sheet (continued)

Computer code	Short title	Unit of quantity	Examples and remarks
Class 1 Material			
1170	Struct Steel	–	All structural steel forming part of the permanent works such as RSJs. Fabricated steel, tunnel rings, gantries, cat ladders, checker plate and sundry ductwork. Metal doors and windows.
1180	Iron castings	–	All iron castings, manhole cover, cast iron gates etc.
1190	Pipes & Fittings–metal	–	All types of basic or pre-fabricated pipes and fittings not specifically included in codes 1540, 1560 or 1590.
1200	Bricks	Thousands	Commons, facings, engineering, specials etc.
1210	Brick Sundries	–	Hollow clay pots Floor tiles, wall tiles, air bricks, dampcourse, wall ties, lime, bricktor, exmet. Roofing material if permanent. Plastering material if cost code applied–see also 1080. See 1250 for breeze and concrete blocks.
1220	Fixing Sundries	–	Rawlties, clamps, brackets, bolts, rivets, nails, screws, glue, inserts.
1230	N. Ferrous Metals	–	Brass strips, aluminium windows, mouldings etc.
1240	Filling special	cu m/tonnes or yds/tons	Special fillings on large contracts not covered by code 1100.

MULTIPLE CHOICE QUESTIONS

2.1 Which of the following costs cannot be classified as functional costs?
   (a) Sellings costs.
   (b) Administration costs.
   (c) Production costs.
   (d) Indirect costs.

(a)   (b)   (c)   (d)

2.2 Which of the following costs can be classified as an indirect cost?
   (a) Supervisor's salary.
   (b) Machine maintenance.
   (c) Factory rent.
   (d) Assembly labour cost.

(a)   (a + b)   (a + b + c)   (all)

2.3 Costs which do not fluctuate as the level of activity changes within the business are:
(a) Stepped costs.
(b) Fixed costs.
(c) Relevant costs.
(d) Opportunity costs.

(a)   (b)   (c)   (d)

2.4 The advantages of cost coding do not include:
(a) Relates cost to units produced.
(b) Avoids ambiguity.
(c) Aids data processing.
(d) Reduces data storage.

(a)   (b)   (c)   (d)

2.5 Which of the following costs are not included in the cost of work-in-progress under full absorption costing?
(a) Indirect labour.
(b) Factory overheads
(c) Distribution costs.
(d) Indirect materials.

(a)   (b)   (c)   (d)

EXERCISES

2A (a) Define the terms 'cost centre' and 'cost unit'.
(b) Distinguish between direct and indirect costs, and discuss the factors which should influence whether a particular cost is treated as direct or indirect in relation to a cost unit.

(Association of Certified Accountants)

2B Cost classifications used in costing include:
(i) Period costs.
(ii) Product costs.
(iii) Variable costs.
(iv) Opportunity costs.

Required

Explain each of these classifications with examples of the type of costs that may be included.

(Association of Certified Accountants)

2C   **You are required to**
   (i)   Explain the terms 'cost centre' and 'cost unit'.
   (ii) Suggest suitable cost units which may be used to aid control within the following organizations:
      (1)   a hospital;
      (2)   a road haulage business;
      (3)   a hotel with 40 double rooms and 5 single rooms;
      (4)   public transport authority.

(Chartered Institute of Management Accountants)

PART II

COST DETERMINATION

3 The Costing Treatment of Materials – Material Control

OBJECTIVE

The objective of this chapter is to explain the system by which the cost of materials is recorded. The provision of materials can be seen as a cycle of events:
1. Recognition that stocks are running low and a requisition from stores or the user department requesting the purchasing department to purchase materials.
2. Calculation of the economic order quantity and placing an order.
3. Receipt of the goods and their inspection on arrival.
4. Entry of the material into the stores, and recording it in the stock records.
5. Issuing material to production, and calculating an appropriate cost to charge to the manufacturing process.

Control can be maintained only if an optimum stock level is recognized and if purchasing is organized to buy the economic order quantity. Stock turnover figures also provide control information.

MATERIAL CONTROL

Control of materials is derived from the provision of adequate information about their ordering, receipt, storage and usage. The routines for buying and storing raw materials are designed to minimize theft and wastage and to ensure that adequate stocks are available for production when required. A secondary purpose of the control system is to provide information to assist managers in deciding how much material to store or to buy. Efficient material control implies a system where authorization to purchase is limited to buying materials of appropriate quality, in quantities and at times when their purchase makes the best use of the resources of the business. The system includes the selection of suppliers, the buying department using its experience to ensure appropriate quality and prompt delivery; the system should also ensure that materials entering the factory are properly inspected and that documents recording their arrival and dispatch to the stores are created. Further control of materials is derived from documenting and properly recording quantities entering the stores, held in the stores, and charged out from the stores to production processes. Accurate stocktaking at the end of an accounting period is another feature of materials control.

The prime objective of the whole system is to provide the right material of the right quality and quantity, at the right time for the production processes.

IMPORTANT DOCUMENTS IN THE MATERIALS CONTROL SYSTEM

Materials requisition

When a production department draws materials from the stores it raises a requisition, which is an order on the stores for the material required. The requisition will contain an accurate description of the materials with quantities, dates required, and other special information. A responsible official must sign the requisition to authorize materials to be withdrawn from the stores.

Figure 3.1 gives an example of a materials requisition.

From: Assembly department			To: Raw materials stores
Date:			
Please supply	Item	Quantity	Description
Date required:			
Authorized by:			
....			
Job number:...........................		Serial number:	

Figure 3.1   Materials requisition

Stores ledger card

A separate record is maintained for each type of material stored, sometimes on a stock record card or stores ledger card, and sometimes in the form of computer tape. This record shows details of movements in and out of the stores for the particular raw material, and is rather like a ledger account for the item of stock. The materials requisition acts as a voucher to show the quantity of material which must be credited to the stores ledger card when materials leave the stores. The value of these materials depends on the cost flow assumption and the valuation method adopted by the company as a matter of accounting policy. The debit side of the stores ledger card is written up from the goods received note, which evidences the arrival of materials from suppliers.

It is only too easy to make mistakes on a stores ledger card so it is wise to make a physical check of the quantities in the stores from time to time. Such a check will ensure that the balances on the stock record cards are correct.

Purchase requisition

This document is raised by the storekeeper to request the purchasing department to replenish the stocks of material. A precise definition and details of quantity, quality, delivery date, and address are essential on this record. It must be authorized in accordance with the organization's policy to guard against goods being ordered which are not required by the business.

Figure 3.2 shows a form of purchase requisition.

1 Purchasing dept copy	PURCHASE REQUISITION	No: .... Date: ....
Please purchase for	dept or	stores
Item	Quantity	Description	Charge to: Cost code:

Catalogue number:

Special instructions:

Required by:

Purchasing department:
Order number:
Supplier:
Delivery date:

Delivery address:

Authorized by: ....

Figure 3.2   Purchase requisition

Purchase order

When the purchase requisition reaches the purchasing department, the buyer will contact suppliers, and ensure that the order is for goods with the correct description, delivery date, and delivery address, and at the best possible price. It is important that only the buyers are authorized to order goods, to avoid managers with little buying expertise committing the company, or unauthorized persons buying what they require at the company's expense. All orders must therefore go through the purchasing department to ensure that goods are not ordered twice, and to enable small orders to be grouped together to obtain a better price.

Figure 3.3 shows a form of purchase order.

Goods received note

Deliveries of materials at the factory should be inspected against the order, to ensure that the quantity and quality are correct. Once this inspection is successfully completed a goods received note is raised, detailing the quantity and

1 Supplier's copy	CLIFTON CASTORS plc		OFFICIAL ORDER

To:

Serial number:
Date:

Please supply:

Quantity	Cost code	Description	Price: Unit:
			Total:
		Catalogue number:	

Delivery address:

Delivery date: Special conditions:	Authorization: .... *signed* Purchasing officer

Figure 3.3   Purchase order

quality of goods, which are then transferred into the stores.

Discrepancy note or inspection note

If goods delivered are found on inspection to be inadequate in any way the checker raises a discrepancy note, which is sent to the supplier and copied to the purchasing and accounts departments.

Materials returned note

If materials issued from the store are found to be of doubtful quality or if they are surplus to the requirements of a job, they are returned to the stores with a materials returned note as evidence of this movement of materials about the factory. Likewise a materials transfer note records the transfer of material from one job to another.

THE MULTI-COPY SYSTEM

A good system is adequately documented. Thus it is necessary to raise several copies of each of the documents outlined above. A materials requisition from a production department to the stores will be raised in duplicate at least so that a copy stays with the requisitioning department while the top copy goes to the stores. With a purchase requisition the storekeeper will keep a copy as a record of what has been requested of the purchasing department. When an order is placed the original is sent to the supplier but the purchasing department will retain a copy and supply copies to the stores to show that their requisition has been attended to, and to the accounts department to check against the supplier's invoice. Several copies of the goods received note are necessary: as a record of deliveries; to notify the purchasing department that orders placed have been completed; and to the accounts department so that order, invoice and goods received note can be matched before payment is made.

Figure 3.4 shows diagrammatically the documentation involved in the ordering and storage of and payment for materials.

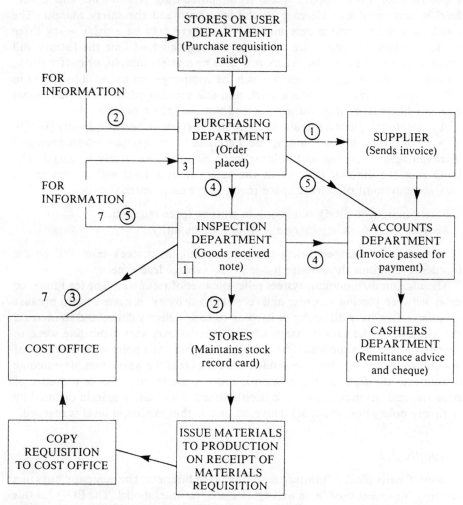

The diagram indicates the documents raised by the system and their distribution. The copies required are shown by numbering those circulated in circles, e.g. ③, and those retained in a box, e.g. ③.

Figure 3.4   Documentation of the ordering, storage of and payment for materials

MAXIMUM/MINIMUM STOCK CONTROL SYSTEM

Where stocks are kept in separate bins or racks, a bin card is an important part of the stock control system. This card is positioned near to the bin or rack and whenever materials are removed or added an entry is made on the card, which will then automatically show the balance remaining in the bin. The bin card can take the form of computerized information on a visual display unit. This is part of the Perpetual Inventory System.

It is essential to reorder stocks in good time to avoid a stock-out. Therefore the reorder level is printed in large type on the bin card, and when it is reached a requisition for more supplies is sent to the purchasing department. The reorder level is calculated by reference to the lead time and the safety margin. The purchasing department orders materials but there may be a delay – say three weeks – before the goods are delivered. During this lead time the factory will continue to use the material. There may also be a safety margin, or buffer stock, fixed as a matter of policy, below which the company does not wish its stocks to fall. This is the minimum stock level, and this amount added to the maximum quantity likely to be used during the lead time sets the reorder level.

A separate calculation is made to compute the economic order quantity (EOQ). This is the optimum amount to be purchased, so that the advantages and disadvantages of buying and holding large quantities are finely balanced. The EOQ plus the amount in store at the safety margin level will determine the maximum amount of storage space required for each material stored.

Safety margin + EOQ = maximum storage space required.
Reorder level = safety margin + lead time quantity.

If there is no prescribed safety margin, the minimum stock level will be the reorder level minus the average usage in the average lead time.

The maximum/minimum system relies on a set of estimates. The lead time, or delay between placing an order and receiving a delivery, is never certain because suppliers often have difficulty in keeping to their delivery dates, and to increase the uncertainty the rate of usage of the material may vary from one week to another. Sometimes the lead time can be quoted only as a point within a range of possible outcomes: in this case prudence dictates that the worst possible outcome is built into the figures. The economic order quantity may also be a matter of estimate, and the maximum stock is established as the safety margin dictated by company policy plus the EOQ delivered just as that minimum level is reached.

Example 3.1

Chiltern Chairs plc is a furniture manufacturing business. The company buys in a certain component used in its well-established 'recliner' model. The EOQ for this component is 8,000 units, and the company has established a minimum stock of 500 units, to ensure that a 'stock-out' does not disrupt production. The supplier has quoted a lead time of from two to four weeks and the factory manager estimates consumption of the components at 450 to 600 per week according to the level of production planned.

The reorder level would be 500 + (4 × 600) = 2,900 units. This is the stock quantity at which an order must be placed if the stock is never to drop below the minimum of 500. If, however, there were rapid delivery and low usage during the lead time, the stores would hold 2900 − [500 + (2 × 450)] = 1,500 when the new order of 8,000 units arrived. Therefore a maximum storage space to accommodate 9,500 (8,000 + 1,500) units would be required.

In formula terms:

Reorder level = Minimum stock + Maximum usage in the maximum lead time.

Maximum stock = Reorder level − Minimum usage in minimum lead time + EOQ.

THE CENTRALIZATION OF PURCHASING AND STORES

The successful control of materials depends upon co-ordination between buyers, storekeepers, checkers and accountants. If purchasing is centralized in the hands of a department of expert buyers, unauthorized and unskilled personnel cannot waste resources. Material requirements should be standardized whenever possible and programmed well in advance. The use of standard forms and a cost code, together with budgetary control, and internal check will improve the efficiency of the system.

There is a constant debate as to whether it is preferable to centralize the stores, or to operate a system of small decentralized stores serving particular segments of the business. Centralization reduces the risk of duplication, and gives closer control on a single site with a consequent reduction in losses through pilferage. With all stores under one roof stocktaking is facilitated, transfers to sub-stores are eliminated and machinery to handle goods in may be employed. By combining the demands of all users, it may be possible to satisfy them from a smaller stock, thus tying up less of the capital employed in the business. The advocates of decentralization point to delays in receiving materials from stock experienced by some departments which are far from the stores. They argue that it is more convenient to have a local store catering for local needs, and able to break down bulk deliveries into more manageable quantities. The answer to this debate seems to be in the rapidity of response of the central store, and the ease of communication felt by the departments.

OPTIMUM STOCK LEVEL

The decision to determine the best possible stock level for a company is a matter of balance. It is necessary to set off the costs of holding a large stock against the advantages derived from holding it. A centralized purchasing department may prove expensive, incurring costs of premises, telephones, stationery and staff. It is also expensive to operate storage premises. Thus a delicate balance must be set between the advantages and disadvantages in order to discover the optimum or best possible stock level in the circumstances of the business.

The advantages of holding large stocks may be summarized as follows.

1. Large stocks form a buffer against the fear of a 'stock-out' and thus are an insurance against disruption to production, delivery delays and the high costs of small urgent purchases. In a retail setting large stocks mean that customer orders can be satisfied without delay thus reducing the chance of losing an order and future business.

2. Large stocks mean that large orders can be placed so that buyers can negotiate favourable discounts from normal trade prices.

3. A large stock replenished from a large order will mean that the materials held in store maintain a constant quality, whereas the frequent purchase of small batches of material will result in variations of quality and colour which bring difficulties to the manufacturing and retailing process.

4. If large stocks are maintained they need to be replenished at less frequent intervals so that the costs of buying will be reduced.

5. If prices rise a large stock puchased at pre-inflation prices will protect a firm against price increases and thus give it a competitive edge over its rivals.

The costs of holding large stocks may be summarized as follows:

1. Interest on capital is perhaps the most important cost concerned with stocks of raw materials and other items. All goods held in stock must be financed and this means that funds are borrowed, sometimes at high rates of interest, to finance the stock.

2. Storage costs: the premises involved in a large store will generate costs of their own such as rent, rates, light, heating or refrigeration, as well as the salaries of the personnel involved.

3. The larger the stock the greater will be the insurance premium required to protect it against fire and other perils.

4. Spoilage caused by a long delay between delivery to the stores and use in the factory may also be a cost of holding large stocks.

5. Pilfering and protection: the larger the store the more expensive it is to protect what is inside and sometimes the more tempting it is to those who seek to steal.

6. Obsolescence: a large stock of components for which use is small may in time be left unused since that particular component has been designed out of the product.

ECONOMIC ORDER QUANTITY

Once the optimum stock level is determined, a further balancing calculation must be made to compute the economic order quantity (EOQ), or most advantageous buying pattern to adopt. This calculation must find the optimum combination of several factors such as discounts for large orders, the usage rate, stockholding costs, storage capacity, lead time and order processing costs.

Example 3.2

As cost accountant to a manufacturer you are asked to advise the chief buyer on buying policy for components. You will need to compute a schedule to show the costs associated with alternative ordering patterns, which at present vary between an order placed every two months (i.e. six per annum) to one order a year. The company uses 24,000 components at a steady rate throughout each year. The buyer informs you that each one costs £50, however large or small the order may be, and that the cost of placing an order is £450. Your own estimate of stockholding costs is that they amount to 1 per cent of the value of the average stock held. As the order size increases the purchasing cost will fall since fewer orders are placed, but the stockholding costs will increase. The EOQ is at the point where total costs are at a minimum.

Solution

First, divide the annual usage by the number of orders in the alternative patterns, to find the order size for each pattern. From this information the size of the average stock for each ordering pattern can be found and the value of the stock computed.

Number of orders	1	2	3	4	5	6
Order size (units)	24,000	12,000	8,000	6,000	4,800	4,000
Average stock (50% of order size)	12,000	6,000	6,000	3,000	2,400	2,000
Value of average stock at £50 each (£000)	600	300	200	150	120	100

From this data the stockholding and order costs of the alternative patterns can be derived:

	£	£	£	£	£	£
Stockholding cost (1% of stock)	6,000	3,000	2,000	1,500	1,200	1,000
Ordering cost	450	900	1,350	1,800	2,250	2,700
Total cost	6,450	3,900	3,350	3,300	3,450	3,700

Thus the least expensive ordering pattern is to order four times a year. This result can be shown graphically, as in Figure 3.5.

Note that if the average stock is deemed to be half the order size, it is assumed that no safety stock is to be held.

It is difficult to determine the cost of placing an order. The cost of operating a purchasing department could be divided between the number of orders placed to show an average cost, but it must be recognized that a large proportion of the purchasing department costs are 'fixed' in nature, and will be incurred whether the volume of the business is large or small. In this case the marginal cost per order might be a more appropriate figure to use.

In Example 3.2 stockholding costs have remained at a constant percentage over a range of stock volumes. Economies of scale may make it cheaper per unit to

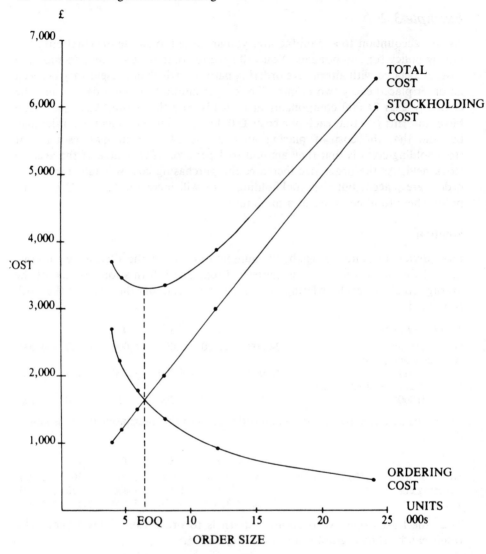

Figure 3.5 Optimum Ordering Pattern

operate a large store than a small one, and the rate of interest on capital tied up may fluctuate over the year. The cost at which materials are purchased may not remain constant during a twelve-month period because of inflation, so it is best to place a large order early in the year. The price at which a large order is placed may be lower per unit than for a smaller order, if a trade discount is given by the supplier. These undoubted advantages must be set against the fact that large stocks are used up only slowly and may deteriorate if held for a long time, and the possibility that existing storage space is inadequate to accommodate a large volume of stock. If a company has a large store but decides to order small quantities, the question of an alternative use for the idle space must be considered.

A MATHEMATICAL SOLUTION

The EOQ can be calculated by means of a formula; but this formula can be applied only if certain unreal conditions are assumed to apply.

$$EOQ = \sqrt{\frac{2AP}{S}}$$

Where:
A = Annual usage of units (24,000)
P = Purchasing cost per order (£450)
S = Stockholding cost of one unit for a year (1% × £50).

There are several versions of this formula, using different symbols but they all mean the same thing.

This formula is somewhat impractical to apply. It assumes that the cost of holding stock is known and will remain constant for different volumes, that the cost of placing an order can be calculated and will also remain constant however many orders are placed, and that the purchasing price per unit in the stockholding cost will also remain constant.

The formula can be applied to the figures in the example above.

$$EOQ = \sqrt{\frac{2 \times 24,000 \times 450}{£0.5}} = \sqrt{43,200,000} = 6,572 \text{ units}$$

This solution substantiates the calculation above, that the least expensive ordering pattern is four times a year because an EOQ of 6,572 units is in the range three to four orders a year, and nearer to four orders.

STOCK TURNOVER RATE

The stock turnover rate is also used in the control of material costs; stock turnover highlights slow-moving or obsolete stocks where action is needed to reduce the stock held. The formula most commonly applied is:

$$\frac{\text{Cost of materials used during a period}}{\text{Average stock of material used during the period}}$$

This formula can be applied to each material or component stored, to show in terms of days the average period which units of that material spend waiting in the stores until they are used.

Example 3.3

Component A: assume that material 239J used during the year cost £480,000, and that the opening stock was £70,000 and the closing stock £90,000.

$$\frac{\text{Cost of component using during the year}}{(\text{Opening stock} + \text{Closing Stock}) \div 2}$$

$$\frac{£480,000}{(70,000 + £90,000) \div 2} = 6 \text{ times}$$

This means that stock is turned over six times during the year. An answer expressed in terms of time can be achieved by a slight variation of the formula:

$$\frac{£80,000}{£480,000} \times \frac{365}{1} = 61 \text{ days}$$

i.e. 61 days × 6 times = 365.

If, for example, there is a lead time of only seven days for this material, one could investigate the reasons for holding such a large stock. A regular review of reorder levels, stock levels etc. will identify over-stocking and slow-moving stocks.

MULTIPLE CHOICE QUESTIONS

3.1   Which of the following records is not part of the material control system?
      (a)   Stores ledger card.
      (b)   Bin card.
      (c)   Remittance advice.
      (d)   Requisition.

(a)   (b)   (c)   (d)

3.2   The safety stock is 200 units; the supplier quotes a delivery delay of two to three weeks; the factory uses 400 to 700 units a week according to activity levels. The reorder level is:
      (a)   1,000.
      (b)   2,300.
      (c)   1,600.
      (d)   1,400.

(a)   (b)   (c)   (d)

3.3   The costs of holding large stocks are:
      (a)   Interest.
      (b)   Premises.
      (c)   Spoilage.
      (d)   Obsolescence.

(a)   (a + b)   (a + b + c)   (all)

3.4   Opening stock £50,000; closing stock £80,000; purchases £370,000; Stock turnover is:
      (a)   49 days.
      (b)   64 days.

    (c)   70 days.
    (d) 58 days.

(a)   (b)   (c)   (d)

3.5   The most advantageous buying pattern to adopt is found by computing the:
    (a)   Reorder level.
    (b)   Optimum stock level.
    (c)   Economic order quantity.
    (d)   Lead time.

(a)   (b)   (c)   (d)

EXERCISES

3A   You are the cost accountant employed by a medium-sized manufacturing company. The materials control system includes the maintenance of a perpetual inventory bin card system.

   Draw a diagram to illustrate the system whereby materials are issued to production, stocks are replenished and suppliers paid. Your chart or diagram should show the department involved, the procedures used and the documents raised, and should give special attention to the position in the system of the costing department and the accounting department which are separated in this company.

3B   After the annual stocktaking at your company, some significant discrepancies between stock records and actual stocks have come to light. You have decided to initiate a system of spot checks on the stores.

You are required to

(i)   Draft a form for use by the stock checkers, and show how you would use it to record the following information resulting from a stock check:

Item	Stock card	Stores ledger	Physical check	Cost per unit
Camera prisms	600	600	560	£60
Flash units	380	380	385	£40
Shutter mechanisms	750	780	720	£10

(ii)   What action should be taken to record the information shown above?
(iii) Suggest reasons for the shortage and discrepancies disclosed above, and recommend a possible course of action by management to prevent future losses.

3C   (a) Explain the rationale underlying the economic order quantity model using a diagram to illustrate your answer. (The mathematical derivation is not required.) State the formula used for calculating economic order quantity.

(b)   Given the data below for material HV700, calculate:

   (i)   the economic order quantity;
   (ii)   the number of orders needed per year, and
   (iii) the total cost of ordering and holding material HC700 for the year.

Annual requirements for material HC700: 14,400 units

Ordering cost: £12.50 per order

Holding cost per annum: 20% of purchase price

Purchase price per unit: £5.00

Safety stock requirements: None

(c)   Although stocks of materials may be planned to maximize profitability, when stock record cards are compared to actual physical stocks, differences may arise. Discuss possible reasons for these differences.

4 Stock Valuation Concepts

OBJECTIVE

The objective of this chapter is to discuss the significance, for the cost of materials, of the valuation method selected by the management accountant. Stock valuation in financial accounting is governed by a basic rule resting on conservatism, and expressed in Statement of Standard Accounting Practice 9 (SSAP 9). While the principles contained in SSAP 9 are of interest to the management accountant, the rules in the Standard cannot constrain the methods applied in management accounting.

THE SIMPLE FORMULA

The formula *opening stock plus purchases less closing stock* computes the cost of goods sold or the cost of materials used. The amounts assigned to opening and closing stock in this calculation have a direct effect on the cost of materials used and therefore on the profit measured. At first glance it seems straightforward to take stock at the end of a costing period by counting the items in the stores, giving them a value, and computing the amount of the closing stock. The difficulty, however, is to decide what value to assign to the stocks at the end of a period. Usually materials purchased during a costing period have been delivered in several different batches and probably purchased at different prices. These materials are probably mixed together in the stores so that it is impossible to say whether the items remaining at the end of the period are part of the original opening stock, or part of what has been purchased during the period. A cost flow assumption must be made, which will determine whether the items remaining in stock at the end of a period are deemed to come from the batch most recently purchased or from a batch purchased at the beginning of the period. If batches are purchased at different prices, it is clear that the cost flow assumption will influence the profit disclosed. The assumption to be adopted is the subject of a policy decision. In some companies materials are charged out at standard costs, that is, costs predetermined at the beginning of the year. In this system any difference between the standard cost and the actual cost incurred to purchase the material is written off to the profit and loss account as a variance. In cases where a batch of materials can be directly attributed to a department or a job, they can be charged out at the exact purchase price.

THE BASIC RULE OF STOCK VALUATION

The basic rule in accounting is that stocks are shown in the balance sheet at the lower of cost or net realizable value, to conform to the concept of prudence or conservatism. Thus, if stock is worth less than its cost on the valuation date, the loss is provided for, but if the stock is worth more than its cost, the apparent profit is not taken into account until it is realized. This rule is set out in the Companies Act 1985 and in SSAP 9. The term 'cost' in this situation is the purchase price plus transport costs plus any duties that have been paid to import materials into the country. In short, cost means amounts incurred to bring the stock to its present location and condition. In the case of stocks of work-in-progress this cost can also include a share of the overhead expenses of the factory. Selling and administrative costs are normally excluded from the value of stock since it is considered best to write them off as period costs. Net realizable value (NRV) is the likely selling price of the materials less any costs needed to put them into a saleable condition and to distribute and sell them.

FIRST IN FIRST OUT (FIFO)

Some firms assume a *first in first out* (FIFO) cost flow pattern. It is logical to assume that materials are used in the order in which they are purchased, and good stores practice to ensure that raw materials leave the stores in a chronological order based on their age. There is no certainty that materials which have been in stock longest will be used, if they are mixed in with other materials bought at a later date. The factory may have a tank of oil, or a large bin full of components, or a heap of sand, and if succeeding batches purchased are merely added to the stock there is no way of telling from which delivery batch the units used up in production have been drawn. The difficulty arises when the various batches delivered to the stores are bought at different prices, so that a FIFO assumption will lead to a charge to production based on the price at which early batches were purchased. The early batches will be the cheapest if prices have been rising steadily, so that the charge to production will reflect lower pre-inflation prices, and the profit derived from such cost will therefore be overstated. Meanwhile the remaining stock, which appears as a current asset in the balance sheet, will be valued at the price paid for later batches. The FIFO system may therefore overstate the profit but will produce an accurate current cost for the stock in the balance sheet.

Example 4.1

Material code 2973 has the following receipts and issues:

Date	Receipts from suppliers	Issue to production
1May	GRN 712: 2,000 at £1.00	
3May		Requisition 59: 1,000
5May	GRN 865: 1,600 at £1.30	
14 May		Requisition 71: 1,000
15 May		Requisition 74: 1,000
18 May	GRN 901: 1,400 at £1.70	
25 May		Requisition 86: 1,000

Required

Write up a stock record for May, using the FIFO basis of valuation.
See Figure 4.1 on page 46.

LAST IN FIRST OUT (LIFO)

The *last in first out* (LIFO) method assumes a pattern of stores issues which is opposite to the FIFO basis, i.e. that the most recent materials received are the first to be used. Therefore those remaining in stock at the end of the period are assumed to be drawn from batches delivered earlier in the year which had not been entirely used up before a subsequent batch was received. During a period of rising prices the charge for the use of raw materials under this method will be at more recent (current) prices, while the stocks remaining at the balance sheet date will be priced at an outdated cost paid for batches received at some time in the past. Therefore under LIFO the profit figure will be measured on a conservative basis using the most recent cost of batches delivered, but the balance sheet figure for stock will show a low pre-inflation value for the materials at the end of the year. Of course good practical storekeeping will attempt to use up the oldest materials first, but as already mentioned LIFO is an assumption of a cost flow pattern and is not intended to represent the true physical flow of materials through the stores. This method is not acceptable to the UK Inland Revenue and is discouraged by SSAP 9 'Stocks and Work in Progress' although it is widely used in the USA and is now permissible in the UK under the Companies Act 1985.

Figure 4.2 shows a stock record card using the same information as in Figure 4.1 but prepared on a LIFO basis.

AVERAGE COST METHOD (AVCO)

The *average cost method* (AVCO) prices raw materials issued to production at an average figure, and therefore it produces both a cost of sales and a balance sheet figure for stocks remaining at the end of the year in between the extremes produced by FIFO and LIFO. A simple average cost could be found by adding the different prices paid during the period for the batches purchased and dividing by the number of batches. However, this method would obscure the fact that the

Date	Receipts		Issues		Balance	
	GRN	£	*Requisition*	£		£
1 May	712 2,000 × 1.00	2,000			2,000 × 1.00	2,000
3 May			59 1,000 × 1.00	1,000	1,000 × 1.00	1,000
5 May	865 1,600 × 1.30	2,080			1,000 × 1.00 } 1,600 × 1.30 }	3,080
14 May			71 1,000 × 1.00	1,000	1,600 × 1.30	2,080
15 May			74 1,000 × 1.30	1,300	600 × 1.30	780
18 May	901 1,400 × 1.70	2,380			600 × 1.30 } 1,400 × 1.30 }	3,160
25 May			86 600 × 1.30	780		
			400 × 1.70	680	1,000 × 1.70	1,700
					(Closing stock)	
			Charge to			
			production	£4,760		

Note: The lines drawn across the issues and receipts columns help to show where each batch is used up.

Figure 4.1   Stock record card: material code 2973 on the FIFO basis

Date	Receipts		Issues		Balance	
	GRN	£	*Requisition*	£		£
1 May	712 2,000 × 1.00	2,000			2,000 × 1.00	2,000
3 May			59 1,000 × 1.00	1,000	1,000 × 1.00	1,000
5 May	865 1,600 × 1.30	2,080			1,000 × 1.00 } 1,600 × 1.30 }	3,080
14 May			71 1,000 × 1.30	1,300	1,000 × 1.00 600 × 1.30	1,780
15 May			74 600 × 1.30	780	600 × 1.00	600
			400 × 1.00	400		
18 May	901 1,400 × 1.70	2,380			600 × 1.00 } 1,400 × 1.70 }	2,980
25 May			86 1,000 × 1.70	1,700	600 × 1.00 } 400 × 1.70 }	1,280
					(Closing stock)	
			Charge to			
			production	£5,180		

Note: The charge to production is greater under LIFO than under FIFO, but with LIFO some material in stock on 1 May is deemed to be still there on 30 May.

Figure 4.2   Stock record card: material code 2973 on the LIFO basis

quantities purchased in each batch might not be the same, and therefore if a large number of components are purchased at a low price and then the next batch is much smaller but priced higher, a simple average between the two prices would not express correctly the true average paid per unit purchased. This problem is avoided by using a weighted average. The calculation is 'weighted' for quantities purchased at different prices. In formula terms it is:

The aggregate of price × weight (units) ÷ total weights

The disadvantages of this method are that the average must be recalculated each time there is a fresh delivery, and the average produced by the calculation may not equal any price actually paid.

Suppose 20,000 kg of chemical are purchased for a fertilizer process, at £15 per kg, and then a second batch of 2,000 kg for £20 per kg a simple average price would work out at (15 + 20) ÷ 2 = £17.50. A weighted average is calculated as follows:

	Price ×	Weight	= Aggregate
	£	kg	£
Batch 1	15	20,000	300,000
Batch 2	20	2,000	40,000
		22,000	340,000

$$\frac{£340,000}{22,000 \text{ kg}} = £15.45 \text{ per kg}$$

The weighted average reflects the greater volume in batch 1 bought at the lower price.

Figure 4.3 shows a stock record card using the same information as in Figures 4.1 and 4.2 but prepared on an AVCO basis.

STANDARD COST

This method prices issues at a preset figure based on budget expectations. Any difference between the actual purchase price and the standard issue price is calculated and written off to profit and loss as a variance. Further information concerning standard costing appears in Chapter 15.

REPLACEMENT COST

Some accountants believe that the true cost of using a material is what it will cost to replace the material, and they advocate the use of replacement cost to price issues from the stores and for balance sheet purposes. SSAP 9 rejects this method since it reflects a cost which has not really been paid. If stocks are held at replacement cost for balance sheet purposes when they have been bought at a lower price, an element of profit which has not yet been realized will be built into

Date	Receipts			Issues			Balance	
	GRN		£	*Requisition*		£		£
1 May	712	2,000 × 1.00	2,000				2,000 × 1.00	2,000
3 May				59	1,000 × 1.00	1,000	1,000 × 1.00	1,000
5 May	865	1,600 × 1.30	2,080				2,600 × 1.18	3,080
14 May				71	1,000 × 1.18	1,180	1,600 × 1.18	1,888
15 May				74	1,000 × 1.18	1,180	600 × 1.18	708
18 May	901	1,400 × 1.70	2,380				2,000 × 1.54	3,088
25 May				86	1,000 × 1.54	1,540	1,000 × 1.54	1,540
							(Closing stock)	
				Charge to production		£4,900		

Notes:
1. A fresh weighted average is computed after each receipt.
2. Materials are charged to production at £1.18 and £1.54 but none has been purchased at this price.
3. AVCO gives a charge to production which is between the amounts derived by FIFO and LIFO.

Workings	£			£
1,000 × 1.00	1,000		600 × £1.18	708
1,600 × 1.30	2,080		1,400 × £1.70	2,380
2,600	3,080		2,000	3,088

$\dfrac{3,080}{2,600}$ = say £1.18 $\dfrac{3,088}{2,000}$ = say £1.54

Figure 4.3   Stock record card: material code 2973 on the AVCO basis

the profit and loss account. Notwithstanding this argument the Companies Act 1985 recognizes replacement cost as a stock valuation method.

BASE STOCK

This is a somewhat outdated method of valuing stocks for balance sheet purposes, which assumes that a definite weight or volume of material will be maintained at all times as stock in a process or manufacturing system. Since there is a definite quantity, 'the base stock', this amount can be carried forward from one costing period to another as the stock figure. The advantage of this method is that it reduces fluctuations in annual profits that would otherwise appear as a result of price changes. The method was discouraged by SSAP 9 and is not widely used, but the Companies Act 1985 recognized the legality of using such a method. The stock value produced by this method is totally unrealistic for balance sheet purposes. The method is not used for pricing issues from the stores.

STOCK VALUATION AND PROFIT

In a period of *falling* prices it is conservative or prudent to value stocks on the

FIFO or AVCO method because the older or more expensive items are assumed to be used up, and the closing stock will be valued according to the most recent (lower) prices. In a period of *rising* prices the FIFO method will overstate profit because the method assumes that batches purchased pre-inflation at lower prices are used up first so that the cost of materials used calculated by this method will not be at later, current prices.

In a period of rising prices the LIFO method will charge materials at a recent or current cost against production but will asume that older batches bought pre-inflation remain in stock at the end of the period for balance sheet purposes. If in a subsequent period stocks are run down, the effect on the cost of materials used is that these older batches of material, priced at very outdated levels, appear to be used. Thus, if stocks are reduced under the LIFO method, a very overstated profit can be the result. While the LIFO method is advantageous for profit measurement in that current prices are used to set against revenue, the balance sheet amount for stock may be understated.

LIFO is difficult to record, with stocks appearing to be made up of several partly charged batches, if later batches are delivered to the stores before earlier batches are exhausted.

WASTAGE

If wastage occurs in the stores through spillage, pilferage or deterioration, the amount can be shown as a separate expense (an overhead) or it can be absorbed into the cost of good material issued to production.

Example 4.2

Assume 2,000 units of material Z413 are purchased for £3,500; 1,760 units are issued to production and at the end of the month 142 units are left in stock. Thus 98 units have been 'lost'.

Material Z413

	Quantity	Rate £	Amount £		Quantity	Rate £	Amount £
Purchases	2,000	1.75	3,500	Wastage	98	–	–
				Issued to production	1,760	1.84	3,238
				Closing stock c/f	142	1.84	262
	2,000		3,500		2,000		3,500

$$\frac{\text{Total cost}}{\text{Good units}} = \frac{£\,3,500}{1,902} = £1.84$$

Thus the wastage is absorbed in the cost of good material charged to production, but an element of this month's wastage is carried forward to next month in the closing stock figure. Some accountants would argue that it contravenes the matching principle to carry forward part of this month's wastage as a cost next month. If the cost of wastage is absorbed into the cost of good material, the production process is penalized, since it bears the cost of inefficiency or waste in the stores. Stores management must take responsibility for these costs.

SSAP 9 'STOCKS AND WORK-IN-PROGRESS'

This statement has some significant comments to make as to the method selected to cost raw material stocks. It recognizes that it is frequently not practicable to relate expenditure to specific units of stock and shows that two further problems stem from this fact:
1. The selection of an appropriate method to relate costs to stocks and work-in-progress, for example, job costing, batch costing, process costing and standard costing;
2. The selection of an appropriate method to find the related cost when a number of identical items, purchased at different times, are mixed together in the stores, for example, unit cost, AVCO and FIFO.

   Management must use judgement to ensure that the method chosen provides a fair approximation to actual cost. The Standard considers that methods such as LIFO and the base stock method do not meet this criterion. It is also considered bad practice to value closing stocks at the price ruling at the accounting date (replacement cost) since in a time of rising prices this method will take into account a profit which has not yet been realized.

MULTIPLE CHOICE QUESTIONS

4.1   The FIFO assumption of cost flow when applied in a period of rising prices:
   (a)   overstates profit and closing stock;
   (b)   overstates profit and understates closing stock;
   (c)   overstates profit and shows closing stock at current prices;
   (d)   understates profit and overstates closing stock.

(a)   (b)   (c)   (d)

4.2   The LIFO assumption of cost flow when applied in a period of rising prices:
   (a)   overstates profit and closing stock;
   (b)   charges stock to profit at current prices and understates closing stock;
   (c)   charges stock to profit at current prices and overstates closing stock;
   (d)   understates profit and closing stock;

(a)   (b)   (c)   (d)

4.3   Purchased 10,000 at £4; 18,000 at £5; 25,000 at £6; the weighted average
cost is:
(a)   £5.
(b)   £5.28
(c)   £6.13.
(d)   £4.90.

(a)   (b)   (c)   (d)

4.4   Materials are purchased and any difference between the unit price and a
preset figure is written off to the profit and loss account. This describes
which method of stock valuation?
(a)   Replacement cost method.
(b)   Base stock method.
(c)   Standard cost method.
(d)   Next in first out method.

(a)   (b)   (c)   (d)

4.5   Stocks are valued at the lower of cost or NRV. Cost in this context includes:
(a)   Duties and tariff charges.
(b)   Transport costs.
(c)   A fair proportion of factory overheads.
(d)   A fair proportion of selling and administrative overheads.

(a)   (a + b)   (a + b + c)   (all)

EXERCISES

4A   Describe and discuss the relative merits of the various methods that may be
used for pricing the issue of raw materials to production.

(Association of Certified Accountants)

4B   On 1 January Mr G started a small business buying and selling a special
yarn, investing his savings of £40,000 in the business. During the next six months
the following transactions occurred:

Yarn purchases			Yarn sales		
Date of receipt	Quantity (boxes)	Total cost £	Date of dispatch	Quantity (boxes)	Total value £
13 January	200	7,200	10 February	500	25,000
8 February	400	15,200			
11 March	600	24,000			
12 April	400	14,000	20 April	600	27,000
15 June	500	14,000	25 June	400	15,200

The yarn is stored in premises which Mr G has rented, and the closing stock, counted on 30 June, was 500 boxes. Other expenses incurred and paid in cash during the six-month period amounted to £2,300.

Required

(a)   Calculate the value of the material issues during the six-month period, and the value of the closing stock at the end of June, using the following methods of pricing:
  (i) first in first out;
  (ii) last in first out; and
  (iii) weighted average (calculations to two decimal places only).
(b)   Calculate and discuss the effect each of the three methods of material pricing will have on the reported profit of the business and examine the performance of the business during the first six-month period.

(Association of Certified Accountants)

5 Accounting for Labour Costs

OBJECTIVE

The objective of this chapter is to review the major items which influence the cost accounting treatment of labour. The costing treatment of labour falls naturally into four distinct parts:
1. the design of the system whereby labour costs are recorded;
2. systems of remuneration used to reward and encourage effort;
3. ledger accounts compiled from the labour cost recording system;
4. labour cost reports which act as an analysis and provide control information for management.

RECORDING LABOUR COSTS

The costing system should be capable of producing data to disclose the amount earned by each employee, what extra remuneration has been paid above the norm, what work has been done to earn this remuneration, and what costs other than remuneration arise from employing each individual. The cost of labour covers wages and overtime payments but also includes holiday and sick pay, pension premiums and the cost of sports and social clubs operated by the firm for its employees, as well as national insurance contributions. Labour costs are recorded by the production of the following documents.

Employee record card

This card (or space on a computer tape) contains the basic information concerning the employee. The card is raised when the employee is engaged and shows a history of progress through the firm with dates, rates of pay, promotion, training, departments in which experience has been gained, and a record of sickness, absenteeism and time-keeping. When the employee leaves, the card is completed with the closing date and if possible the reason for leaving. The employee record card is the source document for the rate of pay which is used in the compilation of other labour records.

Figure 5.1 gives an example of an employee record card.

Clock card

Employees whose wage is calculated on a time basis will need to clock in and out of their place of employment so that the time period to be paid can be ascertained. A clock number is assigned to each employee and a card is prepared for that number. The cards are kept in a rack near to the clock, usually at the gate of the factory. Employees must stamp their time of arrival and departure on to the time card. Thus pay office clerks (or computer software) can calculate the hours to be paid according to the wage sheet. The operation of the time clock should be supervised by a responsible employee: since it is easy to stamp another employee's card with a false time, fraud may take place. The card can also form part of the control system to check on time-keeping and absenteeism.

The wage sheet

All employees are listed on the wage sheet in alphabetical order, or by gangs or departments. Thus each employee has his or her own line extending across the wage sheet. The hours worked are entered on the wage sheet from the clock card and multiplied by the rate of pay, and a figure for total gross pay is computed. Any extra payments such as overtime, bonus or shift premium are added at this point, together with such allowances as subsistence and 'dirty' money, extra payments for difficult or anti-social tasks. Deductions for a holiday club or sports and social club are also made. Statutory deductions for tax and national insurance are included for each employee on his or her line of the wage sheet, which will then show a figure for gross pay, plus allowances less deductions, amounting to the net amount to be paid in cash. This amount can either be put into a pay envelope or be written up as a cheque. When this information is entered on the wage sheet, other records can be produced by means of carbon-impregnated inlays, e.g. a strip for each employee to show the make-up of his or her net pay which can be put into the individual pay envelope, and a tax deduction card for each employee.

The analysis columns on the wage sheet are totalled to provide figures for entry in the cost accounts for such items as basic pay, overtime, allowances and deductions. Clearly these repetitive clerical operations can be computerized but the same totals and basic documents must be produced (see Figure 5.2).

The time sheet

As the wage sheet analyses the amounts paid to employees so the time sheet analyses the hours worked for which payment has been made. Some employees will work in a single department or at a single job throughout the week but

EMPLOYEE RECORD CARD	Surname	Address	Clock no.
	Other names		Pension fund

Personal details	Employment record			
Date of birth	Date	Department	Grade	Job
Marital status				
Date of engagement				
References				
	Wage rate record					
Previous employment	Date	Rate	Detail	Date	Rate	Detail
Notes						

Notes
1. The back of this form would contain information concerning timekeeping/attendance record/health and accident record/training/merit rating/qualifications.
2. There would also be a box on the form to record the date and reason for leaving.

Figure 5.1   Employee record card

others, perhaps organized into groups or gangs, will move from job to job or department to department, e.g. a machine maintenance team. A daily or weekly time sheet will analyse this movement, and when signed by the foreman (a control technique) an analysis of the labour cost of that gang can be made to the various tasks undertaken by the group. The time sheet is written up in terms of hours rather than in terms of money, and can be designed to show other important information such as overtime, idle time and travelling time.

Piece work tickets

Some companies pay their employees on the basis of work completed rather than for the time they have spent at the factory. Payment is 'per piece' so that it is necessary to record the number of 'pieces' and multiply that figure by the piece rate negotiated beforehand. Clearly work completed under a piece work system must be carefully checked by a trusted inspector who will initial the piece work ticket to signify that the work is free from faults. The gross pay is calculated according to the number of tickets initialled for each worker or group.

PAYMENT OF WAGES

It is important to have a proper internal check system when wages are calculated

1. Bottom copy –Sheet of payslips to go into each pay envelope – perforated for tearing

Employees' Payslips

HOURS		RATE	WAGES						PAYE				DEDUCTIONS				
Day	O/Time		Pay	O/Time	Bonus	Sick	Allow-ances	Gross	Free	Taxable	Tax to date	Gross to date	Tax	N.I.	Holiday – Sports	Total	NET	Name & number

2. Middle copy – Wage sheet or payroll – totals of certain columns provide figures for posting into the cost accounts

Wage sheet for week ending .... Costing Week No ....

HOURS		RATE	WAGES						PAYE				DEDUCTIONS					
Day	O/Time		Pay	O/Time	Bonus	Sick	Allow-ances	Gross	Free	Taxable	Tax to date	Gross to date	Tax	N.I.	Holiday – Sports	Total	NET	Name & number	Employer's NI

3. Top copy – Tax deduction card for each employee

Personal tax deduction card

Name
Clock number
Department

Rate of pay .... Tax code .... N.I. ....

Tax Week	RATE	WAGES						PAYE				DEDUCTIONS			
		Pay	O/Time	Bonus	Sick	Allow-ances	Gross	Free	Taxable	Tax to date	Gross to date	Tax	N.I.	Holiday – Sports	Total	NET
1															
2															

Note: NI = national insurance – a social security deduction paid to the government by the employee and the employer, but collected by the employer as a deduction from wages or salaries paid.

Figure 5.2 Example of a wage sheet (and two documents which can be produced at the same time if a carbon system is used)

and paid. The pay out should be witnessed by a responsible supervisor who can identify the workers receiving their pay packets. Some companies make payment when the employee presents him or herself to the wages clerk at a counter or window. Wages must be checked by the employee immediately so that discrepancies can be reported. The provision of window envelopes enables such a check to be made easily. Any dispute as to hours worked can be settled by reference to the time card or clock card. In other organizations the wage packets are taken by the wage clerks to the appropriate departments and workers are paid while they are at work. Payment by cheque is much more convenient.

Internal checks should be built into the wage payment system, in such a way that the task of preparing the wage sheet and making the payment is divided between two or more employees. In this way fraud can be committed only if there is collusion between the wage clerks. The system for recording time or completed piece work, or the calculation of bonus payments, should be the subject of check or authorization by a responsible senior employee. All overtime should be authorized and verified to the extent that the work has been undertaken.

The completed wage sheet should be scrutinized by a senior manager to ensure that all names on the wage sheet correspond to employees in the plant. In this way 'dummy' workers can be identified. A careful system for handling and storing unclaimed wage packets is essential, to prevent wages being paid to an employee who has not earned them, and to increase the difficulty of defrauding the company by inserting 'dummy' workers on the payroll.

A well-organized system should prevent fraud, but the wage payment routine does present many opportunities for employees to receive more than their true entitlement. Fraud may be committed by employees changing the hours recorded on the clock card, by clocking in and out for a colleague who is not present, or by clocking in and out but failing to work in a production department. Some companies place the time clock at the factory gate to control workers entering and leaving the premises, others install a time clock in the workshop or department, in order to maintain closer supervision of each production team.

If the wage rates to be applied in the pay calculation are derived from the employee record card, and if the employee is isolated from the wage calculation activity, fraud to change wage rates or tax codes can be prevented, unless the employee has an accomplice working within the wages office. Payment based on production achieved rather than time worked demands strict control of production records, e.g. piece work tickets. If the amount of work recorded can be changed, or if tickets can be submitted for payment more than once, the wages paid will not reconcile to the work actually undertaken.

REMUNERATION

The labour cost attributable to a unit of production may depend on the time taken to produce the unit, or on a predetermined rate (a piece rate) paid for its production.

Piece rates

These work well in a situation where there is a long, uninterrupted production run, of products which are homogeneous and can easily be checked for quantity and quality. If the labour cost per unit is fixed in advance, employees will be encouraged to work hard, since the more they produce the more they will be paid. The introduction of new technology which increases output per employee will be welcomed if piece rates are paid. A sensible rate negotiated for difficult tasks will ensure that skilled employees will be able to earn an adequate wage and at the same time use their skills to produce work of a high standard. With piece rates reward is linked to effort but this may encourage some workers to work quickly rather than carefully, so that a system of inspection is required. This generates further costs and the cost of wastage from rejected work may be high.

The task of setting a piece rate is often difficult, since the wrong rate can provoke disputes between employees and management. A high rate will increase the cost per unit and may price the company out of its market, but if the rate is too low the morale of employees will suffer and there will be little incentive for them to work hard. If workers in one department earn widely differing amounts because of the operation of a piece work system, jealousy and dissention may reduce productivity.

Time rates

Comparatively few situations in industry allow for the payment of piece rates, so most employees are paid per hour, day or week. In a business where quality is important, or measurement of production difficult, a time rate will be the best method by which to remunerate the labour force. However, time rates give employees no inducement to work hard, so that the employer is presented with the difficulty of encouraging effort from the labour force during the hours which they work in the factory. Supervision is essential to reduce time wasting but of course this is expensive, and the atmosphere of co-operation between management and labour can be harmed if supervision is applied with an over-zealous attitude. Time rates do not give an incentive to a skilled or conscientious worker since all employees are paid the same for the time they work.

An extension of the time rate system is to pay *high day rates* (a rate of pay above normal rates), which allows the company to select only the best workers and then to expect them to work hard and well. In some schemes the high day rates are used as an incentive for labour to achieve preset targets. This is a simple system involving much less clerical effort than piece work or a bonus system, but it still encourages efficient standards of output. The drawback is that high wages may be seen as the norm rather than as a reward for good production. Careful work study and timing are essential to measure the expected production levels, so the system cannot be applied to all circumstances. A further problem arises if the required production levels are not achieved.

INCENTIVE SCHEMES

It is expensive to install and operate an incentive scheme, so the benefits to be derived must be clearly recognized when the scheme is planned. A bonus or reward for good production will improve the morale of the labour force and attract good quality labour. A successful incentive scheme enables employees to profit from their own skill and effort. Increased production will spread the fixed overheads over a larger volume of goods produced thus reducing the cost per unit. The design and introduction of an incentive scheme should follow certain basic principles.

1. The scheme must be simple to understand and to administer. Complexity increases cost.
2. There must be adequate consultation between employer and employee, involving unions, during the design stage of the scheme so that it is seen as fair by all parties.
3. Adequate steps must be taken to ensure that all parties understand the scheme and that there is a recognized procedure to resolve disputes.
4. Incentive payments should be related to effort and should be made soon after the effort has taken place. This is to ensure that employees appreciate the reason for the extra payments and will thus be motivated to work hard in the future.
5. Incentive schemes should be guaranteed to operate for a long period. If they are cancelled or altered after a short time, employees will lose faith in the scheme. A good incentive scheme should not limit the amount that can be earned.
6. Circumstances outside the control of employees should not be allowed to affect the amount they earn. A smooth flow of work on the production line is important; e.g. if it stops due to a material 'stock-out' or machine breakdown so that workers are prevented from earning up to and beyond the incentive level, some form of guaranteed day rate must be used to compensate for a reduction in pay caused by no fault of their own.
7. Incentive payments must apply only for 'good' production and there must be adequate control to prevent falsification of figures for work done or the acceptance of substandard work.
8. When standards are set they must be recognized as feasible so that it is possible for the average worker to raise output to the level which qualifies for the bonus. A small bonus will not provide sufficient incentive for extra effort.
9. The incentive scheme should cover as many of the employees as possible. Any workers excluded from the scheme may well feel a sense of grievance.

ADVANTAGES OF PAYMENT ON A TIME BASIS

To summarize, the advantages of payment on a time basis are as follows.
1. The system can be easily understood.
2. A minimum of clerical time is required.
3. The worker has no incentive to hurry the job, so will concentrate on quality and the full use of his or her skills.

The disadvantage of payment on a time basis is that it provides no incentive to increase production and the lazy worker gets as much in an hour as a hard-working employee.

PIECE RATES EVALUATED

The advantages of piece rates are:
(a) simplicity;
(b) incentive;
(c) increasing rates of production, which spreads overheads over a larger volume thus reducing the cost per unit;
(d) the exact labour cost for each unit is known in advance thus facilitating budgeting and estimating;
(e) careful time study is necessary to set piece rates, and this alone provides valuable information on which to base production control and standard costs.
Piece rates do, however, have disadvantages.

1. The design and introduction of the scheme take time and are expensive.
2. If rates are badly measured at the outset of the scheme it is difficult later to reduce an unduly high rate. Revisions can be made only when machine speeds or methods are changed.
3. An expensive system of inspection is necessary to ensure that quality is maintained.
4. Lateness and absenteeism may increase since, under a piece rate scheme, employees consider that they are paid for what they do, not how long they attend. However, a machine standing idle represents a loss of production. Production departments are often interlinked in a 'line' relationship, so that a steady flow of production is required from a piece work department to maintain production in other departments.
5. If the same rate is paid regardless of the quantity produced there may still be little incentive for exceptional effort. Accordingly some piece work schemes can be combined with the payment of bonus based on production achieved beyond a set norm. By the same token there is no penalty under a piece work scheme for substandard effort.

PREMIUM BONUS SCHEMES

A premium bonus scheme computes remuneration on the basis of the difference between a preset time allowed to complete a job or task and the actual time taken by an individual employee or a team. The object of the scheme is to relate pay to both time worked and output achieved. A normal time for each job or task is fixed by time and motion study and negotiation. If the employee completes the task in less than the time allowed, a bonus is paid based on the time saved.

Various schemes are in operation which share the time saved between the employee and the company, for example:

1. The Halsey Scheme – the bonus paid is based on half the time saved.
2. The Halsey/Weir Scheme – bonus paid is based on one-third of the time saved.
3. The Rowan Scheme – bonus paid is based on a proportion of time saved computed by the formula:

$$\frac{\text{Time taken}}{\text{Time allowed}} \times \text{Time saved}$$

Example 5.1

An employee is operating a lathe to produce a standard component in a bicycle factory. The normal working week is 37 hours, for a rate of £4 per hour – £148 per week.

Each component is timed to take ten minutes on the lathe (including normal idle time), so each worker should produce 222 components in a week, at a direct labour cost of £4 ÷ 6 = 66.7p each.

An employee produces 300 components during a week.

The production is worth a standard time of 300 ÷ 6 per hour = 50 hours, but has been achieved in 37 hours. Time saved is 13 hours. The remuneration would be calculated as follows under the three schemes.

1. *Halsey Scheme*   £
   Basic: 37 hours at £4 per hour   148.00
   Bonus: half time saved
       13 hours ÷ 2 = 6.5 hours × £4   26.00
                                 174.00

2. *Halsey/Weir Scheme*
   Basic: 37 hours at £4 per hour   148.00
   Bonus: one-third time saved
       13 hours ÷ 3 = 4.33 hours × 4   17.33
                                 165.33

3. *Rowan Scheme*
   Basic: 37 hours at £4 per hour   148.00
   Bonus: $\dfrac{\text{Time taken}}{\text{Time allowed}} \times \text{time saved}$

   $$= \frac{37 \text{ hours}}{50 \text{ hours}} \times 13 \text{ hours}$$

   $$= 9.62 \text{ hours} \times £4 \qquad\qquad 38.48$$
                                 186.48

OTHER INCENTIVE SCHEMES

There are many forms of incentive scheme other than those based on recorded time and preset norms. Some are based on points awarded for efficiency or time-keeping, but such schemes may rely on supervisors making value judgements about employees. It is easy to see that under such a scheme favouritism may enhance the prospects of one employee at the cost of another so that this type of incentive scheme may increase conflict within the workplace rather than encourage co-operation. Some tasks cannot be analysed to the effort of individual workers, e.g. a gang working at the face of a coal mine, and for them group bonus schemes can be organized. A good group scheme will help to create team spirit among the employees.

Incentives for direct workers can be related to production but it would be unfair to exclude indirect workers from bonus payments since their efforts are vital if production operations are to run smoothly. The efforts of indirect workers must be recognized, perhaps with some form of bonus based on the overall results of the organization or of a particular department, so that they feel they are appreciated for their role in the organization. Such schemes are quite simple to organize, and may be used to encourage flexible working arrangements and closer co-operation from indirect workers who form part of the production team. No scheme is perfect, however, and the bonus may become remote as an incentive and perhaps be seen instead as an amount to which indirect workers have a right, whether or not extra production or profit has been achieved.

COST ACCOUNTING FOR WAGES

The principles of double entry apply in cost accounting just as they do in financial accounting. The wage sheet records the gross amount earned by employees, which can be analysed to direct and indirect labour, and then to appropriate cost centres or units or to production overhead control. It is important to be able to analyse labour costs between direct workers who work on production units and indirect workers who service the production process. Further analysis is required to reveal the cost of normal time, and overheads such as overtime, bonus and allowances made to employees. The employer's national insurance contributions are recorded as a separate column on the wage sheet and also treated as a production overhead.

Deductions for items such as the employee's national insurance contributions and Schedule E income tax reduce gross pay to net pay. These deductions are made by the employer when wages are paid, weekly or monthly, and held and paid over to the appropriate government agency at certain stated intervals. Where a contributary pension scheme is in operation, pension contributions are deducted from wages and channelled into the pension fund.

The basic data for these entries can be taken from the totals of columns on the wage sheet. Gross pay is a debit, being the cost of direct labour charged to work in progress and indirect labour charged to production overheads. The deductions are credit entries since they are owed to other parties. The net pay is credited to the cash book because that is the amount paid out in the form of cash or cheques. These entries can also be passed through a wages control account and are further explained in Figure 5.3. The appropriate boxes in Figure 5.3 show figures for gross wages of £20,000 with deductions of £3,000 for Schedule E tax, £1,000 for employees' national insurance, £1,000 for pension fund contributions, and cash paid out of £15,000. The gross pay comprises direct labour £10,000, indirect labour £7,000, bonus £2,000 and overtime £1,000. The wages control account for these transactions would be as follows:

Wages control account

	£		£
Cash paid	15,000	Work-in-progress control	10,000
Taxation: Schedule E	3,000	Production overhead	
NI deductions	1,000	control	10,000
Pension fund	1,000		
	20,000		20,000

Overtime occurs when employees work for periods in excess of the normal agreed hours for a working day or week. This extra time is paid for by the employer at a premium rate, e.g. time and a half, which means that the employee receives one and a half time the normal hourly rate for each overtime hour worked. Overtime hours at the normal rate are treated as a direct labour cost and charged to production on the same basis as time worked during normal hours, but the premium paid during the overtime period is not a direct charge against production. The overtime premium is treated as an overhead expense unless the overtime has been worked on a specific job, perhaps to complete it by a certain date, in which case the entire labour cost can be charged as direct labour to that job.

National insurance contributions are made by the employer as part of the labour cost but cannot be allocated to individual hours worked or jobs completed. It is possible to average the contributions over the hours worked in a normal week so that they are automatically charged out as part of the labour rate, but it seems much simpler to treat them as an overhead expense. National insurance contributions are paid by employers and employees, as a contribution towards social security benefits. The employer collects the employees' contributions and pays them to the government. The employer's contribution is treated as an extra cost of employing labour.

Labour analysis is often undertaken as a weekly task in many companies. Employees or their supervisors fill in time sheets which show how the workers or groups have spent their time during the week. Such time sheets must be initialled by a supervisor to authenticate the information they contain, since any difference between total time allocated to jobs and the total time paid will count as 'idle time'.

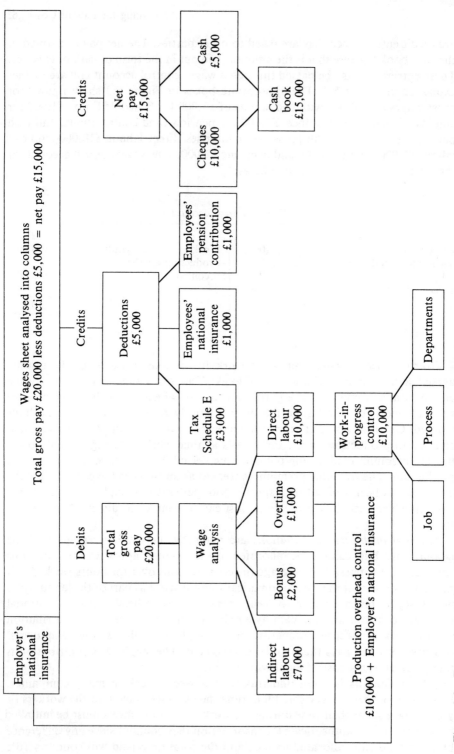

Figure 5.3 Entry of totals from the wage sheet into the cost accounting system

Example 5.2

Packers Ltd makes wooden packing cases in a small factory. The wage sheet for the week has been compiled and the following information is available. The company operates two eight-hour shifts, and a premium is paid to workers for working unsocial hours. A bonus is paid if production targets are exceeded.

	Direct workers	Indirect workers
Total attendance time (hours)	2,200	960
Basic rate of pay per hour	£4.20	£3.60
Overtime hours worked	250	120
Shift premium	£430	£190
Group bonus	£370	£240
Deductions from pay:		
Income tax	£700	£520
Employees' national insurance	£220	£130
Employer's national insurance	£280	£160

Overtime is paid at time and a half.

Half the overtime worked during the week was incurred on one particular batch of production to meet a deadline on an export order. An analysis of time records shows that the direct workers' time has been spent as follows:

	Hours
Production	1,580
Non-production time:	
Stock-out of materials	153
Power failure	188
Machine breakdown	137
Idle time	142
	2,200

i.e. 620 hours of non-productive time.

Required

Record these events in the cost accounts.

Solution

1. *How to treat awkward items*

The employer's national insurance contribution is best charged to production overhead because it cannot be allocated to any specific batch of production, unless the hourly wage rate is grossed up to include this amount. A similar comment applies to the group bonus, which cannot be identified to any particular batch produced. The shift premium is paid to recompense the labour force for working unsocial hours, so that too is an overhead.

Overtime is worked as a result of a policy decision to increase production, and as such it should be spread over all products as an overhead, not charged only to the goods produced during the overtime period. However, if some overtime is worked to complete a specific batch, as in this case, the extra direct labour cost should be charged to work-in-progress on that job.

The cost of indirect labour is an overhead expense.

2. Workings

Direct workers		£	Indirect workers		£
Attendance time					
2,200 hours × £4.20		9,240	960 hours × £3.60		3,456
Overtime					
250 hours × £2.10		525	120 hours × £1.80		216
Shift premium		430			190
Group bonus		370			240
Gross wage		10,565			4,102
Less deductions					
Tax	700			130	
Insurance	220	920		160	290
Take-home pay		9,645			3,812

Note: Overtime is calculated here at half the normal rate, since the overtime hours are included with attendance time, and have been entered in the computation at basic rates. Thus half the basic rate needs to be added on to complete that calculation for time and a half.

3. Analysis of direct workers' gross wage

	Direct £		Indirect £
Production time 1,580 × £4.20	6,636.0	620 × £4.20	2,604.0
Overtime 125 × £2.10	262.5	125 × £2.10	262.5
Shift premium and bonus	–	430 + 370	800.0
	6,898.5		3,666.5

Total £10,565.

4. Analysis of indirect workers' gross wage

	Direct £		Indirect £
Attendance time 60 × £3.60	216	900 × £3.60	3,240
Overtime 60 × £1.80	108	60 × £1.80	108
Shift and premium bonds	–	190 + 240	430
	324		3,778

Total £4,102.

Note: Half the overtime (120 hours) was spent on a particular batch. This means that 60 hours at time and a half (60 × £5.40 = £324) should be charged direct to production in the work-in-progress accounts. The remaining 60 hours of overtime count as indirect labour. If total indirect labour hours are 960, and 60 of these are spent on direct production, 900 hours must be spent on indirect tasks.

Wages control a/c

	£		£
Cash		Work-in-progress	6,898.5
Direct	9,645	Production overhead	3,666.5
Indirect	3,812	Work-in-progress	324.0
Inc. tax a/c	700	Production overhead	3,778.0
Inc. tax a/c	130		
Nat. ins. a/c	220		
Nat. ins. a/c	160		
	14,667		14,667.0

Income tax a/c

	£		£
		Wages control	
		Direct	700
		Indirect	130

Cash book

	£		£
		Wages control	9,645
		Wages control	3,812

Production overhead a/c

	£		£
Wages control	3,666.5		
Wages control	3,778.0		
Nat. ins.			
(Employer's)	280.0		
(Employer's)	160.0		

Work-in-progress a/c

	£		£
Direct labour			
Wages control	6,898.5		
Wages control	324.0		

National insurance a/c

	£		£
		Wages control (Employees)	220
		Wages control "	160
		Production overhead (Employers)	280
		Production overhead "	160

MANAGERIAL APPLICATIONS OF LABOUR COST

Cost control is immeasurably improved by an analysis of labour costs.

Labour turnover

When employees leave a business, costs are incurred to recruit and train replacements. The labour turnover ratio for a company can be compared to the norm for the industry, or figures for the same company in previous years. This ratio is computed as the relationship of the number of employees leaving and arriving during a period to the average number employed by the company during that period. The formula is:

$$\frac{\text{Leavers + newcomers}}{\text{Average employees}} \times \frac{100}{1}$$

Alternatively, less sophisticated companies use the formula:

$$\frac{\text{Leavers}}{\text{Average employees}} \times \frac{100}{1}$$

Labour turnover indicates the proportion of the labour force in a company which moves during a period. The cost implications of employees leaving the business are as follows:

(a)   administrative cost of dealing with the leaver, for example paperwork to be completed and disruption to production if a sudden loss occurs;

(b)   cost of advertising for a replacement;

(c)   expenditure needed to screen applicants and then to interview for a replacement;

(d)   cost of training new employees;

(e)   spoilt work produced by a recruit during the learning period;

(f)   accidents and damage to machines caused by unskilled learners operating them;

(g)   production lost when a slow-working recruit replaces a skilled operative;

(h)   the whole investment in the development of an existing employee is lost to the company when that employee leaves.

Low labour turnover indicates a stable workforce, whereas increasing labour turnover points to employees' dissatisfaction with pay and/or conditions. A turnover ratio should be computed for different grades and types of labour in case an overall low ratio hides an adverse position for one sector of the workforce. When considering labour turnover certain significant factors should be identified, as their presence will help in interpreting the situation.

1.   Any particular departments which have a high labour turnover: this may mean that the fault if any can be isolated to one part of the company and identified more easily.

2.   The skill ratings of those who are leaving the business: some employees may join a company merely to take part in its training scheme, without seeking

permanent employment there.
3. The length of service of those leaving the business: it is interesting to discover whether a small number of employees join and then depart after only a short time, thereby requiring replacement and increasing the turnover ratio. Perhaps the recruitment procedure could be adjusted to improve this situation.
4. An analysis of employees leaving the company might show that a high proportion were dismissed, or that some left through natural wastage, i.e. retirement, or through the seasonality of the business.
5. Particulars of new employers in the region who might be attracting skilled workers away from the company are also significant for labour turnover.

High labour turnover may be a symptom of poor employee facilities at a company, e.g. canteen, sports club, crèche etc., or that wage rates paid by the business are below the norm. Poor recruitment techniques will result in employing the wrong person for a job so that he or she leaves after only a short period. Poor working conditions, a lack of job security or prospects of promotion and indeed the attitude of certain departmental managers can also increase labour turnover.

Idle time

It is important for management to know what proportion of the labour hours paid for have not resulted in actual production. The difference between hours paid and hours worked is called *idle time*. Some idle time is unavoidable and is considered as a normal occurrence in the factory, e.g. teabreaks, travelling time from one job or department to another, *down time* when direct workers wait for routine maintenance on their machines to be completed and *setting-up time*, which is the delay between one job and another while machinery is adjusted. The labour force is paid during these periods but of course no production takes place and this cost is a production overhead expense. It is not sufficient to inform management of the total idle time, since an analysis of the reasons for this non-productive time will be useful in formulating action to remove the cause and improve efficiency.

Avoidable idle time requires a separate cost statement. It is caused by stock-outs, machine breakdowns, production bottlenecks, strikes etc., and other unfortunate mishaps which disrupt production. Management need to know the reasons for avoidable idle time so that corrective action can be formulated and past mistakes avoided in the future. Other reasons for lost time should also be identified by a comment on lateness or absenteeism; an employee who is absent is not paid but his or her absence will result in under-used production facilities, and may well cause problems in other parts of the production cycle which rely on that employee for component parts.

An idle time report is compiled in terms of hours rather than money, and attempts to reconcile hours paid with hours spent on actual production. Figure 5.4 gives an example of a report.

XYZ Ltd	IDLE TIME STATEMENT		Week ended..............	
	This week		Average of year to date	
	Hours	%	Hours	%
Production time paid for – normal rates				
Production time paid for – overtime rates				
	Hours		Hours	
Idle time avoidable – waiting for instructions – waiting for materials – waiting for tools – maintenance – waiting for machine setter				
Idle time unavoidable – power failure – breakdown – –				
Idle time ratio (Idle time/time paid for)		%		%

Figure 5.4   Idle time report

Effectiveness

Labour efficiency reports comment on the effectiveness of an employee or a team in completing the task for which they have been paid. An inefficient employee may well attend the factory in good time but because his or her rate of production is not fast enough or because he or she is careless and finished production is rejected, production time may be wasted. The efficiency of labour is usually measured in terms of standard hours, i.e. the number of hours allowed for production which has taken place, as opposed to the hours actually taken to produce that production. This is part of the standard costing system and the term used to express the effectiveness of labour is *productivity*.

MULTIPLE CHOICE QUESTIONS

5.1   The period of time for which a work station is available for production but is not utilized due to shortage of tooling, materials, operators etc. This statement defines:

(a)   Down time.
(b)   Idle time.
(c)   Operation time.
(d)   Set-up time.

(a)   (b)   (c)   (d)

5.2   Wages analysis may include:
(a)   Gross wages per department or operation.
(b)   Gross wages per labour classification.
(c)   Gross wages per product.
(d)   Analysis of constituent parts of gross wages – direct/lost time.

(a)   (a + c)   (a + b + c)   (all)

5.3   Favourable conditions for the operation of piece rates include:
(a)   Long uninterrupted run of production.
(b)   Homogeneous products.
(c)   Ease of inspection.
(d)   High proportion of indirect labour.

(a)   (a + b)   (a + b + c)   (all)

5.4   Employees leaving during the quarter – 750; employees joining during the quarter – 600; total employees at the start of the quarter – 14,630.
   Calculate labour turnover as:
(a)   5.13 per cent.
(b)   9.23 per cent.
(c)   9.28 per cent.
(d)   9.32 per cent.

(a)   (b)   (c)   (d)

5.5   Which of the following items is not a cost implication of labour turnover?
(a)   Training.
(b)   Recruiting.
(c)   Damage to machines.
(d)   Ageing labour force.

(a)   (b)   (c)   (d)

EXERCISES

5A   Shown below is one week's basic payroll data for the assembly department of Wooden Ltd, a manufacturer of a range of domestic furniture.

	Direct workers	*Indirect workers*
Total attendance time (hours)	800	350
Basic hourly rate of pay	£1.50	£1.00
Overtime hours worked	100	40
Shift premium	£150	£50
Group bonus	£160	£70
Employees' deductions:		
Income tax	£250	£100
National insurance	£75	£35
Employer's contributions:		
National insurance	£125	£55

Overtime, which is paid at basic time rate plus one half, is used as a means of generally increasing the factory output. However, 20 per cent of the overtime shown above, for both direct and indirect workers, was incurred at the specific request of a special customer who requires, and is paying for, a particular batch of coffee tables to be completed quickly.

Analysis of the direct workers' time from returned work tickets shows:

Productive time:	590 hours
Non-productive time:	
Machine breakdown	50 hours
Waiting for materials	40 hours
Waiting for instructions	45 hours
Idle time	75 hours

Required
(a)   Assuming the company operates a historical batch costing system, fully integrated with the financial accounts, write up the assembly department's wages, work-in-progress and production overhead control accounts, and other relevant accounts.
(b)   Explain the reasons for, and effect on product costs of, your treatment of the following items:
    (i)   employer's national insurance contributions;
    (ii)   group bonus;
    (iii)   overtime earnings.

(Association of Certified Accountants)

5B   (a) Shown below is a summary of the previous week's payroll data for the moulding department in Peal plc, a company manufacturing two different types of telephone receiver.

	Direct workers	Indirect workers
Hours worked:		
Ordinary time	3,600	800
Overtime	630	80
Basic hourly rate of pay	£3.60	£2.10
Net wages paid	£12,864	£1,420
Analysis of direct workers' time:		
Productive time (hours):		
Type 1 receiver - 4,800 units	2,400	
Type 2 receiver - 1,500 units	1,125	
Non-productive down time (hours)	705	

The moulding department employs 90 direct and 20 indirect operatives. All operatives are paid at hourly time rates; overtime, which is regularly worked to meet budgeted production targets, is paid at time rate plus one-third.

The company operates a batch costing system, using actual costs, which is fully integrated with the financial accounts.

Required

Construct the moulding department's wages control account for the previous week *clearly* indicating the accounts into which the corresponding entries would be posted.

(b) The works manager of Peal plc is considering introducing a piece work incentive scheme for the direct workers in the moulding department. Work Study Services have examined the manufacturing process in the moulding department and consider that the operation to produce Type 1 receivers should be performed under normal conditions, by one operative in 24 minutes, for a Type 2 receiver the corresponding time is 36 minutes. Unavoidable non-productive down time is expected to remain at approximately 20 per cent of productive time.

Having considered the above times the works manager suggests that direct operatives should be paid a piece rate of £1.90 for each Type 1 receiver produced; £2.85 for each Type 2 receiver produced; and non-productive down time should be paid at £2.50 per hour.

As the accountant of Peal plc you have been asked to appraise the above scheme. It should be assumed that the previous week's payroll data shown in (a) above represents an average week in the moulding department; although the weekly volume of production and consequent wages do fluctuate around this mean figure. No further information has been provided.

Required

(i) Examine the effect of the proposed scheme on the labour costs in the moulding department.

Any assumptions you consider necessary should be clearly stated.

(ii) Briefly discuss any additional considerations which would need to be thoroughly examined before the feasibility of the proposed incentive scheme could be finally assessed.

(Association of Certified Accountants)

5C   In production, an employee often works on several jobs each day, and it is necessary to keep a record of how much the employee has earned as well as the labour cost of each job.

Outline a costing system which will enable the wages department and the cost department to maintain accurate records.

6 The Cost Accounting Treatment of Overheads

OBJECTIVE

The objective of this chapter is to identify overhead costs, and demonstrate how they should be treated in the cost accounts.

The term 'overhead' covers all those costs which cannot be directly attributed to cost units produced. Included in this classification of costs are indirect materials, indirect labour, and other indirect expenses whether incurred at the factory or as distribution, selling or administrative expenses. The costing treatment of overheads concerns methods whereby these indirect expenses can be related to cost units. If each unit is allotted its share of indirected expenses, a full absorbed cost for that unit will be computed. It is relatively easy to determine the cost of direct material or direct labour built into a cost unit, but the allotment of indirect costs first to cost centres and then to cost units requires a complex system of allocation and apportionment. The usual method is to allocate certain expenses to cost centres to which they logically belong. Costs which cannot be allocated are then apportioned, or divided up on a logical basis, so that each cost centre is given its appropriate share. Once overheads are attributed to various cost centres they can be attached to cost units by means of absorption rates as those units pass through the cost centres.

The costing treatment therefore comprises the three processes of *allocation, apportionment and absorption*.

WHAT ARE OVERHEADS?

The following costs might be included as part of the factory overhead expense. The list is not exhaustive.

1. Indirect materials: any material required in the production process but not necessarily built into the product. A good example of an indirect material is

the chemical required for water softening in a laundry. This material softens the water used in all departments and thus cannot be directly connected to any cost unit.

2. Indirect labour: this category covers all employees who do not work on units of production, e.g. storemen, labourers etc. Indirect labour was discussed in the previous chapter.

3. Supervisory labour: chargehands and managers who work for a salary rather than a weekly wage are an overhead expense because their efforts cannot be directly attributed to individual units of production. Note that bonuses and even overtime for direct labour are counted as an indirect labour cost.

4. National insurance contributions paid by the employer are part of the cost of employing the labour force, but even for direct employees this cost cannot be analysed to cost units.

5. The maintenance of plant and buildings.

6. The cost of fuel and power to operate the machinery.

7. The general administrative costs of the factory such as rent, heating, lighting, telephones and stationery.

8. Insurance: this is often an important overhead expense since the risks of fire, accident and other perils experienced in the factory must be provided for.

9. Depreciation of plant and any fixtures and fittings which are part of the factory.

The cost of selling, distribution, research, development and administration are main headings for groups of non-factory overhead expenses. A factory can be divided into cost centres some of which are direct, i.e. they produce cost units, and others indirect, i.e. they produce services to the production departments. Examples of indirect cost centres are the cost office, the stores, the canteen, the tool room, the power house etc. One of the difficulties of cost accounting is that, once allocated and apportioned to indirect cost centres, overheads must then be reallocated to direct cost centres so that they can eventually be attributed to cost units by means of absorption rates applied as the cost units pass through the production cost centres.

ALLOCATION AND APPORTIONMENT

Overhead costs by their nature cannot often be related to one particular cost centre. Where a cost is directly attributable to a department, e.g. electricity metered to that department, allocation can take place. Non-allocable costs, however, must be apportioned on some logical basis to be divided between the cost centres concerned. Selection of an appropriate base is important because an inappropriate base will result in unreliable overhead costs per cost centre, on which decisions may be based. The following list shows some apportionment bases which can be applied to certain overhead costs.

1. Supervisory labour can be apportioned on the basis of time sheets filled in by each individual. A time sheet will analyse the activity of the supervisor between production departments.

2. Indirect wages: this is the cost of support workers who provide services to production departments. If they cannot be allocated directly to one or other of the production departments the general cost of indirect wages can be apportioned according to the number of direct workers in each production department.
3. Rent: this expense can be apportioned in proportion to the floor area of each department.
4. Depreciation: this overhead can be apportioned according to the cost of machines in each department as shown by the plant register.
5. Light and heat: this cost may be apportioned according to area, but some cost accountants prefer to use the cubic capacity of the premises concerned since heating rooms with high ceilings will require more heat.
6. Electricity: this cost can be apportioned according to the number of outlet points in each department, but some account must be taken of the use made of these points if a logical apportionment is to be derived.
7. Power: this cost is apportioned by the number of machines, but the capacity of the machines should be considered since one large machine may use more power than several small machines in another department.
8. Maintenance: this cost is apportioned according to the time sheet of the maintenance gang.
9. Canteen: the number of employees in each department is a logical basis for the apportionment of canteen costs, but this assumes that all employees will make use of the canteen.
10. Insurance: the premium to insure machines might well be apportioned according to the number or value of the machines in each department, but the cost of fire insurance might be better apportioned according to floor area or capital value.

Example 6.1: Apportionment

Maxi Manufacturers plc's budgeted overhead for the year is as follows:

	£
Supervision	47,525
Indirect labour	86,008
Holiday pay and national insurance	26,226
Tooling cost	19,400
Machine maintenance labour cost	34,500
Power	42,528
Small tools and supplies	11,171
Insurance of machinery	2,185
Insurance of buildings	1,170
Rent	18,000
Depreciation of machinery	29,184
Total	317,897

The company operates four production departments: milling, casting, drilling and polishing. The budgeted overhead cost must be allocated or apportioned to these cost centres using the following information.

| | Factory departments | | | | |
	Milling	Casting	Drilling	Polishing	Total
Floor space (square feet)	2,800	2,500	1,800	1,900	9,000
Kilowatt hours (000s)	370	166	185	165	886
Capital cost of machines (£000s)	130	120	18	116	384
Indirect workers	5	4	2	2	13
Total workers	21	34	22	17	94
Machine maintenance hours (000s)	3	3	3	1	10
Tooling costs (£)	5,500	6,300	5,000	2,600	19,400
Supervision costs (£)	12,050	12,200	11,775	11,500	47,525
Small tools and supplies (£)	2,991	4,441	1,566	2,173	11,171
Machine running hours (000s)	60	56	29	18	163

Allocation and apportionment

	Milling £	Casting £	Drilling £	Polishing £	Total £
Supervision – allocation	12,050	12,200	11,775	11,500	47,525
Indirect labour – persons	33,080	26,464	13,232	13,232	86,008
Holiday pay – total workers	5,859	9,486	6,138	4,743	26,226
Tooling cost – allocation	5,500	6,300	5,000	2,600	19,400
Machine maintenance – hours	10,350	10,350	10,350	3,450	34,500
Power – kilowatt hours	17,760	7,968	8,880	7,920	42,528
Tools – allocation	2,991	4,441	1,566	2,173	11,171
Insurance of machinery – cost of machine	740	683	102	660	2,185
Insurance of buildings – floor space	364	325	234	247	1,170
Rent – floor space	5,600	5,000	3,600	3,800	18,000
Depreciation – cost of machines	9,880	9,120	1,368	8,816	29,184
Overhead per cost centre	104,174	92,337	62,245	59,141	317,897

ABSORPTION

Once the overhead expenses have been allocated or apportioned to direct cost centres, they can be charged out from those cost centres to cost units. This procedure is undertaken by calculating a predetermined absorption rate which, if applied to cost units passing through the cost centre, will absorb or charge out all the overheads attributable to that cost centre. The rate is calculated for the forthcoming year as part of the budgeting procedure, using estimates for the cost to be incurred and the basis on which it is to be absorbed. In a less sophisticated system, a single rate can be computed for an entire factory, but as the cost structure becomes more complicated, with a series of direct cost centres in the factory, a rate for each centre should be calculated. This technique recognizes the different use made of cost centres by various products and builds this factor into the calculation when the overheads are charged out to production.

A simple system is possible if only one product is made, which goes through all the productive cost centres. However, suppose product A is produced in the moulding and assembly departments but not the painting department, while product B is manufactured in the assembly department and the painting department. Clearly, the use made of factory cost centres by these two products is different, and should influence their cost. Products which use the services of all three production departments may not make the same use of those departments. One product may spend much more time in the moulding department than in the assembly department; another may spend comparatively little time in the moulding department but take a long time to assemble. Accordingly, the absorption of cost centre overheads should recognize the overheads attributable to each cost centre and reflect the relative use made of cost centre facilities by different products.

OVER- AND UNDER-ABSORPTION

Because the overhead absorption rates are calculated in advance of the year by means of estimated costs, they cannot be expected to be completely accurate. Therefore when they are applied to actual volumes of units produced they may absorb more or less than the actual overhead cost incurred. Over- or under-absorbed should be written off at once to the costing profit and loss account. The costs are accumulated in a total or control account, and then charged out from that control account to the manufacturing account or work-in-progress control account. If less is charged out than has been incurred the balance on the overhead control account will show the under-absorbed amount, and this should be written off to the costing profit and loss account. If more overhead is charged out than is incurred, the surplus is credited to the costing profit and loss account. Under- or over-absorbed overhead may be caused by faulty estimates when the rates are set, and should be communicated to management since it may indicate that the planned level of capacity usage has not been achieved, or that the planned level of overhead cost has been exceeded.

Example 6.2

The ABC Company Limited computes an overhead absorption rate by dividing the factory overhead cost expected to be incurred by the number of labour hours expected to be worked:

$$\frac{\text{Expected overheads}}{\text{Expected labour hours}} = \frac{£80,000}{160,000 \text{ hours}} = 50\text{p per hour}$$

The actual cost incurred during the period is £85,000, and labour hours worked amount to 165,000.

Factory overhead control a/c

	£		£
Cost incurred from various overhead expense accounts	85,000	Amount absorbed to the work-in-progress a/c (165,000 × £0.5)	82,500
		Overheads under-absorbed written off to costing profit and loss a/c	2,500
	£85,000		£85,000

Work-in progress a/c

	£		£
Direct material	xxx	Completed production transferred to	
Direct labour	xxx	finished goods stores	xxx
Factory overhead absorbed to production	82,500	Balance of WiP stock c/f	xxx

Costing profit and loss account

	£		£
Administrative overheads	xxx	Operating profit	xxx
Factory overheads under-absorbed	2,500		

Under-absorbed overhead is written off to profit and loss as a separate item. Any over-absorbed overhead appears as a credit in the costing profit and loss.

ABSORPTION RATES: THE ALTERNATIVES

The selection of an appropriate rate which overheads can be absorbed to cost units as they pass through a cost centre is of the greatest significance if the resulting cost allocation of overheads to individual products or jobs is to be meaningful and therefore reliable as a true cost. The rate selected should attempt to relate the absorption of overheads to whatever factors have contributed most to the overhead cost which has been incurred. In a department which is highly mechanized the bulk of the overheads will stem from machinery, for example depreciation, maintenance, power, insurance etc., and a rate expressing the usage of that machinery per cost unit would be appropriate. Accordingly, in this situation departmental overheads would be absorbed according to the machine hours worked on each product or job. A high proportion of the departmental overheads caused by the cost of operating a store suggests the use of a rate based on the cost of materials used in production. In the case of a labour-intensive department using hand-operated techniques a rate based on labour cost or labour time per unit would be appropriate.

The simplest basis on which to absorb overheads to production is to divide the expected cost by the number of units to be made, according to the production budget. However, a unit rate is possible only where the output of a cost centre is homogeneous. If the department produces several different types of product, other methods must be used to relate overhead to the cost of production.

There are four main methods by which overhead can be charged to production.

Direct material percentage

$$\frac{\text{Estimated overheads for the year}}{\text{Estimated direct material costs}} \times \frac{100}{1} = \text{The rate}$$

The estimated overhead expenses are divided by the estimated cost of raw materials to be used in the department during the period. The percentage thus derived relates overheads to be charged to each job to the amount of materials built into that job. This method is useful if materials are a major part of the cost of units made in the department. The direct material percentage method has the disadvantage, however, that when material prices change (as they can do under the FIFO or LIFO pricing rules) the overheads borne by a job will change, even though there has been no change in the overhead costs themselves. A second disadvantage of this basis for absorption is that it is unfair to charge more overheads to a job merely because it uses expensive materials whereas other jobs are built with cheaper items. A third disadvantage is that the rate has no relation to either time or machinery and thus is not appropriate in a cost centre where overheads stem from machine costs or are time-orientated.

Direct labour percentage

This method uses a similar formula to the one above but is preferable because it does indirectly take time into account through the labour cost, and because labour costs are less likely to fluctuate between production units than are material costs. Many overhead expenses are related to time, e.g. salaries, rent, depreciation etc., so that an absorption method which is based on the wages of hourly paid direct labour may be reliable and fair.

The formula for calculating the rate is:

$$\frac{\text{Estimated overheads for the year}}{\text{Estimated direct wages for the year}} \times \frac{100}{1} = \text{The rate}$$

If this rate is applied to the direct labour cost of a job or product the resultant amount will be the share of overhead expense to be absorbed or charged to that job. This method can be applied successfully where labour is an important part of the direct cost, and where the same grade of labour is used throughout the cost centre. It does not relate directly to time or to machine costs, nor does it take account of the relative efficiency of those who work on the job concerned. A job undertaken by a skilled employee may have a higher labour cost than one undertaken by an apprentice, but if the two jobs take equal amounts of time to complete, it might be unfair to charge different amounts of overhead to them.

Direct labour hour rate

$$\frac{\text{Estimated overheads for the year}}{\text{Estimated direct labour hours for the year}} = \text{Rate per hour}$$

This absorption rate is time-orientated but should be applied only in a business where the manufacturing techniques are hand-operated rather than mechanized. It is expensive to maintain records which show the labour hours spent on each job or product, but perhaps this expense is worthwhile since it is a clear advantage to link the overhead charge to the time taken by each job in the department. A disadvantage is that a job completed by an inefficient worker will be charged more overhead merely because it has spent more time in the department.

Machine hour rate

$$\frac{\text{Estimated overheads for the year}}{\text{Estimated machine hours for the year}} = \text{Rate per hour}$$

For example, £50,000 ÷ 40,000 hours = £1.25 per hour. If £1.25 is charged to jobs for every hour of machine time used in the cost centre, the total overhead allotted to that cost centre will be absorbed by production. In a normal mechanized factory, the overheads will be machine-orientated, so this method is appropriate for most modern situations. A machine hour rate will be able to account for the varying lengths of time taken by products or jobs as they are worked on by the various machines in the department. However, it cannot take into account the fact that an hour spent on an expensive machine should perhaps charge more overheads to a job than an hour spent on a cheaper, less important machine, unless the departmental overheads are further analysed to each group of machines and separated rates are computed.

The success of full absorption costing depends on the correct logic used in the selection of apportionment bases, and also on the choice of an appropriate absorption rate.

Example 6.3: Absorption

Maxi Manufacturers plc charges overhead to jobs as a percentage of direct labour cost. The rate in use is 120 per cent. The overhead budget of the company is set out in Example 6.1, where overhead costs were allocated and apportioned to cost centres as follows:

	Milling	*Casting*	*Drilling*	*Polishing*
	£104,174	£92,337	£62,245	£59,141
Machine Running hours	60000	56000	29,000	18000

The company is concerned that the single 'blanket' overhead absorption rate used at present is not appropriate to the circumstances of its business. It is proposed therefore to introduce a new system whereby overheads are absorbed on the basis of a separate machine hour rate for each of the four cost centres.

Required

As adviser to the business recommending the change to the machine hour basis you are required to:
(a)   state the arguments in favour of the change;
(b)   calculate a machine hour rate for each of the four departments;
(c)   calculate the overhead to be absorbed by job A, involving six hours in milling, eight hours in casting, two hours in drilling and four hours in polishing, using the machine hour rates calculated by you in answer to (b);
(d)   calculate the overhead to be absorbed by job A when the labour cost is £70 and the present method is used.

Solution

(a) The case for the change from a blanket rate should contain the following points.

1. A machine hour rate is more appropriate since costs in the budget are related more closely to machinery than to labour.
2. A rate per machine group is more flexible and takes closer account of machine time for different jobs. For example, why should a job which does not use the milling department bear part of the overhead of that cost centre?
3. The rate per machine group is different. Why should ten hours on polishing be charged the same as ten hours on drilling?

(b)	Milling	Casting	Drilling	Polishing
Overhead per cost centre	£104,174	£92,337	£62,245	£59,141
Machine running hours (000s)	60	56	29	18
Rate per hour (pence)	173.6	164.9	214.6	328.6

(c) Job A	£
6 hours' milling × 173.6p	10.42
8 hours' casting × 164.9p	13.19
2 hours' drilling × 214.6p	4.29
4 hours' polishing × 328.6p	13.14
Overhead on job A	41.04

(d) 120% × £70 = £84.

Note: A different overhead costing method has changed the cost of job A and thus affected its profitability. Any reliance placed by management on this profit measurement will be affected by the respect they have for the bases used in the apportionment. If this costing is used as a basis for pricing or tendering the firm may well win job A from a competitor. Faulty overhead costing can underprice jobs, thereby taking on loss-making work, or overprice jobs, thereby losing out to the competition.

THE APPORTIONMENT OF SERVICE CENTRE COSTS

Some departments provide a service to the direct production cost centres. However, overhead costs will be apportioned to these indirect cost centres and these costs must be reallocated in some way to direct cost centres. This matter is made more complex when one service department is used by another and vice versa.

Example 6.4

The Mini Manufacturing Company has two production departments, namely machining and finishing, and two service departments, maintenance and materials handling.

The overhead budgets per four-week costing period are £22,000 for the machine department and £25,000 for the finishing department. The machining department overhead is absorbed on a machine hour basis (400 per period) and the finishing department overhead is absorbed on the basis of direct labour hours (5,000 per period).

In establishing the overhead budgets of the production departments the service department costs have been allocated as follows:

1. Maintenance department:
   (a) 60 per cent to machining department;
   (b) 30 per cent to finishing department; and
   (c) 10 per cent to materials handling.
2. Materials handling:
   (a) 30 per cent to machining department;
   (b) 50 per cent to finishing department; and
   (c) 20 per cent to maintenance department.

During May the machining department was in operation for 392 hours, and the number of direct labour hours worked by the finishing department personnel was 5,400. Overheads incurred during May were as follows:

	£
Machining	15,200
Finishing	18,600
Maintenance	9,600
Materials handling	8,000
Total	51,400

Required

(a) Write up the overhead accounts for each of the production departments for May showing the disposition of any under/over-absorption.
(b) Analyse the factors which give rise to the under/over-absorption.

Solution (using the repeated distribution method)

First redistribute the service department costs according to the allocation system followed in establishing the overhead budgets, e.g. £9,600 for maintenance is allocated to the other three departments in the ratio 60:30:10, and the cost of handling materials is spread in the ratio 30:50:20.

	Machining £	Finishing £	Maintenance £	Materials handling £
Overhead incurred	15,200	18,600	9,600	8,000
Maintenance redistributed	5,760	2,880	(9,600)	960
Handling redistributed	2,688	4,480	1,792	(8,960)
Maintenance redistributed	1,075	538	(1,792)	179
Handling redistributed	54	89	36	(179)
Maintenance redistributed	24	12	(36)	Negligible
Overhead incurred	24,801	26,599		

Absorption rates are calculated using the estimated budget figures, i.e.

$$\text{Machining} \quad \frac{£22,000}{400 \text{ hours}} = £55 \text{ per hour}$$

Finishing $\dfrac{£25,000}{5000 \text{ hours}}$ = £5 per hour

Note that over- and under-absorbed overheads are written off to the costing profit and loss.

The factors which have caused the over- and under-absorption are both concerned with the estimates of cost and hours worked, which vary from actual performance. The under/over-absorption can be expressed as ledger accounts:

Machining dept overhead a/c

	£		£
Cost incurred per		Cost absorbed to WiP	
schedule	24,801	(392 hours × £55)	21,560
		Under-absorbed to P. and L. a/c	3,241
	24,801		24,801

Finishing dept overhead a/c

	£		£
Cost incurred per		Cost absorbed to WiP	
schedule	26,599	(5,400 hours × £5)	27,000
Over-absorbed to P. and L. a/c	401		
	27,000		27,000

Further analysis reveals information which is of interest to management.

Machining

Activity:	Worked eight hours less than budget, therefore absorbed 8 × £55 less than expected	£ 440	adverse
Expenditure:	Incurred £24,801 against budget of £22,000	£2,801	adverse
	Under-absorbed	£3,241	

Finishing

Activity:	Worked 400 more hours than budget, therefore over-absorbed 400 × £5	£2,000	favourable
Expenditure:	Incurred £26,599 against budget £25,000	£1,599	adverse
	Over-absorbed	£401	

In this case the factors affecting absorption pull in opposite directions, and a small variance of £401 masks much greater departures from budget.

ALGEBRAIC SOLUTION TO THE APPORTIONMENT OF SERVICE DEPARTMENT COSTS

An alternative solution to this problem can be derived by the use of simultaneous equations.

Let X = total overhead of the maintenance department, and let Y = total overhead of the handling department. Two equations can then be formulated as follows:

$$X = £9,600 + 0.2Y$$

$$Y = £8,000 + 0.1X$$

These formulae can be rearranged and multiplied out to eliminate the decimals. Two further formulae are the result of this calculation:

(a) $10X - 2Y = £96,000$

(b) $-X + 10Y = £80,000$

Equation (a) includes $-2Y$ so if it is multiplied by 5 an equation is derived which includes $-10Y$. When that equation is added to equation (b), Y is eliminated.

$$[50X - 10Y = £480,000] + [-X + 10Y = £80,000]$$
$$49X = £560,000$$
$$\text{Therefore } X = £11,428$$

60 per cent of X should be allocated to the machining department = £6,857.
30 per cent of X should be allocated to the finishing department = £3,429.

Now that X is known, Y can be calculated by substitution in formula (a):

$$10 \times £11,428 - 2Y = £96,000$$
$$£114,280 - 2Y = £96,000$$
$$£18,280 = 2Y$$
$$£9,140 = Y$$

30 per cent of Y should be allocated to the machining department = £2,742.
50 per cent of Y should be allocated to the finishing department = £4,570.

The overhead can now be apportioned as follows:

	Machining £	Finishing £
Overhead incurred	15,200	18,600
Maintenance department	6,857	3,429
Handling department	2,742	4,570
	24,799	26,599

Note: The total overhead apportioned has lost £2. This is caused by rounding in the calculation.

This method works well if there are two service departments, but if more than two are involved the equations can become complicated.

MACHINE HOUR RATES

In some companies a single machine is treated as a cost centre, or alternatively a small group of machines forming only part of the activity within a department or workshop can be costed as a separate cost centre. The costs associated with such a machine complex can be identified and estimated for a year ahead. The total cost for the group can then be spread across the hours of activity which are planned in the budget. This calculation will compute a charging out rate which can be applied to all jobs which come through the cost centre. The same technique can be applied to a mobile machine such as a crane or a bulldozer, to calculate the rate at which the machine and sometimes the driver can be hired out to customers.

Example 6.5

A machine shop cost centre contains six machines of equivalent capacities. Three operators are employed on each machine, one at £5 an hour and two assistants at £3 per hour each. The factory works a forty-hour week which includes four hours per week for set-up and gauge time. This work is done jointly by the operators. An average bonus of 15 per cent on productive time is paid. Costs are reported in this company on the basis of thirteen four-weekly periods, and the direct wages of the operators are included in a single machine hour rate which also recoups the factory overhead allocated to the machines. The following details of factory overheads applicable to the cost centre are available:

1. Set-up times as described above.
2. Depreciation: 15 per cent per annum on each machine (cost £10,000 each).
3. Maintenance and repairs: £20 per week per machine.
4. Consumable stores: £23.19 per week per machine.
5. Electric power: 15 units per hour per machine at 20p each.
6. Apportionment to the cost centre: rent £2,260 per annum, heat and light £2,195 per annum, foreman's salary £14,650 per annum.

Required

Compute the cost of running one machine for a four-week period and the hourly rate to be applied to recover the operating cost of each machine.

Solution

	£	£
Direct costs – per hour:		
Labour [£5 + (2 × £3)]		11.00
Power (15 × 20p)		3.00
Indirect costs – per week:		
Set-up and gauge time (4 hours × £11)	44.00	
Depreciation (£10,000 × 15% ÷ 52)	28.85	
Maintenance	20.00	
Consumable stores	23.19	
Bonus [(£11 × 15%) × 36 hours)	59.40	

Apportionments: £
Rent 2,260 p.a.
Heat and light 2,195 p.a.
Foreman 14,650 p.a.
————
19,105

£19,105 ÷ 6 ÷ 52	61.23	
Weekly cost	236.67	
£236.67 ÷ 36 hours		6.57
Hourly rate to recover operating cost		£20.57

The cost of running one machine for a four-week costing period is:

£20.57 × 36 × 4 = £2,962.08

However the behaviour of costs under different circumstances is significant when calculating machine hour rates. It must not be assumed that if a machine is sold, for example, the cost of running that machine for a week will be saved. Some of the costs involved, e.g the annual apportionments, are fixed costs, and will be incurred whether or not the machine is in operation, or even in the premises.

OVERHEADS AND STOCKS OF FINISHED GOODS AND WORK-IN-PROGRESS

Statement of Standard Accounting Practice (SSAP) 9 is quite specific as to the relationship of overhead expenses to stocks. If the cost of stock carried forward is to be matched fairly with revenue from its eventual sale, it should include any expenditure incurred in the normal course of business to bring the stock or work-in-progress to its present location and condition. This means that even though they accrue on a time basis, a proportion of production overheads should be included in the valuation of the stock of finished goods and work-in-progress.

The term 'cost' when applied to stocks and work-in-progress includes all expenditure on purchasing the material and converting it to semi-finished products. Purchase cost in this sense covers the price of raw materials plus any import duties, transport and handling costs, less discounts and rebates received. The cost of converting the materials to semi-finished work-in-progress is then added to this material cost. Conversion costs comprise direct labour, direct expenses and subcontract costs as well as production overheads and any other overheads which may be directly attributable to that product. (These production overheads (including depreciation) should be based on a normal level of activity for the year.) Thus production costs, even though incurred on a time basis, can be included as part of the cost of bringing the stock to its present condition and location. Abnormal conversion costs such as exceptional spoilage or idle time must be excluded from this calculation since they are avoidable under normal operating conditions, and should therefore be written off against profit in the period in which they are incurred. Overheads relating to design, marketing and selling are not normally included in the cost of stock but this rule is relaxed if a firm sales contract exists so that a proportion of their costs can be carried forward within the value of the stock. The cost of general management cannot normally be treated as part of the cost of conversion, but the costs of central servicing departments which can reasonably be allocated to production are considered to be part of the cost of conversion. Costs derived from unused production capacity must be written off and cannot be carried forward in the value of stock. The SSAP does not recognize the argument that it is prudent to write off all overheads in the year in which they are incurred; in this case the matching concept appears to override that of prudence.

DEPRECIATION

Depreciation is an important factory overhead, and as such merits some extra discussion.

Fixed assets gradually lose their value during the course of their useful economic life. This fall in value experienced during successive costing periods is an overhead expense of the period concerned. Depreciation can be defined as the diminution in value of a fixed asset due to the use and/or the passage of time; alternatively it is the measure of the wearing out, consumption or other loss of value of a fixed asset whether arising from use, the passage of time, or obsolescence through technology and market change.

Plant and machinery employed in a business may lose value because they are worn out by the work they have done and eventually become so inefficient that they must be scrapped. Other assets may, however, be just as efficient as on the day they were purchased, but nevertheless may have lost value because improved technology has developed new machines which can do the same work with greater efficiency. Alternatively, a machine that is physically effficient even though old may lose value because, due to market changes, there is no longer a demand for the product it makes. A loss in value caused by improved technology or market changes is said to be the result of obsolescence. Assets whose life is limited to a certain period, such as a lease, will lose value simply by the passage of time. Thus depreciation is a loss in value of a fixed asset either through physical deterioration or wear and tear related to the work done by the asset, or resulting from the passage of time.

The cost accountant must calculate the cost of depreciation suffered during a costing period, and charge it as an overhead expense to the cost units produced during that period. Depreciation is therefore an estimated cost charged to account for an uncertain fall in value on the part of fixed assets. Since it is an uncertain cost the accountant uses the term 'provision'; depreciation is 'provided for' out of the profit and loss account. To the cost accountant depreciation is the charge that must be made for the use of plant or machinery in the factory: from a financial accounting standpoint depreciation is seen as a means of spreading the capital cost of fixed assets over the years of their useful life and matching that cost to the revenue derived from their use. A more conceptual view of depreciation is that the provision of depreciation out of profits sets aside funds which might otherwise be distributed as dividend, which funds will be available to replace the capital tied up in fixed assets when those assets are worthless.

Example 6.6

A machine costing £10,500 has a useful economic life of four years, at the end of which period it is expected to realize £500 as scrap. Accordingly, £10,000 must be spread across the four-year working life of this asset. Depreciation of £2,500 is provided out of the profits each year so that a fair charge is made against revenue earned during each year of the asset's working life. At the end of that life, an amount of £10,000 has been set aside out of profit and automatically reinvested in the business, and this amount together with the cash received from the scrap sale, will be available to replace the old machine, if management consider that such a replacement is appropriate.

If replacement of the machine is not required, the funds originally tied up in it will be available for some other use in the business, so that productive capability of the business is maintained. Thus depreciation is not a provision out of profits to replace a machine, but rather to maintain the capital employed in the business and to avoid the overstatement of profits which would eventually deplete the capital invested. Depreciation is an estimated cost since the amount charged depends upon the method selected by management, and it is a non-cash cost since no payment is involved each year when depreciation is provided out of profits.

METHODS OF DEPRECIATION

Several methods can be applied to provide for depreciation. Selecting an appropriate method is often an arbitrary matter since businesses tend to use the method they have used in the past rather than select the most appropriate method for the asset concerned. The methods available also reflect the uncertain nature of depreciation, which relies upon estimates of the useful economic life of the asset and of its eventual residual value. Some methods are based on time, others use activity as a prime constituent in the calculation.

As an example, assume a machine purchased for £25,000, with an estimated scrap (residual) value of £1,000 and a useful economic life of four years. The machine can work for 2,000 hours per year, and produce a certain product in thirty minutes. The various methods of depreciating the machine are described below.

Straight line method

This method gives an equal charge for depreciation to each year of the useful economic life of the machine. The formula for its calculation is:

$$\frac{\text{Cost} - \text{Estimated scrap value}}{\text{Forecast economic life}} = \text{Annual charge}$$

$$\frac{£25,000 - £1,000}{4 \text{ years}} = £6,000$$

The obsolescence factor can be built into the estimate of the useful economic life. This method is simple to calculate and widely used, although it does not pay attention to the fact that the machine may work for a much greater time in one costing period than another. However, if a machine does not work during a costing period it may nevertheless lose value through obsolescence. Conceptually this method supports the idea that it is better to match the cost of a machine to the period and show it as the cost of holding the machine during that period, rather than to match the cost of the machine to the revenue produced from the sale of its production. The annual charge can be divided by 12 or 13 to give a cost per calendar month/four-weekly cost period.

The production unit method

This method attempts to relate the depreciation charge to the use made of the machine during the period. The cost of the asset, net of scrap value, is divided by the number of units it is expected to produce during its useful life. A rate is computed which can be applied to the units produced in each costing period so that an appropriate charge can be calculated. The formula for this method is:

$$\frac{\text{Cost} - \text{Estimated scrap value}}{\text{Expected units}} = \text{Unit rate}$$

At 2,000 hours per annum, two products per hour, and a four-year life, 16,000 units will be produced.

$$\frac{£25,000 - £1,000}{16,000 \text{ units}} = £1.5 \text{ per unit}$$

If 3,800 units are made this year a depreciation charge of £5,700 will be computed.

This method can be applied only if the units expected from a machine during its useful economic life can be forecast with some degree of accuracy, and if those units are similar or have the same work value. It is sometimes used to depreciate the cost of excavating a mine, where a forecast is made of the amount of ore or coal to be produced before the mine is worked out. Alternatively, a press which is designed to perform a certain number of operations before it is worn out may be depreciated in this way. A charge under this method is made only when the machine works, so that during an idle period there will be no depreciation to account for the obsolescence which may have taken place.

The production hour method

This method of depreciation calculates a rate per hour rather than a rate per unit, which is applied to the activity of the asset during a costing period to calculate the depreciation to be charged to that period. The formula which is applied is:

$$\frac{\text{Cost} - \text{Estimated scrap value}}{\text{Hours of useful economic life}} = \text{Rate per hour}$$

At 2,000 hours per annum over a four-year life, there will be 8,000 hours of use.

$$\frac{£25,000 - £1,000}{8,000 \text{ hours}} = £3 \text{ per hour}$$

If 1,900 hours are worked this year the depreciation charge would be £5,700.

A machine which produces a number of dissimilar products, perhaps taking different amounts of time in their production, can be depreciated by this method. A lathe, for example, can be employed on many different tasks and depreciation can be attached as a cost to those tasks according to the time taken.

With both the production unit and production hour methods, it is necessary to document the amount of work undertaken by the machine. With these methods, since depreciation is directly related to activity it may well become a variable rather than fixed cost.

The reducing balance method

This method calculates depreciation each year as a constant proportion of a continually reducing balance. An asset purchased for £10,000 and depreciated at 20 per cent will be written down by £2,000 during the first year of its life, then by 20 per cent of the reducing balance of £8,000 (£1,600) during the second year, by 20 per cent of the reducing balance of £6,400 (£1,280) during the third year, and so on. This method is not related to time or production, but seeks to charge a greater amount of depreciation during the earlier years of the life of the asset, with a correspondingly reduced amount in later years. The merit of this method is that a large proportion of the cost is written off when the machine is at its most efficient in the early years of its life, and that the charge falls in later years to balance the effect of increasing repair bills. Some authorities see this as an advantage, but perhaps the reduced depreciation in later years only masks the increasing cost of using an old machine. There is no certainty as to the rate which should be applied in the reducing balance method, although a formula exists for its calculation. It is usual practice to adopt the percentage consistently used by the business in the past. A further advantage of this method is that it writes off depreciation early in the life and is thus a good method to use if sudden obsolescence is expected from a machine which might be subject to technological change.

The formula which can be used to find the rate required, is:

$$1 - N\sqrt{\frac{S}{C}}$$

Where N = the number of years in the useful economic life
S = estimated scrap value
C = capital cost.

In terms of the original example above this can be calculated as:

$$1 - 4\sqrt{\frac{£1,000}{£25,000}} = 1 - 4\sqrt{0.04} = 1 - 0.447 = 0.553 \text{ or } 55.3\%$$

The depreciation each year would be calculated as:

	£
Cost	25,000
Depreciation: year 1 (25,000 × 0.553)	13,825
Written down value	11,175
Depreciation: year 2 (11,175 × 0.553)	6,180
Written down value	4,995
Depreciation: year 3 (4,995 × 0.553)	2,762
Written down value	2,233
Depreciation: year 4 (2,233 × 0.553)	1,234
Approximately scrap value of £1,000	999 *

*Slight difference due to working to three decimal places.

The revaluation method

This method of depreciation revalues the machine or other asset at the beginning and end of a costing period. The difference in value is the depreciation to be charged for that period. Although accurate unless the valuation is biased, this method is cumbersome in that the valuation takes time and may be influenced by increases in value caused by inflation, which mask the true depreciation charge.

In terms of our original example:

	£	Depreciation
Cost	25,000	
Value at end of year 1	21,000	4,000
Written down value	21,000	
Value at end of year 2	16,000	5,000
Written down value	16,000	
Value at end of year 3	11,500	4,500
Written down value	11,500	
Value at end of year 4	5,000	6,500

Clearly, if the machine is worth £5,000 at the end of year 4, the estimated scrap value on which the preceding calculations were based was not a very accurate estimate.

MULTIPLE CHOICE QUESTIONS

6.1 Which of the following is not a means whereby factory overheads can be charged out to production?
   (a) Direct labour rate.
   (b) Overtime rate.
   (c) Machine hour rate.
   (d) Blanket rate.

(a)   (b)   (c)   (d)

6.2 'The charging of discrete identifiable items of cost to cost centres or cost

units' describes:
- (a)   Cost absorption.
- (b)   Cost apportionment.
- (c)   Cost allocation.
- (d)   Cost conversion.

(a)   (b)   (c)   (d)

6.3   Which of the following costs is not a factory overhead expense?
- (a)   Salary of quality control inspector.
- (b)   Machine maintenance labour cost.
- (c)   Depreciation of equipment used in the research department.
- (d)   Overtime premium paid to direct labour.

(a)   (b)   (c)   (d)

6.4   Which of the following bases would be most appropriate to apportion the cost of electric power to factory departments?
- (a)   Amount metered out.
- (b)   Number of outlet points.
- (c)   Cubic capacity of premises.
- (d)   Kilowatt capacity of machines in department.

(a)   (b)   (c)   (d)

6.5   Department A absorbs factory overhead to work in progress by means of a DLH rate, worked out for each thirteen-week quarter. The department employs thirty skilled operatives and ten general labourers, who work a forty-hour week.

The budget reveals expected factory overhead for the quarter of £93,600. This week the skilled operatives have each worked one hour's overtime, and the general labourers have each worked two hours' overtime. Factory overhead incurred for the week is £7,200.

Calculate the amount of factory overhead over-or under-absorbed.
- (a)   Under-absorbed – £180.
- (b)   Over-absorbed   – £225.
- (c)   Over-absorbed   – £300.
- (d)   Over-absorbed   – £180.

(a)   (b)   (c)   (d)

EXERCISES

6A   Bookdon plc manufactures three products in two production departments, a machine shop and a fitting section; it also has two service departments, a canteen and a machine maintenance section. Shown below are next year's budgeted production data and manufacturing costs for the company.

Product	X	Y	Z
Production (units)	4,200	6,900	1,700
Prime cost, per unit:			
Direct materials	£11	£14	£17
Direct labour:			
Machine shop	£6	£4	£2
Fitting section	£12	£3	£21
Machine hours, per unit	6	3	4

Budgeted overheads:	Machine shop	Fitting section	Canteen	Machine maintenance section	Total
	£	£	£	£	£
Allocated overheads	27,660	19,470	16,600	26,650	90,380
Rent, heat and light					17,000
Depreciation and insurance of equipment					25,000
Additional data:					
Gross book value of equipment	£150,000	£75,000	£30,000	£45,000	
Number of employees	18	14	4	4	
Floor space occupied (square metres)	3,600	1,400	1,000	800	

It has been estimated that approximately 70 per cent of the machine maintenance section's costs are incurred servicing the machine shop and the remainder incurred servicing the fitting section.

Required

(a) (i) Calculate the following budgeted overhead absorption rates:
  • a machine hour rate for the machine shop;
  • a rate expressed as a percentage of direct wages for the fitting section.
  All workings and assumptions should be clearly shown.
  (ii) Calculate the budgeted manufacturing overhead cost per unit of product X.

(b) The production director of Bookdon plc has suggested that, 'as the actual overheads incurred and units produced are usually different from that budgeted and as a consequence profits at each month-end are distorted by over/under-absorbed overheads, it would be more accurate to calculate the actual overhead cost per unit each month-end by dividing the total number of all units actually produced during the month into the actual overheads incurred'.
  Critically examine the production director's suggestion.

(Association of Certified Accountants)

6B TCK Ltd manufactures three products known as T, C and K. Each product is started in the machining department and completed in the finishing section. It also has two service departments, a canteen and a machine maintenance section. Shown below are next year's budgeting production data and manufacturing costs for the company.

Budgeted overheads	Machining Department	Finishing Section	Canteen	Machine Maintenance Section	Total
	£	£	£	£	£
Allocated overheads	31,172	25,198	12,850	11,760	80,980
Depreciation and insurance of equipment					28,000
Rent, rates, heat and light					18,000
Additional data:					
Gross book value of equipment	120,000	45,000	15,000	60,000	240,000
Floor space occupied (square metres)	3,600	2,400	1,800	3,000	10,800
Number of employees	8	5	4	3	

Product:	T	C	K
Production (units)	3,400	2,800	1,600
Prime cost, per unit:			
Direct materials	£10	£8	£9
Direct labour:			
Machining department	£4	£5	£6
Finishing section	£8	£6	£4
Machine hours, per unit in the machining department	2	4	8

It has been estimated that approximately 80 per cent of the machine maintenance section's costs are incurred servicing the machining department and the remainder incurred servicing the finishing section.

Required

(a) Critically examine the objectives of calculating manufacturing overhead absorption rates.

(b) (i) Calculate the following budgeted overhead absorption rates:
  • a machine hour rate for the machining department;
  • a rate expressed as a percentage of direct wages for the finishing section.

  (ii) Calculate the budgeted manufacturing overhead cost per unit of product K.

(c) Comment briefly on the problems associated with apportioning service department costs to production departments.

6C   Kegworth Cats Ltd makes hulls for sale to other manufacturers of racing dinghies and leisure craft. The hulls are moulded and machined from glass reinforced plastic, fitted with joinery surfaces, and filled with a buoyancy foam. The processes are mechanized where possible with electricity supplied from the firm's own generator and machine repair services provided by the maintenance department.

The overhead expense budgets of the three production departments have been compiled by allocating the service department costs on the following bases:

Generating plant:
  Moulding and machining - 55%
  Joinery - 15%
  Filling - 20%
  Maintenance - 10%
Maintenance Department:
  Moulding and machining - 35%
  Joinery - 30%
  Filling - 20%
  Generating plant - 15%

Overhead expenses are budgeted on an annual basis and apportioned to thirteen four-week costing periods. This budgeted overhead is absorbed to production on the basis of machine hours. The budget for period 9 shows costs of £60,000 for moulding, £27,000 for joinery, and £35,000 for filling. The overhead is absorbed to production on the basis of machine hours, using the standard hours available each month for moulding 15,000 hours, joinery 18,000 hours, and filling 5,000 hours.

During period 9 actual costs and machine hours worked were as follows:

	Moulding	Joinery	Filling	Generator	Maintenance
Overheads incurred	£35,800	£19,600	£22,700	£29,400	£11,600
Machine hours worked	15,730	18,650	4,630		

Required

(a)   Prepare a simple statement to show overheads over- or under-absorbed by the production departments in period 9 and identify likely causes of the over- or under-absorption.
(b)   Briefly discuss the usefulness of overhead absorption rates for managerial purposes.

6D   A company is preparing its production overhead budgets and determining the apportionment of these overheads to products.

Cost centre expenses and related information have been budgeted as follows:

	Total	Machine shop A	Machine shop B	Assembly	Canteen	Maintenance
Indirect wages (£)	78,560	8,586	9,190	15,674	29,650	15,460
Consumable materials (incl. maintenance) (£)	16,900	6,400	8,700	1,200	600	–
Rent and rates (£)	16,700					
Buildings insurance (£)	2,400					
Power (£)	8,600					
Heat and light (£)	3,400					
Depreciation of machinery (£)	40,200					
Area (sq. ft)	45,000	10,000	12,000	15,000	6,000	2,000
Value of machinery (£)	402,000	201,000	179,000	22,000	–	–
Power usage – technical estimates (%)	100	55	40	3	–	2
Direct labour (hours)	35,000	8,000	6,200	20,800	–	–
Machine usage (hours)	25,200	7,200	18,000	–	–	–

Required

(a)   Determine budgeted overhead absorption rates for each of the production departments, using bases of apportionment and absorption which you consider most appropriate from the information provided.

(b)   On the assumption that actual activity was:

	Machine shop A	Machine shop B	Assembly
Direct labour hours	8,200	6,500	21,900
Machine usage hours	7,300	18,700	–

and total production overhead expenditure was £176,533, prepare the production overhead control account for the year (you are to assume that the company has a separate cost accounting system).

(c)   Explain the meaning of the word 'control' in the title of the account prepared in answer to (b).

(*Association of Certified Accountants*)

6E   Viking Engineering Limited has two production departments: machining and assembly. There are two service departments: maintenance and stores.

The budgeted overheads for May 1986 were:

Machining   £90,000
Assembly   £75,000

The machining department uses a machine hour rate basis for overhead absorption. (The budgeted machine hours being 3,600 hours for May.)

The assembly department uses a direct labour hour rate. (The budgeted labour hours being 24,000 hours for May.)

When production department overheads were prepared, service department overheads were dealt with as follows:

Maintenance department:
   70% to machining department
   20% to assembly department
   10% to stores department

Stores department:
  40% to machining department
  30% to assembly department
  30% to maintenance department

During May 1986 the machine department worked for 3,515 machine hours and the direct labour hours recorded in the assembly department were 26,280.

Overhead incurred was as follows:

	Machining £	Assembly £	Maintenance £	Stores £
Directly allocated:				
Material	12,000	18,000	21,000	4,000
Labour	7,000	9,000	30,000	11,500
Expenses	8,500	7,500	3,000	2,000
	27,500	34,500	54,000	17,500
Apportioned	11,000	15,500	8,500	5,000
	38,500	50,000	62,500	22,500

Required

(a)   The overhead account for each production department.
(b)   Give an explanation of how the under/over-absorption occurred for each department.
(c)   From your explanation in (b) give a numerical analysis of the under/over-absorption for each department.

6F   The costs listed below have been estimated for the forthcoming year for a company which makes sheet metal air-conditioning equipment.

	£000
Energy costs and water (heating and general)	20
Electricity for machines	14
Rent and rates	180
Repairs and maintenance: machinery	25
buildings	10
Raw materials	750
Maintenance and patterns and jigs	45
Direct wages	1,040
Direct wage-related costs	115
Indirect wages – production, absorb on direct labour hours	83
Indirect wage-related costs	10
Production management salaries	133
Depreciation of machinery	150
Security	10
Inspection and commissioning (production)	60
Carriage on raw materials	49
Carriage outwards	88
Salesforce salaries and commissions	100
Salesforce expenses	50
Design and estimating related to sales function	75
General management and administration	232
Advertising	40

Additional information:

Function	Area occupied (sq. ft)
Production	80,000
Sales/design and estimating	5,000
General office and administration	15,000

	Expected to be worked in current year	Budget for next year
Machine hours	160,000	180,000
Direct labour hours	180,000	200,000

Budgeted sales for next year are £4,550,000.

The production is mainly for specific orders from customers and the units made may be formed by machine, or involve intensive labour input, or be a mixture of both.

(a) **You are required to**
(i) Prepare an overhead analysis sheet to cover the classifications of:
    1. production overhead to be absorbed by machine hours;
    2. production overhead to be absorbed by direct labour hours;
    3. selling and distribution costs;
    4. administration costs.
(ii) Calculate the rates of absorption for *each* of the items (1) and (4) above.

(b)   Job 1019, which has been completed and was previously quoted to sell at £12,000, has had 300 machine hours booked to it and the following costs recorded on the job card:

Raw materials   £2,888
Direct wages   £3,500 (for 700 direct labour hours)

You are required to

(i) Compute the total cost of job 1019, using the rates of absorption you have calculated for the forthcoming year, show the expected profit and express that profit as a percentage of the selling price.
(ii) Compare and comment on the percentage profit on job 1019 with the percentage profit expected overall for the forthcoming year.
(Chartered Institute of Management Accountants)

7 Cost Bookkeeping

OBJECTIVE

The objective of this chapter is to examine the double entry aspect of cost accounting, and the relationship of formal ledger accounts for costing to the financial accounting system.

Business transactions are recorded and entered into the financial accounts of the organization, according to the principles of the double entry system. Cost accounting analyses these same transactions. Cost statements prepared for management can be derived from the financial accounting system adapted for cost accounting purposes, or from a separate bookkeeping system set up for cost accounting purposes and running alongside the financial accounts. It would seem at first glance that such duplication would be extremely wasteful. The accuracy of either method depends on the efficiency with which the system of recognizing and recording transactions is operated. Unless the basic data is complete and accurate, the ledger accounts written up from it will not be reliable, and cost or financial accounting statements based on information extracted from those ledger accounts will not show a true and fair view.

THE PRINCIPLES OF DOUBLE ENTRY

The double entry system has proved its worth over a long period of years as a means of recording financial transactions. Its principles can be adapted for use by cost accountants, whether the information is being recorded by hand on the pages of a ledger, by machine on cards, or by computer on tapes or discs. The principle of duality maintains that every transaction has a double effect on the business, and therefore should be recorded twice to account for this effect. Thus the double entry bookkeeping system records transactions twice, once on the 'debit' side and once on the 'credit' side. The following are examples of this dual effect.
1. A company borrows money from the bank. This transaction will increase its

liabilities, and at the same time increase the asset cash. Therefore the change in liabilities has balanced the change in assets.
2. A company sells products. Sales income will increase and at the same time the asset cash will increase. If the sale made is on credit terms, the increase in sales will be balanced by an increase in debtors.
3. A company purchases raw materials on credit terms. Purchases will increase and this will be balanced by an increase in liabilities in respect of the amount owed to the supplier.

There is not transaction which does not have a similar dual effect on the ledger accounts of the business. The ledgers are divided into accounts, not for each individual transaction, but to summarize transactions of a similar nature on the same page, e.g. factory direct wages, factory indirect wages, rent, power, sales revenue. The ledger account records transactions of a similar type, but if there are too many of one type to fit into an account a separate book or ledger will be opened to accommodate them, e.g. the debtors ledger, which has a separate page for each individual debtor's account, or the cash book, which summarizes all cash payments and receipts. With many companies the cash transactions, in and out, are too many for a separate ledger, and subsidiary ledgers are used to provide totals which are entered into the main cash book. As already stated accounts and ledgers need not be maintained in written form. Records held on computer tape or disc can be reproduced quickly as a printout, or on a visual display unit.

In bookkeeping terms each ledger account has two sides, one for debits and one for credits. In the days of handwritten ledgers, the debits were always listed on the left-hand side and the credits on the right-hand side and this practice still persists. When the two sides are totalled, the balance on the account can be found by deducting the lower total from the greater. If the entries on the credit ('Cr.') side total more than those on the debit ('Dr.') side of an account, that account is said to have a credit balance.

Example 7.1

Electricity cost

Dr.		£		Cr. £
4 April	Bill	893	Factory overhead control	2,499
5 July	Bill	761		
10 Oct.	Bill	845		
		2,499		2,499

East Midlands Electricity Board

Dr.		£			Cr. £
10 July	Cash	1,654	4 April	Bill	893
Balance c/f		845	5 July	Bill	761
			10 Oct.	Bill	845
		2,499			2,499
			Balance b/d		845

There are two accounts: one to show the cost (debits) and the other to record the liability (credits) owed to EMEB. When the bills for April and July are paid the EMEB account is debited and cash in turn is credited. The balance owing to EMEB is £845, a credit showing the liability at the year-end.

The costs of electricity consumed are totalled and written off to factory overhead account – credit electricity and debit factory overheads – eventually to be charged out to production.

THE FOUR BASIC RULES

The double entry system has four basic rules.

1. Each transaction has a dual effect on the business, and therefore should be recorded twice, once on the credit side and once on the debit side of the ledger. Although the associated debit and credit will not be in the same ledger account, and perhaps not even in the same book, the total of the debits must equal the total of the credits if this rule has been correctly followed. For example, sales made for cash will appear on the credit side of the sales account in the general ledger as income, and on the debit side of the cash book as cash received. In Example 7.1 the EMEB account would be maintained in the creditors' ledger, with the accounts of amounts owing to other suppliers, but the electricity cost account would be in the general ledger as an expense.

2. Assets and expenses are debit balances, and liabilities and revenues are credit balances. Assets purchased by a business are financed by funds invested in or lent to the business by the shareholders or creditors who then have a claim against the company for the return of their funds. Thus every asset is balanced by a corresponding liability as expressed in the balance sheet. In the profit and loss account, if income exceeds cost the balance – a profit – is on the credit side and since that profit belongs to the shareholders it forms part of the balance of shareholders' funds in the balance sheet. Figure 7.1 illustrates this in simple, diagrammatical form.

   The debit balances to the left of the vertical line must always equal the credit balances to the right of the line. If revenue exceeds cost, the surplus is a profit which belongs to shareholders. Thus a net profit disclosed by the income statement is posted to the credit of reserves which form part of the capital of the company.

3. An increase to an asset account or a cost account will be on the debit side and an increase to a liability account or to sales revenue will be on the credit side. If, however, an account is to be decreased the amount is not deducted from the side on which the balance is shown, but is instead posted to the opposite side of the account, so that the effect is to reduce the balance. See Example 7.1 when cash was paid to EMEB to reduce the amount owed. An asset account for motor vehicles has a balance on the debit side but if a vehicle is

DEBITS	CREDITS	
ASSETS	LIABILITIES AND CAPITAL	BALANCE SHEET
COSTS AND EXPENSES	REVENUE – SALES ETC.	PROFIT AND LOSS ACCOUNT OR INCOME STATEMENT

Figure 7.1   The quadrant

scrapped, that balance must be reduced. Accordingly the cost of the scrapped vehicle is posted to the credit side which in turn reduces the balance remaining on the debit side of the account.

Motor vehicles

	£		£
1984		1988	
Vehicle purchased for cash	5,000	Vehicle scrapped to disposal a/c	5,000
1985			
Vehicle purchased for cash	9,000	Balance c/f	9,000
	14,000		14,000
Balance b/d	9,000		

4. A useful aid to separate debit from credit is that the giving account is credited and the receiving account is debited. For example, when a sale is made on credit terms, the debtor receives and is debited, while sales give and are credited; but when the debtor pays cash in settlement of the debt, cash receives and is debited and the debtor gives and is credited. In Example 7.1, when EMEB was paid in cash it received and its account was debited, while cash, the giving account, was credited.

RECORDING TRANSACTIONS: PRIME DOCUMENTS AND THE DAY BOOK

The system must recognize and record transactions when they take place, and provide evidence of what has happened. This evidence takes the form of working documents or vouchers which are sometimes called 'prime documents'. For example, when an order is placed a copy is sent to the accounts department to evidence the transaction. When the goods arrive, a goods received note is prepared which evidences that part of the transaction, and a copy is also sent to the accounts department. When the invoice for the goods arrives it can be matched with the order and goods received note in the accounts department. Thus there is evidence that the goods which the company is being asked to pay for have not only been correctly ordered but have also been received. When this evidence is all gathered together, the invoice is passed and can then enter the ledger accounts as a debit to the purchaser's account (a cost) and a credit to the supplier's account (a creditor). Other prime documents: include credit notes to record invoices cancelled or goods returned; cheque book stubs to record cash paid out; the bank paying in book to record cash received from sales or debtors; clock cards and wages sheets to show the amount paid for labour; and sales invoices to record the amounts that have been sold and the customers to whom the sales have been made.

A large business will have many customers to whom it will make sales on credit terms from day to day. At the same time such a business will make purchases from a large number of suppliers again on a day-to-day basis. With such a large volume of transactions the prime documents need to be brought into some form of order so the device of a day book, or journal, has been interposed between the prime documents and the ledger accounts. For sales the sales invoices for the day are entered individually in the day book so that at the end of the day, week, or month, as the case may be, the total can be credited to the sales account in the general ledger, and the individual amounts debited to each customer who has received goods on credit, in the debtors ledger. The sales figure can also be analysed to various products which have been sold. A similar system works well for purchases, in that all purchase invoices passed each day, week or month can be listed in the purchase day book with the total debited to purchases at the end of the period, and the individual items credited to each supplier (or creditor) in the creditors' ledger. Clearly, handwritten books of prime entry such as those described above can easily be replaced by machine-prepared lists or computer entries. Debits and credits can exist as positive or negative pulses on a computer tape, which can be organized by the software and printed out on demand.

The term 'journal', however, persists for a special ledger which is used to record internal transactions and alterations made between the other ledgers. For example, if rent paid by cheque (£1,000) has been correctly entered as a credit in the cash book but has been debited in error to the insurance account, a journal entry will be required to credit insurance and debit rent, thus correcting the mistake. A journal entry will record the appropriate account to be debited and credited, with a 'narrative' giving the reason for the alteration. In some systems even this book has been replaced by a file of journal vouchers which evidence the debit and credit entries made in the mechanized or computer system. The journal entries to correct the error described above would be as follows:

Journal	Debit £	Credit £
Rent a/c	1,000	
Insurance a/c		1,000
Being correction of misposting to insurance a/c		

INTERLOCKING AND INTEGRATED ACCOUNTS

Some companies prefer to separate the financial accounting system from the cost records, others prefer to integrate cost analysis into the financial accounting system. *Interlocking accounts* can be defined as a system in which the cost accounts are distinct from the financial accounts, the two sets of accounts being kept continuously in agreement by the use of control accounts, or made readily reconcilable by other means. In this case the cost records will not record the relationship of the company with the outside world since that is the province of the financial accounting system with its ledgers containing accounts for creditors, debtors, capital and cash.

Integrated accounts can be defined as a set of accounting records which provide both financial and cost accounts using a common input of data for all accounting purposes. With the integrated system the ledger accounts must include a control account for each main cost heading, e.g. materials, direct labour, factory overheads, selling overheads, administration overheads and sales analysis. An integrated system produces a manufacturing account, a finished goods stores account, a trading account and a profit and loss account, but the figures contained in these accounts are the subject of much greater analysis from their related control accounts. This analysis is especially important in the absorption of overheads.

In an integrated system the general ledger is of the utmost importance. It contains the control accounts for other sub-ledgers and other accounts for assets, liabilities and capital etc. The system merges cost and financial accounting into one accounting function and avoids the cost of duplicating the processing of records relating to the same business transactions. Financial accountants tend to produce accounts for users other than managers and it is an important part of the integrated system that adequate cost statements are made available to management on an appropriate time scale. A costing profit and loss account, sometimes termed an 'operating statement' is produced rather than the more traditional profit and loss account usually associated with financial accounts.

An interlocking system implies that the source data for the financial accounts will be passed to a separate cost accounting department for reprocessing and classification into a different form of costing analysis. The overriding need for cost statements to be available soon after the event means that the costing department may have the first use of the transaction data. A separate cost accounting system will of course be more closely connected to such production statistics as labour analysis, machine usage, scrap reports and an analysis of idle time. The separate cost accounts will not record transactions outside the firm, e.g. debtors, creditors, share capital, long-term liabilities etc., and in order to balance as a double entry system, a financial ledger control account will be required to carry the double entry of transactions which are partly outside the costing system.

Figures 7.2, 7.3 and 7.4 show these various types of system diagrammatically.

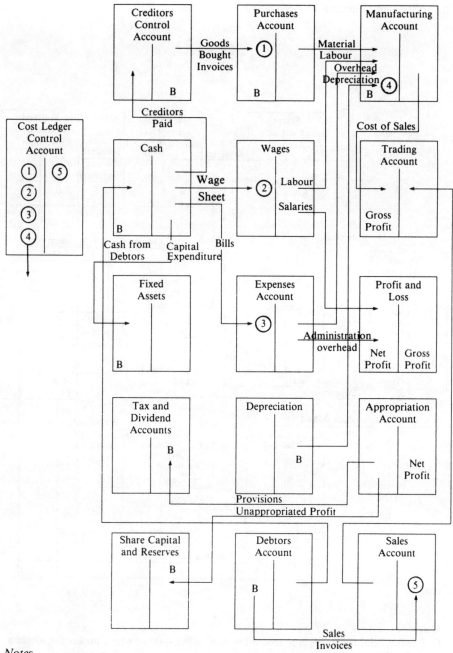

Notes
1. The cost ledger control account is a memorandum account and does not affect the balance of the system. However, the balance on the account must reconcile to the balance on the financial ledger control account (see Figure 7.3).
2. Numerals in circles correspond to similar items in Figures 7.3 and 7.4.
3. B = Balance at end of period.
4. ⟶ indicates direction of accounting entry.

Figure 7.2 Interlocking accounts: 1 The financial accounting system

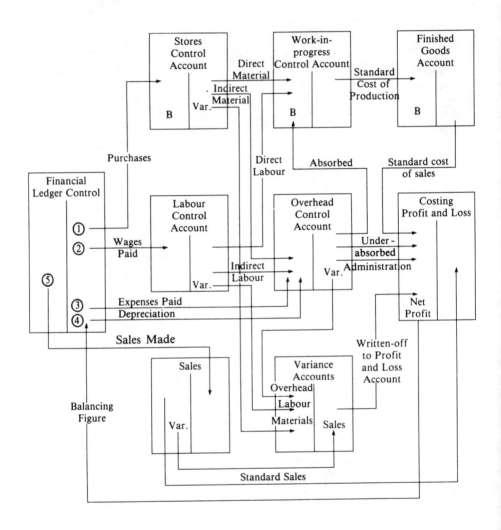

Notes
1. The financial ledger control account is part of the system, which makes the whole a self-balancing set of accounts.
2. The standard costing is used in the system illustrated here, and the variances ('var') are shown as one account. Those for materials, labour and overheads are adverse; those for sales are favourable.
3. Numerals in circles correspond with similar items in Figures 7.2 and 7.4.
4. B = Balance at end of period.
5. ⟶ indicates direction of accounting entry.

Figure 7.3   Interlocking accounts: 2 The cost accounting system

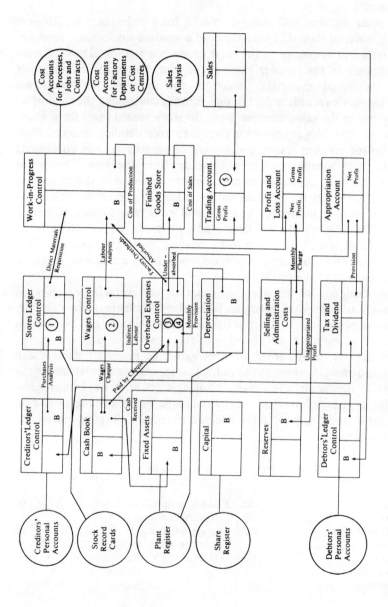

Notes
1. Large circles indicate analysis controlled by accounts – subsidiary ledgers or individual memorandum accounts.
2. Numerals in circles correspond to similar items in Figures 7.2 and 7.3.
3. B = Balance for balance sheet.
4. ⟶ indicates direction of accounting entry.

Figure 7.4   Integrated cost and financial accounting system

CONTROL ACCOUNTS

A control account is an account to which totals of similar transactions are posted, so that the control shows the total balances of many individual accounts in a subsidiary ledger.

A manufacturing business will maintain stocks for a wide range of different materials. Each material should be the subject of a separate stock record card, the balances of which will aggregate to the total of materials stock. Thus the asset stock which appears in the balance sheet is the total figure for a number of balances for individual materials. Accounts for individual materials are maintained in the stock record cards, but one account controlling the total of all those cards appears in the general ledger. Thus the stock record cards form a sub-ledger or memorandum ledger whose purpose is to keep detailed records, while the total or control account shows a summary of all transactions concerning materials. This total account can be written up from the total figures for purchases, or credit notes, or requisitions for materials issued to the factory. It automatically follows that the balance on the materials control account must equal the total of all the balances on the individual stock record cards. If there is no such reconciliation a mistake has been made, probably in the posting of an item to an individual card, and that mistake must be found and rectified. Thus the total account controls the many transactions which are accounted for in the individual records kept in the sub-ledger.

A total account can be used to control the situation wherever a large number of postings are made to individual accounts in a subsidiary ledger. For example, direct labour control account, work-in-progress control account and production overheads control account are all posted with the totals of a large number of individual transactions mainly involved with gathering materials, labour and overhead costs and charging them out to individual jobs or batches which are the subject of work in the factory. The manufacturing account or work-in-progress control account is the recipient of the total charge made for the period to individual jobs for direct labour, materials and overheads. Typical entries for control accounts are as follows:

Work-in progress control account

	£		£
Opening balance b/f (stock at start)	xx	Finished goods control a/c (transfer to stores)	xx
Stores ledger control a/c (material issued)	xx	Closing balance c/f (closing stock per stock take of work-in-progress)	xx
Wages control a/c (cost of direct labour)	xx		
Production overhead control a/c (overheads absorbed)	xx		
Stock gain to P. and L. a/c	?	Stock loss to P. and L. a/c	?
	xx		xxx

The account should balance, but if as a result of the physical stock check a debit or credit balance is found to exist, then it should be written off to the profit and loss account.

Production overhead control account

	£		£
Prepayments b/f	xx	Creditors and accruals b/f	xx
Stores ledger control a/c	xx	Work-in-progress control a/c	xx
(indirect materials)		(total absorbed to	
Wages control a/c		production)	
Direct labour	xx	Capital under construction	xx
Indirect labour	xx	Prepayments c/f	xx
Cash (expenses paid)	xx	P. and L. a/c	xx
Accruals c/f	xx	(under-absorbed)	
	xxx		xxx

Overheads over- or under-absorbed will appear as the balancing figure on the account. If overheads are over-absorbed the amount will appear as a debit balance to the account, to be written off to profit and loss account.

THE RECONCILIATION OF COST AND FINANCIAL ACCOUNTS

In circumstances where the financial accounting system is not integrated with the cost accounting system, it is both beneficial and necessary to attempt to reconcile the costing profit for twelve monthly periods to the financial profit for the year. The transactions covered by accounting statements from the two systems are the same, so that they should show the same profit unless different rules have been used to measure that profit. It is a very useful check on the accuracy of both systems to analyse the reasons for a different profit figure. This analysis may discover mistakes made in either system, thus improving the reliability of the figures, and the very fact that differences have been investigated and analysed will increase managers' understanding of the profit figure. Differences between cost and financial accounts can be classified into groups as follows.

Appropriations of profit

Appropriations occur only in the financial accounts of the business because they are amounts set aside out of profits after the profit figure has been struck. They characterize the way in which the profit measured has been disseminated. Cost accounting is more concerned with the measurement of profit on a month-to-month basis, and its analysis to department or product etc. Amounts set aside for taxation, for the payment of a dividend, or to be added to reserves or sinking funds, are examples of appropriations.

Costs which are a matter of policy rather than a business expense

Certain costs may be the result of a board decision rather than an expense incurred in the normal way. The board may consider it a matter of financial prudence to provide extra depreciation, to write off goodwill according to a certain profile, to write down stocks, or to provide an extra amount to cover doubtful debts or to top up the company's pension fund. These provisions, which are artificial in that they stem from managerial decision rather than cost incurred, will affect the financial accounts but will not form part of the cost accounting records.

Items excluded from the cost accounts

Miscellaneous income from investments or bank interest may be excluded from the cost accounts. Rents received on property may also not find its way into the costing system since they do not concern a particular product or department. If property rental is a significant activity in the business, a separate management account should be prepared for it. Other costs which are purely of a financial nature will also be excluded from the cost accounting system, e.g. damages and costs from legal actions, penalties payable under certain contracts, and interest on debentures or unsecured loan stock. Interest should perhaps be treated as a fixed overhead expense. The capital profit or loss made when a fixed asset or investment is sold may appear in the financial accounts but be excluded from the cost accounts, on the ground that it does not form part of the normal operating activity of the business. However, if such items are included in the budget, and fixed asset changes are important enough to be preplanned, then perhaps there is a place for them within the cost accounting system.

Accounting policies

Some items in the cost accounts may receive a different accounting treatment from the accounting policy applied to them to them in the financial accounts. Stocks of material or work-in-progress may be valued for costing purposes using a different method from the financial accounts, e.g. the costing system may use LIFO – but as this basis is not accepted by the Inland Revenue or encouraged by SSAP 9 the financial accounts may be based on a FIFO valuation. Different methods of depreciation may be used in the cost accounts from those applied in financial accounting. In a full absorption costing system overhead expenses may be over- or under-recovered by the application of preset absorption rates. The over- or under-recovery will appear in the costing profit and loss account but will not form part of the financial accounts.

Items appearing only in the cost accounts

Some cost accounting systems include 'notional' amounts for certain costs which, although not necessarily incurred, it is considered be covered by the surplus from business operations. A notional rent is often charged for a factory building owned by a company, and notional interest on capital employed may be set against the profit of a department or product to ensure that it is making the required return on the resources at its disposal. These notional costs will not be found in the financial accounts. In some companies interest on capital and a notional rent for premises may be included in the budgeted overheads. These costs are introduced by the cost accountant in an attempt to show the full cost of the department or product. Premises and capital have been used by certain production processes, and it is logical that they should be charged for the use of these scarce resources if a true profit on their activities is to be measured. A common charge for interest or rent facilitates inter-firm comparison, and comparison of the operating performance of various departments or divisions within the same group of companies.

Example 7.2

A company operates a financial accounting system separate from its costing system. The profit according to the financial accounts was £156,200 after tax, but including:

	£
Overdraft interest	13,000
Interest received	12,000
Discount allowed	19,000
Discount received	14,000

Depreciation was provided according to the straight line method on a ten-year life.

Stock valuations were:

	Opening stock £	Closing stock £
Raw material	261,000	306,000
Work-in-progress	169,000	175,000
Finished goods	191,000	194,000

Corporation tax was provided as £35,000.

The plant cost £150,000 when new, and had just completed its third year of life. The costing profit was calculated after the inclusion of:

	£
Debenture interest	31,720
Notional rent	45,000
Administration overhead over-absorbed	8,000
Production overhead under-absorbed	27,000

Stock valuations in the cost accounts were:

	Opening stock £	Closing stock £
Raw material	271,000	294,000
Work-in-progress	165,000	172,000
Finished goods	197,000	202,000

Depreciation was provided in the cost accounts at 15 per cent on the reducing balance.

Required

Prepare a statement which reconciles the profit shown in the financial accounts to the costing profit figure.

Solution

The question provides the financial profit, so the reconciliation should adjust that figure only. The data in the question about items in the costing profit is not all relevant: debenture interest would already be in the financial accounts. Overhead over- or under-absorbed would be written off to costing profit and so would have no effect, as total overheads are charged in the financial accounts. Notional rent must be taken away from financial profit.

Depreciation of £150,000 over a ten-year life = £15,000 per annum in financial accounts. However, for the cost accounts:

	£
Cost	150,000
15% year 1	22,500
	127,500
15% year 2	19,125
	108,375
15% year 3	16,256 − 15,000 = £1,256

Depreciation in year 3 on the reducing balance method is £1,256 higher than the 10 per cent straight line figure, so £1,256 must be subtracted from the financial profit.

Stock differences (effect on profit):

	Opening stock £	Closing stock £	Net £
Raw material:			
Financial accounts	261,000	306,000	
Cost accounts	271,000	294,000	
	− 10,000	− 12,000	− 22,000
Work-in-progress:			
Financial accounts	169,000	175,000	
Cost accounts	165,000	172,000	
	+ 4,000	− 3,000	+ 1,000
Finished goods:			
Financial accounts	191,000	194,000	
Costs accounts	197,000	202,000	
	− 6,000	+ 8,000	+ 2,000

Reconciliation statement:

	£	£	£
Net profit before tax per the			
financial accounts (156,200 + 35,000)			191,200
Adjustments:	*Add*	*Subtract*	
Overdraft interest	13,000		
Interest received		12,000	
Discount allowed	19,000		
Discount received		14,000	
Depreciation		1,256	
Notional rent		45,000	
Stock differences			
Raw materials		22,000	
Work-in-progress	1,000		
Finished goods	2,000		
	35,000	94,256	(59,256)
Net profit per cost accounts			131,944

EXERCISES

7A (a) Describe the distinguishing characteristics of integrated and interlocking accounting systems. What is the function of a financial ledger control account in the cost accounts?

(b) A company which maintains interlocking cost and financial ledgers has the following balances at the end of a period:

Cost ledger control account in the financial ledger	£199,800
Financial ledger control account in the cost ledger	£172,200

On comparing the financial and cost ledger records the following facts emerged:

1. Sales made on the last day of the month were entered in the cost ledger, but the financial ledger clerk failed to make any record of the transaction. The sales value was £11,500 and the factory cost of sales £7,500. The cost of sales account is kept in the financial ledger; the finished goods account is kept in the cost ledger.
2. Depreciation of plant and equipment of £24,000 was provided for in the financial ledger. No memo had been sent to the cost ledger clerk.
3. Raw materials costing £8,000 had been received into stores and recorded in the cost ledger. The transaction had not yet been entered in the financial ledger.
4. The factory overhead account shows an over-absorbed balance of £12,400. Any under/over-absorption remaining at the end of the period is to be transferred to the profit and loss account.
5. Work, costing £4,100, completed by factory personnel on an extension to the factory buildings, has been adjusted through the financial ledger control account. No entries have been made in the financial ledger.

Required:

 (i) Prepare adjustments to the control account in both the financial and cost ledgers, showing clearly the corrected balance on each account.
(ii) Prepare correcting journal entries in the cost ledger, where necessary (no narrative is required).

(Association of Certified Accountants)

7B   Below are incomplete cost accounts for a period for which final accounts are to be prepared:

Stores ledger control

	£		£
Opening balance	6,000	(ii) Job ledger control	19,000
(i) General ledger control	27,000	(iii)	

Production wages control

	£		£
(iv) General ledger control	25,000	(v)	
		(vi)	

Production overhead control

	£		£
(iii)		(x)	
(vi)			
(vii) General ledger control	26,000		

Job ledger control

	£		£
Opening balance	20,000	(xi)	
(ii) Stores ledger control	19,000		
(v)			
(x)			

Selling and administration overheads

	£		£
(viii) General ledger control	12,000	(xii)	

Cost of sales

	£		£
(xi)			
(xii)			

Sales

	£		£
		(ix) General ledger control	110,000

General ledger control

		£			£
(ix)	Sales	110,000	Opening balance		26,000
			(i)	Stores ledger control	27,000
			(iv)	Production wages control	25,000
			(vii)	Production overhead control	26,000
			(viii)	Selling and administration overhead	12,000

The closing stock balances are:

Stores ledger	£12,000
Job ledger	£10,000

Of the production wages incurred 80 per cent are charged directly to jobs. Production overheads are absorbed at a predetermined rate of 150 per cent of direct wages, and selling and administration overheads at 10 per cent of sales.

Required

(a) Identify any distinguishing features of the cost accounting system.
(b) Complete the cost accounts for the period, by listing the missing amounts. determining the profit/(loss), and showing the balances to be carried forward to the following period.
(c) Provide a brief description of the accounting entries numbered (i) to (xii).

(Association of Certified Accountants)

7C   a) Using journal entries account for the following transactions within the integrated accounting system of Integer plc.

The company uses standard costing, charging out materials from stores at standard cost, and writing off the difference between the standard cost of a material and its purchase price to a price variance account. The standard cost of material 539 is £12 per kg.

2 May: Integer plc bought and received 2,000 kg of material 539 from Supplies plc for £25,500. The standard cost of this material was (2,000 kg × £12) £24,000.
5 May: 1,400 kg of material 539 were issued to production.
8 May: 120 kg of material 539 were spoiled in the stores. This material had no scrap value.
10 May: 100 of the 1,400 kg issued to production on 5 May were found to be substandard and were returned to the stores. These 100 kg were immediately returned to Supplies plc. Replacement material was issued to production with additional requirements against a requisition note for 400 kg.

(b) 'For cost accounting purposes an integrated accounting system is preferable to a non-integrated accounting system.'

Comment on the above and explain two advantages and two limitations of an integrated system.

7D   A company maintains an interlocking system for financial and cost accounts, and prepares a profit and loss account from each of the two sets of records. For the financial year just ended, the figure of 'profit' in the cost accounting records is substantially different from the figure of 'profit' in the financial accounting records.

Itemize the transactions which might form part of the reconciliation of financial and cost accounts.

PART III

COST ACCOUNTING METHODS

---

8   Job and Batch Costing

OBJECTIVE

In previous chapters the discussion has stressed the need for cost accounting, and the means whereby costs are determined for materials, labour and overheads. This part of the book reviews the methods by which the analysis of cost accounts can be made useful to management when applied in certain business situations. The cost accounting system will reveal the cost of materials, labour and overheads, but having produced the data, it is next important for the cost accountant to analyse that data and use it in the production of a cost statement, relating the costs to the output of the business. The term 'output' may be applied to individual jobs which pass through the works, or to a batch of similar items produced as a group, or as a stream of homogeneous items in continuous production as they pass from process to process. Production in the business by job, batch or process will determine the method to be applied; the ease with which each cost unit can be separated from the others and seen as an individual, is the criterion on which the choice of costing method will be based.

JOB COSTING

Where production is organized for significant individual cost units, probably the result of a specific order, or where work is undertaken to a customer's special requirements, the work carried out will be treated as a separate job as it moves through the processes and operations within the factory. In circumstances where each job is capable of separate identification, the job becomes a convenient cost unit so that the cost of that job can be accumulated as it passes through the separate operations up to its completion. Costs are added as each process is undertaken. This method of costing is practised in heavy engineering, foundry work, the machine tool industry and printing, where jobs are the subject of separate orders or contracts.

The normal procedure is that each job is identified by a number and perhaps a name, and a separate job card is raised for that job. The card may accompany the job as it goes through the processes or departments in the factory, or alternatively the job card is maintained in the cost office. Materials are requisitioned separately on to the job, labour is analysed according to time spent on the job, and overheads are absorbed to the job according to the rate applicable for each cost centre. A batch of production of similar items can be treated as a separate job in this way. Thus, instead of producing a single manufacturing account or work-in-progress account, the factory activity is broken down into a number of job or batch accounts which, in aggregate, would equal the items normally entered into the manufacturing account.

Cost coding is particularly helpful for job and batch costing, since if material requisitions are coded with the appropriate job number, the materials used on a job can be separately identified. Time record cards analyse the labour time spent by teams or individual direct workers on each job. At the end of a week or month a labour analysis will then divide the total direct labour cost to the various jobs undertaken during the period, and the amount of idle time can then be reported to management.

Advantages of job costing

The advantages of job costing are:

1. The profit or loss made on each job can be measured if cost is set against the price tended for the job.
2. Since job costs build up as the job is completed, reference to the job cost card will reveal the current situation at a glance. In this way any excessive costs can be identified at an early stage.
3. Comparison of the job cost with the estimate on which the tender price was based, again reveals costs which are exceeding the estimate and also acts as useful check on the estimating procedure. Faulty estimating may result in inaccuracies in the prices quoted for future jobs. Work taken on at low prices will result in losses or little profit, while estimates which are too high may cause jobs to be lost to competitors as a result of high pricing.
4. Job costing enables a comparison to be made with performance on other jobs so that inefficiencies are identified.
5. 'Cost plus' jobs: if there is difficulty in estimating a price for a certain job, negotiation between the company and its customer may produce a contract where the customer agrees to pay the cost of the job plus an agreed percentage as a profit margin. In these circumstances it is essential to maintain reliable costing records.

DOCUMENTATION: THE JOB COST CARD

A good system of documentation is essential if job costing is to be successful.

Requisitions for materials, and materials returned notes for surplus goods returned to the stores, will identify the material cost to be entered on the job cost card. Accurate labour analysis by time sheet and meticulous recording of machine time used by each job will again identify direct labour cost and provide a means by which departmental or process overheads can be charged out to individual jobs. Some jobs require special materials or components, and the invoice for these items can be allocated direct to the job cost card.

An example of a job cost card appears in Figure 8.2, which forms part of Exercise 8A at the end of this chapter. The information on the card includes:

(a) order number;
(b) job number;
(c) customer description;
(d) delivery date;
(e) material cost to date;
(f) labour cost to date;
(g) overheads charged to the job;
(h) miscellaneous expenses;
(i) completion date;
(j) invoice price;
(k) profit summary.

An accurate record of cost to date on all the jobs in the factory at one point in time facilitates period-end stocktaking for work-in-progress so that a monthly operating cost statement can be produced.

Explanation of the flow of documents in the job costing system

A customer may invite a company to give an estimate of the price to be charged for a certain job. This estimate, if accepted, forms the basis of the contract with the customer. Once a firm order is received a works order is issued, with a job number, specifying the job in detail. This document is copied to factory departments, cost office, wages office stores and accounts department, so that all interested parties have full information.

A job cost card is raised for the job, and charged with the cost of direct materials, labour and overheads. Any special items purchased for a job will reach the job cost card via the invoice section of the accounts department. The total cost on the job cost card forms part of the work-in-progress total on the work-in-progress control account. The completed job cost card forms the basis of the production of an invoice to the customer.

Figure 8.1 shows this document flow diagrammatically. Figure 8.2 gives an example of a job cost card.

SMALL WORKS

Cost information is expensive to provide and, in the case of small orders, the profit derived from the job may be insufficient to warrant the expense of a separate cost treatment. It is expensive to take the order, acknowledge it, accept

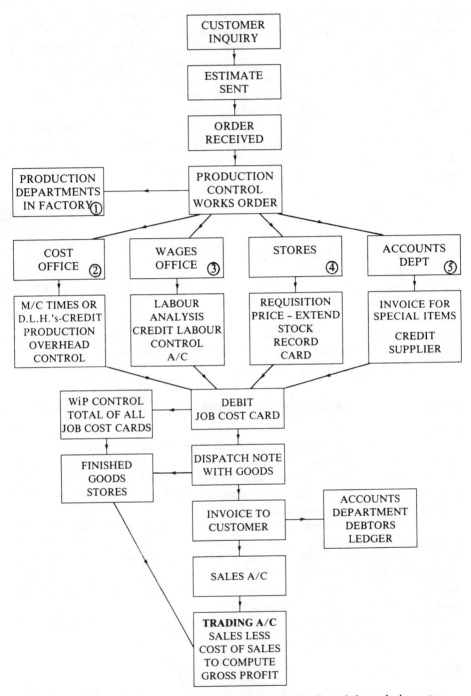

Note Five copies of the works order are produced and distributed through the system. Colour-coding would assist this distribution.

Figure 8.1   Documentation of a job costing system

THRUSH SWITCHGEAR PLC Customer: British Coal		Order number 517/88 Job number 2/88–4 Start date – 1 June Delivery date – 1 July			Price £20,000
Descripton Pit switchgear			Despatch date – 1 August		Despatch note – 1791
Date	Reference	Material	Labour	Overhead	Miscellaneous
		Estimate £7,213	Estimate £6,000	Estimate £3,600 d.l.h rate £1.80	Estimate £1,260
		Cost £ Cum £	Hours Cum Cum £ £	Cost £ Cum £	Cost £ Cum £
	c/f	3,843	1,800 5,400	3,240	1,083
1 July	MR 971	984 4,827			
2 July	MRN 81	(128) 4,699			
20 July	Packing				210 1,293
24 July	MR 1062	2,841 7,540			
31 July	Labour analysis		280 1,260 6,660	504 3,744	

Summary	£	Comments Invoice 1791 dated 25 October
Material	7,540	
Labour	6,660	
Overhead	3,744	
Misc.	1,293	
Total cost	19,237	
Price	20,000	
Profit	763	

Figure 8.2   Job cost card

or reject it, and then issue a production order. If the expense of analysing cost information to small works is added to these administrative costs, much of the profit margin on the job could be used up. In some businesses a minimum standing charge is imposed on all small orders to cover these expenses. In the absence of a job cost card for each small job, a general jobbing account can be maintained. This is merely a ledger account, or some other form of record, containing the cost and revenue from small orders. The overall profit made by this activity is thereby revealed on a monthly basis if required. However, no record is maintained of the profitability of individual jobs, so that pricing is undertaken without the aid of information as to past costs, and control of the small work situation may be lost.

Records of time and materials spent on small works must be maintained if fraud is to be avoided. One particular area of difficulty concerns the travelling time of employees from one small job to another. It is one thing to design and organize a system of record keeping, but often a good system falls into disuse so that a series of spot checks is required to ensure cost data is being accurately returned. A further difficulty for the cost accountant is to determine the size of job below which individual cost records will not be kept, and the small works system will be operated.

BATCH COSTING

A batch is a group of similar products and is treated as a single cost unit; e.g. bricks are costed per thousand since it would be counter-productive to attempt to analyse the cost to produce a cost per brick. The conditions needed for batch costing are that identical products should be produced and that it should be convenient to group them into a production batch rather than to attempt to separate them and cost them individually. The costs of a batch are ascertained in much the same way as for an individual job. Each batch is identified by a number, and careful recording of materials issued, scrap, labour time and overheads for the batch will build up the cost record of the batch on a cost card. In this way the costs of batches can be compared and variations investigated. A unit cost can be found by dividing the cost of the batch by the number of units in the batch.

organization of production before the machines start work, and covers the time spent adjusting jigs, tools and machinery so that they are ready to receive the production batch. The larger the batch, the smaller the unit cost of setting up. This fixed cost is therefore spread over the volume of production, so that the size of batch will directly influence the unit cost. It is possible to calculate an optimum batch size by a similar method to that for the economic order quantity, by setting the advantages gained by increasing batch sizes against the cost of storing the greater volume of production.

SCRAP AND RECTIFICATION

When work is undertaken it is normal to expect a certain amount of scrap material to be produced, e.g. off-cuts, shreddage, turnings etc. The cost of this waste material is regarded as part of the normal cost of the job and an allowance for normal scrap is usually built into the tender price for a job. Alternatively, if an abnormal level of loss from scrap is experienced on a job it will in the first instance be charged to the job cost card since extra material will be requisitioned from the stores to make up for the items lost. While this cost analysis will show the true cost of the job concerned, the exact losses experienced through abnormal scrap may be obscured if the total is divided between a number of different jobs. The cost of abnormal scrap should be recognized as an individual item and notified to management so that corrective action can be taken. It therefore follows that abnormal scrap losses should be credited to individual jobs and charged as a separate item to a departmental or cost centre scrap account or to the costing profit and loss. A good costing system should lead to control of the situation by managers, so that if the cost of abnormal scrap is identified in a scrap report, remedial action can be planned.

Another feature of job costing is the inspection which takes place as the job moves from one process or department to another. In this way faulty work is recognized at an early stage and either the expenditure of further cost on such rejected jobs is avoided, or rectification can take place immediately. An analysis of reject tickets issued by inspectors, and or the cost of rectification, is important information for factory management.

Work scrapped is costed out as a separate item, with the expenditure to date on the items scrapped. Normal losses to be expected in a process are absorbed in the cost of 'good' production passed on to the next process or into the finished goods stores, but the cost of abnormal scrap is a factory overhead expense. Losses from abnormal scrap may not necessarily be caused by faults within the production process; faulty materials bought by the purchasing department will inevitably increase scrap losses when they are worked. The cost of scrap materials within the stores can be absorbed by inflating the rate at which the material is charged out. However, if an abnormal level of wastage or breakages is experienced, this cost should be shown as a separate item. Material rejected for one purpose may well be useful in some other product. It would be wrong to transfer such scrap material to another job at the full cost incurred up to its wastage on the first job. A reasonable market value may appear to be a useful compromise to use as a basis for charging out such materials. When scrap is sold the revenue produced may be credited to individual jobs, but if the revenue produced is small the cash received from scrap sales is posted to a general scrap account.

Scrap and rectification reports showing the amount of scrap and rectification work undertaken by each cost centre should be prepared at frequent intervals and submitted to all levels of management. Management may need to decide whether to sell scrap material at once or to undertake further work on the material to increase the revenue which it can earn. The cost incurred on producing the scrap material up to its point of rejection must be ignored when this decision is made. The scrap should be regarded as being worthless at that point in time so that the manager must decide between the revenue derived from an immediate sale and the net revenue derived from further processing.

MULTIPLE CHOICE QUESTIONS

8.1 'A costing method which applies where each order is of comparatively short duration, where the work moves through processes and operations as a continuously identifiable unit.' The description refers to:
   (a) Batch costing.
   (b) Job costing.
   (c) Process costing.
   (d) Operations costing.

   (a)   (b)   (c)   (d)

8.2 What information would be found on a job cost card?
   (a) Direct labour hours.
   (b) Idle time.
   (c) Materials returned to store.
   (d) Indirect labour hours.

   (a)   (a + b)   (a + c)   (b + d)

8.3   Which of the following documents does not form part of a job costing system?
   (a)   Materials requisition.
   (b)   Labour analysis.
   (c)   Works order.
   (d)   Stock record card.

(a)   (b)   (c)   (d)

8.4   Setting-up time is:
   (a)   Time-lag between placing an order and receiving materials.
   (b)   The time required to prepare a work station from a standard condition to readiness.
   (c)   The period of time between the completion of an operation and the availability of the material at succeeding work stations.
   (d)   The period of time for which a work station is not available for production due to a functional failure.

(a)   (b)   (c)   (d)

8.5   The cost of scrap is treated as:
   (a)   Part of the cost of good production.
   (b)   Raw material cost on another product.
   (c)   Miscellaneous income.
   (d)   A factory overhead expense.

(a)   (b)   (a + c)   (a + d)

EXERCISES

8A   Thrush Switchgear plc specializes in the manufacture of electrical switchgear to customers' specific requirements. Each job is costed separately on a job cost card (see Figure 8.2).

Required

Comment on the information disclosed by the job card with references to:
(a)   the costing system in operation;
(b)   profitability of the job;
(c)   control action required;
(d)   improvements in design of job cost card.

8B   (a) What advantages would you expect to be derived from a system of job costing?

(b) Midland Jobbing Engineers plc undertakes engineering work on a contract basis.

The factory is organized as three departments: foundry, assembly and painting. In the foundry the basic shape of each piece of equipment is made, in the assembly department components are added and the job is completed by skilled engineers, while jobs that require painting are then put through a highly mechanized finishing process in the painting department.

Fixed overhead costs are budgeted quarterly, and in the present quarter are estimated to be: foundry £75,000, assembly £72,250 and painting £64,500. The budget also plans machine hours for the quarter in the three departments as 20,000, 5,000 and 30,000 respectively, and direct labour hours as 8,000, 17,000 and 4,000 respectively.

Job no. 1473 is now complete. Analysis of materials requisitions and time sheets for the job shows that materials cost £4,680 in the foundry, components costing £950 were added in the assembly department and paint cost £211. Direct labour hours worked on the job were foundry 17, assembly 59, and painting 11. The job also used 26 hours of machine time in the foundry, 6 hours of machine time in assembly, and 11 hours in the painting department.

Wage rates per hour paid by the company are:

	Foundry £	Assembly £	Painting £
Direct labour	7.00	9.00	5.00
Indirect labour	4.00	4.50	3.50

Required

Prepare a cost statement for job no. 1473.

9 Contract Cost Accounting

INTRODUCTION

Accounting in the construction industry must of necessity adapt the principles of accounting to the particular conditions experienced in that industry. Civil engineering contracts are often completed over a period of years, which means that cost must be recorded and profit measured in more than one financial accounting period. The strict legal position is that the client does not take over the building from the contractor until it is completed. Therefore, technically speaking, the contractor cannot make a sale until the building is accepted by the client. However, it may take two or three years to complete a large building contract, so it would seem less than fair to show all the profit for three years of effort as being earned in the third year. Therefore the accountant must find a way to evaluate the work-in-progress during the period of the contract, so that a profit can be measured up to a particular point in time.

The financial accounting treatment of long-term contracts does not differ very much from the cost accounting treatment, since if a monthly cost statement showing profit for the month and to date is to be submitted to management, the cost accountant will meet the same profit measurement problems.

SITE ORGANIZATION

A civil engineering contract acts as a self-contained cost centre while, at the same time, it can be seen as a cost unit. On a large building site there is a separate management team of engineers, quantity surveyors, storekeepers and perhaps even a wages clerk, under the leadership of an agent or clerk of the works, so it is possible to keep all the costs of that contract separate from other expenditure incurred by the business. Materials are delivered to the site and often the invoice is sent to the site for checking before payment. A separate wage sheet will show the direct and indirect labour cost incurred by the contract. Indirect costs will be generated by each contract, and a share of the main company administrative expenses can be computed and charged to the contract. Thus the difficulties of apportionment and absorption are avoided.

Some companies organize their activities by setting up a separate plant department or plant company to administer the use of construction machinery owned by the company, and charge out plant to the various contracts currently undertaken. For a civil engineering company the main manufacturing account is divided into a number of individual contract accounts. Cost coding by number and name is extensively used to identify contracts and to enable costs to be analysed and entered into the recording system.

Very large amounts of money are involved in contract costing since the cost of building, say, a power station or a large reservoir and dam may well run into many millions of pounds. Cost analysis is necessary within the contract account, to divide costs between materials, labour, subcontracting, transport, loose tools etc. The materials built into a complex civil engineering job may need to be analysed under fifty or more sub-cost classifications. Complexity can be overcome by analysis, to enable management to maintain control over a large variety of raw materials. Some contractors divide costs according to processes as well as making an analysis to contracts; they will, for example, produce a cost per cubic yard of concrete laid, or per square yard of shuttering erected. An alternative analysis may be to compare the actual costs incurred against the cost headings specified in the tender document on which the contract was awarded. This analysis divides the cost according to parts of the work, e.g. site clearance, foundation work, erection of a chimney or cooling tower, or the mechanical installation of complex plant.

PLANT ON CONSTRUCTION SITES

A plant register should be maintained to record all items of plant which arrive on the construction site. On a large contract plant may be lost, stolen, misused or even forgotten. Therefore it is necessary to have clear information to control the situation, especially when plant is transferred from one contract to another. If items of machinery are to be used on a contract for several years it is convenient to charge the original cost of the new plant (or its written down value if it is second-hand) direct to the contract. When the contract is completed or the plant is no longer required it may be sold at the site or transferred to another contract. In the intervening period the depreciation of that plant should be charged to the contract. This depreciation can be calculated by any one of the methods described in Chapter 6.

Another feature of plant on civil engineering sites is that there is often a large quantity of small tools and implements such as shovels, wheelbarrows etc. Clearly it would not be worthwhile to maintain separate records for such small items, so a revaluation at the end of each period will show the value of small plant on the contract. A simple calculation taking opening valuation plus purchases less closing valuation will show the cost of plant used up during the period. The quantity surveyors prove helpful in this valuation exercise. It is difficult to forecast a working life for plant on civil engineering contracts because, unlike machinery in a factory, accidents and extreme working conditions can render a machine worthless very quickly. Prudence must therefore be used when the economic life of contractors' plant is forecast. Some companies prefer to operate the central plant yard system whereby machinery is charged out to contracts on a monthly or weekly basis. If an invoice is sent from the plant department to the contract each month it will act as a regular reminder to the site management of the costs that they are incurring by using the plant. This may cause them to dispense with its services as soon as the task is over, returning it as soon as possible to the plant yard for use on other jobs.

PROFIT IN UNCOMPLETED CONTRACTS: CONCEPTS

Legally the contract is not completed until the finished building is taken over by the customer. This may be two or more years from the start date. If profit is deferred until the end of the contract, the fair view of the company's activities disclosed by the profit and loss account will be distorted, both in a year before the contract is completed and in the year of completion. In that year the profit on several years' activity is credited to the profit and loss account. Accordingly, SSAP 9 encourages the financial accountant to take credit for 'reasonably ascertained profit' while a contract is in progress, and this practice is also followed in monthly contract cost accounts. There are a number of rules for the recognition of profit on contracts, but the overriding principle is to act prudently when estimates are made.

1. Profit should be taken only on work covered by an architect's certificate. The architect certifies that a certain part of the job has been satisfactorily completed, and on the basis of this certificate the accountant can act as though a sale has been made. The certificate is also used as the basis for progress payments made by the client to the contractor during the course of the contract.

2. It is reasonable to assume that work covered by a certificate has been satisfactorily completed, but if the final outcome of the contract cannot reasonably be assessed, it is prudent not to take profit that appears to be made up to the current date. This is especially true of contracts in the early stage of building, when the final result cannot be forecast since it is several years in the future. The cost of work on such a contract must be carried forward at cost.

3. The profit taken should reflect the proportion of the work carried out at the accounting date, and should take into account any known inequalities of profitability in the various stages of the contract. This implies that if a contract is half-completed, half the profit can be taken to date, but if 50 per cent of the profit will be earned on the last 30 per cent of building activity that fact must also be taken into account.

4. A prudent view of future events must be taken at all times. Any loss disclosed

to date should be provided for in full and if it is estimated that a loss will eventually be made, prudence dictates that provision should be made for the whole loss as soon as it is recognized. Thus work-in-progress on a loss-making contract will be carried forward at cost less attributable loss. This valuation is in accordance with the Companies Act 1985, which stipulates that stocks must be valued at the lower of cost or net realizable value. If the architect's certificate is for an amount less than the cost of work covered by it, the certificate will be the equivalent of the net realizable value.

5. No attributable profit should be taken until the outcome of the contract can be foreseen with a reasonable degree of certainty. Cost accountants use a number of methods to inject prudence into their profit measurement. Large and costly mistakes can be made on a civil engineering job, which can turn a profit shown in the first two years of a job into an eventual loss.

STANDARDS AND RULES

SSAP 9 states that work-in-progress on profitable contracts can be carried forward at cost plus the attributable profit on the contract taken to date. This rule does not coincide with the Companies Act 1985, which states that stocks of work-in-progress must be shown at the lower of cost or net realizable value. The 1985 Act further requires that a figure for turnover should be shown in the accounts, but as we have already seen there is no sale until the end of the contract so it is difficult to follow the legal rule for contract accounting. The Accounting Standards Committee has reviewed SSAP 9 to try to bridge this gap.

International Accounting Standard 11

'Accounting for Construction Contracts' suggests two methods by which profit on construction contracts can be measured. The *percentage of completion* method recognizes revenue according to the stage of completion, as the contract progresses. Costs to date are set against that revenue. A figure for revenue may be derived from a certificate based on measurement of the work, or as a proportion of the final price by calculating the proportion of cost to date to the total cost expected on the contract. Progress payments cannot be used to estimate revenue. Expected losses on stages of the contract not yet completed must be the subject of a full provision against costs to date under the percentage of completion method.

This international standard suggests as an alternative the *completed contract* method, where revenue is recognized only when the contract is substantially completed. Any costs attributable to gaining the contract (tendering expenses etc.) can be deferred and set off against the contract if such costs can be clearly identified and if it is reasonably certain that the contract will be obtained. The percentage of completion method can be used only if the outcome of the contract can be reliably estimated by the application of firm figures for the price, the cost to completion, and the stage of the contract completed to date. Clearly the completed contract method does not allow reported income to reflect activity since profits disclosed will fluctuate as contracts are completed.

PROFIT MEASUREMENT: THE METHODS

The manner in which prudence is injected into the measurement of profit on long-term contracts varies in practice. Different companies use different methods, and in the context of monthly or quarterly management accounts those methods are often informal and rely on estimates of future costs and activity. A formal approach is to carry forward work not covered by a certificate at cost, and to set the cost of certified work against the value of the certificate, so calculating an attributable profit. As a matter of prudence this profit is then further reduced to reflect uncertainties up to the end of the contract, and also the risk that the client will not make the progress payments.

A formula which can be applied is:

$$\frac{2}{3} \times \frac{\text{Cash}}{\text{Certificate}} \times \text{Attributable profit} = \text{Profit recognized to date}$$

The fraction employed in the formula can vary according to the degree of prudence required by the company concerned, e.g. 3/4 can be used. If profit on a contract has been recognized in a previous period, that amount is deducted from the profit to date, to show the profit attributable to the current period.

Example 9.1

Construction plc has four contracts outstanding at the year-end: contracts A, B, C and D.

Contract A

Contract A was started this year and is half finished. The agreed price is £400,000, and a certificate in the sum of £180,000 has been received which is subject to a 10 per cent retention. New plant has been purchased during the year, which is expected to have a five-year life. Stocks of raw material on the contract at the year-end had cost £6,000. Work not covered by the certificate is estimated to have cost £12,000.

Costs incurred during the year are: materials £100,000, labour £60,000, overheads £8,000, plant £40,000 and accruals £4,000. Materials costing £1,000 were returned to the suppliers during the year, and scrap materials were sold for £2,000.

Contract A

	£000		£000
Materials	100.0	Returns	1.0
Labour	60.0	Scrap sales	2.0
Overhead	8.0	Plant c/f at w.d.v.	32.0
Plant	40.0	Material stock c/f	6.0
Accruals c/f	4.0	Work-in-progress c/f	183.6
	212.0		
Attributable profit to			
P. and L.	12.6		
	224.6		224.6
Work-in-progress b/d	183.6		
Material stock b/d	6.0		
Plant b/d	32.0	Accrued costs b/d	4.0

A well-established contract. It may be assumed that a successful conclusion can be reasonably foreseen.

Calculation

	£
Cost to date (£212,000 − £41,000)	171,000
Less cost of work not certified	12,000
Cost of work certified	159,000
Certificate	180,000
Profit	21,000

Formula

$$\frac{2}{3} \times \frac{\text{Cash}}{\text{Certificate}} \times £21,000$$

$$\frac{2}{3} \times \frac{162,000}{180,000} \times £21,000 = £12,600 \text{ to P. and L.}$$

Work-in-progress c/f is cost to date £171,000 + profit of £12,600 = £183,600.

Contract B

Contract B was started this year and is half finished. The agreed price was £240,000, and a certificate in the sum of £110,000 has been received with cash of £60,000. The plant on the site at the year-end is reckoned to be worth £20,000 and materials in stock cost £8,000. Work not covered by the certificate is estimated to have cost £8,000.

Costs incurred during the year are: materials £60,000, labour £40,000, overheads £6,000, plant £48,000 and accruals £2,000. Depreciation on the contract is by the revaluation method – it certainly seems to have fallen in value.

Contract B

	£000		£000
Materials	60	Plant c/f	20
Labour	40	Materials c/f	8
Overhead	6	Loss to P. and L. a/c	10
Plant	48	Work-in-progress	118
Accruals	2		
	156		156
Plant b/d	20		
Materials b/d	8		
Work-in-progress	118	Accrued costs b/d	2

This contract has made a loss which is written off at once to the profit and loss account. If it is considered that further losses are to be made before completion, a provision to cover foreseeable losses must be charged to the profit and loss account.

Calculation	£
Cost to date (£156,000 − £28,000)	128,000
Less cost of work not certified	8,000
Cost of work certified	120,000
Certificate	110,000
Loss	10,000

Work-in-progress is cost to date £128,000 less loss £10,000 = £118,000.

Contract C

Contract C was started only three months before the year-end. The contract price is £67,000, and no certificates for completed work have yet been issued. The closing stock of materials was worth £2,000 at cost, and it is estimated that half a year's depreciation should be charged on the plant, based on a five-year working life.

Costs incurred during the year were: materials £8,000, labour £5,000, overheads £1,000, plant £20,000 and accruals £2,000.

Contract C

	£000		£000
Materials	8	Plant c/f	18
Labour	5	Materials c/f	2
Overhead	1	Work-in-progress	16
Plant	20		
Accruals c/f	2		
	36		36
Plant b/d	18		
Materials b/d	2		
Work-in-progress b/d	16	Accrued costs b/d	2

No certificates have been issued. This contract is in its early stages and, even if a certificate had been issued, it would have been too early to be certain of a successful completion of the contract. Therefore the work to date is carried forward at cost in the work-in-progress figure.

An alternative method

An alternative method which can be applied to contracts nearing completion is to take cost to date and add to it an estimate of the cost to complete the work. This total cost is then deducted from the price, to reveal the likely final profit on the contract. That profit can then be reduced to the formula:

$$\frac{\text{Cash}}{\text{Certificate}} \times \frac{\text{Certificate}}{\text{Price}} \times \text{Final profit} = \text{Profit recognized to date}$$

Once again, any profit taken in previous periods on a contract is deducted from the profit to date derived by the formula. An element of prudence is injected into the calculation by setting cash received against the certificate figure of progress payments to be made by the client. The formula is, however, based on the proportion of work completed to the total price of the contract.

Example 9.1 (continued)

Contract D

Contract D is nearing completion. Work-in-progress brought forward at the beginning of the year was £400,000 which included profit of £20,000. The opening stock of material on the contract was worth £24,000, and plant brought forward at that time was worth £46,000.

At the end of the year the plant was worth £20,000, and material stocks at cost were £8,000. Both the plant and material were expected to be used up completely by the end of the job. Rectification and guarantee work is expected to cost £15,000.

The contract price is £680,000, and a certificate for £600,000 has been received from the architect, together with progress payments totalling £560,000. The site agent reckons a further £10,000 of cost will be incurred to complete the contract, and wishes to provide £8,000 against contingencies. Costs not covered by the certificate are £5,000.

Costs incurred during the year were: materials £80,000, labour £60,000, and overheads £10,000.

Contract D

	£000		£000
Work-in-progress b/d	400.0	Plant c/f	20.0
Materials stock b/d	24.0	Materials c/f	8.0
Plant b/d	46.0	Work-in-progress c/f	610.7
Materials	80.0		
Labour	60.0		
Overhead	10.0		
	620.0		
Profit to P. and L. a/c	18.7		
	638.7		638.7
Plant b/d	20.0		
Material b/d	8.0		
Work-in-progress b/d	610.7		

This contract is nearing completion, so the attributable profit calculation can be made by estimating the final profit, and taking a proportion of that profit to the profit and loss account.

Calculation		£
Total debits to date		620,000
Less profit taken in a previous year		(20,000)
Less amounts carried forward (20,000 + 8,000)		(28,000)
Cost to date		572,000
Add Cost to completion	£	
Plant	20,000	
Stocks used up	8,000	
Costs	10,000	
Contingencies	8,000	
Rectification	15,000	61,000
Total cost		633,000
Price		680,000
Expected final profit		47,000

The formula for contract D is as follows:

$$\frac{\text{Cash}}{\text{Certificate}} \times \frac{\text{Certificate}}{\text{Price}} \times £47,000 = \text{Profit to date}$$

$$\frac{£560,000}{£600,000} \times \frac{£600,000}{£680,000} \times £47,000 = £38,706$$

Less Profit taken in previous years	£20,000
Profit taken this year	£18,706

Work-in-progress c/f is: Cost to date	£572,000
Plus profit to date	£38,706
	£610,706

Under both these methods work-in-progress is carried forward at cost *plus attributable profit to date*, which is in defiance of the Companies Act 1985 rule that all stocks are to be shown at the lower of cost or net realizable value. The Standard requires that profit taken in any year should reflect the appropriate proportion of the total profit on the job, by reference to the work done to date.

A further formula can be applied which follows the rule in the Standard:

$$\frac{\text{Cost of work completed}}{\text{Total estimated contract cost}} \times \text{Expected final profit} = \text{Profit to date}$$

For contract D this would be:

$$\frac{£572,000 - £5,000}{£633,000} \times £47,000 = £42,099$$

In this calculation £5,000 is deducted because this is the cost of work not covered by a certificate, and therefore not completed.

In calculating the estimated total cost, the accountant must bear in mind likely increases in wages and raw material prices, and future costs of rectification and guarantee work. How far the requirements of the Standard and the law will apply to monthly cost accounts produced for managers is at present not at all clear.

THE NEW RULES

Under the new rules suggested for financial accounting by a restatement of SSAP 9, contract D in Example 9.1 might be accounted for as follows.

1. The cost of work not certified is carried forward as work-in-progress *at cost*, as per the Companies Act 1985.
2. The cost of work certified is taken to a special profit and loss account where it is set against the value of the contract as measured by the certificate, and any profit derived is either taken to profit and loss, or held in suspense if prudence requires that it is not yet available for distribution.

The accounts would show

Contract D account

	£		£
Costs to date net of		Plant c/f	20,000
profit taken so far	600,000	Material c/f	8,000
		WiP c/f	
		[cost not certified]	5,000
		Costs w/o to P. and L.	567,000
	600,000		600,000
Plant b/d	20,000		
Material b/d	8,000		
WiP b/d	5,000		

Contract profit and loss account

	£		£
Cost of work certified	567,000	Value of work certified	600,000
Profit taken last year	20,000		
Profit taken this year to			
P. and L.	8,000		
Profit in suspense c/f	5,000		
	600,000		600,000
		Profit in suspense b/d	5,000

A profit of £33,000 is computed on work completed so far, but £20,000 has been taken in a previous period, and the managers wish to provide £5,000 against contingencies, so this amount of profit is held is suspense.

A further alternative method which can be applied is to use the formula:

$$\frac{\text{Cost of work certified}}{\text{Estimated total cost}} \times \text{Estimated final profit}$$

For contract D this would compute: $\dfrac{£567,000}{£633,000} \times £47,000 \times £42,099$

Deduct profit taken in a previous year	£20,000
Profit attributable to this year	£22,099

This calculation ensures that profit taken reflects the proportion of work done on the contract.

With so many alternatives available to the financial accountant, the cost accountant cannot be blamed for continuing to use outdated 'rule of thumb' methods which reflect the degree of prudence appropriate for the company concerned.

MULTIPLE CHOICE QUESTIONS

9.1   Which of the following features apply to contract cost accounting?
  (a)   Job completed over a period of years.
  (b)   Progress payments received before completion.
  (c)   Contract is cost centre and cost unit.
  (d)   High proportion of direct costs.

(a)   (a + b)   (a + b + c)   (all)

9.2   Which of the following conditions must exist before profit is taken on a civil engineering contract?
  (a)   Progress payments up to date.
  (b)   All work to date covered by an architect's certificate.
  (c)   The outcome of the contract can be seen with a reasonable degree of certainty.

(d)   Costs to completion forecast with accuracy.

(a)   (b)   (c)   (d)

9.3   Useful formulae which can be applied when computing profit taken in one
period on a long-term contract are:

(a) $\dfrac{2}{3} \times \dfrac{\text{Cash}}{\text{Certificate}} \times$ Attributable profit

(b) $\dfrac{\text{Cash}}{\text{Certificate}} \times \dfrac{\text{Certificate}}{\text{Price}} \times$ Final expected profit

(c) $\dfrac{\text{Cost of work completed}}{\text{Total estimated contract cost}} \times$ Estimated contract profit

(d) $\dfrac{3}{4} \times \dfrac{\text{Cash}}{\text{Certificate}} \times$ Attributable profit

(a)   (a + b)   (a + b + c)   (all)

9.4   Plant on a contract cost £80,000 at the start of the period. At the end of
twelve months it is carried forward at written down value as £65,000. Which
method of depreciation has been used?
(a)   Straight line method with a life of five years.
(b)   Straight line method, life of five years, residual value £10,000.
(c)   Reducing balance method – 15 per cent, nil scrap value.
(d)   Revaluation method.

(a)   (b)   (c)   (d)

9.5   The stock of work-in-progress on construction sites should be carried in the
balance sheet as:
(a)   Cost plus attributable profit to date.
(b)   Cost of work certified.
(c)   The lower of cost and net realizable value.
(d)   Cost less attributable losses to date if any.

(a)   (b)   (c)   (c + d)

EXERCISES

9A   One of the building contracts currently engaged in by a construction
company commenced fifteen months ago and remains unfinished. The following
information relating to work on the contract has been prepared for the year just
ended.

	£000
Contract price	2,100
Value of work certified at end of year	1,840
Cost of work not yet certified	35
Costs incurred:	
Opening balance	
Cost of work completed	250
Materials on site (physical stock)	10
During the year	
Materials delivered to site	512
Wages	487
Hire of plant	96
Other expenses	74
Closing balance	
Materials on site (physical stock)	18

As soon as materials are delivered to the site, they are charged to the contract account. A record is also kept of materials as they are actually used on the contract. Periodically a stock check is made and any discrepancy between book stock and physical stock is transferred to a general contract materials discrepancy account. This is absorbed back into each contract, currently at a rate of 0.4 per cent of materials booked. The stock check at the end of the year revealed a stock shortage of £4,000.

In addition to the direct charges listed above, general overheads of the company are charged to contracts at 5 per cent of the value of work certified. General overheads of £13,000 had been absorbed into the cost of work completed at the beginning of the year.

It has been estimated that further costs to complete the contract will be £215,000. This estimate includes the cost of materials on site at the end of the year just finished and also a provision for rectification.

Required

(a)   Explain briefly the distinguishing features of contract costing.

(b)   Determine the profitability of the above contract, and recommend how much profit (to the nearest £000) should be taken for the year just ended. (Provide a detailed schedule of costs.)

(c)   State how your recommendation in (b) would be affected if the contract price was £3,500,000 (rather than £2,100,000) and if no estimate has been made of costs to completion.

(Association of Certified Accountants)

9B   The Simon Construction Company is currently undertaking two building contracts. Information available is as follows:

	Peterborough development	Nottingham development
Contract price	£400,000	£200,000
Estimated period of contract	3 years	2 years
Date of commencement	1.1.87	1.4.87
Retention	10%	15%

Balances b/fwd 1 April 1987:	£	£
Cost of work not yet certified	14,000	
Plant on site at written down value	204,000	
Stock of materials on site	6,000	
Reserve of profit b/fwd	3,000	
Value of work certified to date		
	76,000	
Less cash received	68,400	
Retention money due from contractee	7,600	
Transactions during 1987–88:		
Materials delivered direct to site	47,720	24,540
Issues from stores	4,280	2,460
Plant sent to site	12,000	166,000
Wages	32,560	34,820
Overheads	16,800	16,180
Other expenses	4,640	4,000
Value of certificates issued	194,000	100,000
Cash received from contractee	174,600	85,000
Balances at 31 March 1988 include:		
Cost of work not yet certified	16,000	6,000
Plant on site at written down value	146,000	130,000
Stock of materials on site	16,000	8,000

The company uses the following formula to calculate profit taken on uncompleted contracts:

$$\frac{2}{3} \times \text{Apparent profit} \times \frac{\text{Cash received}}{\text{Value of work certified}}$$

Required

(a) Prepare the contract account for the two contracts as at 31 March 1988.
(b) Show clearly your calculation of profits to be taken for the year to 31 March 1988, and profit in suspense as at 31 March 1988.
(c) Show the entries in the balance sheet as at 31 March 1988.

9C The Eveready Contractors Ltd is working on three major contracts at the date of its year-end on 31 March, 19—; details of the contracts are as follows.
1. Contract A is for £150,000, a certificate has been issued for £75,000 and cash has been received, of £60,000.
2. Contract B for £100,000 has a certificate for £35,000 and cash received of £25,000.
3. Contract C for £210,000 has a certificate in the sum of £200,000 and cash amounting to £190,000 has been received. This contract was commenced in a previous accounting year.
The quantity surveyors employed by Eveready Contractors estimate that the cost of work not certified on contract A is £3,700, on contract B £1,500 and contract C £500. Work-in-progress brought forward on contract C is £150,000 which includes profit of £5,000 taken into account in the previous year. The plant on contract C at the beginning of the year is valued at £20,000, and the stock of raw materials at £1,000.

Costs charged to the contracts during the year are as follows:

	A £	B £	C £
Materials	40,000	25,000	9,000
Labour	30,000	10,000	10,000
Overhead expenses	2,500	1,000	5,000

New plant costing £15,000 has been charged to contract A. This plant is to be written off on a straight line basis over five years. Plant valued at £8,000 has been charged to contract B during the year and is revalued at the year-end at £4,000. The plant at contract C is revalued on 31 March at £4,000. You discover that accrued expenses amount to £1,000 for contract A, £500 for contract B and £1,000 for contract C.

Stocks of materials at the year-end are contract A £4,100, contract B £3,000 and contract C £1,000. During the year materials valued at £500 have been returned to stores from contract A. Scrap sales during the year on contract A total £200.

The contract manager estimates that an extra £4,000 will be incurred to complete contract C. He informs you that the plant on that contract will be worth £3,000 at the completion date and that all materials will have been used up by that time. He points out, however, that his estimates of future costs may be optimistic by as much as £1,000.

Required

(a) Write up the contract account and compute the profit or loss taken to the profit and loss account for the year on each contract.

(b) Show the entries which will appear in the balance sheet for each contract.

9D   AB plc contractors and civil engineers, are building a new wing to a hospital. The quoted fixed price for the contract is £3 million. Work commenced on 7 January 1985 and is expected to be completed on schedule by 30 June 1986. The company's financial year ended on 31 March 1986 and it is company policy to apply the requirements concerning long-term contracts which are contained in SSAP 9 'Stocks and Work-in-Progress'.

Data relating to the contract at 31 March 1986:

During the fifteen months to 31 March

	£000
Plant sent to site at commencement of contract	240
Hire of plant and equipment	77
Materials sent to site	662
Materials returned from site	47
Direct wages paid	960
Wage-related costs	132
Direct expenses incurred	34
Supervisory staff salaries – direct	90
– indirect	20
Regional office expenses apportioned to contract	50
Head office expenses apportioned to contract	30
Surveyor's fees	27
Progress payments received from health authority	1,800

The following points are also to be considered:
1. Plant is to be depreciated at the rate of 25 per cent per annum, straight line basis, with no residual value.
2. Unused materials on site at 31 March are estimated at £50,000.
3. Wages owed to direct workers total £40,000.
4. No profit in respect of this contract was included in the year ended 31 March 1985.
5. Budgeted profit on the contract is £800,000.
6. Whilst the contract is expected to be completed by the scheduled date without encountering difficulties, it is obvious to the management that the budgeted profit will not be realized. However, to calculate the attributable profit to date you are to assume that further costs to completion will be £300,000.

You are required to

(a)   (i) prepare the account for the hospital contract for the fifteen months ended 31 March, 1986;
      (ii) show the work-in-progress valuation as it will appear in the company's balance sheet at 31 March;
      (iii) calculate the profit on the contract by one other method, taking a more prudent view than that advocated in SSAP 9 and assuming for *this part of your answer* that the cost of work *not* certified is £500,000 and that the invoice value of work certified is £2 million. (Show clearly any formulae you use and your workings.)
(b)   explain and comment on the following statement which was printed in the 'Notes on Accounts' section of the 1983 published accounts of a contracting company.

In accordance with the provisions of SSAP 9 the attributable profit amounting to £8,048 (last year £303,357) is included in the value of long-term contracts. The inclusion of this attributable profit is a departure from the statutory valuation rules for current assets but is required to enable the accounts to give a true and fair view.

(Chartered Institute of Management Accountants)

10 Process Costing

CONTINUOUS PRODUCTION

Some products are produced by the application of a series of processes; as the product is transferred from one process to another it is gradually transformed from raw material into the completed article. By adding a component or undertaking some operation each process will make its contribution to the completed article. Each one of this series of operations or processes forms a natural cost centre for the accountant.

The costs of labour, materials and overhead normally shown in the manufacturing account can be analysed to the various processes which make up the manufacturing operation. Cost analysis will need to report to management on the number of units of output from each process and the cost added per unit. The term 'throughput' is often used rather than output, since in process operations units are fed into the process at the beginning and emerge at the end. The completed production of one process becomes the raw material for the following process, and must therefore be transferred to that process at a figure of cost to date per unit. It is difficult in such circumstances to distinguish one cost unit from another since they are homogeneous and may well be mixed together, e.g. as a liquid in a vat, so that the cost per process is averaged over the units produced to compute a unit cost. Process costing can be readily applied in such industries as refining, distilling, soap making, brewing, and the chemical or plastic industries, where raw materials are blended together in a process and then further raw materials are added or manufacturing operations undertaken in later processes.

The costing system needs to identify and measure the cost of raw material, labour and overhead incurred by each process and allocate those costs to batches of cost units as they are put through the process. It is therefore advisable to express a process cost statement in terms of units as well as in terms of cost.

PROCESS COSTING AND JOB COSTING

With job costing each job acts as a cost unit, and costs are identified to the job. Process costing, however, is the exact opposite of this situation since individual cost units cannot be identified, and the costs of the process as a whole (the cost centre) are averaged as the cost of each unit passing through the process. Process costing would thus appear to be less accurate than job costing since it computes only an average cost for each unit in a batch of similar products. The recording systems for process and job costing have similar features. Requisitions are used to transfer materials from the store to the production department, and labour costs can be analysed to a process as easily as to a job. In both cases indirect labour forms part of the production overheads. With job costing, factory overhead costs need to be allocated and apportioned to the cost centres through which the job passes on its way to completion, and those overheads are then absorbed to the job by means of preset rates. With process costing, however, the overheads can be more easily allocated direct to the process so that part of the inaccuracies experienced by the apportionment and absorption procedures can be avoided.

Job costs require a continuous updating of the job cost card, and a degree of clerical error can affect the accuracy of the figures. Process costing suffers from the arbitrary assessment of the degree of completion of stocks of work-in-progress, which is made at the end of a costing period and on which is based the calculation of effective units which will determine the cost of completed production. If a process produces joint products, or a main product and a by-product, further inaccuracies arise in the means which the joint costs are allotted to the products concerned.

Example 10.1

Blank Discs Ltd is a small company in the record industry which undertakes production by two processes, the first to mix the ingredients and the second to stamp out the record blanks. The cost of materials, labour and production overheads can be analysed per process, and the process accounts prepared as follows:

Process 1: Mixing

	kg	£		kg	£
Raw material A	28,000	6,500	Completed production		
Raw material B	12,000	2,500	Transferred to		
			process 2	40,000	13,230
Labour	–	2,820			
Production overhead	–	1,410			
	40,000	13,230		40,000	13,230

Cost per kg transferred: £13,230 ÷ 40,000 = 33.1p.

Process 2: Stamping (100 blanks per kg)

	Blanks	£		Blanks	£
Received from			Completed production		
process 1	400,000	13,230	Passed to stores	400,000	20,055
Labour	-	2,370			
Production overhead	-	4,095			
	400,000	20,055		400,000	20,055

Cost per blank: £20,055 ÷ 400,000 = 5p each.

Note that the raw material of process 2 is transferred from process 1.

There are four major difficulties associated with process costing.

1. The treatment of waste and scrap materials in the cost accounts: part of the production of a process may be rejected when it is inspected for quality, and cannot therefore be passed to the next process in the manufacturing sequence.

2. Normal and abnormal losses or gains in process: when materials are mixed in a process the quantity of mixture derived from the process may be less in volume or weight then the aggregate of the inputs. This loss in process may be caused by evaporation or chemical reaction when the materials are mixed. Such losses are usually treated in the accounts by estimating the normal loss that is likely to be experienced in the process, and to charge that loss to the 'good' production so that normal losses are averaged out within the unit cost of production. Abnormal losses or gains in the process need to be shown to management as a separate item.

3. Joint and by-products: if a process produces more than one product from its inputs, it may be difficult to apportion the joint or common costs of the process between the products produced.

4. Semi-completed production: at the end of a costing period there may be semi-completed stocks of work in process, which must be valued for accounting purposes. This value will of course affect the amount of process costs which are charged to completed units.

WASTE AND SCRAP IN PROCESS COSTING

Waste

Waste is a discarded substance having no value. It is that part of the material input of the process which is lost during production, or which when emerging from the process has no recovery value. If two liquids are mixed in a process and 200 litres of each are introduced into that process, the heat treatment within the process will evaporate some of the mixture. Accordingly, if at the end of the process 380 litres of mixture are produced, the process has lost 5 per cent in volume of its input materials. The chemical reaction within the process will determine what loss is to be experienced, and this process loss or waste is considered to be a normal cost of that process.

The basic rule in cost accounting for normal waste is that it should be absorbed into the cost of 'good' production. The total process cost is divided by the number of good units produced, thus calculating an average unit cost which bears a proportion of the cost of the waste products. However, if waste is experienced beyond the expected level abnormal waste has been incurred and this extra cost above the norm must be credited to the process account and debited to an abnormal waste account. This is an unplanned cost so it should be shown as a separate item in the costing profit and loss account.

Example 10.2

Suppose that in process 1 referred to in Example 10.1 a 10 per cent wastage is experienced; the process account would record waste as follows:

Process 1 account

	kg	£		kg	£
Raw material A	28,000	6,500	Waste	4,000	–
Raw material B	12,000	2,500	Transferred to		
			process 2	36,000	13,230
Labour	–	2,820			
Overhead	–	1,410			
	40,000	13,230		40,000	13,230

The unit cost of good production is: £13,230 ÷ 36,000 kg = 36.75p per kg.

Scrap

Scrap is discarded material which has some recovery value and which is usually sold when it is produced, without further treatment, or reintroduced into the production process as raw material. An appropriate costing treatment for scrap will depend upon the circumstances of its production. The alternatives are:
1. If the material can be used elsewhere in the business, credit the process and debit the stores with the original cost of the material which should then be returned to stores for reissue to some other manufacturing process.
2. If the scrap is sold the process should be credited with the income derived, the corresponding debit being made in the cash book.
3. In the case of insignificant scrap sales, a simple debit to cash and corresponding credit in the production overhead control account will record the transaction adequately.

Scrap sales credited to the process account will influence the average cost of the good production.

Example 10.3

Suppose that the 10 per cent loss in process described in Example 10.2 produces scrap material which can be sold for 5p per kg.

Process 1 account

	kg	£		kg	£
Raw material A	28,000	6,500	Scrap sold for cash	4,000	200
Raw material B	12,000	2,500			
Labour	–	2,820	Transferred to	36,000	13,030
			process 2		
Overhead	–	1,410			
	40,000	13,230		40,000	13,230

The unit cost of good production is now: £13,230 – £200 ÷ 36,000 kg = 36.19p per kg.

NORMAL AND ABNORMAL LOSSES AND GAINS IN PROCESS

As discussed above, normal losses experienced in a process are treated as waste and averaged out to the cost of good production. If losses experienced in a process are greater than the normal expected amount, the abnormal loss – being the difference between loss experienced and the loss expected – should be costed, credited to the process, and debited through an abnormal loss account to the costing profit and loss. If the loss experienced on a process is less than the norm, an abnormal gain has occurred. Such gains should be debited to the process, and credited to an abnormal gains account whence it will eventually be posted to the costing profit and loss account.

Example 10.4

Suppose that in process 1 shown in Example 10.3 only 35,000 kg were transferred to process 2. This means that the loss in process was 5,000 kg, as opposed to a normal loss of 4,000 kg, an abnormal loss of 1000 kg. We will assume that scrap sales whether normal or abnormal can be made at 5p per kg.

Therefore 35,000 kg are transferred to process 2 at a cost of 36.19p each (say £12,668), and the cost of 1,000 kg of abnormal loss of 36.19p per kg (say £362) is credited to the process account and debited to an abnormal loss account. The sale of abnormal scrap should be credited to the abnormal loss account so that the net cost of abnormal scrap is revealed and transferred to the costing profit and loss account.

Process 1 account

	kg	£		kg	£
Raw material A	28,000	6,500	Normal loss – scrap sale	4,000	200
Raw material B	12,000	2,500	Abnormal loss	1,000	362
Labour	–	2,820	Transferred to process 2	35,000	12,668
Overhead	–	1,410			
	40,000	13,230		40,000	13,230

The cost of normal production is: £13,230 − £200 = £13,030 for 36,000 kg, and the unit cost is 36.19p per kg for abnormal loss and good production.

Abnormal loss account

	£		£
Process 1 account	362	Scrap sales	
		1,000 kg at 2.5p	·50
		Costing P. and L. a/c	312
	362		362

Example 10.5: Abnormal gains

Suppose that in process 1 above 37,000 kg are produced, 1,000 kg more than the normal expected production. As before, the cost of normal production is found by dividing the number of expected units into the process cost (£13,030 divided by 36,000 = 36.19p). The actual volume of production is credited to the process, at 36.19p per unit (37,000 × 36.19p = say £13,390), and debited to the next process. The abnormal gain is debited to the process account (1,000 kg × 36.19p = £362) and credited to the normal gain account.

Process 1 Account

	kg	£		kg	£
Raw material A	28,000	6,500	Normal loss – scrap sales	4,000	200
Raw material B	12,000	2,500	Transferred to process 2	37,000	13,392
Labour	–	2,820			
Overhead	–	1,410			
Abnormal gain at 36.19p	1,000	362			
	41,000	13,592		41,000	13,592

The position disclosed by the ledger accounts at this stage is unreal in that scrap sales of 4,000 units have been credited to the process account, whereas in reality only 3,000 kg of scrap have been sold. This fiction is necessary to calculate the normal cost of production transferred to process 2, and the position is corrected by debiting the abnormal gain account with the amount of the apparent error (1,000 kg × 5p = £50).

Abnormal gain account

	£		£
Scrap sales	50	Process 1 - 1,000 kg at 36.19p	362
Costing profit and loss	312		
	362		362

Scrap sales account

	£		£
Process 1 - 4,000 kg	200	Abnormal gain - 1,000 kg at 5p	50
		Cash - 3,000 kg at 5p	150
	200		200

JOINT PRODUCTS

It cannot be assumed that a process will always produce only one product; sometimes two or more are separated in the course of processing. If these products are of equal significance they are termed joint products; alternatively, if one is more significant than the others it will be a main product, the others by-products. The by-product is recovered incidentally from the material used in the manufacture of the main product. Often joint and by-products require further processing before they can be marketed: when crude oil is refined, for example, major products such as petrol, diesel and fuel oil are produced as well as some by-products of lesser significance such as gas and chemicals. Propane gas produced at an oil refinery may be treated as a waste product and burned away or, alternatively, if it is considered worthwhile the gas may be bottled and sold to consumers.

If two joint products are produced from a process, the costs of that process have been incurred in the production of both the products, and therefore these joint or common costs need to be allotted to the units produced. The difficulty is that pre-separation-point costs cannot easily be allocated to the products which emerge from the process after the separation. At best an apportionment of joint process costs will give some idea of the total production cost of joint products, but the validity of this cost depends upon the basis on which the apportionment was made. Three alternative bases for apportionment can be used:

(a)   a physical measurement to show the proportion of total output attributable to each joint product, i.e. by weight or volume;

(b)   the proportion of total market value of the joint products at the point of separation;

(c)   the proportion of total market value of the joint products when they are eventually sold after further processing.

Example 10.6

A chemical process has total costs for a week of £15,600. These costs include the input of materials, direct labour and production overheads. The output of the process for the week was 4,000 litres of detergent and 3,000 litres of liquid fertilizer (7,000 litres in all). The detergent can be sold for £2 per litre without further processing, and the fertilizer for £5 per litre.

Apportionment on a physical basis (7,000 litres)

	Detergent		Fertilizer		Total
		£		£	£
Sales:	4,000 × £2	8,000	300 × £5	15,000	23,000
Costs:	4/7 × £15,600	8,914	3/7 × £15,600	6,686	15,600
Profit/(Loss):		(914)		8,314	7,400

Apportionment of basis of sales revenue (£23,000)*

	Detergent		Fertilizer		Total
		£		£	£
Sales		8,000		15,000	23,000*
Costs:	8/23 × £15,600	5,426	15/23 × £15,600	10,174	15,600
Profit		2,574		4,826	7,400

Example 10.6 shows that the basis of apportionment applied by the accountant will affect the profit disclosed. Apportionment of joint costs on the basis of physical production is simple to apply and seems reasonable if the same amount of effort and cost is applied to produce each unit of the joint products. However, this method presumes that cost accrues in proportion to the quantity processed, but in reality this may not be the case. Apportionment of joint costs on the basis of sales value may also be unreal in certain situations, since selling price may bear little relationship to the joint process costs. It may be difficult to calculate a market value for joint products at the split-off point since these products may need further processing to put them into a saleable condition. If this is so the eventual selling price earned by joint products may be too remote from the original joint process to act as a reasonable basis for apportionment. Example 10.6 illustrates the difficulty of applying various methods of apportionment to joint costs, in that apportionment on a physical basis shows detergent making a loss, but apportionment on the basis of sales value shows detergent as a profitable product. Clearly, management cannot place any reliance on profit or loss figures produced in this way unless they believe that the method of apportionment used is a reliable one.

Apportionment of joint costs may well act to obscure the relevant figures when a decision is to be made. If the alternatives facing a manager are either to sell a joint product immediately or to incur further costs in processing the product after the split-off point, any joint costs incurred up to the split-off point will not change whether or not further processing takes place. Accordingly, these costs are incurred in any event and should not be allowed to affect the decision. The manager must decide on the basis of revenue to be earned immediately by sale, or the net revenue to be earned by further processing and sale at a higher price.

BY-PRODUCTS

By-products are less significant than the main product but they may nevertheless have a saleable value both at the split-off point and after further processing. There are several methods of treating by-product costs, but as usual the circumstances of the case will determine which method should be applied.

1. The sales revenue from insignificant by-products can be credited direct to the costing profit and loss account. This method ignores any further processing or selling costs incurred but if the by-product is of little significance, those costs are likely to be negligible.

2   An alternative costing treatment for insignificant by-products is to treat them as scrap, so that any sales revenue will be credited to the process which produced the by-product.

3. Where further processing of a by-product is required to put it into a saleable condition, the cost should be set against the sales revenue, and the net revenue then credited to the main product.

Example 10.7

Process 1 produces main product A and a by-product X. Product A is passed on to process 2 for further processing, and the by-product receives further treatment in process 3.

	£	£
Joint costs		17,680
Add subsequent costs of main product		9,760
		27,440
Less sale of by-product	2,315	
Less process cost of by-product post-separation point	1,441	(874)
Net cost of main product		26,566
Revenue from sale of main product		29,000
Profit of main product		2,434

WORK-IN-PROGRESS: EQUIVALENT UNITS

With some processes a stock of semi-finished products remains in the process at the end of the costing period. This stock must be valued at cost, and carried forward as the opening stock of the next accounting period. The value of stock carried forward will therefore reduce the cost of completed production in the first month, and it will be added to the cost of completed production in the second month. The difficulty encountered in computing a precise cost for the closing stock of work-in-progress stems from the fact that the unit cost of items processed is merely an average of process cost divided by the units completed. The closing stock of work-in-progress is not complete. All the materials may be there, but perhaps only half the labour time required to complete each product has been expended on the units at the end of the costing period. If production overhead is absorbed on a labour hour basis, only half the overhead can be charged to the semi-finished goods at the period-end. Thus process costs allocated to finished goods during a period will be affected by the cost of stock carried forward, but the allocation of costs in the next period will also be affected because in that period the opening stock of semi-finished work will be completed.

Process costing merely averages the costs of the process during a period over the units produced. If, however, some of the units are only 50 or 75 per cent complete, those semi-finished units must be translated into their equivalents with completed units, in order that the averaging technique may proceed. The concept of equivalent units is applied by substituting a notional quantity of completed units for an actual quantity of incomplete physical units in the process at the end of a costing period. Thus the aggregate work content of 100 units which are 75 per cent complete is equal to 75 full units, or equivalent units. Suppose that during a month a process produces 2,000 complete units, and 500 units are in process at the end of the month. These units are deemed to be 60 per cent complete. The total equivalent production would therefore be 2,000 units + (60% × 500) 300 units = 2,300 equivalent units. The term 'effective units' is often used as an alternative. Costs of the process, say £46,000 would be averaged over the 2,300 equivalent units to give a unit cost of £20. The closing stock of work-in-progress would be valued as 300 × £20, i.e. £6,000, as the amount of process cost attributable to the 500 units in process at the end of the month, which are to be carried forward as the opening stock of the next month. In the next month it will take the normal cost of producing 200 units (40% × 500) to complete the semi-finished work-in-progress brought forward.

Example 10.8

Process A has no opening stock of work-in-progress, but 8,000 units of material are put into the process in the month of June. Production during June completes 7,000 units but 1,000 semi-finished units remain in process at the month-end. These semi-finished units are complete for material, but only half-complete for labour and overheads. These circumstances can be expressed in terms of equivalent units as follows.

1. *Raw materials*: 8,000 units of material have been issued, 7,000 units are completed and passed on to the next process, and 1,000 remain. Therefore the cost of materials for the process for the month, £16,000, can be apportioned as:
    (a) 1,000/8,000 to stock of work in progress; and
    (b) 7,000/8,000 to completed production.
    The cost of £16,000 is spread over 8,000 units to give a material cost of £2 per unit.
2. *Labour and overheads*: 8,000 units entered the process in June but only 7,000 were completed. The remaining 1,000 units are half-finished, so that they are the equivalent of 500 completely finished units. Thus the labour cost incurred by the process is divided among 7,500 completed units (7,000 finished and 500 equivalent units representing the work completed to date on the closing stock of work-in-progress).

If the labour and overheads cost for the month of June was £33,750, then dividing by 7,500 equivalent units gives a unit cost of £4.50. Completed production is charged with 7,000 × £4.50, and closing stock valued at 500 × £4.50. The process account can be written up as follows:

Process A - June

	Units	£		Units	£
Material	8,000	16,000	Completed production	7,000	45,500
Labour and overhead	–	33,750	Stock c/f	1,000	4,250
	8,000	49,750		8,000	49,750

	£
Stock:	
1,000 units of material at £2	2,000
500 units of labour and overhead at £4.50	2,250
	4,250
Completion production:	
Material 7,000 units at £2	14,000
Labour and overhead 7,000 units at £4.50	31,500
	45,500

This example can be extended into the month of July, when cost data for process A is: 12,000 new units introduced at a cost of £3 each for material; labour and overhead costs for the month £44,000. During July 11,000 units were completed and a closing stock of 2,000 in process at the end of the month is 25 per cent complete for labour and overheads.

The equivalent units may be calculated as follows:

1. *Opening stock*: 1,000 complete for materials but half-complete for labour and overheads. These units require 500 equivalent units of labour/overhead expenses to complete them.
2. *Introduced and completed*: 10,000 units introduced during July were completed during that month forming 10,000 equivalent units for materials and for labour/overheads.
3. *Closing stock*: 2,000 equivalent units of material were in stock at the month-end. This closing work-in-progress is 25 per cent complete, so 500 equivalent units of labour/overheads have been expended to bring the stock to its present condition. The total equivalent units for July are materials 12,000 and labour/overheads 500 + 10,000 + 500 = 11,000. The equivalent units for labour/overheads are divided into the cost of £44,000 to give a unit cost of £4 each. The process account can be written up as follows:

Process A - July

	Units	£		Units	£
Stock b/d	1,000	4,250	Completed production	11,000	76,250
Material	12,000	36,000	Stock c/f	2,000	8,000
Labour and overhead	–	44,000			
	13,000	84,250		13,000	84,250

Completed production for July comprises:
1. Opening stock finished off: £4,250 plus 500 equivalent units at £4 each (£2,000), giving a total of £6,250.
2. Units introduced and completed: 10.000 units of material at £3, and labour/overhead at £4 = 10,000 × £7 = £70,000.

This gives a total cost of £76,250.

The closing stock is complete for material (2,000 × £3 = £6,000) but represents 500 equivalent units of labour/overhead at £4 (£2,000), giving a total of £8,000.

If waste occurs in a process the cost should be absorbed by the good production, so that the number of equivalent units over which the process cost is averaged will be produced. This calculation can be made more complicated if rejected units have been semi-completed at the point of their rejection. They are merely translated into equivalent units and their portion of the process costs are charged to the rejected work account.

THE FIFO METHOD VERSUS THE AVERAGING METHOD

The calculation of equivalent units so far has followed the logical assumption that units in process are dealt with on a first in first out basis. This assumption means that when the equivalent units are calculated the first work undertaken during a period is deemed to be the completion of the opening stock of work-in-progress. This means that the closing work-in-progress will be valued by reference to the costs of the current month, and any costs of the previous month brought forward in the value of opening work-in-progress will be charged to production during the current month.

An alternative assumption is that the equivalent unit calculation should take into account not only the costs of the current month but also the costs of opening work-in-progress carried forward from the previous month. This has the effect of bringing into the average calculation some costs from a previous month, which could then be carried forward within the calculation of the value of closing work-in-progress, to the succeeding month. A calculation based on such an average could reduce the validity of any comparison of performance between costing periods. Alternatively, in favour of the averaging method is the argument that it helps to reduce the effect of fluctuations in costs experienced from month to month.

When applied to the July data in Example 10.8, the averaging method produces slightly different figures. The opening stocks are considered as full units for the month but their costs from the previous month are brought into the calculation of process costs incurred for the month.

	Materials	Labour/ overhead
Cost	£	£
Opening stock (4.250)	2,000	2,250
July	36,000	44,000
	38,000	46,250

Total cost of £84,250 to be divided between equivalent production units:

Completed	11,000	11,000
Closing stock	2,000	500(25%)
	13,000	11,500

giving a cost per equivalent unit of £38,000 ÷ 13,000 = £2.92 for materials, and £46,250 ÷ 11,500 = £4.02 for labour/overheads.

Completed production: 11,000 × £6.94 (£2.92 + £4.02)		76,340
Closing stock: 2000 × 2.92	5,840	
500 × £4.02	2,010	7,850
		84,190

Note: The two totals (£84,250 and £84,190) differ slightly due to rounding.

MULTIPLE CHOICE QUESTIONS

10.1 Which of the following definitions describes a by-product?
   (a) Units of output which fail to reach the required standard of quality.
   (b) Discarded material which has some recovery value.
   (c) A product which is recovered incidentally from material used in manufacture.
   (d) Products separated in the course of processing which have roughly equal significance.

(a)   (b)   (c)   (d)

10.2 There are four major difficulties associated with process costing. Which of them are listed below?
   (a) The valuation of stocks of work-in-progress.
   (b) Normal or abnormal losses or gains.
   (c) The separation of fixed from variable costs.
   (d) The recognition of the 'split-off' point.

(a)   (a + b)   (c + d)   (b +d)

10.3 Which of the following statements is correct?
   (a) Abnormal losses in process are averaged out to the cost of good production.
   (b) Abnormal losses in process are always sold as scrap.

(a)   (b)   (both)   (neither)

10.4   Equivalent units are:
  (a)   The result of multiplying the financial forecast of the outcome of a course of action by the probability of achieving that outcome.
  (b)   A notional quantity of completed units substituted for an actual quantity of incomplete physical units in progress.
  (c)   A hypothetical cost taken into account in a particular situation to represent a benefit enjoyed by an entity in respect of which no actual expense is incurred.
  (d)   A predetermined calculation of how much unit costs should be under specified working conditions.

(a)   (b)   (a + c)   (b + d)

10.5   Common costs can be apportioned to joint products on the basis of:
  (a)   Physical quantity produced.
  (b)   Ultimate sales revenue.
  (c)   NRV at split-off point.
  (d)   Post-separation-point costs.

(a)   (a + b)   (a + b + c)   (all)

EXERCISES

10A   The Carreau Co Ltd manufactures decorative tiles. The company operates a process whereby tile blanks are produced for further decoration and treatment. Materials are fed into the process and the products, large blanks and small blanks, are produced. The joint costs of the process amount to £9,400 per month and normal output is 20,000 large blanks weighing 0.5 kg, and 20,000 small blanks weighing 0.15 kg. Waste material from the process is sold for £300 each month. The tile blanks are glazed after separation, at a cost of 30p for large and 20p for small tiles. Large tiles sell for 65p each, but small tiles, because of their exquisite design and workmanship, sell for 75p each.

You are required to:

(a)   Report to management on the profitability of the two joint products using three methods of evaluation in your report.
(b)   Discuss the relevance of your analysis in (a) above, and suggest a more meaningful method of reporting to management.
(c)   The company has discovered that by passing the small blanks through a second glazing treatment they can be sold to a wholesaler in the luxury bathroom trade for £1 each. The cost of the further processing is £1,500 for a batch of 10,000 tiles, with a further 5p per tile as a share of fixed overhead expenses to be absorbed by this extra activity. A transport cost of 3p per tile must be paid for delivery to the customer's warehouse, but packaging costs of £500 would be saved on each batch. Advise management whether to follow up this opportunity.

10B   The marketing director of your company has expressed concern about product X, which for some time has shown a loss, and has stated that some action will have to be taken.

Product X is produced from material A, which is one of two raw materials jointly produced by passing chemicals through a process.

Representative data for the process is as follows:

Output:	
Material A	10,000 kg
Material B	30,000 kg
Process costs:	
Raw material	£83,600
Conversion costs	£58,000

Joint costs are apportioned to the two raw materials according to the weight of output.

Production costs incurred in converting material A into product X are £1.80 per kg of material A used. A yield of 90 per cent is achieved. Product X is sold for £5.60 per kg. Material B is sold without further processing for £6.00 per kg.

Required

(a)   Calculate the profit/(loss) per kg of product X and material B respectively.
(b)   Comment upon the marketing director's concern, advising him whether you consider any action should be taken.
(c)   Demonstrate for product X, and comment briefly upon, an alternative method of cost apportionment.

(Association of Certified Accountants)

10C   A chemical company carries on production operations in two processes. Materials first pass through process I, where a compound is produced. A loss in weight takes place at the start of processing. The following data, which can be assumed to be representative, relates to the month just ended:

Quantities	
Material input	200,000
Opening work-in-progress (half-processed)	40,000
Work completed	160,000
Closing work-in-progress (two-thirds processed)	30,000
Costs (£)	
Material input	75,000
Processing costs	96,000
Opening work-in-progress – materials	20,000
– processing costs	12,000

Any quantity of the compound can be sold for £1.60 per kg. Alternatively, it can be transferred to process II for further processing and packing to be sold as Starcomp for £2.00 per kg. Further materials are added in process II such that for every kg of compound used, 2 kg of Starcomp result.

Of the 160,000 kg per month of work completed in process I, 40,000 kg are sold as compound and 120,000 kg are passed through process II for sale as Starcomp. Process II has facilities to handle up to 160,000 kg of compound per month if required. The monthly costs incurred in process II (other than the cost of the compound) are:

	120,000 kg of compound input	160,000 kg of compound input
Materials	£120,000	£160,000
Processing costs	£120,000	140,000

Required

(a) Determine, using the average method, the cost per kg of compound in process I, and the value of both work completed and closing work-in-progress for the month just ended.

(b) Demonstrate that it is worthwhile further processing 120,000 kg of compound.

(c) Calculate the minimum acceptable selling price per kg, if a potential buyer could be found for the additional output of Starcomp that could be produced with the remaining compound.

(Association of Certified Accountants)

10D (a) Explain briefly the term 'joint products' in the context of process costing.

(b) Discuss whether, and if so how, joint process costs should be shared amongst joint products (assume no further processing is required after the split-off point).

(c) Explain briefly the concept of 'equivalent units' in process costing.

(Association of Certified Accountants)

10E A distillation plant, which works continuously, processes 1,000 tonnes of raw material each day. The raw material costs £4 per tonne and the plant operating costs per day are £2,600. From the input of raw material the following output is produced:

	%
Distillate X	40
Distillate Y	30
Distillate Z	20
By-product B	10

From the initial distillation process, distillate X passes through a heat process which costs £1,500 per day and becomes product X, which requires blending before sale.

Distillate Y goes through a second distillation process costing £3,300 per day and produces 75 per cent of product Y and 25 per cent of product X1.

Distillate Z has a second distillation process costing £2,400 per day and produces 60 per cent of product Z and 40 per cent of product X2.

The three streams of products X, X1 and X2 are blended, at a cost of £1,155 per day to become the saleable final product XXX.

There is no loss of material from any of the processes.

By-product B is sold for £3 per tonne and such proceeds are credited to the process from which the by-product is derived.

Joint costs are apportioned on a physical unit basis.

You are required to

(a) Draw a flowchart, flowing from left to right, to show for one day of production the flow of material and the build-up of the operating costs for each product (*hint*: turn your answer book to have the longer edge of the paper at the top or use two facing pages).

(b) Present a statement for management showing for *each* of the products XXX, Y and Z, the output for *one* day, the total cost and the unit cost per tonne.

(c) Suggest an alternative method for the treatment of the income receivable for by-product B than that followed in this question (figures are not required).

(*Chartered Institute of Management Accountants*)

11 Cost Accounting for Service Activities

FUNCTION COSTING

Service, or function, costing concerns specific services or functions found within a business, such as canteens, maintenance, power generation, etc. Functions such as these are often organized in separate departments or service centres.

The operation concerned may provide a service to production departments and/or to customers outside the business, in which case the cost unit would describe some measure of the service provided. The function can be organized as a separate operation within the business, e.g. the transport department or a plant yard operated by a civil engineering company. The operations undertaken may result from specific orders or may be part of a general service to other sectors of the business, but the fact that the operation is seen as a separate function, perhaps providing specialist services on demand to other parts of the business, means that a separate cost treatment is required.

SERVICE ORGANIZATIONS

The provision of services is not confined to separate departments within a business, since some companies exist only to provide a service. Nor is service costing restricted to the profit-making sector of activity since there are many non-profit-making undertakings whose activity is best analysed per unit of service. Examples of such organizations are the provision of a transport service by bus or rail, the provision of electricity by a power station, the provision of patient care by a hospital or local health authority, and the provision of educational services by a college. Clearly these services require significant investment and considerable administrative skills, one of which is the provision of adequate cost information to the management of the undertaking. The service organization may have to overcome the problems of providing an adequate service at peak periods of demand and suffering the penalty of under-utilized capacity at other times, e.g. transport services during the rush hour and electricity demand at certain times of the day. Considerable cost collection and analysis is required to give managerial control of such large operations, and considerable sophistication is needed to define an appropriate cost for services provided at peak periods or during periods of low demand. One solution to this problem is to analyse costs to their fixed and variable categories, and then to price services so that a contribution is made on all services provided, towards the fixed costs of the undertaking.

ADMINISTRATIVE SERVICES

These can form a significant proportion of the total cost in an organization which prefers to organize its own in-house operation, rather than to employ outside specialists. A company with its own transport fleet (owned or leased), its own design and marketing department, and which administers its own pension fund – and perhaps within a large group operating its own insurance agency – will certainly consider service costs as significant. The costing treatment of such service activities is to recognize the service given, identify its recipients, and then compute the cost of providing it. Costs can be attributed to users, by the techniques described under full absorption costing. Some organizations prefer a standard service charge to be applied to all users of the service department, but this approach may be considered inflexible if users make different demands upon the service department, e.g. repetitive operations versus 'one-off' orders, and long and short production runs. If the cost of service departments is to be built into the full absorbed cost of a unit on which prices or tenders are to be based, a mistake in charging out service costs could result in over-pricing and the loss of work to competitors. The costs of service centres, however, must be controlled perhaps by the use of a budget which defines the maximum amount of expenditure on that service within a period, and is also based on the level of service which management wish to provide.

IN-HOUSE VERSUS BOUGHT-IN SERVICES

The evaluation of the benefits derived from services within a firm is difficult, especially if a decision is to be made between the alternatives of buying in a service or providing that service within the business. The value of a service can be measured by the loss felt or extra costs generated were the service to be withdrawn. For example, suppose a company provides its own computing services within a separate department. This department will charge out its costs to other departments which use its service. When deciding whether to close the computing department and substitute the bought-in services of a bureau, it is difficult to take into account all the extra but unrecorded use made of the computing department by other parts of the business, for example seeking advice, securing instant information, or having computing runs brought forward or changes made to the information regularly supplied. With a bureau operation some of these extra services may not be possible, and others will certainly be charged for.

A further difficulty concerns the way in which the service department charges its users. Is the charge to be based on the volume of use made of the service, or is it to be a standard charge for all user departments? A charge based on use will motivate user managers to avoid wasting the service provided by the computing department; a flat rate charge may encourage waste. Further difficulties with the costing treatment of service activities concern the comparison between the service that is provided and the service that should be provided. User managers will always opt for extra services, but whether the benefit is greater than the additional cost of providing such services may be difficult to determine. Opportunity cost is a useful concept in such a comparison since resources tied up to extend a service will limit other activities within the business.

SELECTION OF COST UNITS

Costs in a service industry or in a service department must be expressed per unit of service provided: this facilitates comparison between the cost of units provided in a previous period or the budgeted cost of units to be provided. The cost for the same period last year is also a useful comparator. A transport undertaking may express its costs in terms of the passenger mile or kilometre for passenger traffic, or the ton mile or kilometre for goods transport. Hospitals use the patient day, or the number of out-patients treated, and the cost per major or minor operation. A hotel may measure its activity by the number of occupied bed nights, a theatre can use the proportion of total seats available occupied by the paying public. A restaurant can express its costs as so much per meal served. It must of course be recognized that the application of cost units in this way is merely an averaging device and that the results derived from this averaging can be misleading. With a restaurant, some meals provided for individual customers may use up a significant amount of the service provided by the organization, but twenty meals provided for a party of guests may make less demand per meal upon the services provided.

TRANSPORT COSTS

A road transport business, or the transport department of a large company, experiences similar costing problems. Separate cost centres should be established for certain aspects of the company, e.g. maintenance, administration and operations. Under operations, sub-centres might be established for individual vehicles or groups of similar vehicles. Costs can be allocated as far as possible to the cost centres, and overheads absorbed by the vehicle groups which undertake the operations of the business. A cost per mile can be calculated for individual vehicles or groups, and fluctuations should lead to investigation. Some accountants believe that cost per mile/kilometre is not a useful measure to relate cost to activity, since the vehicle may operate for some of the miles without a load. Efficient organization arranges for return loads so that the vehicle does not run without earning revenue. Perhaps the calculation of costs per ton mile (tonne/kilometre) is a better measure of efficient operation.

Drivers should complete a daily log sheet on which details of journeys, e.g. mileage, load, start and finish times, are recorded. Fuel supplied for journeys can also be entered on this record. The cost office should maintain records which reveal the activity and idle time of each vehicle, its running and operating costs, the mileage and weight carried during a costing period, and other overhead expenses concerning the vehicle. Such costs as road tax, insurance, tyres, spares and overhauls are important if the true cost of operating the vehicle is to be identified. The maintenance department may have its own costing system with a further series of time sheets and stores requisitions so that the cost of repairs undertaken on each vehicle can be determined.

Calculation of the ton mile is made by several different methods, but the simplest is that a vehicle is carrying a load of one ton for a mile equals a ton mile. A 100-mile journey with a load of 5 tons is 500 ton miles. This same statistic can be computed by taking account of the fact that the vehicle has to return 100 miles without a load. The vehicle has therefore travelled 200 miles and a formula $5 \times 200 \div 2$ also gives 500 ton miles as the result. (Return with a full load of 5 tons would result in $10 \times 200 \div 2 = 1,000$ ton miles.) Alternatively, if two smaller vehicles carrying 2.5-ton loads had made the same journey and returned empty the calculation, $2.5 \times 400 \div 2$, would still equal 500 ton miles. The ton mile seems one way in which loads of different sizes and journeys of different lengths may be compared on the basis of a common unit. Perhaps a more meaningful item of managerial information might be to compute the number of miles run by the company's vehicles *without* a load.

MAINTENANCE

The maintenance department can be treated as a separate cost centre and its accumulated costs can be charged out to user departments either in a pre-agreed proportion, say 10 per cent, or on the basis of time spent by department workers on certain jobs. If maintenance activity is significant, a job costing system could be introduced to deal with each maintenance task as a separate job to be costed out by the maintenance department. User managers would therefore be charged the full cost for work done in their departments and, with the true cost being identified, machine replacement decisions might be facilitated. Constant repair work on a single machine must single out that machine as a likely candidate for replacement or at least investigation into the reasons for its constant failure. Managers in user departments who are charged the full cost of repair work may be more willing to join in a programme of preventive maintenance, or to use maintenance services external to the firm which will save money.

Conversely, a manager cannot be responsible for maintenance costs allocated as a pre-agreed proportion. By his or her own efficiency the manager cannot influence the maintenance charge to his or her department (so why bother?); and the manager of the maintenance department has no spur to efficiency if the department costs, however great, are charged to users. This is a wholly unsatisfactory system.

UNIFORM COSTING

The CIMA terminology defines uniform costing as 'the use by several undertakings of the same costing system, i.e. the same basic costing methods, principles and techniques'. It is convenient for organizations with similar interests to analyse cost, and present reports, in a like manner. There are many instances where advantages will flow from the situation where organizations co-operate to promote and use one costing system.

Uniform costing can be used by organizations of the following types.

1. Companies in the same group, which are able to compare the cost of similar products across the group, e.g. laundry plants controlled as subsidiaries by a holding company.
2. Businesses in the same trade association, e.g. the printing industry, which are able to review the efficiency of their own business when compared against cost information for the average of all firms in the industry expressed by an inter-firm comparison scheme.
3. Local authorities may co-operate to cost similar activities by the same method, again providing data to establish relative efficiencies.
4. Businessmen tendering for the same type of contract will follow the uniform costing rules laid down by the client, e.g. government departments for public contracts.

The advantages of uniform costing

The reasons for adopting uniform costing by groups of similar organizations are as follows.

1. To promote the adoption of good costing methods across a group of businesses, thus improving the standard of management information provided in those businesses.
2. To provide the benefit of cost accounting expertise to companies which might otherwise be too small to afford high-calibre management assistants. Managers in small businesses in a trade association may not appreciate the benefits of good costing information, or be able to organize a system to provide such information. The trade association, however, will consult the appropriate experts and produce a system for all to use.
3. To achieve a measure of comparability between companies so that inefficiencies can be identified and the means suggested to improve performance. Comparison of this type takes place within companies in the

same group, or within companies in a trade association by means of an inter-firm comparison scheme, or through a group of local authorities which also compare performance figures against an established norm. Without uniform costing such a comparison cannot be valid.

4.   To establish a common basis for tendering or the calculation of government grants or subsidies. If an industry wishes to make representations to government to influence policy it is necessary to present reliable, industry-wide information to support the case being made. Uniform costing provides a basis for such information. If the prices charged by an industry are based on a carefully designed costing system, used by all companies in the industry, there will be public confidence that the prices are fair and that the industry is not taking advantage of the consumer.

These advantages are significant but uniform costing does have some disadvantages as well. The uniform system must of necessity be a general one to cover cost accounting in a group of companies, and as such may not fit certain parts of each individual business. All companies are different and it is very difficult therefore to provide a uniform system to which they can all subscribe. A good costing system is tailored to fit the circumstances of an individual company but if a company cannot afford expensive tailoring of this nature it is best to join a uniform costing scheme. A further disadvantage is that once set up it is difficult to change or adjust the system. This means that when improvements to the system are suggested, or ways of avoiding disadvantages, they may take time to implement because all members of the group will need to be convinced and perhaps even an industry-organized committee will need to give them official approval.

Fundamentals of a uniform costing system

The organizers of a uniform system need to agree its basic elements before it can be put into operation. There is no complete set of features or requirements of a uniform costing system since each must be developed to serve the specific situation for which it is intended. Decisions concerning the following must be made.

Costing methods

A decision must be made as to which method of cost accounting is best to apply in the circumstances: full absorption costing to marginal costing; job costing or process costing; standard costing or historical costing; or a variation of these methods. Once the method is ascertained an appropriate cost unit and even cost centres can be defined.

Cost statements

The design of a common cost statement to fit the uniform system is important so that the benefits of design expertise are achieved, and the further benefits of easy comparison are available. If an inter-firm comparison is envisaged, entry of information for computerized comparison is significant when the cost statement is designed.

Accounting period

The parties to the uniform costing scheme should use the same accounting period. They must agree on the frequency with which information is to be provided to managers, e.g. weekly or monthly, and perhaps even go so far as to subscribe to a group calendar so that the costing period starts and ends on the same date for all parties to the scheme.

Cost classification

If costing is to be uniform costs must be classified along the same lines. This requires the establishment of definitions of which costs are considered to be direct or indirect, production overhead or administration; and also how common costs are to be apportioned to various cost headings.

Common methods

If uniform costing is to succeed the parties to the scheme must agree a common basis for the valuation of materials charged to production or stocked (FIFO or LIFO), the payment of wages, the allocation of production overheads, and means whereby administrative and selling expenses can also be applied to jobs if such a cost analysis is seen as significant for the scheme. Agreement concerning depreciation methods, useful economic lives and rates to be applied is essential in a uniform costing scheme. Even with such agreement costs will not be comparable unless assets are recorded according to a uniform system. The group must decide whether to apply historic cost accounting without revaluation of assets from time to time or, if it considers revaluation is important, must decide on the frequency and methods to be used when carrying out a revaluation.

INTER-FIRM COMPARISON

Once uniform costing has taken place, with a common classification of costs and the application of similar costing methods, it is possible to undertake an inter-firm comparison (IFC), whereby the performance of a company or department can be compared with that of other similar entities. It is possible to undertake a one-to-one comparison between departments doing a similar job within one company, but inter-firm comparison usually comprises the comparison of performance of one business against the average performance of a set of similar firms. Uniform costing is used to calculate the costs, ratios or other statistics which are to be used in the comparison. These figures are then sent to a central agency which organizes the inter-firm comparison scheme. The agency may be the head office for a group of companies, a trade association or a firm of accountants which audits a number of small businesses within the same trade.

The organizing agency must select the items to be compared: usually certain key ratios considered significant for the type of company within the scheme. The establishment of uniform cost accounting by firms participating in the scheme will ensure the production of comparable costs or other information. A standard form is designed and completed by all participants to the scheme, and then sent to the scheme organizers. This central agency often calculates the ratios for each company and then finds the average for each performance indicator. A report is returned to the participating firm showing its own ratios and the average for the group. It is possible in some schemes to disclose the upper and lower quartiles as well as an average figure.

Benefits of inter-firm comparison

1.   A comparison of cost ratios against a norm will identify those parts of the firm which are performing at less than average profitability or efficiency. In a quartile scheme it is possible to see whether performance is in the top or bottom 25 per cent of the range.
2.   IFC provides a useful comparator which management can use to judge its own performance against that of a group. The fact that the scheme itself has been designed to give a meaningful comparison will save much time and effort in deciding how to compare a firm with its peers.
3.   The IFC statement will focus managerial attention on weak parts of the business and promote early consideration of remedial action to cut costs and improve profit.
4.   The key ratios in an IFC report form a scoreboard, which discloses the extent of the leeway a firm has to make up when compared with the others in a group.
5.   The fact that the figures are processed by a central authority will ensure that they are treated with confidentiality, that the analysis is impartial and that the figures are likely to be accurate. These three features will improve the response rate from participants who might not be willing to join a scheme unless it was operated by an independent agency. If a company thinks that its own figures will be seen by rivals, it is likely to adjust them in such a way as to improve performance but not necessarily to reveal the truth.
6.   The establishment of performance ratios may provide targets when future operations are planned or the strategy of the business is considered.
7.   IFC data may be helpful to disclose trends. If the performance of a company is usually in, say, the third quartile (i.e. above average but below the top 25 per cent of the range) a sudden change of position will indicate that the firm's performance is not changing in line with that of the group. If, for example, it is evident that performance is falling away within a company, it is helpful to know that all firms in the IFC scheme are suffering from the same change of conditions.
8.   Membership of an IFC scheme provides a stimulus to self-criticism within a business.

Problems of inter-firm comparison schemes

A major problem experienced by IFC schemes is to ensure that a large enough sample of firms joins the scheme to be representative of the group and to ensure that participants are of a similar nature. Clearly a scheme which contains firms ranging from small to large will need to be stratified so that a meaningful comparator is established for firms of similar size within the scheme. Other differences between firms, such as whether they are capital- or labour-intensive, should also be recognized and stratified within the scheme. In a seasonal industry the common accounting period should be such that balance sheets represent the position at the end of the busy period rather than in the middle. Some of the major difficulties experienced by IFC schemes are as follows.

Standardization

Even though a uniform costing system is in use and similar accounting policies are used across the group it will be difficult to standardize terms and to ensure that the content of the various ratios used is the same for all participants. It may be necessary to make adjustments to figures in the cost statements of certain companies, thus reducing the reality of what is being compared and consequently the understanding of what the figures mean. (See 'Structural differences', below.)

Comparison with an average

In an IFC scheme the costs or performance figures of one company are compared with the average for all participants. It is questionable whether average performance is sufficiently demanding as a comparator, and whether such a comparison will encourage participant firms to achieve their potential. This argument is to some extent answered by schemes which include quartile analysis or even decile analysis. The latter would allow a firm to compare its performance with the top 10 per cent of the industry and thus provide a real spur to improve efficiency.

Identification of an industry

Some companies operate in more than one industry so that there may be confusion if an attempt is made to unravel its operations and to produce figures for one segment in order to participate in an IFC scheme. Good cost classification and recording should enable segmental figures to be produced with confidence, but the difficulty of allocating central administration costs incurred jointly for all parts of the business may produce figures which cannot be compared with those of other companies. In a company with several divisions which trade between themselves, one segment of the business may subsidize the operation of another by providing raw materials or components at a favourable transfer price.

Structural differences

In order to operate IFC it is necessary to make adjustments to the costs of certain companies to ensure that they are comparable with the other firms in the scheme. Such adjustments inject a measure of unreality into the figures of the company concerned. How can you compare a company which owns its own head office, purchased fifteen years ago, with another company whose head office was purchased last year, with a third company which leases its head office and pays a rent? Either the first two companies must be charged a notional rent for their premises or the capital employed by the third company must be increased to include a notional value for its rented office space. Differences in plant structure require further adjustments. Is it possible to compare two companies whose plant was purchased at different periods, the old plant being well written down but inefficient and the new plant being recorded at post-inflation current costs? The inclusion of plant leased by a company adds to this problem. However, it can be argued that IFC schemes can point out differences in performance caused by plant structures similar to those detailed above.

Differences of capital structure are a further problem. Company A may use its own funds (share capital plus reserves) while company B relies to a greater extent on borrowed funds (long-term loans) on which an interest cost is payable. Once again, adjustments need to be made to even out this structural difference when a figure for capital employed is calculated and when the cost of interest is set against profit figures.

Differences of accounting policy for such items as development expenditure capitalized or written off must also be the subject of adjustment. With so many adjustments it is true to say that the figures which are eventually compared may be quite different from the figures of the company concerned. The non-comparability of parties to the scheme may not invalidate an IFC, because even though the firms are not all the same size, or do not make their products in the same way, operate in the same geographical area or use plant and machinery of a similar type, they may still be compared. Perhaps the object of the IFC is to reveal the effect that such differences will have on their performance. The question of comparability of participants does not invalidate a scheme so long as the firms are sufficiently comparable for helpful conclusions to be drawn from the figures.

IFC schemes and management

IFC schemes will provide helpful information for managers at all levels in the business. The selection of ratios or other information to be compared will determine the type of comparison to be made, e.g. a comparison of operating performance for general management; or of the costs of production (the cost in pence per unit of production for each cost classification such as wages, power, maintenance, depreciation, adding up to the total cost per unit); or of productivity, analysing labour hours for a series of standard operations undertaken by several firms in the same industry.

A chart of ratios suitable for a general management appraisal is given in Figure

11.1. Note that this appraisal compares the company's own figures with the average and first and third quartiles for all participants in the scheme and also shows performance for the current and previous years.

The ratios selected have a significant interrelationship which, when explained, will alone give an insight into the operations of firm 319. Ratio 1 is the primary ratio, which expresses the return on capital employed (ROCE) and the ability of the business to pay a dividend and attract fresh capital. Return on capital is influenced by two factors:

(a)   the profitability of sales – ratio 2;

INTER-FIRM COMPARISON OF OPERATING RATIOS			FIRM 319			
RATIO		First quartile Average Third quartile	All firms		Firm 319	
			This year	Last year	This year	Last year
1. $\dfrac{\text{Post-tax profit}}{\text{Operating assets}}$	%	Q 1 Average Q 3				
2. $\dfrac{\text{Post-tax profit}}{\text{Turnover}}$	%	Q 1 Average Q 3				
3. $\dfrac{\text{Turnover}}{\text{Operating assets}}$	Times	Q 1 Average Q 3				
4. $\dfrac{\text{Production cost}}{\text{Turnover}}$	%	Q 1 Average Q 3				
5. $\dfrac{\text{Distribution cost}}{\text{Turnover}}$	%	Q 1 Average Q 3				
6. $\dfrac{\text{Administration cost}}{\text{Turnover}}$	%	Q 1 Average Q 3				
7. $\dfrac{\text{Fixed assets}}{\text{Total assets}}$	%	Q 1 Average Q 3				
8. $\dfrac{\text{Cost of sales}}{\text{Average stock}}$	Times	Q 1 Average Q 3				
9. $\dfrac{\text{Average debtors}}{\text{Turnover}}$	Days	Q 1 Average Q 3				

Figure 11.1   IFC chart of ratios

(b) the activity of the business expressed as the number of times the operating assets are turned over during the year – ratio 3.

An active firm with a high profit ratio will have a good return on capital employed.

Ratio 2 multipled by ratio 3 equals ratio 1. For example, operating assets of £500,000 and post-tax profit of £50,000 gives a ROCE of 10 per cent; if turnover is £1 million, ratio 2 is 5 per cent and ratio 3 is 2 times – $2 \times 5\% = 10\%$.

Further analysis of the two important factors mentioned above will disclose the significance of the various cost classifications as a proportion of sales during the period – ratios 4, 5 and 6. For example, production cost £600,000, distribution cost £100,000 and administration cost £300,000 (on the same turnover of £1 million) give: ratio 4, 60 per cent; ratio 5, 10 per cent; and ratio 6, 30 per cent. The effective use of operating assets (ratio 2) can be further investigated by ratios 7, 8 and 9. Ratio 7 explores the proportion of total assets which are held as fixed assets and thereby comments on the asset structure of a firm – is it capital-intensive? Fixed assets of £400,000 and working capital of £100,000 give 80 per cent – yes. Ratio 8 investigates the stock turnover of the company and finds whether it is as efficient as the average for the group in managing this important current asset. Opening stock £60,000, closing stock £140,000 equals average stock of £100,000. Cost of sales of £600,000 ÷ 100,000 gives stock turnover of six times per year, which is once every two months.

Ratio 9 investigates debtor turnover by showing the average period of credit allowed by the business to its debtors. Opening debtors £200,000, closing debtors £300,000 equals average debtors £250,000. Applying ratio 9:

$$\frac{\text{Average debtors}}{\text{Turnover}} \text{ i.e. } \frac{£250,000}{£1,000,000} \times \frac{365}{1} = 91 \text{ days}$$

On average, debtors take three months to pay.

EXERCISES

11A The Manchester Manufacturing Company operates a power house as a separate service department to meet the requirements of all production departments in its factory, for heat, light and power.

The costs of the power house are recorded and totalled each month, and then apportioned to the production departments on the basis of a preset ratio calculated at the beginning of the year, to reflect anticipated average power consumption in each department. Budgeted power costs are also apportioned to production departments using this ratio, but the ratio is itself reviewed each year.

Required

(a) Explain the reason for charging service department costs to production departments.

(b) Criticize the existing method for charging actual monthly power costs to production departments at the Manchester Manufacturing Company.

(c) Discuss the usefulness of an alternative system of charging production departments for actual power consumption using a budgeted cost calculated as follows:

(i) budgeted fixed costs of the power house apportioned to production departments according to anticipated usage during the year – a monthly amount;

(ii) a variable charge for each unit of power consumed by a user department based on the budgeted variable costs of operating the power house at normal efficiency.

11B A small private company in a town with 190,000 inhabitants has decided to take advantage of the deregulation of passenger transport services. It is proposing to operate a bus service on six particular routes where, after carrying out market research, it has been identified that there are opportunities to compete with existing services. Currently, the company has five 3-ton trucks which are engaged in light road haulage for regular established customers and has two mini-vans which are used as a courier service for fast delivery of letters and lightweight parcels.

The company has its own garage facilities for the repair and maintenance of its vehicles. The offices are located on the first floor above the garage and an upper floor, currently used for the storage of old records, is being cleared for conversion into office accommodation. At the rear of the garage and offices is a fenced compound where the vehicles are kept overnight. The compound is locked and floodlit during the hours of darkness and a security firm patrols regularly.

A suitably qualified person has been recruited to manage the bus operation and you have been engaged as the accountant for the expanding business. The owner of the company, a former transport manager, looks after selling and control of routing and utilization of the five trucks and two min-vans. His wife and a full-time bookkeeper undertake all the administrative work. Seven drivers and two garage mechanics are employed.

Cost accounting records kept have been of a rudimentary nature but the financial accounts, prepared at the end of every quarter by the company's auditors, show the business to be very profitable. The owner is conscious that with the expansion, better records will have to be maintained. From the accounts and in conjunction with the auditors, you ascertain that costs for the following expense headings are available:

Depreciation
Drivers' wages
Employers' national insurance contributions
Fuel
Holiday pay
Insurance
Management and staff salaries
Mechanics' wages
Oil
Rent and rates for garage, office and compound

Replacement parts and spares
Road fund licences
Security costs
Tyre replacements

The newly engaged passenger transport manager informs you that six minibuses at a total cost of £210,000 are on order. Each bus can seat twenty people and nine people are allowed to stand. The buses will each be operated by one person and the manager is currently interviewing drivers who hold PSV (public service vehicle) driving licences. He indicates that he will need information from you to ascertain the profitability of each route operated.

You are required,
Bearing in mind the objectives of cost accounting:

(a) draft a form for the ascertainment of operating costs for the vehicles currently owned;
(b) draft a form suitable for the proposed passenger service to show income and expenditure;
(c) comment on the allocation *and* apportionment of overheads now that they have been increased substantially following the recruitment of yourself and the passenger transport manager.

(Chartered Institute of Management Accountants)

PART IV

BUDGETARY PLANNING AND CONTROL

12 Budgetary Procedures

THE BUDGET

Business operations are usually planned in advance, on an annual basis. The plan, or budget, is often subdivided to cover a shorter time period, e.g. a calendar month or a four-weekly costing period. The budget details the intended operations of all parts of the business, so that each activity undertaken is carefully fitted into the overall plan, and expressed for a more manageable monthly period. The Chartered Institute of Management Accountants includes in its terminology one definition of a budget as a 'plan quantified in monetary terms, prepared and approved prior to a defined period of time, showing the planned income to be generated and/or expenditure to be incurred during that period, and the capital to be employed to attain a given objective'.

Another definition is that a budget is a 'financial and/or quantitative statement, prepared and approved prior to a period, of the policy to be pursued during that period'. This second definition introduces the term 'quantitative', since the budget for a department or a sector of the business may not be in financial terms, but can be expressed as units to be produced, standard hours of work to be accomplished or machine hours to be worked.

A budget should be expressed in terms which its recipients can best understand. Accordingly, while the master plan or main budget is in financial terms, some of the sub-budgets will show in detail how departments of the business are to help one another to reach goals set by the main budget, and may well be expressed in terms of units, hours or some other measurement which is most helpful to the manager concerned.

BUDGET PREPARATION - A TEAM EFFORT

The budget is prepared in advance of the period but preparation is only part of the activity. The budget must be approved before it is finalized, both by the top management of the business so that is accords with their goals, and by the lower echelons of management on whose efforts the successful attainment of the budgetary objectives will depend. If a budget is to be effective as a plan it must gain the approval of the executives who are to carry it into practice because their acceptance of the plan as being reasonable or feasible is vital for the successful operation of the plan. Unrealistic targets set in a budget will have an adverse effect on the morale of employees, and they may not strive to achieve budgeted goals. The budget is a plan produced by the members of the management team working together which expresses their intentions for the operations of the business during the forthcoming period. This plan is not just an estimate, nor is the profit expressed in the plan just a surplus which emerges at the end of the period. In business, profit is planned just like everything else. Each department or cost centre has its own budget which is built into a master budget or overall plan for the business as a whole in such a way that co-ordination between departments is achieved.

THE BUDGET AS A CO-ORDINATING DECISION

The annual budget forms part of the strategic or corporate plan of a business which charts the long-term course the directors intend to follow. Each department is budgeted within the overall framework so that managers are able to make decisions which will optimize the use of resources. Costs and revenues are planned as an operating budget, and the effect of operations on finance can then be forecast. A cash budget links the operations of a business with capital expenditure, and the planned need for external finance. Drafting the budget is a decision-making process since it requires an analysis of alternative courses of action available to the business and the selection of the most advantageous set of options.

Budgeting is a co-ordinating process since all the disparate departments and cost centres which make up the business are fitted into one plan. It is also an iterative process, since by a series of small steps comprising a process of continual review and revision, the original estimates become firm plans. The various departments or functions within a business are interdependent: a decision concerning sales will affect production and finance, and production decisions within the factory will cause alterations to the purchase of materials, the use of labour, and the amount of machine time or maintenance required. The various parts of a business are not independent but should be co-ordinated together to ensure an optimum combination of resources used in the business, and a steady progress towards the strategic goals expressed by the board. Each part of the business works towards a target which is planned to lead to the best possible result for the business as a whole. The target which seems best for a single segment of the business may not be the most favourable goal for the whole business. Thus a budget prevents sub-optimization, and what might be best for parts of the business is subordinated to the needs of the business as a whole. Thus the budget needs to state the objectives of the business, and to plan the means of attaining those objectives.

The preparation of a budget forces managers to analyse the activities of individual sectors of the business with a critical eye, and to anticipate problems or appreciate opportunities which may arise in the future. Such forethought not only clears away obstacles to the progress of the business but also motivates the managers to find a way round difficulties which may interfere with what they plan to do.

THE OBJECTIVES OF A BUDGETARY SYSTEM

Control

The existence of budgetary figures provides a very useful comparator against which actual performance may be measured, in order to gain control of business activity. Comparing actual performance against budgeted figures which express the planned intensions of management will show up those parts of the organization which are not performing according to plan. If such a comparison takes place on a monthly basis, deviations from planned performance can be recognized quickly and notified to the managers concerned, so that remedial action can be organized at an early stage. The management accountant acts as 'controller' because his or her knowledge of the costing records, and of the budget, enable him or her to make the comparison. Variances from planned costs are disclosed in a management accounting statement which highlights the exceptions to planned performance. When these exceptions are identified managers are able to concentrate their limited resources on those parts of the business which are not performing to plan. The name given to this system of control is 'management by exception'. The very fact that the budget is expressed in terms of the span of control or responsibility of individual managers facilitates the provision of a variance statement expressed in terms of those costs which an individual manager can control. Once having accepted a budget, a manager is responsible for running his or her department within the terms of that budget, and will be responsible if actual performance varies from the plan; this system is called 'responsibility accounting'.

Co-ordination

After planning and control, a further objective of budgeting is co-ordination. When the budget for various parts of the business is drafted, by means of constant review and revision, each part can be made to fit together into one whole unit. The business is one organization so it should not be considered unusual that, when planning its activity, the parts of the business should be co-ordinated. It would be foolish to draw up a production plan which failed to consider the quantities planned to be sold and the projected stock levels for finished goods, and equally foolish to compile a sales budget without reference to the quantity the company's production facilities can manufacture and to the costs of those goods. The business is a single entity, and the operation of all its parts – selling, manufacturing, transporting, storing, finance and personnel – must be keyed in to the master plan, if bottlenecks and over-production etc. are to be avoided. This co-ordination must take place not only in terms of quantities but in terms of time: it is also foolish to co-ordinate production and sales for a year if the sales are to be made in the early months, before production is completed.

Communication

Another objective of budgeting is that it should act as a communicator. Once the budget has been agreed by managers at all levels, and they have taken responsibility for its successful conclusion, the monthly portions of the overall plan act as an executive instruction, telling each manager what he or she should do in that particular month to enable the department or cost centre to play its part in the overall scheme. The budget is analysed to show in detail the costs to be incurred and activity undertaken by even the smallest department of the business, so managers at all levels are instructed what to do, and given a monthly reminder of the part they are to play.

Motivation

A final objective of budgeting is to motivate the managers in the business, and encourage them to strive for its success. Human behaviour is a significant factor in budgetary control since the managers' attitude may determine the success of the planned operations. The mere existence of the budget does not motivate managers, but if they see that it is reasonable, and that their own ideas have influenced its formulation, they will be more ready to accept budgeted standards. The authoritarian system of presenting managers with a budget which they are expected to perform is now out of date; a manager will follow a plan with enthusiasm only if he or she has first accepted it.

Goal congruence and teamwork are important if petty squabbles over the setting of budget levels are to be avoided. Some executives in a business may not be motivated by aims which lead to the maximization of profits. Sales managers may well consider that an increase in market share or the growth of turnover is of the greatest importance for the well-being of the business. Production managers may seek to standardize the product to smooth out problems of production and to reduce the number of components needed, but they will not recognize the significance of the sales manager's requirement for a wide range of products. Financial managers will be interested in credit control rather than sales at any price. They may argue with production managers who plan capital expenditure to increase the machinery in the factory, since the accountant will seek to prove the financial viability of such a scheme before borrowing the funds concerned. Groups with such diverse aims and conflicting goals must be brought together and urged to co-operate, in an atmosphere where suspicion and frustration are removed. If all managers have a part to play in the construction of the budget, they will learn to wòrk together as a team and build their own aspirations into the overall business plan. The aims and conflicting goals of individuals are considered by the budget committee which by iteration, a constant review and revision of the plan, will gradually draft a compromise plan which is acceptable to all.

SETTING THE BUDGET

The principal budget factor

This is the item which limits the activities of a business, and therefore it becomes the figure from which all others in a budget are derived. In some businesses sales is the principal budgeting factor and sales volume will therefore influence the amount to be produced within the production budget, and through that budget the amounts of materials, labour and overheads costs which are to be incurred. The board will lay down its policy for the business, perhaps by calculating the amount to be sold and made if sufficient profit is to be earned to service the capital employed and compensate the investors providing that capital for their risk. Alternatively, the managers of the business will forecast what they consider to be the possible level of future operations, reflecting the capabilities of the business in the forthcoming period. Board policy and the forecasts derived from the 'grass roots' of the business may not coincide. Differences between policy and forecast are considered by the budget committee whose job it is to produce the completed and agreed budget. This committee is usually chaired by the managing director and it comprises the executive heads of the main parts of the business, e.g. sales director, production director and the budget officer (the management accountant, who is very active in the work of the committee). Line managers must be seen to have a participating role in the production of the budget. The budget officer, acting as a communicator, is one way in which the deliberations of the budget committee can be explained to the line executives who must perform the completed budget. The budget officer also acts as a channel for the line managers' views to be introduced into the discussions of the budget committee.

Defining responsibility

If costs are to be controlled effectively, the responsibilities of individual managers must be clearly defined. Thus managers will accept responsibility for certain costs, but some costs can be influenced by several managers while other costs which affect a department may be outside the control of the departmental manager, e.g. power provided to a workshop by a central power house operated by another manager. It is important not to try to make managers answerable for costs which are outside their control, or which can be influenced by other managers. Frequent and accurate reports covering costs controllable by an individual manager, which are easily assimilated and which highlight the problems and deviations from budget in a constructive manner, form an important part of the budgetary control system.

THE BUDGET COMMITTEE

As has been shown, the task of this committee is to draft the final accepted budget, which acts as an executive instruction to all managers by setting out in detail the activity of their departments month by month. Another function of the budget committee is to reconcile the differences which occur between board policy and the forecasts of line managers, and between the budgets of the various departments. This reconciliation takes place by a constant adjustment as part of the planning process, whereby board decisions can change the situation (capital expenditure to increase machine time) and the forecasts of the executives need constant revision to take account of these changes.

Co-ordination

The overall budget covers the activities of all parts of the business, and the budget for each interconnecting department should be compiled in such a way that it is integrated into the plan for the whole organization, e.g. sales and production should be geared to the same level to avoid over-production, and the budgets for labour, materials and machine utilization must be finalized with the same production volume in view.

The consideration of alternatives

The budget committee will review the policy of the business in the light of alternative courses of action which present themselves to the business. They will seek to optimize performance and maximize the return on capital employed, by building into the plan the most profitable projects to utilize scarce resources in the best possible way.

Limiting factors

Any factor which limits the activity of a business or in some way impedes expansion is known as a 'key factor' or 'limiting factor', because it reduces the potential of the business so far as sales, production and profit are concerned. The budget committee identifies limiting factors and plans action to reduce their influence on the budget. For example, if insufficient plant capacity causes production to lag behind sales, a decision by the board to increase capital expenditure will remove this limiting factor. Key factors are dealt with by the budget committee in their order of importance, so that items which restrain the progress of the business most are removed first. Once a board decision has been taken the circumstances under which the original forecasts were made are changed, so those forecasts are returned to the executives concerned with a request for a budget revision to reflect the new conditions. Thus, gradually each limiting factor is removed so that, by a system of iteration, the potential of the business is maximized.

Limiting factors may be classified as follows.

1. Sales may be disappointing because of a lack of demand for the product, poor or insufficient advertising, or the fact that the salesforce itself is ineffectual.
2. Labour can limit the potential of the business if a special skill is in short supply, or through a lack of training facilities within the company, or due to poor labour relations.
3. Materials act as a limiting factor if a scarce raw material cannot be purchased in sufficient quantities, or if company policy concerning the size of stocks limits the size of orders which can be placed and reduces the availability of raw materials; the action of a component supplier who cannot be trusted to deliver parts on time may also limit the potential of the business.
4. Plant and machinery acts as a limiting factor if insufficient productive capacity is available. There may not be enough machine hours to produce the goods the salesforce has budgeted to sell. Plant may further limit the potential of a business if it is too inflexible to produce alternative products, or if it is so old that constant breakdowns lead to disruption of production. Insufficient space or a poor layout of machinery within the factory is also a limiting factor.
5. Management is also a limiting factor if incompetence or a lack of guidance caused by communication problems within the firm results in the inefficiency and losses caused by mistake and poor organization.
6. Capital itself may be a limiting factor. If the business has insufficient funds to finance fixed assets, stocks or debtors, its potential to expand will certainly be reduced.

Board decisions to increase the advertising budget, to authorize shift working or overtime, to change the design of a product to limit the use of a scarce material, or merely to make more capital available within the business, will all in their own way reduce the effect of limiting factors.

Responsibility

Once the budgets for various parts of the business are co-ordinated, the final master budget is produced. Since managers have participated in its production, they are then expected to accept responsibility for its execution. In this way the board can delegate responsibility to a manager, and yet maintain control of the operation through the budget.

Flexibility

Most businesses will benefit from the production of a flexible budget, which provides a plan for the various levels of operation which the business may achieve. A fixed budget may prove misleading in the short term, since it is unrealistic to compare the budgeted cost of one quantity produced with the actual cost for a different volume of production. A fixed budget for a production volume of, say, 200,000 units must be 'flexed' to produce the expected figures for a production of 220,000 units if a realistic comparison with the actual cost of producing 220,000 units is to be made.

THE BUDGETARY CONTROL FRAMEWORK

Each functional or departmental budget is compiled from a number of sub-budgets, e.g. the sales budget is the aggregate of the budgets for the various sales areas, which in turn are made up from the sales expectations of each sales executive in the area. Once budgets have been established for sales revenue, selling expenses, production costs, administration expenses etc., they can be expressed in the master budget, which is the projected profit and loss account for the period covered by the budget. Other aspects of the business are also budgeted, e.g. stocks, debtors, capital expenditure and cash, so that these capital budgets can be combined with the budgeted profit and loss account into a budgeted balance sheet which expresses the position which the company intends to achieve at the end of the period.

These interrelationships, and other topics discussed in this chapter, are shown diagrammatically in Figure 12.1.

THE BUDGET CONTROLLER

The cost accountant who uses the budget figures as comparators with actual costs will be the budget controller. A variance statement can be produced which compares actual performance with the budget and highlights those exceptional points at which the budget has not been achieved. Management by exception focuses the attention of management on those parts of the business which are under-performing the budget, and points to the need for remedial or control action. Action must be taken quickly, and reported to the controller. Some variances are uncontrollable, in so far as they cannot be influenced by the action of any single manager. Such variances are reported to the board, since a top-level decision may be required to eradicate them.

In some companies the controller is responsible for the administration of the budget. It is the controller's task to encourage and assist departmental managers when they make their forecasts, to collect those forecasts and to build them into a co-ordinated budget. The budget officer or controller reviews the estimates of managers, consolidates them into more important budgets, and consults with them when revisions are necessary. He or she forms a link between middle management and the board when the budget is drafted. Much responsibility rests upon the budget officer in this type of system, since he or she must ensure that the plan is feasible, that it will be wholeheartedly accepted by managers and that it falls within the parameters of board policy. The controller is responsible for

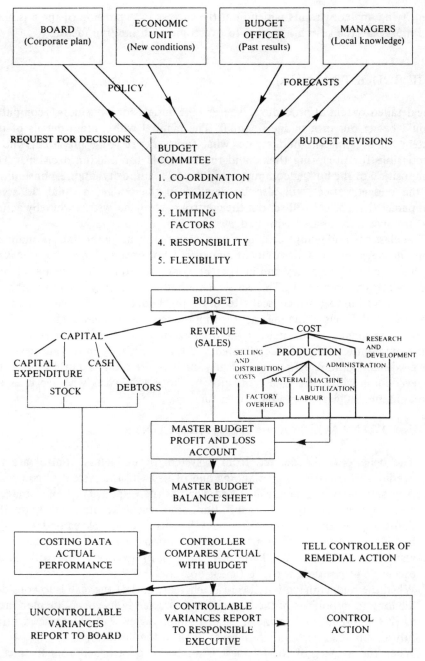

Notes
1. The budget officer may undertake the function of the economic unit in some organizations.
2. The budget officer may fulfil the role of the budget committee in an alternative system.

Figure 12.1   Budgetary control system

identifying any constraints which limit the success or expansion of the business, and must lead the search for ways to overcome such limiting factors.

THE BUDGET MANUAL

The detailed system of procedures whereby the budget for a business is computed should be set out in a budget manual. The manual will contain details of the system for drafting the budget, i.e. what forecasts are to be prepared, who is responsible for preparing them, and the timetable for making decisions. The composition of the budget committee and the role, authority, and responsibilities of the budget officer will also be detailed in the budget manual. In some companies the manual will set out the control part of the system whereby actual performance is compared with budget.

The classical budgeting technique was operated in an authoritarian manner, from the viewpoint of a hierarchy of managers who conceived their major task to be that of pressuring a lazy and inefficient workforce to produce greater efforts and achieve a desired result. This classical method is giving way to a more modern budgeting technique, which seeks to draft the budget from a partnership or coalition of all levels of management within the business. Such a budget will help to motivate managers throughout the organization. An 'ideal' budget assumes that maximum capacity can be attained and that everybody in the business will work with maximum efficiency. Clearly such a situation is not likely to be achieved, nor will it act as a motivator to those employees who see it as an unreasonable budget, not to be striven for.

THE ADVANTAGES OF BUDGETARY CONTROL

1. The benefits to be derived from a system of budgetary control are the products of the system of planning and of its twin, the system of control.
2. Any activity which emphasizes and clarifies the responsibility of managers must be beneficial to the organization, since each executive will know the limits of his or her authority, and harmful squabbles caused through boundary disputes within the organization will be minimized. If responsibilities are clearly laid down, no area of activity will be without an executive responsible for its efficient operation.
3. When the budgeting activity begins each year, part of the task is to consider the long-term policies of the business as expressed in its corporate plan, and to fit the annual budget into that plan. This review will of course identify future opportunities and alternatives open to the business.
4. When the activity of the business is analysed to each department or cost centre, the contribution made by departments or products to the overall profit of the firm will be revealed. Thus management can assess the strengths and weaknesses of the firm, perhaps in terms of return on capital employed for separate segments of the business. The relative importance of the various activities undertaken by the business are revealed.

5. When performance is compared to budget, the efficiency of managers may be judged, and of course the control element of the system will help to show up losses and waste at an early stage and initiate remedial action before too much damage has been done.

6. The budget will act as a communicator of each manager's task, and an executive instruction authorizing each manager to fulfil his or her part of the plan. The existence of a budget in monthly portions acts as a constant reminder to managers of their task, and the fact that variance statements will in due course be produced will help to create a cost-conscious organization.

7. Co-ordination in terms of quantities produced, stored and sold, and quantities of raw materials purchased for production, will ensure a steady flow of production and the most economic use of the resources concerned. Co-ordination is significant for the timing of the various elements in the chain of production and sales, so that bottlenecks are avoided and stock-outs kept to a minimum.

8. Once managers have accepted their departmental budget, they can be safely left to organize its performance. Thus delegation is achieved without any relaxation of control since each manager will be organizing the achievement of major business goals.

BUDGETARY CONTROL: PRACTICAL DIFFICULTIES IN ITS OPERATION

Managerial attitudes

The success of budgetary control within any organization will depend upon the attitude of the managers who must make the system work. If managers do not understand the purpose and objective of budgetary control, its usefulness will be reduced. A lack of understanding may turn to suspicion, which may develop into antagonism either between executives or against the budgetary control system. Co-operation between executives is vital in business, but if managers fail to recognize their role within budgetary control many of the advantages of the system may not be fully realized. A budget should act as an aid to, but it is not a substitute for, management; it is not enough to budget an organization and then to expect that organization to operate efficiently.

Levels of attainment

Setting the levels of attainment to be achieved in various parts of the business is always difficult. If targets are too easy to achieve there will be no incentive; if targets are perceived to be beyond the reach of managers their morale will suffer as they see the budget as an unrealistic measure of their performance. Once the budget is set, and accepted by a manager, superiors should refrain from interfering with the manager's activities. Delegation implies a certain freedom of action so long as the ultimate purpose is achieved. Financial limits which are too restrictive will inhibit management but, conversely, the recipient of a well-padded budget which has plenty of spare capacity may feel impelled to spend all the disposable finance, whether or not needed, for fear that a surplus at the end of the period will lead to the next budget being reduced. The attitude of the accountant is vital to the success of budgetary control; if he or she is seen as a budget cutter, rather than one who helps executives to draft their budgets within the overall plan, suspicion will replace co-operation. Those executives who will be responsible for the successful operation of the budget must be given an appropriate opportunity to make a significant input at the drafting stage, and the management accountant must help them to make their forecasts and revisions.

Timeliness

If the monthly cost accounts which act as a comparator for budgetary performance are not made available soon after the end of each month or budgeting period, the impact of the variances disclosed will be reduced and the opportunities for organizing remedial action may be lost. The fact that the budgets in a business are interrelated, just as the departments are, must be fully understood by all concerned so that the actions of one manager which affect the performance of another must be clearly understood when the efficiency of managers is measured. This interrelationship is shown in Figure 12.1.

THE ROLLING BUDGET

In some businesses it is not feasible to plan for up to a year ahead, perhaps because of seasonality within the trade, or because of changes in taste and fluctuations in demand which can upset long-term plans; e.g. demand in the fashion trade. Selecting an appropriate time horizon for the budget is therefore important. It seems wasteful to attempt to plan operations beyond the limits when reasonable expectations can be forecast. It is equally unfortunate to select budget periods according to the wrong criteria. Suppose, for example, an organization experiences seasonal peaks and troughs in the demand for its services; it would seem only right to link the peak periods together and budget them separately from the slack periods, because the pressures on the organization are very different for the periods of relative activity and inactivity. Departments which are seen by management as long-term activities, e.g. research and development, may need to be planned more than a year ahead.

In an inflationary period a budget for twelve months, compiled before the beginning of the year, will not reflect realistic costs and prices towards the end of the year. A rolling, or continuous, budget provides a more realistic yardstick against which actual figures can be compared. If a twelve-month budget is prepared from, say, January to December, the plan can unfold normally for the first few months. As the year rolls by, a second budget is prepared for the period from July until June in the following year. This second budget will update the last six months of the existing budget and plan ahead for a further six months. The frequency with which the budget is rolled over depends on the planning horizon of the business and the pace of inflation. A flexible approach to adapt to current conditions and speed in the computation of the budget are essential if this tactic is to succeed.

Those weaknesses of orthodox budgets which the rolling budget is intended to remedy are as follows:

1. In conditions of high inflation, detailed forecasting will be inaccurate beyond, say, six months ahead. Costs will change as prices rise and selling prices will have to be adjusted accordingly. An orthodox budget fixed for a year may restrict the flexibility of managers in reacting to inflationary conditions.

2. Business is a continuous activity, not just a series of annual steps. An annual budget prepared from January to December will give the manager operating in September only a further three months of planned activity. A rolling budget will extend this horizon, since in September the manager will have a budget from July to the following June.

3. Budgeting is normally undertaken at one part of the year, e.g. during the autumn for a January start to the plan. If drafting the budget is seen merely as a clerical exercise, the opportunity to challenge the basis on which it is drafted may be missed. A rolling review, whch takes place more often, may therefore be seen as a more realistic plan rather than an annual chore.

4. Under orthodox annual budgeting there is a sudden transformation when the old budget period ends and a new one begins; new standards are introduced and perhaps stocks are written up to reflect the new costs written into the budget. Under such a scheme, orders taken in November on the old basis may show losses when November prices are set against January costs. A more frequent update to the budget may remove this difficulty.

5. A traditional twelve-month budget, prepared two months or so before the period begins, will include assumptions as to business conditions, which extend for fourteen months into the future. Such figures may be useless as comparators with the real situation nine or ten months later.

6. Managers will realize the degree of uncertainty contained in a budget which plans up to a year ahead, and this will affect their respect for it and the accuracy with which they prepare their forecasts which form part of that budget. It is human nature to build in some flexibility, and to pad out a budget rather than provide figures which may give the impression of inefficiency when compared with post-inflation actuals. The more frequent review technique associated with a rolling budget may solve this problem.

EXERCISES

12A You have been appointed as management accountant to a medium-sized manufacturing company. The managing director, an engineer by training, is considering extending the rudimentary system of budgetary control at present operated by the company.

Required

Draft a memorandum to the managing director which explains the objectives and advantages of budgetary control.

12B   **You are required to**

(a)   Compare the operation of fixed budgets (or cash limits) within public sector organizations or local government authorities with the budgeting procedures normally used in commercial organizations, listing *three* advantages and *three* disadvantages from the public sector or local government point of view.

(b)   Explain the use of a budget manual and give an indication of the likely contents. Your explanation must be related to *one* of the following:

(i)   a private sector organization;

(ii)   a public sector organization;

(iii)   a local government authority.

(Chartered Institute of Management Accountants)

13 Budgetary Techniques

The management accountant acting as a budget officer is directly involved in the techniques of compiling the budget. This chapter concentrates on the practical methods used to draft an overall budget for an organization, to fit a cash budget into the system and to flex an otherwise fixed budget.

To ensure that the budget is attainable, it will be necessary to build in an allowance for normal idle time such as set-up time, relaxation time or other allowances for time spent when no production is undertaken. This allowance can be budgeted as a percentage of direct labour or machine time, or it can be included as part of the standard time per unit used in the budget calculation. A productivity ratio (or efficiency ratio) can be applied to translate standard times to expected attainable budgeted hours needed to complete the budgeted volume of work. If a certain volume of work has a standard time of 20,000 hours, this is how long an efficient labour force working at a reasonable speed should take to complete the work. If the labour force is 90 per cent efficient they will be expected to complete the work in $10/9 \times 20,000$ hours = 22,222 hours, that is:

$$\frac{\text{Standard hours}}{\text{Expected hours}} = \frac{20,000}{22,222} \times \frac{100}{1} = 90\%.$$

COMPILING A BUDGET: A COMPREHENSIVE EXAMPLE

Big Togs plc specializes in the manufacture of fashionable clothes for large-sized individuals. The two main products, jackets and trousers, are made up in the factory and sold to retailers. The business prepares a budget for each year on the basis of a full absorption costing system.

The balance sheet of Big Togs plc as at 31 December this year is shown in Table 13.1.

	£	£
Capital		
1,400,000 ordinary shares of £1 each		1,400,000
General reserve		1,359,361
		2,759,361
Current liabilities		
Trade creditors	431,851	
Corporation tax	128,200	560,051
Total capital employed		3,319,412
Represented by:		
Fixed assets		
Land and buildings		1,850,000
Plant and machinery	1,300,000	
Less depreciation to date	920,000	380,000
		2,230,000
Current assets		
Stock materials		
Cloth	180,000	
Lining	135,000	
Finished goods	223,500	
Debtors	445,628	
Cash	105,284	1,089,412
		3,319,412

Table 13.1   Big Tops plc: balance sheet at 31 December

The management of the business are preparing to produce a budget for the year to 31 December *next*. As management accountant you are to help them to co-ordinate their departmental plans. Their forecasts must be realistic in terms of the conditions likely to prevail in the forthcoming year.

Cost estimates

Materials are purchased from a trusted supplier: cloth in standard widths at an expected price of £4.90 per metre and lining fabric at £2.80 per metre, a considerable reduction on prices paid this year. The designer plans to use three metres of cloth and two metres of lining for each jacket, with trousers taking two metres of cloth and one metre of lining.

Direct labour is paid at a rate of £4.10 per hour, whether they are cutters, stitchers or finishers. It is estimated that four hours of direct labour time will be needed to make a jacket, and three hours to make trousers. Production overheads are absorbed on the basis of direct labour hours.

Projected stock changes

The opening stock of cloth is 36,000 metres, lining material 26,000 metres, and it is intended to halve these amounts during the year. The opening stock of finished goods contains 2,000 jackets and 6,000 pairs of trousers. The company intends to build up its stocks of jackets up to 4,000 at the end of the year, but will maintain trouser stocks at current levels. The FIFO system of stock valuation is used by the company, which means that the expensive lining fabric in stock at the beginning of the year is assumed to be used up during the year. Work-in-progress stocks are negligible and should be ignored.

Planning sales

The managing director plans to fix prices for the year at £70 for jackets and £50 for trousers. He estimates that at these prices 76,000 jackets and 58,000 pairs of trousers will be sold. All sales are on credit terms to retailers.

Overheads

Production overheads are expected as follows:

	£
General expenses	148,000
Indirect labour	242,500
Power	73,750
Maintenance	40,000
Depreciation	66,000
Insurance	5,250
Supervision	56,300
	631,800

Indirect labour is considered to be a fixed cost, but general expenses are reckoned to be 50 per cent variable, while power and maintenance have a 40 per cent fixed cost element.

The selling and administration overhead expenses are expected to be as follows:

	£
Advertising	125,000
Commissions	39,500
Salaries of sales executives	196,500
Travelling expenses	167,500
Wages and salaries of general office	221,600
Electricity	14,700
Stationery	23,500
Post and telephone	33,000
General expenses	14,300
	835,600

The principal budget factor

The factor from which all other figures are derived is the sales figure, which sets the level of activity for the business. The quantities which it is planned to sell, when adjusted for the stockholding policy, will set the production budget. Once production quantities are determined, plans can be made for materials to be used and purchased, labour hours required and overheads to be absorbed. The management accountant can draft a production budget, and its subsidiary budgets for materials, labour, overheads and stocks. The budgets for selling and administration expenses can also be computed.

Big Togs plc: Sales budget year to 31 December 19—

Product	Units	Selling price £	Total sales £
Jackets	76,000	70	5,320,000
Trousers	58,000	50	2,900,000
			8,220,000

Normally the sales budget would be compiled from the expected sales of individual area representatives, so that a clear picture of who will sell the goods, and where and when they will be sold, is available as a basis on which to rest the sales forecast. Such a basis will increase the reliance which can be placed on the sales figures.

Budgets for production, materials and labour

Big Togs plc: Production budget year to 31 December 19—

	Jackets	Trousers
Planned sales per budget	76,000	58,000
Planned finished goods stocks at year-end	4,000	6,000
Total requirements	80,000	64,000
Less opening stock of finished goods	2,000	6,000
Units to be produced	78,000	58,000

Note that this budget is in terms of units not costs.

Big Togs plc: Direct material purchases budget year to 31 December 19—

	Cloth (metres)	Lining (metres)
Planned closing stock	18,000	13,000
Required for production	350,000	214,000
Total required	368,000	227,000
Less opening stock	36,000	26,000
Units to be purchased	332,000	201,000
Unit price	£4.90	£2.80
Purchase cost	£1,626,800	£562,800
Total purchase cost: £2,189,600		

Workings

	Cloth (metres)		Lining (metres)	
Quantities required per production budget				
Jackets: 78,000 units	(× 3)	234,000	(× 2)	156,000
Trousers: 58,000 units	(× 2)	116,000	(× 1)	58,000
Total usage		350,000		214,000
Less opening stock		36,000		26,000
To be purchased and used		314,000		188,000

	£	£
To be purchased and used		
Cloth: 314,000 × £4.90	1,538,600	
Lining: 188,000 × £2.80		526,400
Add opening stock	180,000	135,000
Total	1,718,600	661,400
Total cost of materials used in production		2,380,000

Note: under FIFO the opening stock is assumed to be used in production during the year.

The stock turnover ratio can be computed at this stage as a guide to the stockholding policy. The ratios for cloth stocks at the beginning and end of the year are, respectively:

$$\frac{36,000}{350,000} \times \frac{52}{1} = 5.4 \text{ weeks}$$

$$\frac{18,000}{350,000} \times \frac{52}{1} = 2.7 \text{ weeks}$$

Stocks sufficient to support 5.4 weeks' production are held at the beginning of the year, and this amount is to be reduced to 2.7 weeks. It is safe to reduce stocks in this way only if confidence can be placed in the supplier to work with a small lead time. Now work out the stock turnover ratio for lining material. The answer should be 6.3 weeks, reducing to 3.15 weeks.

Big Togs plc: Direct labour budget year to 31 December 19—

Product	Units	Direct labour hours per unit	Total hours	Cost at £4.10 per hour
Jackets	78,000	4	312,000	1,279,200
Trousers	58,000	3	174,000	713,400
			486,000	1,992,600

Note that the units produced figures are derived from the production budget.

Overheads, stock and administration costs

Big Togs plc: Production overhead budget year to 31 December 19—

	Fixed costs £	Variable costs £
General expenses	74,000	74,000
Indirect labour	242,500	–
Power	29,500	44,250
Maintenance	16,000	24,000
Depreciation	66,000	–
Insurance	5,250	–
Supervision	56,300	–
	489,550	142,250

Total cost: £631,800

$$\text{Direct labour hour rate} = \frac{\text{Production overhead}}{\text{Direct labour hours}}$$

$$= \frac{£631,800}{486,000 \text{ hours}} = £1.30 \text{ per hour}$$

Big Togs plc: Stock budget year ending 31 December 19—

Raw materials	Metres	Cost (£)	Totals (£)	
Cloth	18,000	4.90	88,200	
Lining	13,000	2.80	36,400	124,600

Finished goods	Units	Cost (£)	Totals (£)	
Jackets	4,000	41.90	167,600	
Trousers	6,000	28.80	172,800	340,400
				465,000

Workings for cost of finished goods stock:

	Jackets		Trousers	
Cloth	3 × 4.90 =	14.70	2 × 4.90 =	9.80
Lining	2 × 2.80 =	5.60	1 × 2.80 =	2.80
Direct labour	4 × 4.10 =	16.40	3 × 4.10 =	12.30
Production overhead	4 × 1.30 =	5.20	3 × 1.30 =	3.90
		£41.90		£28.80

Big Togs plc: Selling and administration expenses budget year to 31 December 19—

Selling expenses	£	£
Advertising	125,000	
Commissions	39,500	
Sales executives' salaries	196,500	
Travelling expenses	167,500	528,500
Administration expenses		
Salaries and wages	221,600	
Electricity	14,700	
Stationery	23,500	
Post and telephone	33,000	
General expenses	14,300	307,100
Total expenses		835,600

Cash budget

At this stage it would be possible to complete a master budget, in the form of a profit and loss account and balance sheet, but for the fact that debtors and creditors and the cash balance at the year-end are unknown. A cash budget is required to provide further information.

Investigation reveals the following expected cash flows analysed in three-monthly periods:

	1st Qtr £	2nd Qtr £	3rd Qtr £	4th Qtr £
Receipts from customers	1,671,536	1,603,420	2,521,305	2,489,206
Payments:				
Material	510,480	501,290	493,610	516,750
Wages	549,600	600,400	548,200	651,700
Other costs	140,600	141,750	143,200	142,100
Tax	128,200	–	–	–
Plant purchase	–	260,000	200,000	–
Building purchase	450,000	–		–

During the last quarter Big Togs plc purchased an investment in a retail outlet for £2 million.

The cash budget for the year is shown in Table 13.2.

	1st Qtr £	2nd Qtr £	3rd Qtr £	4th Qtr £	Full year £
Opening cash balance	105,284	(2,060)	97,920	1,234,215	105,284
Add receipts from debtors	1,671,536	1,603,420	2,521,305	2,489,206	8,285,467
	1,776,820	1,601,360	2,619,225	3,723,421	8,390,751
Less payments for:					
Materials	510,480	501,290	493,610	516,750	2,022,130
Wages	549,600	600,400	548,200	651,700	2,349,900
Expenses	140,600	141,750	143,200	142,100	567,650
Tax	128,200	–	–	–	128,200
Premises	450,000	–	–	–	450,000
Plant	–	260,000	200,000	–	460,000
Investment	–	–	–	2,000,000	2,000,000
	1,778,880	1,503,440	1,385,010	3,310,550	7,977,880
Closing balance:	(2,060)	97,920	1,234,215	412,871	412,871

Table 13.2 Big Togs plc: Cash budget year ending 31 December 19—

The master budget

Big Togs plc's budgeted profit and loss account is given in Table 13.3. Note that the account acts as a summary of figures from previous budget schedules.

	£	£	£
Sales			8,220,000
Costs			
Materials		2,380,000	
Direct labour		1,992,600	
Production overhead		631,800	
		5,004,400	
Stock adjustment			
Add opening stock of finished goods	223,500		
Less closing stock of finished goods	(340,400)	(116,900)	4,887,500
Gross profit			3,332,500
Less selling and administration			835,600
Net profit			2,496,900
Provision for taxation			840,000
Net profit after tax as increase in reserves			1,656,900
Opening balance of reserves			1,359,361
Closing balance of reserves			3,016,261

Table 13.3 Big Togs plc: Budgeted profit and loss account year ended 31 December 19—

The cost accountant has now attained the position from which one can complete the master budget by preparing a balance sheet as at the end of the budget period. The balance sheet and its workings are shown in Table 13.4.

	£	£
Capital		
1,400,000 ordinary shares of £1 each		1,400,000
General reserve		3,016,261
		4,416,261
Current liabilities		
Trade creditors	1,075,771	
Corporation tax	840,000	1,915,771
Capital employed		6,332,032
Represented by:		
Fixed assets		
Land and buildings (1,850,000 + 450,000)		2,300,000
Plant (1,300,000 + 460,000)	1,760,000	
Less depreciation (920,000 + 66,000)	986,000	774,000
Investment		2,000,000
		5,074,000
Current assets		
Stock		
Materials	124,600	
Finished goods	340,400	
Debtors	380,161	
Cash	412,871	1,258,032
Assets employed		6,332,032

Table 13.4   Big Togs plc: Budgeted balance sheet as at 31 December 19—
Workings

	£	£
Debtors		
Opening balance		445,628
Add sales		8,220,000
		8,665,628
Less cash paid (cash budget)		8,285,467
Closing balance		380,161
Creditors		
Opening balance	431,851	
Add purchases of materials	2,189,600	
Direct labour	1,992,600	
Production overhead (less depreciation)	565,800	
Sales and administration overhead	835,600	6,015,451
Less cash paid		
Materials	2,022,130	
Wages	2,349,900	
Expenses	567,650	4,939,680
Closing balance		1,075,771

Note that depreciation is a non-cash cost and this cannot affect the balance of creditors.

CASH BUDGETING TECHNIQUES

Most transactions within a business will ultimately have an effect upon the cash position. Therefore the cash budget is unique in drawing together the results of other departmental budgets; for example, if sales are the principal budgeting factor the amount sold will influence the amount to be produced, which in turn will set the limit for materials to be used, and material usage when adjusted to the stock policy of the business will reveal the amount of materials to be purchased, which in turn will set the amount of cash to be paid out, and the months during which such payments are to be made.

A cash budget is usually computed on a monthly basis, and shows expected inflows and outflows of cash which enable a forecast to be made of the likely cash balance or overdraft at the end of each month. A shortage of liquid funds is a most serious limiting factor in business, so that a warning of an overdraft required some months in the future will enable a careful approach to be made to the bank to negotiate overdraft facilities. Should such a loan request be turned down, the business still has several months of leeway in which it can plan its way out of the cash shortage by amending its operations or tapping further sources of finance. Plans for capital expenditure or expansion can be made only in the light of the funds available, and the sources which management plan to use to finance this activity. In the absence of a cash budget, a shortage of liquid funds may not be recognized until it is too late to prevent harmful short-term counter-measures. A cash flow forecast can be made as an independent operation or as part of the budgetary system. The success of a cash budget depends upon the accuracy with which forecasts are made as to exactly when payments will be made or received.

Sales revenue

The sales budget will be compiled from monthly forecasts of cash and credit sales in certain sales areas. Cash sales can be assumed to be received during the forecast month, but credit sales will be more difficult to predict. Some debtors may take two months' credit, if this is the norm for the trade concerned, but others may extend the period of credit beyond that which the company may set as its limits. A further complication occurs if debtors are offered a cash discount to pay within one month of the sale, and a proportion of them avail themselves of this opportunity. Some debtors may not pay at all if reckless selling has taken place resulting in bad debts.

Expense and expenditure

The production budget will determine the quantities of material to be used. Usage when combined with planned stock levels will set the materials purchased budget. Payment dates may be forecast for these purchases after taking account of the credit period allowed by suppliers. Two months' credit terms on sales or purchases means that a transaction in January will be settled in cash before the end of March. Wages are paid weekly, but some companies will pay wages like salaries on a monthly basis. The fact that there are thirteen weeks in each quarter means that some months will include four weekly pay-days, in others there will be five. Some costs are paid quarterly, e.g. rent, while others are paid half-yearly, e.g. debenture interest, or even annually, e.g. insurance premiums. The cash budget must take account of this periodicity and ensure that payments are budgeted into the appropriate month.

Certain payments such as capital expenditure, dividends and taxation will also need to be programmed for specific months, and some items, e.g. investments, will improve cash flow at certain times.

Non-cash costs will not affect the cash budget, so items such as depreciation or the provision for bad and doubtful debts, although they appear in the profit and loss account, will not feature in a cash budget. It is possible to reconcile the cash position to the budgeted profit by adjusting for items treated differently in the cash budget and the profit calculation. Timing differences between the date on which a cost is deemed to be incurred and thus appears in the profit and loss account, and the date on which a consequent cash flow takes place, will also influence this reconciliation. Payments for tax or dividend well after the end of the year to which they refer are a further example of such timing differences. Capital items such as the issue of shares, the purchase or sale of fixed assets such as plant or buildings, and receipts or payments concerning loans made, received or repaid, will be found in the cash budget, but do not have a place in the profit and loss account.

Example 13.1

Superskirts Ltd plans to commence trading as a dress wholesaler on 1 July 19—, occupying leased premises from that date. A forecast trading, profit and loss account prepared for the first six months is given in Table 13.5. The account has been prepared using normal accounting principles including accruals and prepayments.

The following information is also available.
1. The business is to be financed (on 1 July 19—) by a long-term loan of £140,000 and share capital of 160,000 £1 ordinary shares. Loan interest is at 15 per cent per annum, and is paid half-yearly in December and June.
2. Sales: sales are expected to develop gradually, being 10 per cent of the total for six months in each of July, August and September, 20 per cent in October and November and 30 per cent in December. Bad debts are expected to be a constant proportion of sales. Terms to customers will be payment by the end of the month following delivery.
3. Initial stocks of £111,000 will be purchased in July and the remainder evenly over the following five months. Terms from suppliers will be as for customers.
4. Wages will be paid at the end of each week, and in August and October there will be five pay-days. The figure for wages includes a Christmas bonus of £5,000 paid on 18 December. Salaries are paid monthly.

	£	£
Sales		1,474,000
Materials		
Purchases	976,000	
Less closing stock	56,000	
	920,000	
Wages and bonus	304,000	1,224,000
Gross profit		250,000
Expenses		
Interest	10,500	
Salaries	36,000	
Rent	14,000	
Royalties (October-December)	1,750	
Power	3,600	
Light and heat	1,300	
Insurance	1,000	
Motor running expenses (MRE)	2,400	
Telephone	1,800	
Repairs and renewals (R & R)	900	
Sundry expenses	1,200	
Bad debts written off	14,000	
Depreciation: Fixtures and fittings	4,000	
Motor vehicles	2,875	
Amortization of lease premium	1,500	
Professional fees	2,425	99,250
Net profit for the first six months		150,750

Table 13.5   *Superskirts Ltd: Forecast trading, profit and loss account for six months to 31 December 19—*

5. The buildings are leased. A lease premium of £15,000 for five years is payable on occupation, and rent is payable quarterly in advance starting 1 July.

6. Royalties are payable to designers half-yearly in advance on 1 April and 1 October.

7. The premises are all-electric and charges are payable quarterly in arrears. The same applies to telephone charges.

8. Insurance is payable annually in advance on 1 July.

9. Motor running expenses, repairs and renewals, and sundry expenses are paid monthly and spread evenly over the period.

10. Superskirts Ltd intends to pay an interim divident of 5p per share in December.

11. On moving into the premises Superskirts Ltd will buy for cash:

	£
Second-hand plant	140,000
Office furniture	26,000
Two motor vans	15,000

12. Professional fees will not be paid until the end of the first year of trading.

Required

1. Prepare a cash budget for the first six months of trading, in columnar format and showing the anticipated bank balance at the end of each month.
2. Prepare a statement for Superskirts Ltd reconciling the net profit as forecast for the period, and the balance in the bank account on 31 December 19—.

Solution

Tables 13.6 and 13.7 give the solutions to requirements 1 and 2 respectively.

	July £	August £	Sept. £	October £	Nov. £	Dec. £
Receipts						
Cash introduced	300,000					
Sales						
(1,474,000 − 14,000)		146,000	146,000	146,000	292,000	292,000
	300,000	146,000	146,000	146,000	292,000	292,000
Payments						
Materials						
(976 − 173) ÷ 5	–	111,000	173,000	173,000	173,000	173,000
Wages/bonus						5,000
4/26 × 299,000	46,000		46,000		46,000	46,000
5/26 × 299,000		57,500		57,500		
Salaries (36,000 ÷ 6)	6,000	6,000	6,000	6,000	6,000	6,000
Rent	7,000			7,000		
Lease premium	15,000					
Royalties						
(half-year to 31.3)				3,500		
Electricity						
(3,600 + 1,300 ÷ 2)			2,450			2,450
Insurance (1000 × 2)	2,000					
Telephone (1,800 ÷ 2)			900			900
R & R, sundries, MRE						
(2,400 + 900 +						
1,200) ÷ 6	750	750	750	750	750	750
Plant	140,000					
Furniture	26,000					
Motor vans	15,000					
Interest						10,500
Dividend						8,000
Total payments	257,750	175,250	229,100	247,750	225,750	252,600
Net surplus (deficit)	42,250	(29,250)	(83,100)	(101,750)	66,250	39,400
Balance carried forward	42,250	13,000	(70,100)	(171,850)	(105,600)	(66,200)

Table 13.6   Superskirts Ltd: Cash budget for the half-year to 31 December 19—

FLEXIBLE BUDGETS

A fixed budget is one which is intended to remain unchanged irrespective of the volume of output or turnover acutally attained. Clearly such a budget will be of

	£	£
Profit per accounts		150,750
Add items not involving cash:		
Depreciation	6,875	
Amortization	1,500	8,375
		159,125
Timing differences:		
December sales	(438,000)	
December materials	173,000	
Royalties prepayment		
(Jan–March)	(1,750)	
Insurance prepaid	(1,000)	
Professional fees	2,425	(265,325)
		(106,200)
Loss		
Balance sheet items:		
Loan and capital	300,000	
Closing stock	(56,000)	
Plant	(140,000)	
Furniture	(26,000)	
Vans	(15,000)	
Lease	(15,000)	
Dividend	(8,000)	40,000
Cash balance as at 31 December 19— - overdrawn		(66,200)

Table 13.7   Superskirts Ltd: Reconciliation statement.

little use as a comparator, since a budget based on the production and sale of, say, 400,000 units will bear little relation to actual costs for the production and sale of 420,000 units. The figures in a fixed budget have been geared to preset estimates of production and sales etc. Therefore such a budget is of little use as a control device when conditions change. A flexible budget recognizes the difference in behaviour between fixed and variable costs, when output and turnover fluctuate and is designed to change in accordance with fluctuations in the level of output etc. Flexibility implies a set of budgets to cover the range of activity levels which may be experienced. Thus, whatever level of actual sales and production is achieved, there is a plan to show what it should have cost, and to act as a comparator for the purpose of control. Cost behaviour is a significant factor when a budget is 'flexed', because the budget must reflect the manner in which costs will react when volumes etc. are changed.

Cost behaviour

The management accountant must first recognize which costs are fixed, variable, or semi-variable, in the context of the new situation, so that the amount of cost change in response to a new level of activity can be calculated. Fixed costs do not change in the short run whatever happens to the level of activity within the business, so such costs as rent, depreciation on the straight line basis and salaries are fixed within the annual period. Variable costs usually vary in direct proportion to volume but they may not always react in this way, since as the quantity produced increase materials may be purchased for cheaper prices, and overtime may need to be paid to the labour force. Semi-variable costs vary in sympathy with, but not in proportion to, a fluctuation in activity. Such costs usually have a fixed and a variable element in their make-up, or tend to increase in a series of steps as activity increases. The management accountant must separate the fixed and variable elements in the cost structure in order to flex a budget. Budgets for such activities as research and development, capital expenditure and advertising are generally considered to be fixed in nature since once a board decision has been taken as to their level this is unlikely to change. It is mainly the costs concerned with production, selling, or distribution which need to be flexed. Some overheads may also vary if activity is increased, e.g. the cost of heat and light in the factory during extra work on an evening shift or at the weekend.

Example 13.2: *Flexible budget*

The management accountant must separate fixed from variable costs since, when volume changes, the fixed costs will remain the same. Variable costs can be expressed in terms of so many machine hours or standard hours. A fixed budget is 'flexed' when the variable and semi-variable cost elements are recalculated for a different volume of production or a series of different activity levels which the business might attain.

The activity ratio expresses:

$$\frac{\text{Standard hours for work produced}}{\text{Budgeted standard hours}} \times \frac{100}{1} = \%$$

This percentage can be applied to variable costs in the budget to find the expected cost for an activity level which varies from that on which the budget was based. A comparison will be meaningful only if the actual cost is compared with a budget for the achieved level of activity rather than for some other level of activity.

Imagine an industrial cleaning company which has gained a contract to clean in a hospital. The budget is drafted to plan the costs of cleaning 100,000 square feet of space: variances A = adverse, F = favourable.

	Cost per sq. ft.	Fixed £	Variable £	Total £	Actual £	Variance £
Materials	25p	–	25,000	25,000	28,000	3,000 (A)
Labour	60p	–	60,000	60,000	69,000	9,000 (A)
Electricity	8p	1,000	8,000	9,000	9,500	500 (A)
Machine rental		8,000	–	8,000	9,000	1,000 (A)
Management		20,000	–	20,000	19,000	1,000 (F)
Maintenance	15p	2,000	15,000	17,000	17,000	–
		31,000	108,000	139,000	151,500	12,500 (A)

These figures appear disastrous until it is realized that 115,000 square feet were ~aned during the period. The fixed budget must be flexed to show the expected ~s for actual activity.

Flexible budget 115,000 square feet

$$\text{Activity ratio} = \frac{\text{Standard units cleaned}}{\text{Budgeted standard units}} = \frac{115,000}{100,000} \times \frac{100}{1} = 115\%$$

	Cost per sq. ft.	Fixed cost £	Variable cost £	Budget total £	Actual £	Variance £	
Materials	25p	–	28,750	28,750	28,000	700	(F)
Labour	60p	–	69,000	69,000	69,000	–	
Electricity	8p	1,000	9,200	10,200	9,500	700	(F)
Rental		8,000	–	8,000	9,000	1,000	(A)
Management		20,000	–	20,000	19,000	1,000	(F)
Maintenance	15p	2,000	17,250	19,250	17,000	2,250	(F)
	108p	31,000	124,200	155,200	151,500	3,700	(F)

$(115,000 \times £1.08) + £31,000 = £155,200.$

The comparison of like with like shows a different picture of the managerial performance on this job.

EXERCISES

13A   (a)   Define the term 'principal budget factor'. Say why the principal budget factor is important in the planning process.
(b)   What are the differences between a fixed budget and a flexible budget? In what ways are fixed budgets and flexible budgets useful for planning and control.
(c)   In its budgets for the period ahead, a company is considering two possible sales forecasts for its three products:

	Product A	Product B	Product C
(i) Sales units	22,000	40,000	6,000
Selling price per unit	£10.00	£6.00	£7.50
(ii) Sales units	30,000	50,000	7,000
Selling price per unit	£9.00	£5.70	£7.10

Variable costs per unit are expected to be the same at the different levels of possible sales. The variable costs per unit are as follows:

	Product A £	Product B £	Product C £
Direct materials	3.00	2.00	4.00
Direct labour	2.00	1.50	1.00
Variable overhead	1.00	0.50	0.50

Fixed overheads are expected to total £150,000. These are expected to be unaffected by the possible changes in activity which are being considered.

Due to recent high labour turnover and problems of recruitment, direct labour will be restricted to a maximum of £135,000 in the period. It can be assumed that all labour is of the same grade and is freely transferable between products. Other resources are expected to be generally available.

Required

Take each of the possible sales forecasts in turn. Say what the principal budget factor is for each of the forecasts.

(Association of Certified Accountants)

13B   A company manufactures three products, extracts from the standard cost data relating to which are as follows:

		Units of material in final product		
Material	*Unit cost*	*Product A*	*Product B*	*Product C*
V	55p	5	4	–
W	50p	3	2	6
X	35p	–	3	5
Y	60p	–	1	4
Z	80p	1	1	–

No losses occur in the use of materials V, W, X and Y. The standard yield on material Z is 90 per cent. This is an ideal standard. The expected yield is 80 per cent.

During the first four-week period budgeted sales are:

Product	Sales units
A	12,000
B	15,000
C	10,000

It is anticipated that 5 per cent of the production of product B will not pass inspection and will be disposed of immediately.

The stocks on hand at the beginning of the period are expected to be:

		Units
Finished goods	A	1,800
	B	2,000
	C	1,600
Materials	V	20,000
	W	30,000
	X	15,000
	Y	5,000
	Z	9,000

It is planned to increase finished goods stocks in order to satisfy orders more quickly. Production in period 1 will be sufficient to increase stocks by 10 per cent by the end of the period. Materials stocks, however, are considered to be too high and a reduction of 10 per cent is planned by the end of period 1.

Required

(a)   Prepare budgets for:
    (i)   production (in quantity);
    (ii)   materials usage (in quantity);
    (iii)   materials purchases (in quantity and value).
    Distinguish between 'ideal' and 'attainable' standards, and consider briefly factors influencing the choice between them.

(Association of Certified Accountants)

13C   Ruddington Bakery Ltd makes only two products, a large loaf and a small loaf. The company uses one basic raw material, flour, and one grade of labour. The bakery works a forty-hour week. The operating statement for this quarter is as follows:

		£	£
Sales:	Large (50p each)	246,000	
	Small (30p each)	180,000	426,000
Cost of sales:	Direct material	110,880	
	Direct labour	247,500	
	Variable overhead	19,800	
	Fixed overhead	30,000	408,180
Operating profit			17,820

Standard material costs for production specify 0.2 kg of flour for a small loaf, 0.4 kg for a large. Actual consumption this quarter was as specified in the standard. The standard wage rate is £2.40 per hour, and the labour cost of a small loaf is 20p, a large loaf 30p. The labour force has achieved standard efficiency this year. The actual rate paid has been 10p per hour above standard. Overhead costs for the year were as specified in the standard, variable overheads varying directly with the labour hours worked.

The sales forecast for the next quarter expects 500,000 large and 550,000 small loaves to be sold. Material stocks are to be reduced by 15,000 kg during the quarter. The material and labour standards are intended to remain the same as for this quarter, except the actual wage rate paid this quarter will be recognized as normal, and a further increase of 20p per hour will be paid in recognition of a productivity agreement by which standard timings for each product will be reduced by 20 per cent and the labour force reduced to 150 workers. Budgeted overheads will be at the same rate as for this year. Material costs are expected to rise by 5 per cent. Overtime is paid at time and a quarter.

Required

(a)   Calculate the budgets for material purchases and wages for the next quarter
(b)   Advise the company of the likely cost saving to be derived from the productivity scheme.

13D   Kerryblue Ltd is a company manufacturing two products using one type of material and a single grade of labour. Shown below is an extract from the company's working papers for the next period's budget.

Product	K	B
Budgeted sales	3,000 units	4,500 units
Budgeted material consumption, per product	6 kg	2 kg
Budgeted material cost; £3 per kg		
Standard hours allowed, per product	5 hours	3 hours

The budgeted wage rate for the direct workers is £4 per hour for a forty-hour week, overtime premium is 50 per cent and there are sixty-five direct operatives.

The target productivity ratio (or efficiency ratio) for the productive hours worked by the direct operatives in actually manufacturing the products is 90 per cent; in addition the amount of non-productive down time is budgeted at 20 per cent of the productive hours worked.

There are twelve five-day weeks in the budget period and it is anticipated that sales and production will occur evenly throughout the whole period.

At the beginning of the period it is anticipated that the stocks will be:

Product K - 1,050 units
Product B - 1,200 units
Raw material - 3,700 kg

The target closing stocks, expressed in terms of the anticipated activity during the budget period are:

Product K - 15 days' sales
Product B - 20 days' sales
Raw material - 10 days' consumption

Required

(a) Calculate the material purchase budget and the wages budget for the direct workers, showing both quantities and values, for the next period.
(b) Describe the additional information required in order to calculate the weekly cash disbursements for materials and wages during the above budget period.

(Association of Certified Accountants)

13E   A redundant manager who received compensation of £80,000 decides to commence business on 4 January 1988, manufacturing a product for which he knows there is a ready market. He intends to employ some of his former workers who were also made redundant but they will not all commence on 4 January. Suitable premises have been found to rent and second-hand machinery costing £60,000 has been bought out of the £80,000. This machinery has an estimated life of five years from January 1988 and no residual value.

Other data is available as follows.

1.   Production will begin on 4 January and 25 per cent of the following month's sales will be manufactured in January. Each month thereafter the production will consist of 75 per cent of the current month's sales and 25 per cent of the following month's sales.

2.   Estimated sales are

	Units	£
January	Nil	Nil
February	3,200	80,000
March	3,600	90,000
April	4,000	100,000
May	4,000	100,000

3. Variable production cost per unit

	£
Direct materials	7
Direct wages	6
Variable overhead	2
	15

4. Raw material stocks costing £10,000 have been purchased (out of the manager's £80,000) to enable production to commence and it is intended to buy, each month, 50 per cent of the materials required for the following month's production requirements. The other 50 per cent will be purchased in the month of production. Payment will be made 30 days after purchase.

5. Direct workers have agreed to have their wages paid into bank accounts on the seventh working day of each month in respect of the previous month's earnings.

6. Variable production overhead: 60 per cent is to be paid in the month following the month it was incurred and 40 per cent is to be paid one month later.

7. Fixed overheads are £4,000 per month. One quarter of this is paid in the month incurred, one half in the following month, and the remainder represents depreciation on the second-hand machinery.

8. Amounts receivable: a 5 per cent cash discount is allowed for payment in the current month and 20 per cent of each month's sales qualify for this discount. Fifty per cent of each month's sales are received in the following month, 20 per cent in the third month and 8 per cent in the fourth month. The balance of 2 per cent represents anticipated bad debts.

You are required to

(a) Prepare a cash budget for each of the first four months of 1988, assuming that overdraft facilities will be available.

(b) State the amount receivable from customers in May.

(Chartered Institute of Management Accountants)

14　Budgetary Control: The Behavioural Connection

RESPONSIBILITY ACCOUNTING AND MOTIVATION

If a budget is drafted in such a way that revenues and costs are segregated into areas of personal responsibility, the performance of managers will be more clearly assessed. A cost centre becomes a responsibility centre, in that its manager has the task of organizing its operations within the budget for the centre, and therefore that manager should be accountable for the performance of the cost centre, and for any remedial action which is required. Variance analysis will focus attention on parts of the organization which are under- or over-achieving the budget. A proper attitude on the part of managers towards the budgetary control system is essential if that system is to succeed. Co-operation and enthusiasm on the part of the managers will ensure that maximum efficiency is attained. Accordingly, human behaviour is an important factor in the successful operation of a budgetary control system. If the right attitude is established, a team of managers will develop so that working together they will achieve the goals and objectives of the organization. The management accountant therefore must understand the behavioural implications of the budget system if he is to be effective in organizing that system.

Responsibility Centres

These are defined within the organization, so that authority for organizing activity within those centres can be delegated from senior to junior managers. Disputes between managers are kept to a minimum if demarcation lines between their respective areas of responsibility are clearly understood. Management reports which compare the actual cost of a department with the budget should be issued to the appropriate manager so that the system will regularly and automatically comment on the success or otherwise with which that manager has fulfilled his or her responsibilities.

GOAL CONGRUENCE

The existence of a budget, and the fact that budget is issued to a manager, will not necessarily motivate the manager to strive for the successful completion of the budget plan. Indeed in an autocratic system, where a budget is handed down to managers as an instruction, the implication is that the manager should perform as planned or accept the consequences. In such a system co-operation may be lost and morale will be low. It is necessary to identify certain factors which will influence a manager not only to accept his or her budget but to strive for its effective performance. Each manager has a set of personal goals, or aspirations, and is motivated to make efforts to reach those goals; if they are perceived to be in line with those of the organization, then by striving to achieve his or her own aspirations the manager will also be working in the best interests of the organization. When a manager accepts the goals of the organization as his or her own, they are said to have been 'internalized', and at that stage the manager's personal goals will be 'congruent' with those of the organization. Goal congruence means that managers accept and support the direction taken by the business as expressed in the budget.

The aspiration levels of an individual may be influenced by several motivating factors.

Motivation

Ambition motivates some individuals to compete for success in an organization, and to perceive the achievement of budgeted performance as a worthwhile ambition which could lead to promotion. Reputation may also motivate a manager in that he or she will be inspired to work hard to maintain a good reputation for always achieving budgeted performance. A budget that sets expected levels of performance which are in line with what a manager realistically expects to achieve will be more readily accepted than a budget set above the realistic expectations derived from the manager's practical experience. An unrealistic budget may well demotivate a manager if it seeks to impose unreasonable levels of performance.

Managers may be motivated by ambition, morale or expectations to strive for their own and the organization's success at one and the same time. This is known as 'intrinsic' motivation, which is different from motivation promoted by the offer of rewards such as a bonus etc. If goal congruence is to be established it is necessary that goals and sub-goals are clearly defined so that confusion is avoided. Too many goals will be counter-productive, since conflict may appear and resources will be spread too thinly for success if effort expended to achieve a certain goal may cause other aims to be neglected.

PARTICIPATION

The budgetary procedure produces a compromise between board policy and the expectations of managers at the grass roots level of the organization. It is vital that those who are to perform the budget recognize that their views have influenced the master budget which is eventually drafted. This recognition will motivate them to accept the budget as being realistic and therefore worthy of extra effort on their part to make it work. The budgeting procedure which adjust estimates in order to co-ordinate the activities of departments, and which seek to reduce the effects of limiting factors, must be made with the full participation of the managers concerned. They will then recognize themselves as participants in the budgetary procedures, and realize that their role is realistic and that it is possible for their personal goals to become congruent with those of the budget. The role of the management accountant at this stage is to advise managers as they express their plans in quantitative terms and to help them with the revisions necessary when conditions are changed. During the iterative co-ordinating process the management accountant forms a vital link between the budget committee and lower levels of management who are making their revisions. Participation means that there must be a genuine expression of views and interplay between all the parties in the development of this joint decision. Line managers may not internalize the budget, or see its targets as realistic, unless genuine consultation has taken place. Effective leadership in this participation process will assist in the development of trust between managers, and the growth of the congruent management team. The absence of participation may lead to junior managers regarding the budget as the vehicle of top management, with the result that they will not be motivated to produce extra effort to ensure that the budget plan works well. Even if the views of junior managers fail to influence a discussion concerning budget levels, the fact that they have participated in that discussion and can appreciate the arguments of their seniors, will enable them to accept the budget.

Group dynamics

Group activity is an important feature of all human behaviour which extends from private life into the work situation. The term 'group dynamics' describes the forces which operate within a group, and which can be used as part of the participation procedure to encourage individual managers to internalize the goals of the group. A manager may value membership of a cohesive group or team, and will work hard to support his or her colleagues in that team. Group dynamics may well act against the organization, in that the group may reject the organization's objectives and thus become a significant disaffected force. Alternatively, strong personalities within the group may influence the managers for their own ends rather than the good of the business.

LEVELS OF PERFORMANCE

The art of setting the performance required by a budget at just the right level is crucial to the success of a budgetary control system. A budget standard should be set at a level which is reasonably attainable and therefore credible in the eyes of managers who are to perform to that standard, and yet not so easy to attain that the organization is budgeted to perform below its optimum level. A good standard will stretch managers to perform at peak efficiency but should not be pitched so far ahead of what is reasonable that their morale suffers from being asked to do too much. Standards which are too easy to attain may also lead to a fall in morale if managers lose respect for them. Standards should be set at a level which is tight and efficient yet still attainable, which means that they are reasonable and can be achieved under normal but not perfect conditions. Such standards are more likely to be internalized by managers.

One behavioural theory holds that standards should be tailored to fit the manager, rather than set at levels which the budget requires. This theory seeks to ease the pressure on individual managers, at the expense of setting goals which are not congruent with organizational policy. When the manager concerned has raised his or her performance to achieve the target set, the target can be increased, so that performance is gradually improved and eventually goal congruence is achieved. It is not always possible to budget parts of a business according to managerial ability, and if individual standards are set they may be seen as favouritism or discrimination by other managers who are expected to achieve more.

EXCEPTION REPORTING

A system of responsibility accounting implies that variances or departures from budget will be reported to each manager as soon as they are recognized. Such feedback enables a greater measure of control. If actual cost is greater than budgeted cost the variance is said to be 'adverse'; if actual cost is less than budget the term 'favourable' is applied to the variance. Thus variance analysis focuses managerial attention on those parts of the business which are not performing according to plan. The system is sometimes referred to as 'exception reporting' or 'management by exception', in that differences between actual and budget are highlighted in the management accounts. The absence of adverse variances means that the manager has been successful in performing according to plan, but adverse variances when disclosed emphasize the significance of under-performance.

Once again, a wrong attitude can influence the success with which management by exception is operated. If the variance statement appears to managers as a means of reporting their failures to senior management, implying that they are inefficient those managers may come to distrust both the variance statement and the management accountant who prepares it. In that case co-operation in formulating the budget and organizing remedial action will be lost.

Exception reporting may not give sufficient significance to those parts of the business which are performing well and may therefore be seen as accentuating executive failure rather than concentrating on success. Such a view can quickly lead to resentment and a lack of trust. The management accountant must try hard to ensure that the variance statement is recognized by managers as a means whereby the accountant can help them to identify departure from the budget at an early stage, so that action can be taken to limit the damage done to the business.

CONTROLLABILITY

A behavioural implication stemming from exception reporting is that managerial performance should be evaluated only on the basis of matters under the control of an individual manager. If efficiency is judged on the basis of adverse variances caused by factors outside the manager's control, such a judgement will be unfair and will forfeit the respect of the manager concerned. It is therefore important that the variance statement should separate variances in controllable costs from those in uncontrollable costs. The acceptance of responsibility implies that the manager concerned can exercise a degree of control over the costs for which he or she is responsible. Very few costs are the sole responsibility of a single manager. Sometimes several managers are able to influence a cost and it may be difficult to ascertain who is ultimately responsible for that cost. Consider whether a factory manager should be held responsible for excess wastage of raw materials from the processes he or she controls, if the machines and employees are operating efficiently and the waste is due to the purchasing department buying cheap materials to create the illusion of their own efficiency by fulfilling the purchase budget at less than expected cost. Eventually responsibility must rest on someone and it seems fair to select the manager who takes the final decision about a certain cost to be responsible for that cost. Once again, considerable delicacy and tact are required if the management accountant is to produce a variance statement which is both useful and which commands the respect of those managers to whom it applies.

DYSFUNCTIONAL BEHAVIOUR

Poor morale on the part of managers is the root cause of most of the disadvantages suffered by a system of budgetary control. Unless adequate attention is given to the behavioural factors and the right atmosphere is created in which the system can flourish, the efficiency of the system may be seriously impaired. Applying budgets without adequate participation, setting standards which are not attainable, reporting exceptions as though they are failures, and fixing responsibility without control, will certainly lead to resentment and distrust on the part of managers within the budgeting system. Being human they will act to defeat what they consider to be a system which disadvantages them, and may link the budget accountant with this action if they consider him to be an adversary, a critic or an investigator.

Dysfunctional behaviour manifests itself in a variety of ways.

1. Line managers faced with the threat of adverse variances will adopt a defensive attitude to avoid responsibility. They may 'build in slack' by increasing their expenditure estimates when the budget is drafted, so that their department is cushioned against adverse conditions, and variances disclosed are usually favourable.

2. A manager may conceal some expected advantage when budget forecasts are made or may delay some profitable activity until it can be used to offset the effect of other losses.

3. A manager who is worried by adverse variances may avoid taking risks: in escaping criticism he or she also forfeits to the business the chance of large profits.

4. Managers who expect their budget to be cut will automatically enlarge their forecast of expected costs. If the costs prove lower than anticipated, they will be entrusted with a greater expenditure budget than they require to run their department efficiently. As the year-end approaches, and they have not spent as much as was expected, in order to escape discovery they will then spend up to the padded budget on items which are not really required.

5. It is not unknown for managers who are pressured by unattainable budgets to falsify information in order to 'beat the budget'.

6. If pressure is put on a manager it will spoil the atmosphere of teamwork and co-ordination in the business, as a pressured manager may try to pass pressure back up the organization by rejecting the budget or the standards imposed by it, or conversely may form a group bond with the employees under his control to express their resentment.

Measures to counter dysfunctional behaviour

While the management accountant has an important role to play in such a situation, it is also significant that managers themselves need to be educated to have a responsible attitude towards variance statements, and not to blame the accountant for what the statement shows. Constructive statements will avoid resentment from managers on whose efficiency they seek to comment. Whenever there is an attempt to apportion blame, behavioural factors will usually provoke argument amongst managers and attempts to 'pass the buck' and blame an executive elsewhere in the business. Managers need to know costs outside their control which are important for their area of responsibility, in order to show them a full picture of what is happening to their department.

It is important to separate arguments concerning efficiency and results from arguments concerning policy. If a department has more than one objective to achieve, it may be that these goals are not congruent. The accountant should not take part in arguments derived from such conflict, since the reconciliation of disparate objectives is the job of those executives who are directly concerned. The role of the management accountant in these circumstances is to provide the protagonists with as much fair and unbiased information as possible in order to enable their decision to be taken on the best possible basis.

MULTIPLE CHOICE QUESTIONS

Note that these questions relate to the whole of Part IV (Chapters 12 to 14) of the book.

14.1   The objectives of budgetary control are planning, control, co-ordination and two others. They are:
(a)   Participation.
(b)   Communication.
(c)   Motivation.
(d)   Delegation.

(a + b)   (b + c)   (c + d)   (b + d)

14.2   'A budget which by recognizing the difference in behaviour between fixed and variable costs in relation to fluctuations in output, or turnover, is designed to change appropriately with such fluctuations.' Which of the following does the statement above define?
(a)   Ideal budget.
(b)   Short-term budget.
(c)   Flexible budget.
(d)   Rolling budget.

(a)   (b)   (c)   (d)

14.3   'A budget which is prepared from and summarizes the functional budgets.' Which of the following does the statement above define?
(a)   Long-term budget.
(b)   Fixed budget.
(c)   Cash budget.
(d)   Master budget.

(a)   (b)   (c)   (d)

14.4   Which of the following is not affected by the production budget?
(a)   Factory overhead budget.
(b)   Research and development budget.
(c)   Machine utilization budget.
(d)   Stock budget.

(a + c)   (b)   (b + d)   (d)

14.5 'The state that exists in a control system when it leads individuals and/or groups to take actions which are both in their self-interest and also in the best interest of the company.' This statement is describing:
    (a) Dysfunctional behaviour.
    (b) Strategic planning.
    (c) Participation.
    (d) Goal congruence.

(a)   (b)   (c)   (d)

14.6 Which of the following factors will not act as a limiting factor?
    (a) An ineffectual salesforce.
    (b) Obsolescent plant.
    (c) Adequate working capital.
    (d) A component supplier.

(a)   (a + b)   (c)   (c + d)

14.7 (1) 'An authoritarian budgeting system harms morale.' (2) 'An ideal budget will act as a motivator.'
    (a) Both true.
    (b) (1) true; (2) false.
    (c) (1) false; (2) true.
    (d) Both false.

(a)   (b)   (c)   (d)

14.8 A rolling budget is intended to remedy:
    (a) Forecasting problems in a period of changing price levels.
    (b) Difficulties associated with a bonus scheme for indirect labour.
    (c) Difficulties associated with a limited time horizon in volatile trades.
    (d) Over-investment in stock.

(a + b)   (a + c)   (c + d)   (a + d)

14.9 The production budget plans to make 25,000 units during the month with a standard time of seven minutes each. The labour force is 85 per cent efficient. The budgeted standard hours are:
    (a) 2,917 hours.
    (b) 2,479 hours.
    (c) 3,431 hours.
    (d) 3,354 hours.

(a)   (b)   (c)   (d)

14.10 If in the example in 14.9, 23,000 units are produced, the activity ratio is:
   (a)   109 per cent.
   (b)   92 per cent.
   (c)   78 per cent.
   (d)   85 per cent.

(a)   (b)   (c)   (d)

14.11 Which items listed below will not appear in a cash budget but will appear in
      a profit and loss account for the same period?
   (a)   Interim dividends.
   (b)   Bad debts written off.
   (c)   Insurance premium paid in advance.
   (d)   Electricity costs accrued.

(a + b)   (a + c)   (c + d)   (b + d)

14.12 Which items listed below will appear in a cash budget but will not appear in
      a profit and loss account for the same period?
   (a)   Cash sales.
   (b)   Depreciation on plant.
   (c)   Purchase of plant.
   (d)   Investment income.

(a)   (b)   (c)   (d)

PART V

STANDARD COSTING AND VARIANCE ANALYSIS

15 The Standard-setting Process

STANDARD COSTS

A standard cost is a predetermined calculation of how much costs should be under certain specified working conditions. Standards are compiled from the various cost elements which are incurred to make a product, e.g. the technical specification of materials required showing the amount and cost of materials needed to produce each unit, standard timings for the labour and machine time involved, and an assessment of fixed and variable overheads. Standard costing as a system uses the standards for costs and revenue to compare actual cost or revenue for a given level of activity with the standard cost or revenue for that same level of activity. The difference between the actual and standard amounts is termed a 'variance'. An analysis of variances during a costing period will focus managerial attention on those parts of the business which are not performing according to budget. Standard costing is a logical extension of the budgetary control system, in that the budgeted amounts of materials, labour etc. can be expressed in terms of preset standards. It is also possible to operate standard costing with variance analysis without a full budgeting system. Standard costing can be applied to processes, in batch costing and in job costing, where standard operations are undertaken as the job passes through a cost centre.

Standard hours

Budgeted production is often expressed in terms of *standard hours*, i.e. the quantity of work which should be achieved during an hour if that work is undertaken at standard performance. Thus, budgeted production can be expressed as so many standard hours, the term being used here more as an amount of work to be undertaken than as a measure of time. The standard hour is a convenient common denominator in circumstances where a number of products are made. It allows production in terms of several different products to be expressed as so many standard hours of work. The standard time for a particular amount of work includes an allowance for normal idle time, i.e. something added on to the actual working time for contingency allowances or relaxation between jobs. Variances of actual cost from standard cost are part of the management by exception system, but such variances should be arranged to show variations from the plan caused by market fluctuations or other factors outside the control of management as opposed to variations caused by inefficiency, which should be controllable.

THE ADVANTAGES OF STANDARD COSTS

Standards derived from the budgetary control activity bring the advantages of facilitating calculations as to costs incurred, providing cost information at an early stage and enabling managers to anticipate changed conditions when compiling the standards. The very fact that standards are prepared involves managers in considering the methods they intend to use, and any sources of inefficiency will be disclosed as part of this consideration. Thus improvements can be built into the system before production begins. When standards are set a consideration of stock volume and buying policy may disclose that a more economic order quantity or buying sequence will reduce costs. The constant search for deviations of actual performance from standard leads to the discovery of inefficiency and the early organization of remedial activity. Predetermined standards facilitate the production and pricing of stock sheets. If standards are adjusted frequently to match current conditions they will be a sound basis on which to compute tenders or estimates for future jobs. A standard represents the intended cost of a unit of production and may thus be a useful guide in pricing.

Standard costing also has some disadvantages. It can be time-consuming and therefore expensive to install and maintain a set of standards. If conditions change during the costing year, e.g. material prices rise, the standards compiled when the system was installed will soon become out of date, and will thus be of little use as comparators to control costs. As with other costing systems, if too much detail is used to calculate and express variances, their usefulness will be limited since busy managers may not have sufficient time available to learn and understand the finer points of variance analysis. A major cause of difficulty with a standard costing system concerns the level at which standards are pitched. Poor standard setting can discount all the advantages to be gained from the system.

TYPES OF STANDARD

If the objective of standard costing is to compare actual costs with standard, the past performance will not provide a reliable yardstick for such a comparison. If past costs are automatically built into standards, there is the danger that future changed circumstances will not be recognized in the standard, and that past uneconomic costs will be perpetuated as comparators in the forthcoming period.

Basic standards

A basic standard is one which is established for use over a long period and from which a current standard can be developed. It remains unaltered for an indefinite period and is not subject to revision when material prices or labour rates vary. The basic standard serves as a baseline from which to measure the extent of changes over time and the direction of trends. Basic standards are soon outdated as conditions change so they cannot be used for the calculation of variances or to comment on current performance. They are there as a foundation from which current standards can be derived by an update based on changed circumstances. A comparison of current performance with basic standards will highlight trends and changes in efficiency.

Ideal standards

An ideal standard is one which can be attained under the most favourable conditions. No provision is built into this standard for normal idle time or other acceptable imperfections in the working system, e.g. spoilage or machine breakdowns. Perfect efficiency is rarely attained so variances derived from ideal standards serve only as an academic exercise to show up the differences between actual performance and perfection. Such unattainable standards cannot be used in useful measurement of managerial efficiency or control. At best an unfavourable variance from an ideal standard serves to remind management of the extent to which actual performance can be improved.

Attainable standards

An attainable standard is one based on normally expected efficiency, e.g. machines properly operated and material correctly used. Allowances are built into an attainable standard for normally acceptable waste or breakdowns or other reasons for acceptable idle time. Attainable standards form the best comparators to use in variance analysis. They have a desirable motivational impact on employees since they are based on what should be achieved in normal, efficient but not perfect operating conditions. This does not imply that attainable standards are easy to perform, since they will be set with reference to efficient performance; they can be attained only at the expense of hard work.

Current standards

A current standard is one established for use over a short period of time and related to current conditions. Normally there would be no difference between a current standard and an attainable standard, but if during the short run conditions change from those built into the attainable standard, a current standard will form a better comparator.

THE STANDARD COST CARD

The standards for materials, labour and overheads for a unit of production are carefully compiled in a standard cost specification. Each standard operation contributing to the eventually complete product will be recorded on a standard cost card. A number of cards will be built into the standard cost specification. The information can be held on card or computer file and it will show in detail the materials, quantities and qualities and prices, the labour times and rates and the machine times and rates so that a total standard cost for the unit of product can be compiled.

There is some discussion among cost accountants as to whether standards should be revised frequently. In a period of inflation the standard material cost of a unit will soon be outdated, and any variance disclosed between actual and standard cost will be much more the result of inflation than of efficiency or inefficiency on the part of management. It is harmful to morale to suggest that adverse material variances are the responsibility of management when they are in reality derived from inflation. Thus frequent revision may be necessary if realistic comparators are to be devised. However, the very fact of revision will make the long-term comparison of performance from year to year difficult to achieve. Small cost changes need to be shown up as variances, so a too frequent revision of standards will be self-defeating.

SETTING STANDARDS

Production planners, designers, buyers, personnel managers and production overseers all co-operate with the management accountant to compile the standard specification for a product. A system must be organized to gather detailed information which can be built into dependable standards. The production department must decide how they are going to produce the product, and from this decision will stem details of materials to be used and component parts bought in, the time of skilled labour and other grades of labour needed, and the amount of machine time to be expended on the production. All this information has a bearing on setting a standard. The standard cost of each part or each operation must be recorded; so far as labour is concerned, it can require time and motion study to establish exactly the standard time for a certain operation.

The technical specification produced by the production engineers will show in great detail the quantities and grades of raw materials and components which are required. When a standard quantity is set a normal allowance for expected waste and other losses in production such as breakages and rejections is built into the quantity. The purchasing department will then price the standard quantities with what they expect to pay during the budget period for the materials required. Past costs are not relevant in this instance. Built into the standard price will be an allowance for trade discounts and likely price increases.

Once the method of manufacture has been decided, work measurement will break down the physical tasks required into constituent parts. Each part will be timed so that work study specialists can produce a standard time in which a task should be completed at standard performance, which includes the basic operating time plus contingency allowances and a relaxation allowance. The personnel department will provide the standard setters with the wage rates which are likely to be paid to the grades of skilled labour specified.

The standard cost of overheads per unit of production will depend upon the absorption basis used to charge out cost centre overheads to products. An overhead absorption rate is usually calculated in advance of production and can be written into the standard according to labour or machine times.

Example 15.1: A standard cost specification

Coffee table pattern AJ75.
Batch size – 200.

	Unit cost £	Per batch £
Material:		
Beech: 2-metre run of 4 cm square × 50p	1.00	
Pine board: 1 metre square × 2 cm thick	1.80	
Veneer	0.80	
Plastic fittings	0.70	
	4.30	860
Labour:		
Planing: 15 minutes × £5 per hour	1.25	
Turning: 10 minutes × £6 per hour	1.00	
Assembly: 15 minutes × £4 per hour	1.00	
Inspection: 5 minutes × £6 per hour	0.50	
Standard production time 45 minutes	3.75	750
Variable overhead	0.60	120
Fixed overhead recovery rates at £5 per hour:		
45 minutes production time	3.75	750
Standard cost	12.40	2,480

EXERCISES

15A   Haskins plc is considering the introduction of a standard costing system. However, somewhat to senior management's surprise, the union representing the direct production workers is suspicious and threatening industrial action.

(a)   Discuss the possible implications of introducing standard costing into this company; and

(b)   describe the information which is significant for management when labour standards are set, and what types of standard are considered during this procedure.

16   Variance Analysis

The CIMA terminology defines a variance as the difference between the planned, budgeted or standard cost, and the actual cost incurred. A variance will focus attention on that part of the business which is not performing according to plan. Analysis of variances into their constituent parts may well raise questions concerning their occurrence and cause even further investigation before remedial action can take place. For example, the materials variance can be divided into a materials price variance and a materials usage variance, thereby setting down a cost amount for each constituent part of the major difference. The main reasons why actual cost of materials is different from that in the budget must be either that the material purchased has cost more than standard, or that the amount used per unit was more than standard.

Variances can be expressed as adverse (ADV) or favourable (FAV) according to whether they show a cost overrun or saving. A cost statement expressing the main difference in terms of a usage variance, a price variance, or in the case of labour an efficiency variance, quantifies the factors which have contributed to the main difference and shows their relative significance. The statement will also separate one cause from another, so that the extent to which a favourable efficiency variance has compensated for an adverse price variance can be recognized. A continuous run of production with the repetition of standard operations and the use of standard components or materials, built into the product in standard labour or machine times, provides the ideal conditions for the use of standard costing.

VARIANCES CLASSIFIED

Variances fall easily into four groups.
1. *Direct materials cost* variance: this variance is the difference between the standard cost of direct materials specified for the output achieved and the

actual cost of direct materials used. The main variance can be analysed into sub-variances focusing attention on *usage* or *price*.

2. *Direct wages cost* variance: this variance is the difference between the standard direct wages specified for the activity achieved and the actual direct wages paid. This main variance can be analys :d into sub-variances which highlight differences derived from the *rate of pay*, the amount of *idle time*, and the *efficiency* factor.

3. *Overhead cost* variance: this variance measures the difference between the standard cost of overheads, both fixed and variable, absorbed in the output achieved and the actual overhead cost. Overheads tend to differ from standard for two main reasons: either more has been spent (an *expenditure* variance); or more units have been produced and more overheads have consequently been charged out to production (a *volume* variance). Factors which will influence the volume produced are abnormal *idle time*, the *efficiency* of the labour force, and the amount of *capacity* used, and sub-variances analyse these items.

4. *Sales margin* variances: if a product has a standard cost and a standard selling price, it is possible to compute a standard profit margin per unit, which when applied to budgeted sales will show the expected sales margin. Clearly this figure will differ from the actual profit margin on actual sales. The sales margin may vary from standard because more or less has been sold than was budgeted, a *quantity* variance, or because sales have been made at *prices* that differ from standard, a *price* variance.

The usual form of a standard costing variance statement is to reconcile the standard profit for actual production or sales to the actual profit for actual production or sales. The difference between these two amounts will be the net effect of the variances disclosed. A chart of variances is shown in Figure 16.1.

PRODUCTION VARIANCES: A COMPREHENSIVE EXAMPLE

The variances in this example are adverse but in practice favourable and adverse variances can exist side by side. A practical point is that the price variance should be computed first, so that all other variances are then calculated at standard prices or rates.

Chiltern Chairs plc produces simple wooden chairs. The accountant's first task is to produce a standard cost specification for each chair. Consultation with the appropriate executives reveals the following specification:

	£
Materials: 2 kg of oak at 60p per kg	1.20
Labour: 2.5 hours at £4 per hour	10.00
Variable overheads per chair	1.00
Fixed overheads per chair: 50p per hour × 2.5 hours	1.25
Standard cost	13.45

The actual time spent by an operative in making a chair is two hours fifteen minutes, but an extra fifteen minutes is allowed in the standard time for the job to

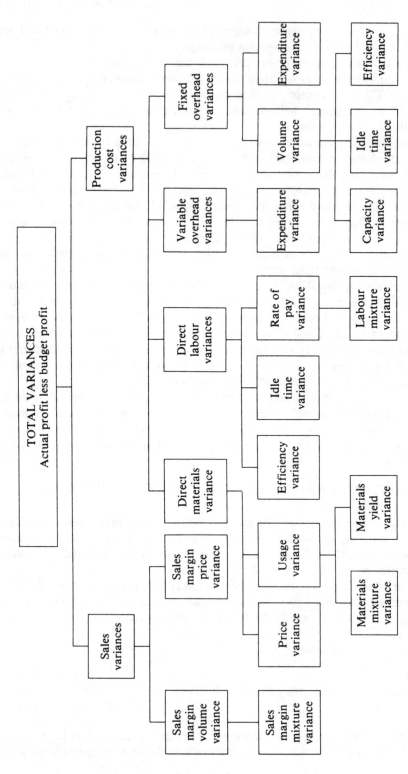

Figure 16.1 Variance classification chart

cover 'normal' idle time, e.g. tea breaks or relaxation time, and other minor reasons for a halt to production. The fixed overheads allocated to each chair produced have been calculated by dividing the overhead expenses of the factory (budgeted at £15,000) by either the number of production hours available if the factory works at planned capacity (30,000 hours) or the standard production equivalent to that time (30,000 divided by 2.5 hours = 12,000 chairs).

```
£15,000 ÷ 12,000 chairs    = £1.25 per chair
£15,000 ÷ 30,000 hours     = 50p per hour
(2.5 hours × 50p per hour  = £1.25 per chair)
```

Planned capacity concerns one month out of a twelve-month budget.

These facts make it possible to compile a budget, by applying the standard cost per unit to the volume of planned production. The budget shows the costs which are expected to be incurred for a given production, so that the actual costs can be compared with this standard to reveal any variances of actual cost from the planned cost.

Suppose 11,000 chairs are produced, and 26,000 hours are worked to produce them.

	£
Standard cost for 11,000 chairs:	
Materials: 22,000 kg of oak × 60p	13,200
Labour: 11,000 chairs × £10	110,000
Variable overheads: £1 per chair	11,000
Fixed overheads charged to production (11,000 × £1.25)	13,750
	147,950

This is a flexed budget since it shows the planned cost of actual production. It is fruitless to compare the budgeted cost of a planned 12,000 chairs with the actual cost of the smaller (11,000) volume produced.

The actual costs and quantities recorded for the period are as follows:

	Actual £	Budget £	Variance £
Materials: 23,000 kg of oak at 65p	14,950	13,200	1,750 ADV
Labour: 29,000 hours at £4.20 per hour	121,800	110,000	11,800 ADV
Variable overheads	15,400	11,000	4,400 ADV
Fixed overheads	16,000	13,750	2,250 ADV
	168,150	147,950	20,200 ADV

A thousand hours of abnormal idle time have been recorded.

It can readily be seen that the actual cost of production exceeds the standard cost for actual production by £20,200. Variance analysis seeks to highlight the reasons for such an excess and to focus the attention of the management on those parts of the organization where action is required to remedy the situation.

Material cost variances

The major variances are the price and usage variances. The price variance isolates the effect on cost of buying the material used at more or less than the standard price while the usage variance shows how much cost has changed because more or less material has been used than was planned. They are computed as follows.

Price variance

This is calculated by the formula: Actual price of actual material used minus standard price of actual material used, i.e.:

£14,950 − £13,800 (i.e. 23,000 kg × 60p) = £1,150

As actual cost exceeds standard cost the variance is adverse (ADV).
Alternatively: (Actual price minus standard price) times actual quantity, i.e.:

(65p − 60p) × 23,000 kg = £1,150

The adverse variance may be outside the control of the purchasing department, since market prices may have moved against them or the material specification may have changed to a requirement for a more expensive substitute material.

Usage variance

The formula for this variance is: Standard cost of actual material used minus standard cost of standard material used, i.e.:

£13,800 − £13,200 (i.e. 11,000 × 2 kg at 60p) = £600 (ADV)

Alternatively: (Standard quantity minus actual quantity) times standard price.
The extra material used is priced at standard cost when this variance is computed, since the price variance has already been extracted.
Higher volumes of scrap from low grade materials or wastage by less experienced labour can increase usage. The variance may not therefore always be the responsibility of the production manager.

The total material variance is therefore £1,750 (adverse).

Labour cost variances

The basic variances are the rate of pay, idle time and efficiency variances. The rate of pay variance (similar to the material price variance) shows the difference between actual and standard cost that has arisen because labour has been paid at rates other than standard, while the idle time variance reveals the standard cost of labour time wasted through production stoppages. Note that an allowance for 'normal' idle time has been built into the standard time for the job, so this variance shows the cost of abnormal idle time. The efficiency variance sets the actual hours worked against the standard hours equivalent to actual production, to test the efficiency of the labour force. The variances are computed as follows.

Rate of pay variance

Apply the formula: Hours paid for at the actual rate minus hours paid at the standard rate, i.e.:

£121,800 − £116,000 (i.e. 29,000 × £4 per hour) = £5,800 (ADV)

Alternatively: (Standard rate minus actual rate) times actual hours.

Non-standard wage rates, overtime or high grade labour may have contributed to this adverse variance.

Having isolated rate differences, all further variances can be calculated at standard labour rate.

Idle time variance

The formula for this variance is: Hours paid for at standard rate minus hours worked at standard rate, i.e.:

£116,000 (i.e. 29,000 × £4) − £112,000 (i.e. 28,000 × £4) = £4,000 (ADV)

One thousand hours of abnormal idle time reduces hours paid to hours worked.

This variance is almost always adverse, and reflects managerial inefficiency in respect of the causes of idle time such as machine breakdown, material stock-out or poor supervision.

Efficiency variance

The formula is: Hours worked times standard rate minus standard hours for actual production times standard rate, i.e.:

£112,000 − £110,000 (i.e. 11,000 chairs × 2.5 hours at £4) = £2,000 (ADV)

This variance sets the time actually taken to do the job against the time which should have been taken at normal efficiency levels and thus comments on the efficiency of labour.

The total labour variance is therefore £11,800 (adverse).

Variances of overheads

Variable overhead expenses vary in direct proportion to production. Any difference between actual and standard cost is usually attributed to an expenditure variance, simply pointing out that more has been spent in this part of the cost structure than was planned. If a significant cost difference is revealed, further analysis into the price and usage elements of the expenditure variance can be made:

Expenditure variance

Apply the formula: Actual expenses minus standard cost for actual production, i.e.:

£15,400 − £11,000 (i.e. 11,000 chairs × £1) = £4,400 (ADV)

Fixed overhead expenses are charged out to production at predetermined rates. Any alteration of the conditions assumed to operate when the rates were computed can lead to amounts of fixed overhead expense over- or under-absorbed. The basic variances (expenditure, capacity, idle time and efficiency) are designed to show why over- or under-absorption has taken place.

They are calculated as follows:

Expenditure variance

Applying the formula: Actual expense minus budgeted expense, gives:

£16,000 − £15,000 = £1,000 (ADV)

This variance shows that actual expenditure exceeds the budget.

Capacity variance

This is calculated by the formula: Planned capacity times rate minus actual capacity times rate, i.e.:

£15,000 (i.e. 30,000 × 50p) − £14,500 (i.e. 29,000 hours paid × 50p) = £500 (ADV)

This variance shows the amount of budgeted fixed overheads not charged out to production because the planned capacity usage was not attained.

Idle time variance

The formula is: Actual capacity used times rate minus actual capacity used productively times rate, i.e.:

£14,500 − £14,000 (i.e. 28,000 hours worked × 50p) = £500 (ADV)

This variance shows the amount of fixed overheads not charged out to production because although the capacity was used it was not productive. Time has been wasted through abnormal idle time, during which time no chairs have been produced to which fixed overhead expenses can be charged.

Efficiency variance

The formula for this variance is: Hours worked times rate minus standard hours for actual production times rate i.e.:

£14,000 − £13,750 (i.e. 11,000 chairs × 2.5 hours at 50p) = £250 (ADV)

The efficiency variance shows the amount of fixed overhead that could not be charged to production because actual production was less than the amount which should have been produced in the hours worked, i.e. inefficiency. In 28,000 hours 11,200 chairs should have been produced, to allow £14,000 to be charged from the fixed overheads control account to the work-in-progress (at £1.25 per chair) control account. Note that a favourable efficiency variance of 1,000 hours would cancel out the adverse idle time variance, if the 11,000 chairs had been produced in 26,500 hours.

If production amounts to only 11,000 chairs, the charge to work-in-progress will be £13,750, leaving £250 of expenses unabsorbed, to be debited to the profit and loss account as an adverse variance.

The total fixed overhead variance is therefore £2,250 (adverse).

Reconciliation of actual to standard cost

	£	£	£
Actual cost incurred			168,150
Variances:	*Favourable*	*Adverse*	
Material – Price	–	1,150	
– Usage	–	600	
Labour – Rate of pay	–	5,800	
– Idle time	–	4,000	
– Efficiency	–	2,000	
Variable overheads – Expenditure	–	4,400	
Fixed overheads – Expenditure	–	1,000	
– Capacity	–	500	
– Idle time	–	500	
– Efficiency	–	250	
Less adverse variances			20,200
Standard cost for actual production (11,000 chairs × £13.45)			147,950

STANDARD COST BOOKKEEPING

The circumstances in the example in the previous section can be expressed as a set of double entry ledger accounts.

Material cost control

	£		£
Cash (actual cost)	14,950	Price variance	1,150
		Usage variance	600
		Work-in-progress	13,200
	14,950		14,950

Labour cost control

	£		£
Cash (actual cost)	121,800	Rate of pay variance	5,800
		Idle time variance	4,000
		Efficiency variance	2,000
		Work-in-progress	110,000
	121,800		121,800

Variable overhead control

	£		£
Cash (actual cost)	15,400	Expenditure variance	4,400
		Work-in-progress	11,000
	15,400		15,400

Fixed overhead control

	£		£
Cash (actual cost)	16,000	Expenditure variance	1,000
		Capacity variance	500
		Idle time variance	500
		Efficiency variance	250
		Work-in-progress	13,750
	16,000		16,000

Work-in-progress control

	£		£
Material	13,200	Standard cost of production	
Labour	110,000	Transferred to finished	
Variable overhead	11,000	goods store	147,950
Fixed overhead	13,750		
	147,950		147,950

Material price variance

	£		£
Material cost control	1,150	Costing profit and loss	1,150

Material usage variance

	£		£
Material cost control	600	Costing profit and loss	600

Labour rate of pay variance

	£		£
Labour cost control	5,800	Costing profit and loss	5,800

Labour idle time variance

	£		£
Labour cost control	4,000	Costing profit and loss	4,000

Labour efficiency variance

	£		£
Labour cost control	2,000	Costing profit and loss	2,000

Other variance accounts would be maintained for fixed and variable overheads.

Notes
1. The standard cost of actual production is compiled in the work-in-progress control account. Stocks if any are carried forward at standard cost.
2. Variances are posted to separate accounts and written off to costing profit and loss accounts at the end of the period.
3. Entries for favourable variances would be debited to the appropriate cost control account and credited to a variance account, and from there credited to the costing profit and loss account.

SOME RATIOS DERIVED FROM STANDARD COSTING

The standard hour is the quantity of output or amount of work that should be achieved in one hour at standard performance. This measure can be used to express certain ratios which are derived from a standard costing system, in an attempt to gain an insight into the current situation in a business. The ratios concerned are the activity ratio, the efficiency ratio and the capacity ratio.

Activity ratio

The activity ratio compares the number of standard hours equivalent to actual production with the standard hours equivalent to budgeted production. It is usually expressed as a percentage, and in formula terms:

$$\frac{\text{Standard hours for actual production}}{\text{Standard hours for budgeted production}} \times \frac{100}{1}$$

This formula is similar to that given in Example 13.2, covering flexible budgeting. The CIMA terminology prefers the term production volume ratio for this relationship which measures the volume of output with budget.

Using the figures from the Chiltern Chairs example above, the company budgeted to produce at full capacity 12,000 chairs, which was equivalent to 30,000 hours of work. In fact it produced 11,000 chairs, equivalent to 27,500 standard hours at a standard time of 2.5 hours per chair. The activity ratio can be computed as:

$$\frac{2.5 \text{ hours} \times 11,000 \text{ chairs}}{2.5 \text{ hours} \times 12,000 \text{ chairs}} = \frac{27,500}{30,000} \times \frac{100}{1} = 91.67\%$$

This ratio is aptly named since it comments on the activity of the management by showing how much of their budget they have achieved. In this case 8.33 per cent of budgeted production has been lost.

Efficiency ratio

The efficiency ratio compares the number of standard hours equivalent to actual production with the actual hours spent in achieving that production. The ratio can be expressed as a percentage, and the appropriate formula is:

$$\frac{\text{Standard hours for actual production}}{\text{Actual hours worked}} \times \frac{100}{1}$$

Using the figures in the Chiltern example:

$$\frac{27,500 \text{ hours}}{28,000 \text{ hours}} \times \frac{100}{1} = 98.2\%$$

This ratio demonstrates efficiency, because it sets the time that should have been taken against the time actually worked to achieve actual production. As computed above, the ratio comments on the efficiency of the labour force: they are 98.2 per cent efficient since they have taken 28,000 hours to produce work which is equivalent to 27,500 hours at standard efficiency.

Alternatively, the actual hours worked may include the abnormal idle time, in which case the comment implied by the efficiency ratio is extended to cover management as well as labour efficiency, since it sets standard hours for actual production against the hours paid for by the firm for that production. There is of course the danger when combining two elements (labour and management) in one ratio that the movement of one element may compensate for a movement by the other, i.e. labour efficiency can make up for abnormal idle time.

Capacity ratio

The capacity ratio compares the actual hours worked with the standard hours for budgeted production, and can be expressed as a percentage by the use of the formula:

$$\frac{\text{Actual hours worked}}{\text{Standard hours worked for budgeted production}} \times \frac{100}{1}$$

Using the figures in the Chiltern example:

$$\frac{28,000 \text{ hours}}{30,000 \text{ hours}} \times \frac{100}{1} = 93.33\%$$

This ratio identifies the use actually made of the standard hours available, to meet the budgeted production target (capacity). In this example 6.66 per cent of budgeted production has been lost through unused capacity and 1.8 per cent has been lost through inefficiency. In this way the 8.33 per cent of lost activity can be set down to efficiency or capacity reasons. Efficiency times capacity equals activity:

$$98.2\% \times 93.3\% = 91.6\%$$

Abnormal idle time may be included in the capacity ratio or the efficiency ratio according to whether comment is required on labour efficiency, and managerial efficiency is considered to be measured by the level of idle time and the amount of unused capacity. If idle time is excluded from hours worked, the ratio comments only on capacity unused and does not cover capacity which stood idle while management were attempting to use it.

An alternative formula for the capacity ratio relates the budgeted working hours to the maximum working hours available in a period. This calculation highlights the use which the management plan to make of the total capacity available in the forthcoming period.

THE PRODUCTION VARIANCES INTERRELATED

Some students consider that standard costing variances are in separate compartments, i.e. materials, labour and overheads. This view is derived from the way in which they are taught to calculate them. In effect all the variances comment on a single entity – the firm – and stem from the budget, which co-ordinates all aspects of the firm. There must therefore be some interconnection or relationship between the variances. Materials, labour and overhead variances may affect one another, or alternatively the price and quantity elements of each may be related. Some of the more obvious relationships are listed below.

1. The labour rate and labour efficiency variances: a favourable rate of pay variance means that each unit of labour has cost less, which in turn may mean that a lower grade of labour has been recruited for the task in hand. Although lower grade labour costs less, it may take longer to complete the work than more expensive labour. Accordingly an adverse labour efficiency variance will be experienced.
2. The material price and usage variances: the purchase of cheap or inferior material may show up a favourable price variance, which prima facie suggests that the purchasing department is efficient. However, the use of inferior material in the factory may cause increased spoilage, and an adverse usage variance. The existence of spoilt work may mean that production time is wasted, as semi-finished products are scrapped or rectified. This will have an impact on the labour and overhead efficiency variances.
3. The labour rate variance and material usage variance: the employment of lower grade labour will generate a favourable labour rate variance, but the use of such labour could lead to an adverse material usage variance, when inexperienced or inefficient workers spoil production, and generate waste.
4. The labour rate variance and fixed overhead efficiency variance: the

employment of labour at a lower grade than that budgeted for the work will produce a favourable rate of pay variance, but may also mean that work takes longer to complete. Accordingly, in a given period there will be less production against which fixed overhead expenses can be charged, and an adverse overhead efficiency variance will reflect this circumstance. The idle time and efficiency variances for both labour and fixed overhead costs are computed on the basis of hours worked, hours idle and standard hours for actual production. A favourable labour efficiency variance will be reflected in a favourable fixed overhead efficiency variance.

5. Labour rates and idle time: if lower grade labour is employed with its consequent favourable rate of pay variance, the unskilled workers may misuse machinery and cause breakdowns. This type of disruption to production will in turn produce adverse idle time variances for both labour and fixed overheads.

6. Just as a favourable rate of pay variance may produce an adverse effect on materials and overheads variances, the opposite situation is equally true: an adverse rate of pay variance, which reflects the employment of labour of a better class, will have a favourable effect on material usage by reducing spoilage, on labour idle time and efficiency, and on fixed overhead idle time and efficiency variances. An adverse labour mixture variance, caused by the use of a larger proportion of good grade labour, will have the same beneficial effect.

7. There may be compensating effects within the labour rate variance, in that an adverse element caused by an increase in rates of pay could be compensated by a reduction in the amount of overtime worked, which will reduce the average price of labour per hour over the total hours worked. It is possible to have a rate of pay variance without a change of rates, if more overtime at say time and a half is worked.

8. A recent question included a strike variance. When a strike takes place a number of hours are lost to production but labour on strike is not paid. Thus the lost hours are not reflected in a labour variance, but if the fixed overheads absorption rate is computed on the basis of hours of capacity intended to be used, the hours lost by a strike will be similar to idle time, and fixed overheads not absorbed to production during the strike will show up as a variance.

THE SALES VARIANCES

These variances seek to explain to management the difference between standard (planned) sales and actual sales. They can be computed in terms of sales revenue but are normally calculated in terms of profit (sales margin). The production variances are computed in terms of cost, so that an adverse cost variance occurs when actual cost is greater than standard. An adverse sales variance occurs, however, when actual performance is less than standard. Variances in terms of turnover, or even in terms of units sold, may perhaps be more suitable for lower levels of sales management.

There are three main sales variances: the price variance, the quantity variance and the sales mixture variance. With sales variances, profit or turnover will differ from standard for two main reasons: variations in the selling price; and variations in the volume sold. The price variance shows the effect on profit or turnover if sales have been made at prices other than the standard price, while the volume variances can be subdivided to show the effect on profit or turnover of a different quantity sold from that specified in the standard. The mixture variance will arise only if a company sells more than one product. When it is computed for a range of products this variance reveals the extent to which sales of individual products are failing to meet budgeted targets. This information will prove useful when a decision is made as to how to allocate funds within the advertising budget. If the mixture of products sold differs from the mixture planned in the budget, it will have an effect on profit, e.g. if more goods with a large profit margin are sold to compensate for reduced sales of those products with a small profit margin.

Example 16.1

A medium-sized company in the motor trade manufactures components for larger companies. Sales for the three major products for the forthcoming month are budgeted as follows:

Product	Price £	Cost £	Profit margin £	Quantity	Budgeted profit £	Budgeted turnover £
Dashboard instruments	30	16	14	3,000	42,000	90,000
Tyres	10	9	1	7,000	7,000	70,000
Batteries	20	18	2	2,000	4,000	40,000
				12,000	53,000	200,000

The actual results for the month are set out below:

Product	Unit sales	Profit margin £	Profit £	Turnover £
Dashboard instruments	2,200	15 (31 – 16)	33,000	68,200
Tyres	10,400	1 (10 – 9)	10,400	104,000
Batteries	2,200	4 (22 – 18)	8,800	48,400
	14,800		52,200	220,600

The fact that profit has fallen slightly while turnover has increased by over 10 per cent is certain to precipitate an investigation into the situation. The variances are computed as follows.

The price variance

The price variance identifies the effect on profit of making sales at prices which differ from the standard prices used to compute the budget. The cost of products is at standard, so an increase in selling price will result in an increase in profit, and a decrease in selling price will have the opposite effect. In simple formula terms the variance is computed as: actual quantity sold at actual profit margin per

product minus the actual quantity sold at standard profit margin per product.
An alternative calculation is:

Actual quantity × (actual price – standard price)

This calculation assumes that costs are at standard, so any change in selling price will have a direct effect on profit.

Product	Actual quantity at actual profit margin £	Actual quantity at standard profit margin £	Price variance £
Dashboard instruments	33,000	30,800 (2,000 × 14)	2,200 (F)
Tyres	10,400	10,400 (10,400 × 1)	–
Batteries	8,800	4,400 (2,200 × 2)	4,400 (F)
	52,200	45,600	6,600 (F)

Alternatively, since cost is taken to be standard, the change in price will have a direct effect on profit and the formula actual quantity × (Actual price – Standard price) can be used:

Product	Actual quantity	Actual price £	Standard price £	Price variance £
Dashboard instruments	2,200	31	30	2,200 (F)
Tyres	10,400	10	10	–
Batteries	2,200	22	20	4,400 (F)
				6,600 (F)

The volume or quantity variance

Once the effect of the price variance has been eliminated, any further difference between standard and actual profit must be the result of a different volume of sales. This volume variance can be analysed into sub-variances, the quantity variance and the mixture variance. A mixture variance will be derived only if more than one product is sold. The volume or quantity variance for single products expresses the change in profit earned because more or less units were sold than the quantities planned to be sold in the budget.

	Actual quantity	Standard quantity	Difference	Standard margin £	Volume variance £
Dashboard instruments	2,200	3,000	– 800	14	(11,200) (A)
Tyres	10,400	7,000	+ 3,400	1	3,400 (F)
Batteries	2,200	2,000	+ 200	2	400 (F)
					(7,400) (A)

The volume variance for each product is as shown above, totalling £7,400 adverse. The total sales variance is calculated as actual profit of £52,200 less expected profit on budgeted sales, £53,000, i.e. adverse £800.

The favourable price variance of £6,600 compensates for part of the adverse volume variance of £7,400, to explain the total adverse sales variance of £800.

There is, however, a *mixture variance* element in these figures because sales of high-profit dashboard instruments have not achieved the budgeted volume, whereas the low-profit-margin tyres and batteries have exceeded budgeted sales. Although aggregate turnover has increased, a less profitable mixture of products has been sold, so that instead of a favourable quantity variance overall, the adverse margin variance for dashboard instruments sales lost is not compensated by the profit margin on the extra tyres and batteries sold.

The company planned to sell 12,000 products in the ratio: dashboard instruments 3,000, tyres 7,000 and batteries 2,000. If the standard mixture had been sold the standard proportion for actual sales of 14,800 units would be:

Dashboard instruments 3,000/12,000 × 14,800 = 3,700
Tyres   7,000/12,000 × 14,800 = 8,633
Batteries   2,000/12,000 × 14,800 = 2,467

The mixture variance is computed by deducting the standard proportion for actual sales from the actual mixture sold, and multiplying the difference by the standard profit margin for each item in the mixture.

Product	Actual mixture	Standard mixture for actual sales	Difference	Standard profit margin £	Variance £	
Dashboard instruments	2,200	3,700	− 1,500	14	− 21,000	(A)
Tyres	10,400	8,633	+ 1,767	1	+ 1,767	(F)
Batteries	2,200	2,467	− 267	2	− 534	(A)
	14,800	14,800			19,767	(A)

The *quantity variance* is calculated by computing the average standard profit margin and multiplying it by the number of products sold in excess of the standard. In the budget 12,000 items sold were planned to produce a profit of £53,000, an average of £4.416 for each product. Actual sales exceeded the budget by 2,800 units. If sales had increased in proportion to the mixture specified in the budget, 2,800 extra profit margins of £4.416 would give a favourable variance of £12,367. The favourable quantity variance of £12,367 when set against the adverse mixture variance of £19,767 gives an overall volume variance of £7,400 adverse, as shown above.

Reconciliation

A reconciliation of these calculations is:

	Dashboard instruments	Tyres	Batteries	£		£
Standard profit						53,000
Price variance	2,200	–	4,400	6,600	(F)	
Mixture variance	(21,000)	1,767	(534)	(19,767)	(A)	
Quantity variance	–	–	–	12,367	(F)	800 (A)
Actual profit						52,200

Note: A small total variance of £800 conceals large detailed variances, disclosed by further analysis.

THE MORE ADVANCED PRODUCTION VARIANCES

Students usually experience difficulty in understanding the mixture variances.

Material mixture variance

This variance can be computed as an extension of the usage variance. Where two or more materials are combined in the production process, there will be a planned or standard formula for the mixture. If the proportions of the different materials used in production are changed an increase or decrease in cost may be experienced, and it is to identify this cost difference that the materials mixture variance is computed. If, for example, a higher proportion of the more expensive ingredient and a lower proportion of a less expensive ingredient are used, a more expensive combination than the standard will have been used, with a consequent rise in the total cost above the budget level computed on the basis of the standard mixture. Indeed, in certain circumstances the material buying price and the total quantity of material used may not change, but an increase of total cost will be experienced because a different mixture of materials has been used.

In simple formula terms, the standard cost of the standard mixture for the actual quantity produced is subtracted from the standard cost of the actual mixture for the actual quantity produced, to calculate the variance.

Example 16.2

Suppose a factory making canned petfood uses two basic materials; A, a protein costing £40 per tonne; and B, a carbohydrate costing £20 per tonne. The standard mixture specifies 50 per cent protein, while in fact the current week's production of 100 tonnes includes only 45 per cent protein.

The mixture variance is computed as follows:

Material	Standard mixture for actual quantity	Standard cost per tonne	Standard cost of standard mixture for actual quantity	Actual mix for actual quantity	Standard cost of actual mix
A	50 tonnes	£40	£2,000	45 tonnes	£1,800
B	50 tonnes	£20	£1,000	55 tonnes	£1,100
	100 tonnes		£3,000*	100 tonnes	£2,900*

* thus there is a favourable materials mixture variance of £100.

The materials mixture variance is rarely found in such simple circumstances. It is in fact a sub-variance of the usage variance. This means that where materials are combined in production, the usage variance can be subdivided to reveal the cost difference caused by the use of a mixture other than the standard mixture, and the cost difference caused because more or less material than standard has been used.

Example 16.3

Suppose three materials, X, Y and Z, are used in the proportions 50:40:10 to manufacture a plastic. The materials cost 50p, 25p and 20p per kg respectively. Budgeted production for the week is 1,000 kg, but both the production and the mixture vary.

The standard cost of producing 1,000 kg is compared with actual production below:

	Standard cost		Actual quantities at standard cost		Total usage variance
X	500 kg × 50p	= £250	600 kg × 50p	= £300	£50 (A)
Y	400 kg × 25p	= £100	360 kg × 25p	= £90	£10 (F)
Z	100 kg × 20p	= £20	80 kg × 20p	= £16	£4 (F)
	1,000 kg	£370	1,040 kg	£406	£36 (A)

The difference of £36 is called a usage variance, but it can be subdivided to show its mixture and usage elements. The mixture variance shows the cost difference caused by the actual proportion differing from the standard proportion in which materials are used. The standard proportion for the actual usage is:

$$X: \frac{500}{1,000} \times 1,040 = 520 \text{ kg} \times 50p = £260.00$$

$$Y: \frac{400}{1,000} \times 1,040 = 416 \text{ kg} \times 25p = £104.00$$

$$Z: \frac{100}{1,000} \times 1,040 = 104 \text{ kg} \times 20p = £20.80$$

Thus, the materials mixture variance is:

	Actual proportion	minus	Standard proportion	×	Price	=	Variance	
X	600 kg	minus	520 kg	×	50p	=	£40.00	(A)
Y	360 kg	minus	416 kg	×	25p	=	£14.00	(F)
Z	80 kg	minus	104 kg	×	20p	=	£4.80	(F)
							£21.20	

Adverse variances occur where actual cost is greater than standard. The difference between the total usage variance and the mixture variance for each material must be caused by excess usage.

Material	Total usage variance £		Material mixture variance £		Usage sub-variance £	
X	50	(A)	40.00	(A)	10.00	(A)
Y	10	(F)	14.00	(F)	4.00	(A)
Z	4	(F)	4.80	(F)	0.80	(A)
	36	(A)	21.20	(A)	14.80	(A)

Materials yield variance

This variance also stems from the usage variance. In some processes materials used are subject to a certain level of wastage in the process, which is accepted by management. The process is said to yield so much good production for every unit of material put into it; the yield usually being expressed as a percentage. Thus it is possible using this percentage to calculate the accepted or standard yield for any given input. If this amount is compared to the actual yield from the process, the difference multiplied by the standard price will be the yield variance.

Example 16.4

Taking the figures for petfoods in Example 16.2, suppose that a 5 per cent loss of all material put into the process is normal, a standard yield of 95 per cent of all material used therefore being expected. Thus, if 100 tonnes of material is used an output of 95 tonnes at a cost of £31.58 (£3,000 ÷ 95) per tonne will be expected – the normal loss being absorbed into the cost of good production. If the actual output is more or less than this standard, a yield variance can be computed by multiplying the difference between standard yield and actual yield by £31.58.

Labour mixture variance

Where different grades of labour paid at different rates are employed on a job, or as a team, a mixture variance can arise. As with the materials mixture variance there will be a standard combination for the various grades of labour, which sets the standard cost per hour of the job. If the grades are employed in a combination that differs from the standard combination, actual cost will differ from the standard; for example, an increased proportion of skilled men and consequently less unskilled men employed in a department may increase efficiency, and increase labour cost.

Example 16.5

The XYZ company employs skilled operatives at £5 per hour in department A. These skilled employees work together in pairs, but each pair has the assistance of one labourer who is paid £3 per hour. The labour force for department A normally comprises twenty skilled employees and ten labourers. Because of illness five labourers were absent for an entire week, and their work was done by apprentices drafted into the department from other parts of the factory. The apprentices were paid £2 per hour. Department A works a forty-hour week.

Labour grade	Standard team	Hourly rate	Standard cost per hour	Actual team	Actual cost per hour
Skilled operatives	2	£5	£10	2	£10
Labourers	1	£3	£3	–	–
Apprentices	–	£2	–	1	£2
			£13		£12

The mixture variance per team is therefore a favourable one of £1 per hour, or £40 for a forty-hour week. As five teams are disrupted by the illness, the total mixture variance will be £200 per week. In formula terms the variance is computed as: (Standard cost per hour of the actual team − Standard cost per hour of the standard team) × Standard hours equivalent to actual production.

MULTIPLE CHOICE QUESTIONS

Note that these questions relate to the whole of Part V (Chapters 15 and 16) of the book.

The following information relates to production for the month, in spreadsheet form.

		Budget (A)	Actual (B)
1.	Units produced	20,000	23,000
		£	£
2.	Direct material cost	60,000	63,000
3.	Direct labour cost	48,000	51,000
4.	Variable overhead cost	24,000	26,000
5.	Fixed overhead cost	20,000	21,000

16.1 The formula to calculate the direct material total variance is:
    (a) A2 − B2
    (b) ([B2 ÷ B1] × A1) − A2
    (c) ([A1 ÷ A2] × B1) − B2
    (d) ([A2 ÷ A1] × B1) − B2

(a)   (b)   (c)   (d)

16.2 The formula to calculate direct labour total variance is:
    (a) (B3 × [A3 ÷ A1]) − A3
    (b) [(B3 ÷ B1) × A1] − A3
    (c) [(A3 ÷ A1) × B1] − B3
    (d) A3 − [B3 × (A1 ÷ B1)]

(a)   (b)   (c)   (d)

16.3 The formula to calculate the total overhead variance is:
    (a) (A4 + A5) − (B4 + B5)
    (b) [A4 × (B1 ÷ A1) + A5] − (B4 + B5)
    (c) [B4 × (A1 ÷ B1) + B5] − (A4 + A5)
    (d) [A4 × (B1 ÷ A1)] + B5 − (B4 + B5)

(a)   (b)   (c)   (d)

16.4   Which of the following quotations defines a standard cost?
    (a)   A predetermined measurable quantity set in defined conditions against which actual performance can be compared.
    (b)   A technique which uses standards for costs and revenues for the purpose of control.
    (c)   A predetermined calculation of how much costs should be under specified working conditions.
    (d)   A cost which a budget centre is expected to incur in a control period.

(a)   (b)   (c)   (d)

16.5   'A standard which can be attained under the most favourable conditions.' This quotation defines which of the following?
    (a)   Attainable standard.
    (b)   Current standard.
    (c)   Basic standard.
    (d)   Ideal standard.

(a)   (b)   (c)   (d)

16.6   For fixed factory overheads, which variance explains the situation when the amount absorbed by production does not coincide with the budget since although the capacity was used it was not productive?
    (a)   Expenditure variance.
    (b)   Capacity variance.
    (c)   Idle time variance.
    (d)   Efficiency variance.

(a)   (b)   (c)   (d)

16.7   The budget for the month plans to produce 3,000 toasters, with a standard time of 4.5 hours each. Hours worked were 15,000, and 3,200 toasters were produced. Calculate the efficiency ratio:
    (a)   106.6 per cent.
    (b)   111.1 per cent.
    (c)   96 per cent.
    (d)   104.16 per cent.

(a)   (b)   (c)   (d)

16.8 From the facts in 16.7, calculate the capacity ratio:
   (a) 90 per cent.
   (b) 111.1 per cent.
   (c) 96 per cent.
   (d) 106.6 per cent.

(a)   (b)   (c)   (d)

16.9 (1) 'An adverse materials usage variance can be caused by the employment
   of unskilled labour.' (2) 'A favourable labour efficiency variance can be
   caused by the purchase of cheap materials.' True or false?
   (a) Both false.
   (b) (1) true; (2) false.
   (c) (1) false; (2) true.
   (d) Both true.

(a)   (b)   (c)   (d)

16.10 An adverse sales margin variance can be caused by:
   (a) Increasing material costs.
   (b) Departure from the standard mixture of products sold.
   (c) A reduction in selling price.
   (d) An increase in prices.

(a + b)   (b + d)   (c + d)   (b + c)

EXERCISES

16A A company produces a product which has a standard variable production
cost of £8 per unit made up as follows:

	£/unit	
Direct materials	4.60	(2 kg × £2.30/kg)
Direct labour	2.10	(0.7 hours × 3.00/hour)
Variable overhead	1.30	

   Fixed manufacturing costs are treated as period costs. The following
information is available for the period just ended:

Variable manufacturing cost of sales (at standard cost)	£263,520
Opening stock of finished goods (at standard cost)	£120,800
Closing stock of finished goods (at standard cost)	£146,080
Direct material price variance	£2,571 unfavourable
Raw materials used in manufacture (at actual cost)	£170,310
Direct labour rate variance	£4,760 unfavourable
Direct labour efficiency variance	£3,240 favourable

Required

(a)   Determine for the period just ended:
  (i) the number of units produced,
  (ii) the raw material usage variance,
  (iii) the total actual direct labour cost, and
  (iv) the actual cost per kg of raw material used.
(b)   Outline the possible causes of the raw material variances.

(Association of Certified Accountants)

Note: The term 'unfavourable' can be applied to variances, instead of the more usually adopted term 'adverse'.

16B   A company had a budget of 200,000 direct labour hours for a period. This was used as the basis for establishing standard factory overhead absorption rates. Fixed factory overhead was budgeted to be £400,000, and variable factory overhead £200,000. Output was budgeted at 400,000 units. In the period 420,000 units were completed in 202,000 direct labour hours, at a labour cost of £787,800. No labour rate variance occurred. The factory overhead incurred during the period was £620,000.

Required

(a)   Calculate the following variances:
  (i) labour efficiency,
  (ii) overhead expenditure,
  (iii) fixed overhead volume,
  (iv) variable overhead efficiency.
(b)   Explain the meaning and significance of the fixed overhead volume variance. How may the fixed overhead volume variance be further analysed?
(c)   (i) Calculate the efficiency ratio in the situation outlined above.
  (ii) What are the implications for both unit costs and profit of such efficiency?

To answer part (c) (ii) you must assume, also, that a bonus scheme is in operation, and that this is related to the level of efficiency.

(Association of Certified Accountants)

16C   In relation to budgetary control you are required to explain and provide your own examples to illustrate each of the following:
(a)   standard hour;
(b)   efficiency (productivity) ratio;
(c)   capacity usage ratio;
(d)   production volume ratio.

16D   Chiltern Chairs plc operates a furniture factory in the home counties. The most recent product to be added to the range is a pine corner cabinet. The standard cost specification for each cabinet contains the following information.

	£
Materials – pine: 6 kg at £2.80 a kg	16.80
– varnish: half a litre at £3 a litre	1.50
Labour – 8 hours at £6 per hour	48.00

During the month of April 620 cabinets were made. Actual costs were:

Pine   – 4,500 kg: £11,250
Varnish – 290 litres: £1,015
Labour – 5,200 hours: £36,400

Abnormal idle time was 400 hours. Hours worked recorded as 4,800 hours.

Required

(a) Calculate materials price and usage variance for both materials.
(b) Calculate labour rate of pay, efficiency and idle time variances.
(c) Suggest possible causes for the pine materials variances.

16E   Shown below is an extract from the April budget for the weaving shed of Textrex Ltd, a canvas manufacturer.

Canvas grade	Economy	Super
Production quantities (standard width)	40,000	32,000
	metres	metres
	per metre	per metre
Standard prime cost:		
Direct materials Yarn A (£3 per kg)	0.2 kg	0.2 kg
Yarn B (£4 per kg)	0.2 kg	0.3 kg
Direct labour (£2 per hour)	12 mins	15 mins

Department overheads	Variable		Fixed	
		£		£
	Power	8,000	Supervision	6,400
	Indirect labour	9,600	Heat and light	2,500
			Depreciation	6,300
	Maintenance	6,400	Rent	4,800
		24,000		20,000

Production overhead is absorbed on the basis of standard hours produced, and it should be assumed that variable overheads do vary directly with this measure of production.

During April the following actual results were achieved:

Production 35,000 metres of Economy: 34,000 metres of Super
Direct materials consumed   Yarn A   13,000 kg, cost £40,500
                             Yarn B   19,000 kg, cost £72,000
Direct labour 15,800 hours worked, cost £30,500.

Department overheads	Variable		Fixed	
		£		£
	Power	8,250	Supervision	6,950
	Indirect labour	9,000	Heat and light	2,900
			Depreciation	6,200
	Maintenance	7,500	Rent	5,000
		24,750		21,050

Required

Produce a working paper calculating and analysing the variances which you consider should be incorporated into the weaving shed's operating statement for April.

(Association of Certified Accountants)

16F   Shown below is the standard prime cost of a tube of industrial adhesive, which is the only product manufactured in one department of Gum plc.

	Industrial adhesive	
	£ per tube	£ per tube
Materials: Powder	1.50	
Chemicals	0.60	
Tube	0.30	2.40
Labour – mixing and pouring		1.80
Total standard prime cost		4.20

The standard material allowance for each tube of adhesive is 2 kg of powder, $\frac{1}{4}$ litre of chemical and one tube. The standard wage rate for mixing and pouring is £4.50 per hour.

During the previous month 4,500 tubes of adhesive were produced, there were no work-in-progress stocks at the beginning or end of the month, and the receipts and issues of materials during the month are shown below:

	Powder	Chemicals	Tubes
Opening stock	1,500 kg	200 litres	100 tubes
Purchases:	10,000 kg	600 litres at	200 tubes at
	at 70p per kg	£2.30 per litre	40p each
		600 litres at	5,000 tubes
		£2.50 per litre	at 30p each
Issues:	9,800 kg	1,050	4,520 tubes

The above materials are used exclusively in the production of the adhesive and it is the policy of the company to calculate any price variance when the materials are purchased.

The direct employees operating the mixing and pouring plant worked a total of 2,050 hours during the previous month and earned gross wages of £8,910.

Required

(a)   Calculate for the previous month the following variances from standard cost:

Materials price variance, analysed as you consider appropriate.

Materials usage variance, analysed as you consider appropriate.

Direct labour efficiency variance.

Direct wages rate variance.

(b)   Discuss the possible causes of the material variances and the direct labour efficiency variance.

(Based on a question from the Association of Certified Accountants)

16G The finishing department of a company manufacturing two different products employs sixty direct operatives working a basic forty hour week. The company operates a standard costing system and the finishing department's standard direct labour cost for each of the two products is, product X £12 per unit and product Y £2 per unit. The standard wage rate for the operatives in the finishing department is £4 per hour and the company offers a guaranteed wage of £160 per week for each direct operative. Overtime premium, which is not included in standard product costs, is paid at time rate plus one third.

The following results occurred in the finishing department during the previous two months:

	Month I	Month 2
Output Product X	2,200 units	2,300 units
Product Y	5,250 units	4,700 units
Gross wages paid to direct operatives	£44,800	£39,600
Productive hours worked by direct operatives	10,800 hours	9,000 hours
Number of hours for which direct		
operatives were paid: Ordinary time	9,600 hours	9,600 hours
Overtime	1,200	NIL

In the second month all sixty direct operatives were standing idle for ten hours as a result of equipment breakdowns.

Required

(a) Calculate the finishing department's productivity (or efficiency) ratio for month 1.
(b) Calculate the efficiency variances, together with any other variances from standard labour cost, which occurred in the finishing department during each of the previous two months.
(c) Write up the entries for the first month's wages in the finishing department's wages control account and work-in-progress control account, including the entries for the appropriate variances calculated in (b) above.
(d) Consider whether the efficiency variances which you have calculated are likely to measure the net effect on the company's profit of direct operatives being more or less efficient than that specified by the standard.

(Association of Certified Accountants)

16H A manufacturing company has the following budgeted costs for one month which are based on a normal capacity level of 40,000 hours. A departmental overhead absorption rate of £4.40 per hour has been calculated, as follows:

Overhead item	Fixed	Variable per hour
	£000	£
Management and supervision	30	–
Shift premium	–	0.10
National insurance and pension costs	6	0.22
Inspection	20	0.25
Consumable supplies	6	0.18

Power for machinery	–	0.20
Lighting and heating	4	–
Rates	9	–
Repairs and maintenance	8	0.15
Materials handling	10	0.30
Depreciation of machinery	15	–
Production administration	12	–
	120	
Overhead rate per hour: variable		1.40
fixed		3.00
total		4.40

During the month of April, the company actually worked 36,000 hours producing 36,000 standard hours of production and incurred the following overhead costs:

	£000
Management and supervision	30.0
Shift premium	4.0
National insurance and pension costs	15.0
Inspection	28.0
Consumable supplies	12.7
Power for machinery	7.8
Lighting and heating	4.2
Rates	9.0
Repairs and maintenance	15.1
Materials handling	21.4
Depreciation of machinery	15.0
Production administration	11.5
Idle time	1.6
	175.3

You are required to

(a)   Prepare a statement showing for April the flexible budget for the month, the actual costs and the variance for each overhead item.

(b)   Comment on each variance of £1,000 or more by suggesting possible reasons for the variances reported.

(c)   State, for control purposes, with reasons to support your conclusions:
   (i) whether (b) above is adequate; and
   (ii) whether the statement prepared in respect of the request in (a) above could be improved and if so, how.

(d)   Calculate:
   (i) the overhead absorbed;
   (ii) the total amount under/over-spent;
   (iii) the overhead volume variance.

(*Chartered Institute of Management Accountants*)

16I   (a)   Discuss in general the ways in which variance analysis helps management to control a business. (*Note* – there is no need to refer to specific variances.)

(b) NC Limited uses flexible budgets and standard costing for its single product P which it makes and sells.

Three kilogrammes of material, having a standard cost of £4.40 per kg, are required for each unit of P. Actual material purchased and used in April cost £336,000 with the actual purchase price being £4.20 per kg. Each unit of P requires thirty minutes of direct labour time and the standard wages rate per hour is £5. The actual wages rate in April was £5.40 per hour. Sufficient direct labour time was utilized to produce 28,000 units of P although actual production in April was 25,000 units.

The company has a normal operating capacity of 15,000 hours per month and flexible overhead budgets are:

Hours of operation	12,500	14,000	15,000
	£	£	£
Variable production overhead	150,000	168,000	180,000
Fixed production overhead	270,000	270,000	270,000
	420,000	438,000	450,000

Actual overhead incurred in April was £430,000 of which £270,000 was fixed.

You are required to

(i) Calculate the appropriate variances for material, labour and overhead.
(ii) Show the variances in a statement suitable for presentation to management, reconciling the standard cost with the actual cost of production.

(Chartered Institute of Management Accountants)

16J   The following data relates to actual output, costs and variances for the four-weekly accounting period number 4 of a company which makes only one product. Opening and closing work-in-progress figures were the same.

Actual production of product XY	18,000 units
Actual costs incurred:	£000
Direct materials purchased and used 150,000 kg	210
Direct wages for 32,000 hours	136
Variable production overhead	38
Variances:	£000
Direct materials price	15 Favourable
Direct materials usage	9 Adverse
Direct labour rate	8 Adverse
Direct labour efficiency	16 Favourable
Variable production overhead expenditure	6 Adverse
Variable production overhead efficiency	4 Favourable

Variable production overhead varies with labour hours worked. A standard marginal costing system is operated.

You are required to

(a) Present a standard product cost sheet for one unit of product XY.
(b) Describe briefly *three* types of standard that can be used for a standard costing system, stating which is usually preferred in practice and why.

(Chartered Institute of Management Accountants)

PART VI

COSTS FOR DECISION-MAKING

17 Marginal Costing

THE CONCEPT OF MARGINAL COSTING

Marginal costing can be defined as a principle whereby variable costs are charged to cost units and the fixed cost attributable to the relevant period is written off in full against the contribution of that period. Although this definition is clear and concise it does need some explanation. Some accountants think of cost accounting as a formal system of cost recording along the lines of the absorption costing system, but marginal costing is more an attitude of mind to be used as an approach in decision-making. A marginal cost is 'the variable cost of one unit of a product or service, or the cost which would be avoided if that unit was not produced'. (CIMA *Terminology*). An alternative definition of a marginal cost is that it is the amount at any given volume of output by which total costs are changed if the volume of output is increased or decreased by one unit. It is the cost of that unit of production which is at the margin, i.e. the last one to be produced. Some authorities prefer the term 'direct costing' instead of marginal costing, since this implies that costs are measured in terms of what is directly attributable to a unit, and the fixed overhead expenses are not allotted to find a unit cost, as with full absorbtion costing.

No discussion of marginal costing can be complete without introducing the term 'cost behaviour'. This term refers to the manner in which certain costs will change when either the volume of production changes or new circumstances are introduced. Clearly some costs will not change and are referred to as fixed costs, while others vary in proportion to any fluctuation in the volume produced and are referred to as variable costs. This distinction is important when short-term business decisions are made, since costs which vary as a result of the decision must be considered as relevant to the decision, but those which do not change can be disregarded. For this reason marginal costs are very significant for decision-making.

THE DISTINCTION BETWEEN VARIABLE AND FIXED COSTS

If the direct material used to make a product costs £20 and the direct labour used in production costs £10, the direct cost of production of the unit will be £30. Accordingly, if 1,000 units are produced direct costs will total £30,000, and the fixed costs of £10,000 incurred as factory overheads will complete the calculation of total costs as £40,000. If one extra unit is produced, the fixed factory overheads will not change but an extra £30 of direct cost will be incurred. Therefore the marginal cost, or the cost of making one more unit, equals the direct or variable cost of £30.

In this example any change in volume will increase or decrease total cost by £30 per unit, the variable cost of producing each unit. This statement is correct up to the point at which spare factory capacity is all used up, say after the production of 50,000 units. If production in excess of 50,000 units is required, it will be necessary to change the circumstances of the business, either to extend the factory or to set up a second factory. In either case the production overheads will increase. If production overheads are doubled to £20,000 by the addition of extra capacity, the marginal cost of producing one more unit after 50,000 units have been produced is £30 (the variable cost) plus £10,000 (the additional fixed cost). This example illustrates the fact that when volumes change the 'incremental' cost is not always equal to the direct cost, since at certain points in the volume scale, and under certain conditions, some costs which have previously been considered fixed may behave in a variable manner, and some costs thought to be variable may prove to be fixed. Clearly the identification of those costs which are incremental when circumstances change is significant when a decision is to be made.

COST BEHAVIOUR

The behaviour of costs when volumes or conditions change is important in marginal costing because of the distinction between fixed and variable costs. Difficulties are experienced in identifying costs to the fixed and variable categories, and in forecasting whether they will stay in those categories as the situation changes. A flexible approach is important in marginal costing since it is all too easy to think of a cost as being fixed and then to continue to categorize it as such even though it changes. Fixed costs are not fixed for ever and sooner or later as the long run succeeds the short run, extra fixed costs will be incurred. A variable cost such as materials cost per unit cannot be expected to remain the same at all parts of the volume range. An order for sufficient materials to manufacture 20,000 units will be supplied at a lower cost than an order for, say, 500 units.

Some costs are termed 'semi-variable' because they change not in proportion to, but in sympathy with, a fluctuation in the volume produced. This cost behaviour usually results from the fact that the cost contains a fixed element and a variable element, e.g. telephone charges have a fixed standing charge and also a cost per unit used. Similarly, electricity or gas charges comprise a fixed standing charge and a variable cost per unit. Some semi-variable costs are fixed for part of the volume range but increase when a certain limit is reached. Such costs are called 'lumpy' costs or 'stepped' fixed costs because they increase in a stepped progression. For example, one supervisor may be able to oversee the work of twelve operatives, but if an extra worker is added to the team a second supervisor will be needed. At this point the cost of supervision will increase by one step. After further expansion, up to say thirty operatives, a third supervisor will be recruited and the cost of supervision will step up yet again. The behaviour of costs can be illustrated graphically as in Figure 17.1.

CONTRIBUTION

Once marginal costs have been recognized and ascertained, it is possible to use them to calculate the effect on profit of changes in the volume or type of production. If the marginal cost of manufacturing one unit of production is subtracted from the sales revenue earned from that unit, the resulting surplus is considered as the 'contribution' to a pool out of which fixed costs will be met, and profit will be provided. The idea of contribution is a significant concept, since contribution is the surplus after variable or direct cost has been covered, and there is no need to apportion or absorb fixed overhead costs since they can be set in total against the total of all the contributions earned by units sold. Therefore the use of contribution instead of net profit (calculated after charging a share of fixed overhead cost) is much more helpful when decisions are made. Contribution can be expressed per unit or as contribution earned by a sector of the business, such as a product, during a certain period. If the contribution earned from sales is greater than the fixed cost incurred, a profit will be made. It is also possible to calculate the amount of sales required to provide a contribution which will just equal the fixed cost incurred, and thus set the business in a 'break-even' situation.

THE ADVANTAGES OF MARGINAL COSTING

The advantages to be derived from marginal costing are as follows.
1. The marginal costing system avoids the arbitrary and sometimes unrealistic charge made to production when fixed costs are apportioned and absorbed. The absorption method is only as good as the assumptions which underlie the apportionments and absorption bases used, so that marginal costing avoids any misleading cost allocations derived from the absorption system.
2. Apportionment and the absorption of overhead expenses is costly and time-consuming. These costs are avoided if marginal costing is employed.
3. Contribution is a much more reliable criterion on which to base decisions than profit derived from full absorption costing. Decisions based on costs which change, rather than an arbitrary allocation of fixed cost, will be based on logical and clear evidence.

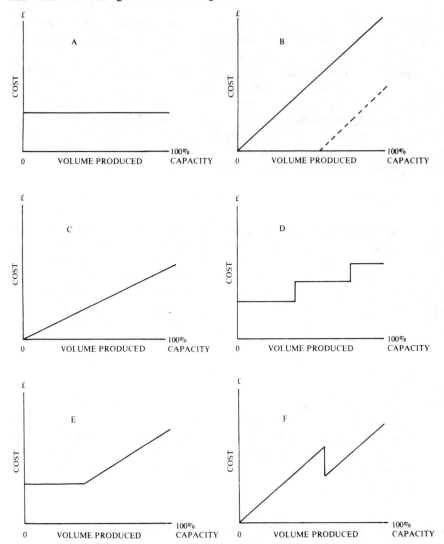

Graph A – shows a fixed cost i.e. the same at all levels of production.

Graph B – shows a variable cost increasing in a linear relationship to production. The dotted line shows a variable cost starting at a certain level – e.g. a bonus.

Graph C – shows a semi-variable cost that increases in sympathy with but not in proportion to an increase in production. The graph represents the equation $y = ax + b$, where there is a fixed element b and a variable cost per unit a. × stands for volume produced.

Graph D – shows a semi-variable cost of the 'lumpy' type with a stepped projection.

Graph E – shows a fixed cost which later becomes variable – e.g. the fixed charge and the first free miles with car hire.

Graph F – shows a serrated profile which is achieved when a trade discount is given on total purchases after a certain level is reached.

Figure 17.1   The behaviour of costs

4. Marginal costing will reveal the effect on profit of volume changes, and facilitates the calculation of a break-even point and other useful managerial information.
5. Marginal costing will value stocks at direct cost without a proportion of fixed overheads. Thus any costs carried forward from one period to another inside the value of stocks will concern only the direct cost of production, so that the fixed overheads incurred in a period are written off against that period.

MARGINAL COSTING VERSUS ABSORPTION COSTING

The major difference between these two concepts concerns the treatment of fixed factory overheads. Under the absorption concept overheads of a period are absorbed to units produced during that period and, if those units are not sold, part of the fixed overhead of one period is carried into the next period inside the cost of finished goods stock. This concept supports the accruals or matching principle in that the full absorbed cost of units is set against revenue whenever those units are sold. The marginal costing concept holds that fixed overheads are a cost of a particular time period, and should be written off against profit in that period regardless of whether all the goods made during that period have been sold. Under marginal costing units completed but not sold during one period are carried forward to the next period at variable cost and not full absorbed cost.

Full absorption costing: advantages and disadvantages

Arguments in favour of the full absorption costing system assert that it is true and fair to include the full cost of production services used to make a product in the cost of that product carried forward and set against eventual revenue from its sale. This argument supports the matching concept and is also in line with Statement of Standard Accounting Practice 9, which decrees that the cost of stock carried forward should contain a fair proportion of the factory overheads incurred in its production. This rule concerns the valuation of stock in financial accounting and it is argued that cost accounting principles should fall in line with the standard, and should recognize the importance of factory overhead expenses. It is further argued that under direct or marginal costing, if a company builds up stock during a period it will be penalized for this activity, since the overhead cost of the increased stock will be charged against the profit for the period during which the stock was created, and not carried forward to the period during which it is intended that the stock should be sold. This it is alleged distorts profit and departs from a true and fair view.

The disadvantages of full absorption costing are that the methods employed to relate fixed costs to production units are both arbitrary and costly, and if mistakes are made in the apportionment or absorption procedures, a misleading result may be obtained. Overhead rates which are calculated in error may charge too much fixed cost to a certain product so that when the full absorbed cost is used in pricing decisions, the business prices itself out of the market by charging too much. Alternatively, if in error insufficient overheads are charged to a certain product, and if prices are subsequently based on this fully absorbed cost, prices may be set too low and work undertaken which in reality leads to little or no profit. These advantages are practical ones, and are reinforced by the conceptual argument that fixed overhead expenses are time costs and should be related to the period during which they are incurred rather than carried forward to the next period inside the cost of stock.

Example 17.1

As cost accountant to a medium-sized manufacturing company you have been asked by the managing director to explain the different profit figures disclosed by full absorption costing and marginal costing when applied to the costs and revenues for the four months from September to December. The company manufactures and sells a single product at £30 per unit, with production costs of £12 for direct materials, £6 for direct labour and £4 for variable overheads. Variable selling expenses are 5 per cent of sales revenue. Fixed costs each month are budgeted as £100,000 for production, £30,000 for selling expenses and £24,000 for administration costs. The production overheads are absorbed on the basis of a normal production of 40,000 units per month. Sales for the months of September to December were 40,000, 44,000, 40,000 and 42,000 units respectively, but production was 46,000 40,000, 40,000 and 40,000.

Thus production and sales are equal for the four-month period, but units sold and units produced do not coincide for September, October and December; only in November does production equal sales. During September stocks will be increased by 6,000 units, to be reduced by 4,000 units in October and 2,000 units in December. Production overheads will be absorbed to units on the basis of £100,000 divided by 40,000 units, i.e. £2.50 per unit. Costing statements based on full absorption and marginal costing are shown in Tables 17.1 and 17.2.

The differences investigated

Differences in the profit figure for the two methods are disclosed for the months of September, October and December. These differences are caused by the fact that the full absorption method transfers the fixed production overhead attributable to units produced but not sold to later months during the period when those units are sold, whereas the marginal costing system writes off the production overheads during the month in which they are incurred.

The difference in September is £15,000 in favour of full absorption costing because stocks of 6,000 units have been created during the month and carried forward to October: 6,000 units at a fixed overhead cost of £2.50 each equals £15,000. In October marginal costing shows £10,000 more profit than the full absorption costing statement. This is because stocks have been reduced by 4,000 units during the month, so that under full absorption costing 4,000 extra unit overhead costs of £2.50 have been charged against revenue. In November the profit figures for the two systems correspond, because the same number of units have been sold and made during that period. In December full absorption costing

Cost of production is £12 + £6 + £4 + £2.50 = £24.50

	September		October		November		December	
Sales (units)	40,000		44,000		40,000		42,000	
Production (units)	46,000		40,000		40,000		40,000	
	£000	£000	£000	£000	£000	£000	£000	£000
Sales		1,200		1,320		1,200		1,260
Opening stock	–		147		49		49	
Production costs	1,127		980		980		980	
	1,127		1,127		1,029		1,029	
Closing stock	147	980	49	1,078	49	980	–	1,029
Gross profit		220		242		220		231
Variable selling costs	60		66		60		63	
Fixed selling costs	30		30		30		30	
Fixed administration costs	24	114	24	120	24	114	24	117
		106		122		106		114
Fixed production overheads over-absorbed*		15		–		–		–
Net profit		121		122		106		114

*Production overheads absorbed in September are 46,000 × £2.50 = £115,500, but only £100,000 of cost is incurred.

Table 17.1 Full absorption costing statement

shows £5,000 less profit than the marginal costing statement because stocks have been reduced during the month by 2,000 units. Thus 2,000 × £2.50 per unit, representing the fixed production overheads of September when those units were made, has been charged against revenue in December when the units were sold. The argument between the supporters of full absorption costing and those who believe in marginal costing has continued for many years and depends upon whether it is right to match fixed production overheads to the time period during which they were incurred, or to attempt to match them to the revenue earned from the eventual sale of products made during the period in which those costs were incurred.

COST/VOLUME/PROFIT ANALYSIS

This technique, sometimes called 'break-even analysis', uses marginal costing and the relationship of fixed and variable costs to interpret or forecast the likely profit or loss at a range of different volumes of production, or the effect on profit of changes in cost or volume sold. The relationship between cost, volume and profit can be expressed on a graph.

Variable production costs is £12 + £6 + £4 = £22.00

	September £000	£000	October £000	£000	November £000	£000	December £000	£000
Sales		1,200		1,320		1,200		1260
Opening stock	–		132		44		44	
Variable production cost	1,012		880		880		880	
	1,012		1,012		924		924	
Closing stock	132		44		44		–	
	880		968		880		924	
Variable selling costs	60	940	66	1,034	60	940	63	987
Contribution		260		286		260		273
Fixed costs:								
Production	100							
Selling	30							
Administration	24	154		154		154		154
Net profit		106		132		106		119
Difference from profit under full absorption (Table 17.1)		– 15		+ 10		nil		+ 5

This difference corresponds exactly to stock changes at £2.50 per unit, the fixed overhead unit cost.

Table 17.2   *Marginal costing statement (using same data as in Table 17.1)*

Example 17.2

A company has production facilities which can be used to make a maximum of 80,000 units during a costing period. Each unit sells for £5, and the variable cost of production is £4. The fixed factory overheads are £50,000 for the period.

Contribution per unit is price £5 less variable or marginal cost £4, i.e. £1. The company budgets to make 70,000 units during the period. Table 17.3 expresses these costs at various levels of production.

Volume in units	Fixed cost £000	Variable cost £000	Total cost £000	Revenue from sales £000
Nil	50	–	50	Nil
10,000	50	40	90	50
20,000	50	80	130	100
30,000	50	120	170	150
40,000	50	160	210	200
50,000	50	200	250	250 Break even
60,000	50	240	290	300
70,000	50	280	330	350
80,000	50	320	370	400

Table 17.3

It can be seen from Table 17.3 that if the volume of production is less than 50,000 units the total cost is greater than the revenue, so that a loss is made. However, if 50,000 units are produced the total cost equals the total revenue so that neither a profit nor a loss is made. This is the 'break-even' point. It can also be seen that at volumes in excess of 50,000 units the revenue exceeds the total cost so that a profit will be made. The marginal cost of making one unit in excess of 50,000 will be £4, and the marginal revenue from its sale £5, so that the excess of price over marginal cost (contribution of £1) will be equal to the extra profit made on that unit. Therefore all contribution on units after the break-even point is profit, because once the break-even volume has been reached, contribution up to that point covers the fixed costs of production.

Fixed and variable costs can be plotted on a graph, together with the revenue line, to demonstrate the information on a break-even chart, as shown in Figure 17.2.

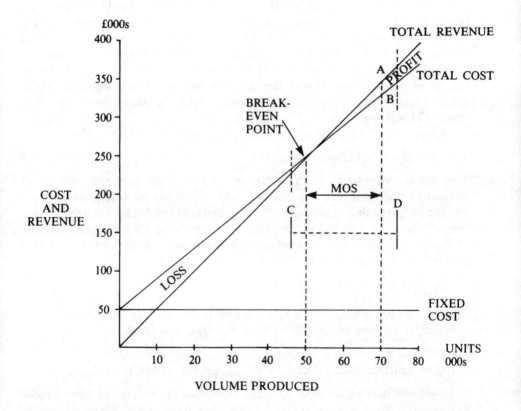

Figure 17.2 Break-even chart

The profit or loss made at certain volumes or capacity levels can be read from the graph. The budgeted profit at a volume of 70,000 units is the distance AB. The margin of safety (MOS) can also be shown, as can the relevant range, CD.

Break-even point

The break-even point can be calculated by the formula:

$$\frac{\text{Fixed cost}}{\text{Contribution}} = \text{Volume break-even point} \quad \frac{£50,000}{£1} = 50,000 \text{ units}$$

In Table 17.3 this would equal £50,000 divided by £1 equals 50,000 units. The profit to volume ratio (P/V ratio) is calculated as:

$$\frac{\text{Contribution}}{\text{Selling price}} \times \frac{100}{1} = \text{P/V ratio (as a percentage)}$$

For the data in Example 17.2 this can be calculated as:

$$\frac{£1}{£5} \times \frac{100}{1} = 20\%$$

Therefore 20 per cent of every sale made is a contribution towards the pool of fixed overhead expenses and towards profit.

It is also possible to calculate the profit or loss which would be made at a certain selected volume of production. This profit would be contribution for that volume less fixed cost. From Table 17.3 it is possible to calculate that for a production of 60,000 units, the contribution would be 60,000 times £1 minus the fixed costs of £50,000 which equals £10,000. In Example 17.2 the budgeted volume of production is 70,000; therefore the budgeted profit would be 70,000 units times £1 of contribution for each unit, minus £50,000 of fixed cost which equals £20,000 profit.

$$(60,000 \times £1) - £50,000 = £10,000 \text{ profit}$$

The margin of safety

The 'margin of safety' is the difference between the budgeted volume of production and the break-even volume. This will show the safety margin built into the budget in that the volume produced and sold can fall by a certain amount before losses are made. In Example 17.2 the margin of safety is budgeted capacity of 70,000 units less break-even capacity of 50,000 units. Therefore the budgeted plan will need to fall short by 20,000 units, or:

$$\frac{20,000}{70,000} \times \frac{100}{1} = 28.6\%$$

before losses are made. Clearly this is a very useful managerial statistic.

Figure 17.3 shows an alternative form of break-even chart.

Further applications of cost/volume/profit analysis

Cost/volume/profit (c–v–p) analysis can be extended to find the turnover needed in order to achieve a required profit figure. The formula for this calculation is:

$$\frac{\text{Fixed cost + required profit}}{\text{Contribution per unit}} = \text{Required volume}$$

In Example 17.2 if a profit of £10,000 is required the calculation would be fixed cost £50,000 plus required profit £10,000, divided by contribution per unit £1 equals a volume of 60,000 units.

Profit to volume ratio

The profit to volume (P/V) ratio can also be used to find the break-even point. The formula to use is:

$$\frac{\text{Fixed cost}}{\text{P/V ratio}} = \text{Break-even sales revenue}$$

In Example 17.2 above the calculation would be:

$$\frac{£50,000}{0.2} = \text{Revenue of } £250,000$$

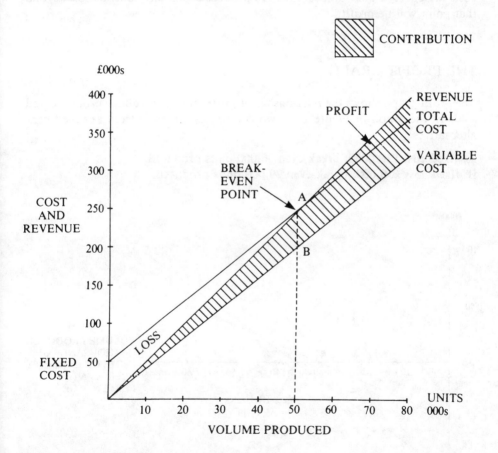

Figure 17.3 Alternative break-even chart

The distance between revenue and variable cost is contribution. The total cost line runs parallel to the variable cost line, because the difference is the constant amount of fixed cost at all volumes. Contribution at the break-even point is AB. All contribution added by production beyond that point is profit.

The P/V ratio is a way in which the contribution per unit can be expressed, e.g. £1 from £5 of sales revenue equals 20 per cent. If all contributions earned after the break-even point are profit, the P/V ratio applied to sales made beyond the break-even point will calculate the profit. In Example 17.2 budgeted sales of 70,000 units will exceed the break-even point by 20,000 units, with a consequent post-break-even revenue of 20,000 times £5. If the P/V ratio is 20 per cent, then 20 per cent of this extra revenue of £100,000 will be the profit earned at volume production of 70,000 units, i.e. £20,000. This reasoning has a particular significance for pricing sales beyond the break-even volume, where goods can be 'dumped' in a market at any price which covers the variable cost. In Example 17.2, once the break-even volume of 50,000 units has been sold further sales can be made at any price which exceeds the variable cost of £4 per unit, since the fixed costs are covered once 50,000 units are produced, and any contribution beyond that point will be profit.

THE PROFIT GRAPH

The profit graph shows the relationship of profit or loss to volume produced and sold. In the graph in Figure 17.4 two companies are considered as investment alternatives:

A: fixed cost £100,000; break-even 35,000 units produced.
B: fixed cost £50,000; break-even 29,000 units produced.

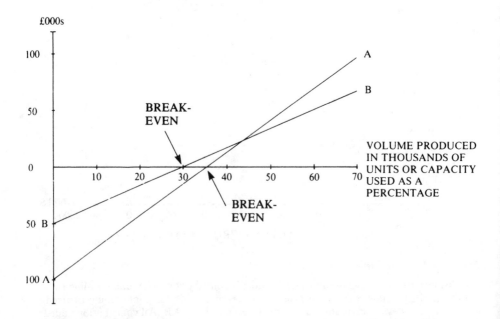

Figure 17.4   The profit graph

If no goods are produced the loss made will equal the fixed cost, since there is no contribution from production. The profit line crosses from the loss sector to the profit sector at the break-even point.

If boom conditions and full employment are forecast, higher production volumes will be achieved, and company A will be preferred as an investment. Alternatively, if recession is forecast company B will be preferred since it breaks even at a lower volume, and makes smaller losses at capacity usage below the break-even point.

LIMITATIONS OF THE BREAK-EVEN CHART

The underlying assumption of traditional break-even, or c–v–p, analysis is that there is a linear relationship between costs, revenue and output, which remains the same throughout the volume range. The break-even chart drawn in terms of straight lines has been criticized for relying too heavily on this assumption of a constant relationship between cost, revenue and volume. The criticisms made of the break-even chart are described below.

Linearity

It is an unreal assumption that selling prices will remain constant whatever the level of sales activity. Economics teaches us that sales revenue will not be the same per product at all volumes, since as more and more of the product is supplied to the market supply will exceed demand and the price will fall. A point may well be reached in this cycle where there is a glut, and total revenue will fall if larger volumes are sold, because price must be reduced significantly if the volume sold is to increase, subject of course to the elasticity of demand.

Costs also have a curvilinear relationship to volume. Unit variable costs may fall as the volume produced increases, if trade discounts are received when purchase orders increase in size, or if the economies of large scale are achieved. If expansion of the firm's production continues, a point may well be reached when variable cost per unit will rise as demand uses up available materials etc., and extra labour can be employed only by offering higher rates or working overtime. If the firm wishes to expand under these circumstances it will be forced to bid for extra resources against other users and thus costs may well increase. For these reasons the assumption of a linear relationship to volume for variable costs and revenue, throughout the entire volume range from nil to full capacity production, cannot be substantiated. It is too simplistic to assume that costs and revenues will behave in the same way across the entire volume scale from the production of nil units up to maximum capacity, and also to suppose that volume alone will affect costs across the range, when other factors such as inflation, changing markets and technical conditions will also influence costs.

Figure 17.5 also demonstrates that there can be more than one break-even point, and that profit is not necessarily maximized when volume is increased to the limit of production.

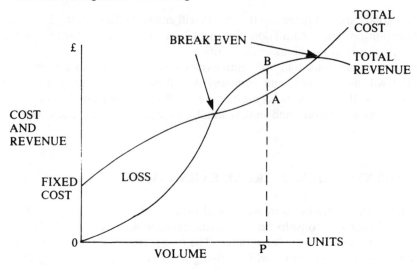

Figure 17.5   Curvilinear break-even chart

The maximum profit is made at volume OP, since at that volume the distance between revenue and cost, BA, is at a maximum. This is the 'optimum' or best possible volume.

Note the eventual fall of total revenue at higher volumes as price is reduced to make increased sales, and the steep rise in costs at higher volumes as scarce resources are purchased at 'inflationary' prices.

Identifying costs

The identification of variable costs and fixed costs is not always a simple and straightforward procedure. If conditions change, some costs which are normally considered to be variable may well become fixed, and others previously thought of as fixed may well become variable. Thus costs may not remain in their normal classification. A fixed cost which increases in a stepped progression, in circumstances where production facilities are fully utilized and must then be expanded if volume produced is to increase, will complicate the analysis of a break-even chart by showing two or perhaps more break-even points. See Figure 17.6

Product mix

The break-even chart works well for a single product, but it may be difficult to apply the concept of break-even analysis to a business which makes more than one product. If the products do not have the same P/V ratio, but instead experience a different relationship between price and variable cost, it will be possible to combine them on a break-even chart only if the mixture of products made remains the same across the volume range. The break-even chart is predictive, so that if the actual mixture of products made departs from the mixture on which the chart has been drafted, its conclusions will not be reliable. Thus the use of the break-even chart is limited to the analysis of individual products.

Stocks

The break-even chart sets revenue against the cost of sales rather than the cost of production. Therefore if stocks are increased or reduced during the period, the cost of using a certain level of production capacity within the firm will not be truly comparable with the revenue earned from selling a different volume of products.

Estimates

A further assumption which reduces the validity of break-even analysis is that prices and costs will either remain constant or will inflate at an equivalent rate. This is unlikely to be true since selling prices may increase faster than costs, and material costs may increase faster than labour costs. This phenomenon reflects an overall weakness in accounting rather than simply a weakness in break-even analysis.

Managers may not be very interested in costs and revenues at the extremes of low or high volume, but will require an analysis covering a range of output volumes relevant to their operation. Accordingly, the idea of the 'relevant range' is significant in reducing the effect of the limitations discussed above. It is reasonable to assume that costs and revenue will behave in a linear way over a small range within the total scale. Thus within this relevant range, say from just below the break-even point to above the budgeted output, break-even analysis can be used to forecast the relationship of costs to volume to profit (Figure 17.2). The fact remains, however, that the break-even chart shows a static picture as at one point in time, and this may quickly be outdated if conditions change.

Example 17.3

A company with one factory can produce 40,000 units, but if expansion is planned beyond this volume extra production facilities will double the fixed factory overhead costs from £60,000 to £120,000. The facilities then provided have a maximum productive capability of 80,000 units, and if further expansion beyond this limit is required a further £60,000 must be spent on extra fixed costs beyond this point. Assuming that all production can be sold across the volume range at £5 per unit, and that variable costs are linear at £3 per unit, a break-even chart can be drawn as shown in Figure 17.6.

There are several break-even points on this graph, and the validity of using a third factory is brought into question. The profit AB from one factory at full production is less than the profit CD when a second factory is employed at full

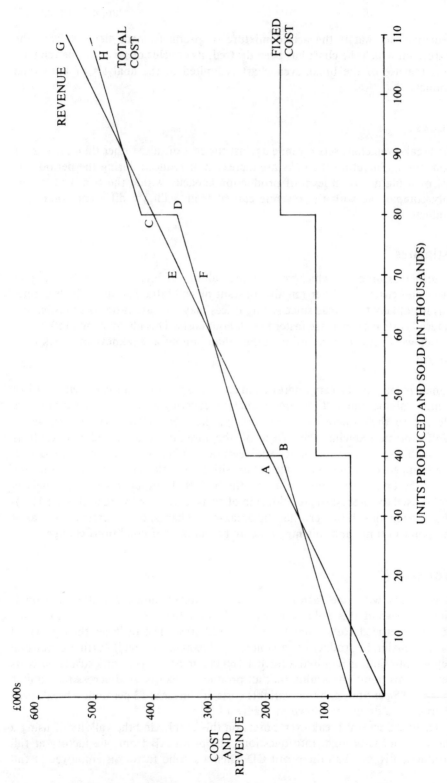

Figure 17.6   Break-even chart for Example 17.3

capacity, but if extra production facilities are to be made available, sales must be guaranteed to increase from 40,000 to at least 70,000 units because only at this volume is the profit EF equal to the profit AB earned by the use of one factory. Using the same logic, expansion into a third factory is worthwhile only if sales can be guaranteed beyond 110,000 units, since only when this volume is reached does the profit GH achieve the amount equal to the profit CD earned when two factories are employed at full capacity.

THE APPLICATION OF COST/VOLUME/PROFIT ANALYSIS TO BUSINESS DECISIONS

Within its limitations c–v–p analysis can be applied to a number of business decisions. It is particularly useful to compute the likely profit to be achieved across a range of possible sales volumes.

Example 17.4

A large company which operates a chain of chemist's shops and household stores is considering the feasibility of installing photocopying facilities, for the use of its customers, in certain of its shops. The customer would pay 10p per copy and at this price it is estimated that average sales per machine would be 2,500 copies per week. The operating costs of each machine are forecast as a direct cost of 3p per copy with additional weekly costs of £60 for rental and £12 for electricity. The company expects the machine to take up a quarter of the time of a shop assistant who is normally paid £120 per week. A maintenance agreement for one year would cost £1,300, but this would cover emergency calls as well as routine maintenance visits.

Required

Use c–v–p analysis to advise the management.

Solution

A selling price of 10p per copy less a direct cost of 3p per copy gives a contribution of 7p per copy. Fixed cost must be covered by the contribution each week:

	£
Rental	60
Electricity	12
Labour	30
Maintenance	25
	127

The break-even point is calculated as:

$$\frac{\text{Fixed cost}}{\text{Contribution per unit}} = \frac{£127}{7p} = 1,814 \text{ copies}$$

Profit at estimated sales is:

Contributions beyond B/E point $(2,500 - 1,814) \times 7p = £48$ per week

The margin of safety is the difference between the break-even point and estimated sales, expressed as a percentage of estimated sales:

$$\frac{2,500 - 1,814}{2,500} = \frac{100}{1} = 27\%$$

This means that estimated sales can be down 27 per cent before the project ceases to be profitable; a sizeable safety margin against over-optimistic forecasts and unforeseen perils.

The analysis in this problem can be extended by any of the following situations.

1. The company requires a return of at least £30 per week from the shop space occupied by the copier.
2. The company fears that once it has committed itself to the scheme, the supplier might raise the machine rental by 15 per cent.
3. The company fears that once it has committed itself to the scheme the supplier might increase the direct cost to 5p per copy.

Advice can be given to the management concerning each of these extensions by the application of c–v–p analysis.

1. With a profit of £48 a week, the machine covers the required return of £30 for the space which it occupies, but a new break-even point and margin of safety should be computed:

$$B/E = \frac{\text{Fixed cost + required profit}}{\text{Contribution per unit}} = \frac{£127 + £30}{7p} = 2,242 \text{ copies}$$

$$MOS = \frac{2,500 - 2,242}{2,500} \times \frac{100}{1} = 10\%$$

2. A rental increase of 15 per cent raises the fixed cost by £9 to £136. A new break-even point margin of safety can be calculated:

$$B/E = \frac{£136}{7p} = 1,943 \text{ copies}$$

$$MOS = \frac{2,500 - 1,943}{2,500} \times \frac{100}{1} = 22\%$$

The safety margin has been reduced but there is still a significant margin for error in the forecasts. The new profit margin would be calculated as the contribution earned beyond the break-even point. Therefore the amount would be 2,500 copies − 1,943 copies at 7p each, a total of £39. This new weekly profit figure is in excess of the £30 required by the company as a profit to be made by the shop space occupied by the copier.

3. If direct cost is increased to 5p per unit the contribution would be reduced to 5p, and a new break-even point should be calculated:

$$B/E = \frac{£127}{5p} = 2,540 \text{ copies}$$

This new break-even point is above the budgeted sales, so that the safety margin disappears. The loss in these new circumstances would be £2 per week (40 copies below break-even at 5p each). Revenue at this level would not cover the profit required from the shop space occupied, or any increased rental which might also be charged.

The figures disclosed in this analysis do not make the decision, but will be very useful to management when they have to exercise their judgement in the decision-making situation.

Example 17.5

A trade union operates a convalescent home in the country, for its members and other guests. The home is open for thirty weeks of the year. Parties of from six to fifteen guests are accepted on terms of £200 per person per week.

Weekly costs per guest incurred by the convalescent home are:

	£
Food – special diets	50
Electricity for heating and cooking	6
Domestic (laundry, cleaning etc.) expenses	10
Use of minibus for outings	20

Local staff supervise and carry out the necessary duties at the home at a cost of £22,000 for the thirty-week period. This provides staffing sufficient for six to ten guests per week but if eleven or more are to be accommodated, additional staff at a total cost of £400 per week are engaged for the whole of the thirty-week period.

Rent for the property, is £8,000 per annum and the garden of the home is maintained by a part-time gardener for a fee of £1,500 per annum.

Required

1. Tabulate the appropriate figures in such a way as to show the break-even point(s) and to comment on your figures.
2. Draw a chart to illustrate your answer to (1) above.

Solution

Convalescent home: costs and income statement

Guests in residence	Income p.a. £	Variable costs £	Contribution £	Fixed costs £	Surplus (deficit) £
6	36,000	15,480	20,520	31,500	(10,980)
7	42,000	18,060	23,940	31,500	(7,560)
8	48,000	20,640	27,360	31,500	(4,140)
9	54,000	23,220	30,780	31,500	(720)
10	60,000	25,800	34,200	31,500	2,700
11	66,000	28,380	37,620	43,500	(5,880)
12	72,000	30,960	41,040	43,500	(2,460)
13	78,000	33,540	44,460	43,500	960
14	84,000	36,120	47,880	43,500	4,380
15	90,000	38,700	51,300	43,500	7,800

The break-even point occurs at two different levels of activity, but it is not possible to specify the exact number of guests required to break even precisely. The first break-even point occurs just in excess of nine guests per day, but clearly there can only be whole numbers, so management could work on a figure of ten. Similarly, when fixed costs rise in excess of ten guests per week the break-even point would change to thirteen guests per week.

In the statement shown above:

1. Variable costs are £50 + £6 + £10 + £20 = £86 per guest, or £2,580 for thirty weeks.
2. Contribution per guest per week is £200 − £86 = £114.
3. Fixed costs are £22,000 + £8,000 + £1,500 = £31,500, with a step of £12,000 beyond ten guests.

The solution is plotted on a graph in Figure 17.7.

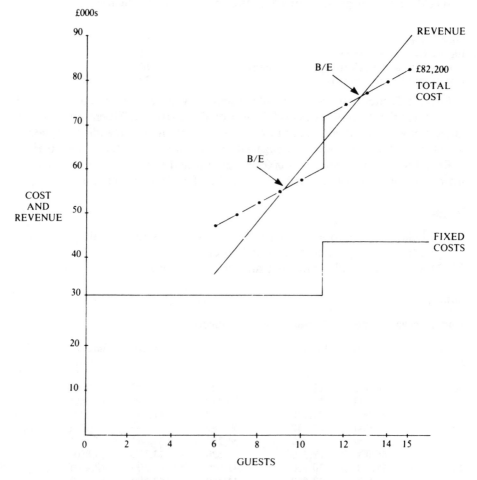

TOTAL COST = FIXED COST PLUS VARIABLE COST

Figure 17.7   Break-even chart for Example 17.5

STANDARD MARGINAL COSTING

The application of standard costing in an industrial situation, usually entails full absorption costing as explained in Chapter 16. However, standards and variances can be produced on the basis of marginal costing. A standard marginal costing system incorporates only costs which are variable, or direct to the product. Therefore the absorption of fixed costs, and the variances derived therefrom, do not feature in a standard marginal costing system. The standard cost card is computed in terms of direct materials, labour and variable overheads only. Standard marginal cost plus a standard contribution per unit equals standard selling price. Therefore, instead of a standard sales margin or profit a standard contribution can be used. Fixed costs, of course, form part of the budgeting system, but they are not allotted to individual cost centres or cost units; instead the total fixed cost is subtracted from the budgeted contribution, to calculate the budgeted profit.

Variance analysis concentrates on materials, labour and variable overheads. For fixed overheads the only variance which needs to be calculated is the expenditure variance, which identifies the difference between the total budgeted fixed cost and the actual cost incurred. The volume variance and its sub-variances (capacity, idle time, and efficiency) are not required under the marginal costing system, because fixed overheads are not related to individual units and they are not absorbed to production.

The sales variances (the sales margin price variance and sales margin quantity variance) are replaced by a sales contribution price variance and a sales contribution quantity variance. These new variances would be calculated in exactly the same way as the previous sales variances.

Example 17.6: Standard marginal costing

This example applies standard marginal costing to the circumstances of Chiltern Chairs plc, in the comprehensive example given in Chapter 16.

The standard cost card or specification would comprise only variable costs, e.g.:

	£
Materials: 2 kg of oak at 60p per kg	1.20
Labour: 2.5 hours at £4 per hour	10.00
Variable overhead per chair	1.00
Standard marginal cost	12.20

Fixed overhead budgeted at £15,000

The standard marginal cost of 11,000 chairs, produced at £12.20, would be £134,200. The variances would be computed exactly as in Chapter 16, with the exception of fixed overhead variances. The difference between actual expenditure and budget for fixed overheads would appear as an expenditure variance. The variance statement would appear as follows:

			£
Actual marginal cost incurred (£168,150 − £16,000)			152,150

	£	£	
	Favourable	*Adverse*	
Variances:			
Material – Price	–	1,150	
– Usage	–	600	
Labour – Rate of pay	–	5,800	
– Idle time	–	4,000	
– Efficiency	–	2,000	
Variable overhead – Expenditure	–	4,400	
		17,950	17,950
Standard marginal cost of actual production			134,200
Fixed overhead incurred		16,000	
Less adverse expenditure variance		1,000	15,000
Standard cost of actual production			
(11,000 × £12.20 + £15,000)			149,200

To extend this example, assume that 10,000 chairs are budgeted to be sold at £15 each. The standard contribution would be £15 − £12.20 = £2.80, and the standard profit 10,000 × £2.80 − £15,000 = £13,000. Further assume that 10,500 chairs are sold at £16 each. The actual contribution is now £16 - £12.20 = £3.80, and a contribution price variance would be calculated at 10,500 × (£3.80 - £2.80) = £10,500 favourable.

A contribution quantity variance would be calculated as £2.80 × (10,500 − 10,000) = £1,400 favourable.

As 11,000 units have been produced but only 10,500 have been sold, the closing stock of 500 chairs would be valued at variable cost of £12.20 each (£6,100).

A management statement might be drafted to show:

	£	£	
Actual sales (10,500 × £16)		168,000	
Standard marginal cost of actual production	134,200		
Less closing stock (at marginal cost)	6,100		
Standard marginal cost of actual sales		128,100	
Actual contribution on actual sales (10,500 × £3.80)		39,900	
Sales variances – Price	10,500		
– Quantity	1,400	11,900	(FAV)
Standard contribution on standard sales (10,000 × £2.80)		28,000	
Fixed costs		15,000	
Budgeted profit		13,000	

Alternatively:

	£
Actual contribution on actual sales	39,900
Less actual fixed costs	16,000
	23,900
Less adverse production variances	17,950
Actual net profit	5,950

Add back to this the adverse production variances of £17,950 and fixed overhead variances of £1,000, and deduct the favourable sales variance of £11,900 = budgeted profit of £13,000.

EXERCISES

17A (a) Discuss the arguments put forward for the use of absorption and marginal costing systems respectively.
(b) The following information is available for a firm producing and selling a single product:

Budgeted costs (at normal activity)	£000
Direct materials and labour	264
Variable production overhead	48
Fixed production overhead	144
Variable selling and administration overhead	24
Fixed selling and administration overhead	96

The overhead absorption rates are based upon normal activity of 240,000 units per period.

During the period just ended 260,000 units of product were produced, and 230,000 units were sold at £3 per unit.

At the beginning of the period 40,000 units were in stock. These were valued at the budgeted costs shown above.

Actual costs incurred were as per budget.

Required

(i)   Calculate the fixed production overhead absorbed during the period, and the extent of any under/over-absorption. For both of these calculations you should use absorption costing.
(ii) Calculate profits for the period using absorption costing and marginal costing respectively.
(iii) Reconcile the profit figures which you calculated in (ii) above.
(iv) State the situations in which the profit figures calculated under both absorption costing and marginal costing would be the same.

(Association of Certified Accountants)

17B   A company produces and sells two products with the following costs:

	Product X	Product Y
Variable costs (per £ of sales)	£0.45	£0.6
Fixed costs	£1,212,000 per period	

Total sales revenue is currently generated by the two products in the following proportions:

Product X	70 per cent
Product Y	30 per cent

Required

(a) Calculate the break-even sales revenue per period, based on the sales mix assumed above.

(b) Prepare a profit volume chart of the above situation for sales revenue up to £4,000,000. Show on the same chart the effect of a change in the sales mix to product X 50 per cent, product Y 50 per cent. Clearly indicate on the chart the break-even point for each situation.

(c) Of the fixed costs £455,000 are attributable to product X. Calculate the sales revenue required on product X in order to recover the attributable fixed costs and provide a net contribution of £700,000 towards general fixed costs and profit.

(Association of Certified Accountants)

17C A company producing and selling a single product expects the following trading results for the year just ending:

	£000	£000
Sales		900
Costs: Materials: direct	200	
Labour: direct	120	
indirect, fixed	38	
Other production overhead: variable	50	
fixed	80	
Administration overhead: fixed	78	
Selling overhead: variable	63	
fixed	44	
Distribution overhead: variable	36	
fixed	20	729
Net profit		171

Budgets are now being prepared for the year ahead. The following information is provided.

1. A selling price reduction from £9 to £8 per unit is expected to increase sales volume by 50 per cent.

2. Because of increased quantities purchased a 5 per cent quantity discount will be obtained on the purchase of raw materials. Material usage per unit of output is expected to be 98 per cent of the current year.

3. Hourly direct wage rates will increase by 10 per cent. Labour efficiency should remain the same. Twenty thousand units will be produced in overtime hours at a premium of 25 per cent. Overtime premium is treated as a direct cost.

4. Variable selling overhead is expected to increase in total proportionately with total sales revenue.

5. Variable production and distribution overhead should increase in total in proportion to the increase in sales volume.

6. Fixed overhead is forecast at 20 per cent above the level for the current year.

7. Monthly production will be scheduled so that finished goods stocks at the end of a month are sufficient to meet sales quantities forecast for the following one and a half months.

8. Materials will be purchased so that closing stocks of materials at the end of a month are sufficient to meet production requirements in the following month.
9. Monthly sales for the first six months are forecast as:

Month	1	2	3	4	5	6
Units (000s)	10	12	15	11	12	12

You are to assume that:

1. Prices and efficiency have been at a constant level throughout the year just ending.
2. Stocks of materials and finished goods by the end of the current year are consistent with the above assumptions for the year ahead, e.g. closing stock of raw materials will be sufficient for production requirements in month 1 of the new year.

Required

(a) Prepare a budgeted profit statement for the year ahead in marginal costing format.

(b) Calculate and compare the break-even points for the two years.

(c) Prepare a monthly production budget for the first quarter of the new year.

(Association of Certified Accountants)

17D (a) Autoparts plc markets a range of vehicle service packs for motoring enthusiasts. The products are sold on a franchise basis from selected garages and petrol stations. The company is planning to introduce as a new pack on to the market a rear window de-mister kit, but is uncertain which alternative to use to promote sales of the kit. Autoparts can either pay a commission on each sale or increase the salaries paid to sales staff. Data for the de-mister kit is:

Selling price	£25
Cost of Autoparts from the manufacturer	£14
Fixed costs of Autoparts directly attributable to the de-mister	£85,056

The fixed costs include the salaries of the sales staff.

Commision on each sale would be £1.40 per pack. Increased salaries to sales staff would cost an extra £14,989. Budgeted sales for the year are 11,000 packs.

Required

(i)   Calculate the break-even point if commission is paid.
(ii) Calculate the break-even point if sales staff salaries are increased.
(iii) Calculate the margin of safety for the two alternatives.
(iv) Comment to Autoparts on their decision.

(b) Discuss the assumptions which underpin break-even analysis, and limit its utility as a management tool.

17E (a) SAP 9 appears to support full absorption costing as opposed to marginal costing.

State the advantages of marginal costing to the management accountant.
(b)   Water Margin plc manufactures and sells aquaria for home use. The company makes a single size of product with a selling price of £45. Unit production costs are: materials £18, direct labour £9 and variable overheads £6. Variable selling expenses are 5 per cent of sales revenue. Fixed costs are: production £75,000, selling £45,000 and administration £36,000, all spent each month.

Production overheads are absorbed on the basis of a normal production of 20,000 units a month.

Unit sales were: January 20,000, February 22,000, March 20,000. Unit production was: January 23,000, February 20,000, March 19,000.

Required

Draft costing statements for each of January, February and March on the basis of full absorption costing and marginal costing, and suggest reasons for the differences in profit disclosed.

17F   X Limited commenced business on 1 March making one product only, the standard cost of which is as follows:

	£
Direct labour	5
Direct material	8
Variable production overhead	2
Fixed production overhead	5
Standard production cost	20

The fixed production overhead figure has been calculated on the basis of a budgeted normal output of 36,000 units per annum.

You are to assume that there were no expenditure or efficiency variances and that all the budgeted fixed expenses are incurred evenly over the year. March and April are to be taken as equal period months.

Selling distribution and administration expenses are:

Fixed	£120,000 per annum
Variable	15 per cent of the sales value

The selling price per unit is £35 and the number of units produced and sold were:

	March Units	April Units
Production	2,000	3,200
Sales	1,500	3,000

You are required to

(a) Prepare profit statements for each of the months of March and April using:
(i)   marginal costing; and
(ii) absorption costing.
(b) Present a reconciliation of the profit or loss figures given in your answers to (a) (i) and (a) (ii) accompanied by a brief explanation;
(c) Comment briefly on which costing principle, i.e. marginal or absorption,

should be used for what purpose(s) and why, referring to any statuory or other mandatory constraints.

(Chartered Institute of Management Accountants)

17G (a) Identify and discuss briefly *five* assumptions underlying cost-volume–profit analysis.

(b) A local authority, whose area includes a holiday resort situated on the east coast, operates, for thirty weeks each year, a holiday home which is let to visiting parties of children in care from other authorities. The children are accompanied by their own house mothers who supervise them throughout their holiday. From six to fifteen guests are accepted on terms of £100 per person per week. No differential charges exist for adults and children.

Weekly costs per guest incurred by the host authority are:

	£
Food	25
Electricity for heating and cooking	3
Domestic (laundry, cleaning etc.) expenses	5
Use of minibus	10

Seasonal staff supervise and carry out the necessary duties at the home at a cost of £11,000 for the thirty-week period. This provides staffing sufficient for six to ten guests per week but if eleven or more guests are to be accommodated, additional staff at a total cost of £200 per week are engaged for the whole of the thirty-week period.

Rent, including rates for the property, is £4,000 per annum and the garden of the home is maintained by the council's recreation department which charges a nominal fee of £1,000 per annum.

You are required to

(i) Tabulate the appropriate figures in such a way as to show the break-even point(s) and to comment on your figures.

(ii) Draw a chart to illustrate your answer to (b) (i) above.

(Chartered Institute of Management Accountants)

18   Cost Concepts and Short-term Decision-making

RELEVANT COSTS

When a short-term decision is made it is important to recognize the costs and revenues that are relevant to the decision, and therefore to exclude non-relevant data from the decision calculations. Relevant costs may be defined as those which are appropriate to aiding the making of specific management decisions, which means in effect those costs which change as a result of the decision. It is logical to make a decision on the basis of such costs, and common sense to exclude non-relevant costs from the calculations to simplify the data on which the decision is based. This is a variation of the use of contribution, since incremental revenue (extra revenue earned as a result of the decision) less incremental costs (extra costs incurred as a result of the decision) will be the contribution derived from the decision, towards the pool of fixed costs and profit. Cost behaviour is a significant factor in decision-making because the circumstances of the decision may be different from normal conditions in the business, so that costs will behave in a somewhat different fashion from their normal expected pattern. Rent, for example, is seen as a fixed cost, but a decision to close rented premises will make that cost variable once the lease is sold.

Factors other than cost should also be taken into account when decisions are made. There are many items which influence a decision, but which cannot be accurately measured in monetary terms. These factors are referred to as 'qualitative factors', e.g. the effect a decision may have on the morale and subsequent performance of the labour force will have an unquantifiable effect on future costs. These qualitative factors are most significant if the quantitative analysis does not give a clear-cut answer as to how the decision should be made.

COSTS FOR DECISION-MAKING – A SPECIAL LOGIC

When short-term decisions are taken, the costs to be used are derived from a special set of rules which consider those costs solely from the point of view of the decision.

Relevant costs

These are incremental costs, the extra costs resulting from a decision, or 'differential' costs, which are the cost differences between alternative courses of action concerned in the decision. The cost of a proposed course of action is best defined as the extra cost incurred thereby, and is best measured as the extra cash paid out consequent upon that decision. Revenue lost as a result of a decision counts as a cost and costs saved can be seen as revenue. The best way to define and measure these incremental or differential items is in terms of cash received or paid out, i.e. cash flow.

Sunk costs

These costs are not relevant to a decision because they have already been incurred before the point at which the decision is made. Sunk cost incurred may concern data which aids the decision-making process, and may be related to the items about which the decision is to be made, but since the cost has been incurred before the decision point is reached, a sunk cost will not affect the decision and thus should not be considered as part of the decision cost statement.

An alternative term for sunk cost is 'committed' costs, since this too expresses the idea of costs incurred before the decision point is reached. Examples of sunk costs include a feasibility study concerning the installation of a computer which is undertaken before the decision to install the computer is finalized, so that whether the business decides to accept or reject the computer, the cost of a feasibility study has been incurred; similarly, the cost of a market survey used to provide evidence to assist a decision on the development of a product is incurred before the decision is made and should not therefore play a part in the decision analysis.

Disposal costs

The loss on disposal of an old machine which is to be replaced as a result of a decision to purchase a new and more sophisticated model cannot be considered as a cost when the replacement decision is made. The loss represents past profits overstated because depreciation was inadequate, and this loss is in no way connected to the future profitability of the new machine. Any cash received from the sale of an old machine would, however, be part of the differential cash flow caused by the replacement decision, and should be considered in this way.

Non-cash costs

Costs which allocate, or provide for, other expenses which have already been spent cannot be considered in the decision analysis. For example, the share of group overhead expenses allocated to a particular project should not count against the project in the decision, because those overhead expenses will be incurred whether or not the project is accepted. Similarly, depreciation or an amount written off old plant made valueless by the decision should not be taken into account since these are book entries and no cash movement has taken place.

Opportunity cost

This concept concerns the value of a benefit sacrificed in favour of an alternative course of action. Decision-making concerns the selection of one course of action from two or more alternatives and, while the differential cash flow to be received by acceptance is an important criterion to use when the decision is made, the cash flow forgone because an alternative idea is rejected should also be considered. It is often difficult to identify the next best alternative, or to compute an expected cash flow forgone if that alternative is rejected. Some companies rank competing projects in order of their cash flow, so that the opportunity cost of choosing project A as opposed to project B can be seen in terms of the return forgone from project B. Thus opportunity cost can be defined as the net revenue or contribution which could be earned by resources in their next best use if they were not committed to their present activity.

The 'ripple' effect

A decision made concerning one part of the business may have a significant effect on another part of the business. This is known as the ripple effect since the ripples caused by one change to costs or revenues following a decision may either harm or enhance the activities of other departments or divisions. A good example would be a publishing company considering the launch of a new monthly magazine, which must recognize as a cost of the new venture the fact that its new publication will gain some circulation at the expense of its existing periodicals. The loss of revenue on other magazines is a cost of the new venture. Alternatively, a new product may use the same raw material already used by other products, and the increased quantity purchased from the supplier may benefit the other products if improved buying prices or trade discounts are received as a result of the increased quantity purchased.

Materials

If a material required for a special contract or job is in regular use elsewhere in the business, the material used on the new product will have to be replaced, so that the cost of using it on the new product or contract is its replacement cost. Thus replacement, not historic, cost is relevant in the context of the decision concerning the new product or contract. Surplus materials which would otherwise be sold or scrapped should be charged to a new product or contract at their net realizable value, i.e. the cash forgone if they are not sold as scrap. Some materials, especially those of a toxic nature, may incur considerable disposal costs, so that if the material is used up on a contract instead of being scrapped the disposal costs avoided will act as a revenue to the contract or product concerned. The original historic cost of material is rarely a relevant cost, because it is 'sunk and gone' and will not affect the future cash flows consequent upon the decision to be taken. If a scarce raw material which cannot be replaced is to be used on a particular contract or product, the cost of its use will be the profit forgone by not using the material on an alternative product, i.e. the opportunity cost.

Labour

The labour cost on a project is the cash paid out for the labour used. Overtime is an incremental cost but if the labour is already paid and would be idle if not otherwise employed, no extra labour cost is incurred. Skilled labour is a scarce resource, and the cost of using it on one product may be the profit forgone if production of another product is thereby curtailed. A manager whose retirement or redundancy is postponed as a result of a project will cost the amount of his or her salary less the pension avoided.

Example 18.1: Relevant costs

A specialist manufacturer of components in the electronics industry has been offered a contract to supply 800 identical components over the next twelve months.

The data relating to the production of each component is as follows:

Material required

Material A1: 4 kg	–	see note 1 below.
Material A2: 3 kg	–	see note 2 below.
Part No. 479: 1	–	see note 3 below.

Notes
1. Material A1 is in continuous use by the company. Current stock is 2,000 kg at a book value of £10.70 per kg but it is known that future purchases will cost £12.50 per kg.
2. A stock of 1,200 kg of material A2 is held. The original cost of this material was £6.30 per kg but as the material has not been required for the last two years it has been written down to £4.50 per kg scrap value. The only forseeable alternative use is as a substitute for material A4 (in current use) but this would involve further processing costs of £2.60 per kg. The current cost of material A4 is £4.60 per kg.
3. It is estimated that the Part No. 479 could be bought for £70 each.

Labour requirements

Each component would require six hours of skilled labour and four hours of semi-skilled. An employee possessing the necessary skills is available and is currently paid £6 per hour. A replacement would, however, have to be obtained at a rate of £5 per hour for the work which would otherwise be done by the skilled employee. The current rate for semi-skilled work is £4 per hour and an additional employee could be appointed for this work.

Overhead

The company absorbs overhead by a machine hour rate, currently £25 per hour of which £9 is for variable overhead and £16 for fixed overhead. If this contract is undertaken it is estimated that fixed costs will increase for the duration of the contract by £5,200. Spare machine capacity is available and each component would require six machine hours.

A price of £240 per component has been suggested by the offeror company.

Required

1. State whether or not the contract should be accepted and support your conclusion with appropriate figures for presentation to management.
2. Comment briefly on three factors which management ought to consider and which may influence their decision.

Proposed contract cost			Unit cost
	£	£	£
4 kg A1 at replacement cost (£12.50)		50.00	
3 kg A2 at replacement cost of A4, i.e. £4.60	13.80		
Less further processing cost of currently held A2 (3 × £2.60)	7.80	6.00	56.00
Part No. 479			70.00
			126.00
Labour:			
6 hours' skilled at replacement cost of £5.00		30.00	
4 hours semi-skilled at £4.00		16.00	46.00
Variable overhead – 6 machine hours at £9			54.00
Total variable costs			226,00
Add incremental fixed costs £5,200			6.50
800			
Total incremental (out of pocket) costs			232.50
Profit			7.50
Selling price			240.00

The contract for 800 components should be accepted at the offered price of £240 each because this is greater than the incremental costs of production. In no circumstances should the work be undertaken at a price of less than £232.50.

Factors to be considered:
1. Will this job lead to repeat orders from this or other manufacturers? It might be worth accepting a small order at a loss, to demonstrate the ability of the company, which might lead to a large future order at an improved price.
2. The contract provides employment for the labour force, and a contribution towards overhead and profit. Production facilities help to earn their keep.
3. Where stocks are used up, they have been charged at replacement cost – but in terms of profit disclosed, lower historic cost would be used, and the profit disclosed would be greater.

SHORT-TERM BUSINESS DECISIONS

Management decisions taken in the short run are a matter of fine tuning to improve the efficiency of the business or to adapt to change. Such decisions are taken within the parameters of existing production facilities, and usually concern closure, pricing, the use of limiting factors, and make or buy decisions.

CLOSURE OR WITHDRAWAL OF A PRODUCT LINE

A common mistake in the context of business is to measure the profitability of departments or products using the full absorption costing system, so that any product which makes a loss under this system will be considered as a prospect for closure. Closure decisions taken on the basis of full absorption cost statements may fail to consider the fact that certain fixed costs allotted to the product to be discontinued are fixed and may continue if the product is discontinued. Sales revenue and variable costs will certainly be affected if a product line is dropped, so these items must certainly influence the decision. Accordingly, a closure or withdrawal decision should be taken on the basis of contribution rather than on the basis of profit, which may include fixed costs which are not relevant to the decision. There are five basic rules for such a decision.
1. Cost behaviour in the context of the changed circumstances of the decision must be taken into account. Costs which may be considered as fixed in the context of an ongoing business may become variable if that business closes, e.g. the rent of premises considered to be fixed under the terms of the lease will cease as a cost if that lease is sold.
2. Any product, department or sales area which shows a negative contribution should be discontinued, because the revenue from its operation does not cover the variable cost of earning that revenue. If closure avoids a negative contribution the remaining total contribution from other sectors of the business will be increased. Before closure is effected, however, serious consideration must be given to the possibility of improving the sector with a negative contribution, to make a positive contribution in future. Closure is a permanent matter and should take place only when management are convinced that a return to profitability is impossible.

3. A business sector which shows a positive contribution should not be closed even though it appears to make a loss under the full absorption system. Closure will lose the positive contribution made towards the fixed costs, but the fixed costs allocated to the business sector will remain and therefore the overall profit of the business will be reduced.
4. A business sector with a positive contribution should be closed, however, if an alternative use of the resources invested in that sector will make an even greater contribution.
5. The 'ripple' effect must be considered in a closure decision, because the withdrawal of one product or the closure of a branch may have an effect on other products or sectors of the business.

Example 18.2

A medium-sized engineering company manufactures four products on separate production lines in its factory. Each product has its own marketing and transport facilities. Products A and D use the same raw material. A full absorption costing system is in operation and the costing department has provided the following profit forecast for the year:

	A		B		C		D	
	£000	£000	£000	£000	£000	£000	£000	£000
Sales		790		1,550		1,250		420
Costs:								
Materials	270		280		460		240	
Labour	300		441		365		200	
Factory overhead	79		155		125		42	
Transport	90		190		140		22	
Marketing	54	793	150	1,216	295	1,385	18	522
Profit/Loss		(3)		334		(135)		(102)

Total net profit
£94,000
Factory overhead cost totals £401,000

Consequent upon this statement, the managing director considers that the company should make only product B and discontinue production of A, C and D since they all show a loss. A management accountant is consulted for advice concerning this decision. Further investigation reveals that:

1. If the marketing facilities of product D are utilized in product C, sales of that product would increase by £220,000. No extra transport costs will be incurred.
2. If the materials used from product D are no longer purchased, a quantity rebate of 10 per cent of the cost of raw material purchased from that supplier will be lost.
3. Transport costs are partly fixed since they cover the lease rental on vehicles, insurance and road tax, and partly variable since they also cover fuel, maintenance and drivers' wages.
4. Marketing costs are considered to be fixed in nature since a predetermined amount is set aside for this activity.

5.   Material and labour are considered to be variable costs of production.

The management accountant would redraft the profit forecast using contribution, and would then be able to make helpful comments to the management.

Redrafted profit forecast

	A		B		C		D	
	£000	£000	£000	£000	£000	£000	£000	£000
Sales		790		1,550		1,250		420
Direct costs:								
Materials	270		280		460		240	
Labour	300		441		365		200	
Transport	90		190		140		22	
Marketing	54	714	150	1,061	295	1,260	18	480
Contribution		76		489		(10)		(60)

Total contribution	£495,000	
Factory overhead	£401,000	401
Net profit	£ 94,000	88

If product B only is produced, a contribution of £489,000 will be achieved, so that the net profit will fall by £6,000 to £88,000. If the managing director's plan is carried out, the negative contributions of products C and D will be avoided, but the positive contribution of product A will also be lost. A better plan would be to produce products A and B thus earning a contribution of £565,000 with a net profit of £164,000. Thus the application of the simple rules stated above will avoid a drop in profit as a result of a faulty decision, and point the way to an improvement in the forecast profit.

If the marketing facilities of product D are transferred to C, the contribution of that product becomes positive at £57,000 (see note below), so that profit is increased to £221,000 if C is then retained. Withdrawal of product D has a ripple effect on product C which then shows a positive contribution. The ripple effect is further demonstrated by the loss of quantity rebate on raw materials. If product D is withdrawn, the quantity rebate of 10 per cent on materials used to make product A will be lost and this will cost the company £30,000 (1/9 × £270,000). Therefore the eventual profit will fall to £191,000.

Although seen as fixed in the context of ongoing business operations, transport and marketing costs become variable if closure is under consideration. Separate marketing and transport facilities will not be required for products which are discontinued, so these former fixed costs will no longer be incurred. However, the cancellation of these services may lead to other *ad hoc* costs which cannot be quantified at the moment.

Note: The material and labour costs of product C equal £825,000, which is 66 per cent of the sales revenue of £1,250,000. Therefore extra sales of product C in the sum of £220,000 will incur direct material and labour costs equal to 66 per cent of the revenue, so that a contribution of £75,000 will be derived from those sales. No extra transport costs are incurred. If the marketing expenses of £18,000 are deducted from this contribution, the former negative contribution of £10,000 becomes positive at £57,000.

THE OPTIMUM USE OF A LIMITING FACTOR

Once the limiting factor has been identified, it is possible to maximize profit by ensuring that the best use is made of the factor which limits expansion. Contribution per unit of limiting factor is a useful guide to the allocation of the scarce resources, and when applied will concentrate production on the most profitable plan. Fixed costs should not be allowed to form part of this decision, since whichever course is taken they will not change.

Example 18.3

A company manufactures two products, A and B, with cost structures as follows. Production is limited since only twenty skilled operatives can be employed, and they will each work only forty hours per week.

Direct unit cost		A		B
		£		£
Materials: 6 components at £15		90	12 components at £15	180
Labour: 9 hours at £5		45	4 hours at £5	20
Marginal cost		135		200
Selling price		162		220
Contribution		27		20

Contribution per unit of limiting factor – labour:

$$A: \frac{£27}{9 \text{ hours}} = £3 \qquad\qquad B: \frac{£20}{4 \text{ hours}} = £5$$

Contribution and therefore profit are maximized if production is concentrated on B.

Proof: twenty operatives work in the factory for a forty-hour week; labour time is therefore limited to 800 hours per week, in which 89 As (9 hours each) or 200 Bs (4 hours each) can be made. The contribution of 89 As at £27 = £2,403; of 200 Bs at £20 = £4,000. Concentration of production on B optimizes the use of scarce resources.

Suppose alternatively that materials are in short supply, and are the limiting factor. Contribution per unit of limiting factor – materials:

$$A: \frac{£27}{6 \text{ components}} = £4.50 \qquad\qquad B: \frac{£20}{12 \text{ components}} = £1.66$$

In this case A is best since it earns a greater contribution than B for each unit of scarce resource used up.

Proof: assume that only 900 components per week are available, which make 150 As or 75 Bs. Contribution earned by 150 As = £4,050; that earned by 75 Bs = £1,500. Therefore A is better.

MAKE OR BUY DECISIONS

A frequent problem in industry is to decide whether to make a component within the business or to buy it from an outside subcontractor. The price offered by the subcontractor must be set against the direct or marginal cost of production within the business. Fixed costs are irrelevant in this decision, since they will still be incurred whether the company makes the component or buys it outside.

Example 18.4

A company uses three components, A, B and C, and must decide whether to make them or buy them from a subcontractor. The significant figures are as follows:

	A	B	C
	£	£	£
Marginal cost	10	12	8
Bought-out price	7	16	14
Excess	(3)	4	6
Machine time (hours)		2	6

Clearly, component A should be bought rather than made, because buying outside saves £3 on each component used. It is equally clear that components B and C should be manufactured in the factory rather than purchased from a subcontractor, thus saving £4 and £6 respectively for each component. To complicate this decision consider the effect of a limiting factor. Assume that production is restricted by the number of available machine hours. Component A must still be bought rather than made, but if there is insufficient machine time to make all the Bs and Cs which the company requires, a decision must be made whether to buy B or C. This decision rests on the *excess per unit of limiting factor*, since it is most profitable to buy the product with the least excess per unit of limiting factor.

$$\text{Excess per unit of limiting factor B} = \frac{£4}{2 \text{ machine hours}} = £2$$

$$\text{Excess per unit of limiting factor C} = \frac{£6}{6 \text{ machine hours}} = £1$$

Therefore C would be bought and the limited resources of the business would be used to make B, thus saving the company from buying the component.

Whose production makes the best use of limited resources?

To prove the logic of this calculation, assume that 600 machine hours are available during a costing period. This machine time can be used to make either 300 Bs (2 hours each) or 100 Cs (6 hours each). Scarce machine time used to make component B will save the excess of £4 of the bought-out price over marginal cost each time a component is made. Therefore if 300 Bs are made costs are reduced by £1,200. If, however, the scarce machine hours are used to make component C, only 100 Cs will be produced, and at an excess of £6 per component only £600 will be saved. Thus it is better to make 300 Bs and buy 100 Cs. The certainty of this proof depends on the need within the business for 300 Bs and 100 Cs each week.

Alternatively a production budget can be drafted, to maximize the contribution earned by the quantity of limiting factor available. If 600 machine hours are available each week either 300 Bs or 100 Cs could be made. If demand is limited to 200 Bs and 80 Cs each week the most profitable course of action would be to concentrate production on the product which maximizes contribution per unit of limiting factor, and to buy the remainder.

Proof

Plan 1: Concentrate on B

Make 200 Bs	use	400 hours	
Machine hours available		600 hours	
Surplus		200 hours	÷ 6 = 33 Cs

Make 33 Cs and buy 47 Cs.

Plan 2: Concentrate on C

Make 80 Cs	use	480 hours	
Machine hours available		600 hours	
Surplus		120 hours	÷ 2 = 60 Bs

Make 60 Bs and buy 140 Bs.

Costs

	£
Plan 1: Make 200 Bs × £12	2,400
Make 33 Cs × £8	264
Buy 47 Cs × £14	658
Total cost	3,322
Plan 2: Make 80 Cs × £8	640
Make 60 Bs × £12	720
Buy 140 Bs × £16	2,240
Total cost	3,600

These figures prove that the cheapest way to provide 200 Bs and 80 Cs would be plan 1, which concentrates production on B and buys C if internal factory capacity is insufficient to produce the volume required.

QUALITATIVE FACTORS AFFECTING A MAKE OR BUY DECISION

Qualitative factors may override the quantitative answer in a make or buy decision. A company may prefer to make a component, even though it could be bought cheaper from a subcontractor, if there is a lack of trust in the subcontractor to maintain supplies and prices. The impact of qualitative factors on costs cannot be forecast or measured with accuracy, but nevertheless these factors are of great significance to a make or buy decision. The major factors are as follows:

1. Doubt as to the subcontractor's ability or intention to maintain the price quoted for the supply of components. If the supplier increases prices after the buying company has committed itself and dismantled its own production facilities, this changed circumstance may reverse the logic of the original decision based on careful calculations. The possibility of a price increase, especially if the supplier knows the buying company is dependent on the supplier for components, may therefore be a reason to make a component, even though it can be purchased at a lower cost outside the business.

2. A lack of trust in the supplier to maintain the quality of the components will also influence a business to make rather than buy. Poor quality components from a subcontractor can harm the reputation of the main product and its manufacturer, if they fail in service.

3. The possibility that the subcontractor will fail to meet delivery dates is another reason for producing a component rather than buying it. Late delivery can disrupt production, causing a failure to co-ordinate supply from the factory to demand, perhaps induced by a pre-planned advertising campaign, or alternatively causing extensive and costly idle time in the factory. A strike or plant breakdown at the subcontractor's factory is outside the control of the buying company, yet such circumstances can have a marked effect on its activities.

4. If a subcontractor restricts supplies of components after the buying company has committed itself and dismantled its own component production facilities, it will be extremely harmful to the buying company. If a rival company makes a takeover bid for the supplier, or offers the supplier a higher price for the use of its specialist machinery, the buying company might be cut off from production capacity for its components.

5. The introduction of product improvements or new designs should remain secret from rival producers for as long as possible. If components are to be produced by a subcontractor, ongoing discussions concerning future changes will be notified outside the business, so that rival companies may gain a foreknowledge of projected developments.

6. Developments and production improvements require close liaison between engineers and production team. Such liaison will not be possible if the production team of the supplier company is distant from the main factory, and not particularly interested in developments of what to them is just another subcontract job.

7. Buying a component may mean that a skilled team of operatives will be dismissed. No business likes to break up such a team, in which it has invested considerable training resources. Redundancies caused by buying components may hinder good industrial relations within the main factory.

8. Work contracted out will reduce the size and influence of the major company. If too much production is contracted out, the main company is left merely with the task of assembly rather than the more sophisticated manufacturing operations. A company which is confident of its ability to supply its own components can demonstrate to other subcontractors that it is still a strong and capable organization. Such a demonstration may prevent other component suppliers from attempting to take advantage of the company when quoting for future orders.

9. As a matter of policy or strategy the management may wish to ensure that the company is self-sufficient and experiencing a steady growth of its operations. Such a policy may be achieved by manufacturing all components within the business rather than using the services of subcontractors.

DECISIONS TO SELL OR PROCESS FURTHER

Differential costs and revenues are important when a manufacturer must decide whether to sell a by-product or joint product at once, or to process it beyond the split-off point. The extra or incremental revenue per unit, which is the increase in value earned by the further processing, must be set against the extra cost of putting the material into a more saleable condition. The revenue forgone by not selling at the split-off point acts as an opportunity cost of the alternative to process further, and only incremental revenue is relevant to the decision.

A similar decision-making logic can be applied to a decision investigating whether it is worthwhile to process or rework scrap materials. The costs up to the by-product split-off point, or the scrap point, are already incurred and, since they will not change whether extra processing is undertaken or not, they are not relevant to the decision.

Example 18.5: Further processing decisions

A company produces a by-product from its chemical process, which could be sold immediately at a price of £6 per litre. Further processing would cost £2 per litre, and packaging 50p per litre. Should it accept an offer from a customer to buy the reprocessed by-product at £9 per litre?

	£
Further processing cost	2.00
Packaging	0.50
Scrap sales revenue forgone	6.00
Incremental cost	8.50
Price	9.00
Surplus	0.50

The offer should be accepted since the incremental cost is less than the incremental revenue. Since the margin of surplus is small, any qualitative factors affecting this decision may become more significant.

Note that process costs up to the split-off point form no part of this decision, and that revenue forgone from the alternative of immediate sale is treated as an opportunity cost of further processing.

As a second example, a publisher has stocks of unsold copies of a book, held in an unbound condition, and receives an offer from a dealer for their purchase.

The stocks comprise 5,000 copies, and the dealer offers £2,000. The full absorbed cost of production is not relevant to the decision, although an examiner may produce convincing figures that make it appear so. These costs have been incurred, and whichever way it goes the decision will not change them.

Relevant costs are the cost of binding, say 20p per copy, and the cost of scrap sales forgone, say £500. Thus these stocks can be sold for £2,000, at a relevant incremental cost of £500 + (5,000 × 20p) = £1,500, and the offer would be accepted.

The problem can be posed by informing the student of the offer price and the binding cost, and asking how much should be expected from a scrap sale. With the facts above, incremental revenue would be £2,000 less the binding cost of £1,000, so the offer would be accepted unless a scrap sale of more than £1,000 could be made.

A further complication might be to introduce the possibility of another offer for the stock, in six months' time (say £2,800). The difference between the existing offer and the expected offer is the incremental revenue (£800) and this must be set against the cost of storing the stock for the next six months, the incremental cost, to see if the current offer should be accepted or whether it is worth waiting.

The ripple effect can also be built into this type of decision. A deal to sell off unsold copies of a book (5,000 for £2,000 means that the dealer can sell them at any price in excess of 40p plus transport and other costs) may affect retailers with unsold stocks, customers who have already bought the book at the full price, and other rival books sold by the same publisher. This ripple effect is a qualitative factor affecting the decision.

COST INFORMATION AND PRICING

The decision as to how much to charge for a product is an important one which draws together many different factors having a bearing on market price. The cost of the product is an important factor in this decision, but marketing specialists must use this information together with data concerning the interaction of supply and demand, any imperfections in the market, and the strategy of the marketing team. In the short run a series of strategies or ploys may be adopted in the price decision of a product, but in the long run price should cover the full absorbed cost of the product if an overall loss is to be avoided.

Short-term pricing strategies cover the following activities.

1. A product may be marketed at a low price even to make a loss, to act as a loss leader or fighting brand which will beat off competition and then allow other products marketed by the company to occupy a more significant place in the market.
2. A new product being introduced to the market may be offered at a low price to ensure a smooth introduction and to establish customer demand for it.
3. Alternatively, a high price may be asked for a new product if it is well advertised and demand is ensured, in order to 'skim-off' early profits from demand stimulated by product launching techniques.
4. If the volume of a product sold exceeds the break-even point, so that fixed costs are covered by contribution up to that point, a different pricing strategy can be used. The contribution earned by sales beyond the break-even point is all profit so prices can be cut to an amount which is in excess of the variable cost of the product. This means that products can be 'dumped' in a foreign market at very low prices so long as the price exceeds the variable cost.

In general, price should not be allowed to fall below variable cost, since a negative contribution would then be earned, unless the product is to be used as 'loss leader' to stimulate demand for other products. The concept of differential revenues and costs is applicable in pricing decisions.

CONTRIBUTION AND PRICING

Decisions to raise or lower the price of a product must be taken in the light of the elasticity of demand. If price can be increased without an adverse effect on demand profit will increase, and if when price is reduced demand proves elastic and sales increase extra profits will be made. Contribution has a part to play in such decisions since it is possible to use it to show by how much demand must respond to a change in price if extra profit is to be made.

Example 18.6

A company sells 20,000 units of a product at £8 each, and incurs variable costs of £4.65 for each product and £50,000 of fixed overhead expenses. There is a suggestion from the sales director that price should be increased by 10 per cent, and from the production director that it should be cut by 10 per cent. As a management accountant what is your advice?

First calculate the profit made under the current situation:

Contribution × volume − Fixed cost = Profit

£3.35 × 20,000 − £50,000   = £17,000

This is the profit required since no price strategy will be accepted if it provides a smaller profit than is earned at present.

Contribution required = £50,000 + £17,000 = £67,000

	Raise 10%		Reduce 10%
Price	8.80		7.20
Direct costs	4.65		4.65
Contribution	4.15		2.55

P/V ratio $\dfrac{4.15}{8.80} \times \dfrac{100}{1}$ = 47.16% $\dfrac{2.55}{7.20} \times \dfrac{100}{1}$ = 35.4%

Contribution required is (Fixed cost + profit)	= £67,000	=	£67,000
Therefore sales required £67,000 ÷ .4716	= £142,070	£67,000 ÷ .354 =	£189,265
Therefore volume sold (units) £142,070 ÷ £8.8	= 16,144	£189,265 ÷ £7.2 =	26,287
Present Volume	20,000		20,000
Change	− 3,856 units		+ 6,287 units

Thus, if prices are raised by 10 per cent the company must be certain that sales volume will not fall by more than 19.28 per cent ($3,866/20,000 \times 100/1$) if profit is to be maintained, and if prices are cut by 10 per cent sales volume must increase by at least 31 per cent ($6,287/20,000 \times 100/1$) if profit is to be maintained.

This information will assist when the decision is made but must be used in conjunction with other data concerning price elasticity of demand for the product.

MULTIPLE CHOICE QUESTIONS

Note that these questions relate to Chapters 17 and 18 of the book.

18.1 Which of the following definitions describes marginal cost?
  (a) A principle whereby variable costs are charged to cost units and the fixed cost attributable to the relevant period is written off in full against the contribution for that period.
  (b) Costs appropriate to aiding the making of specific management decisions.
  (c) The price at which material identical to that which is used up could be replaced on the date of usage.
  (d) The variable cost of one unit of product or service.

(a)   (b)   (c)   (d)

18.2 Which of the following definitions describes opportunity cost?
  (a) A hypothetical cost taken into account in a particular situation to represent a benefit enjoyed by a business in respect of which no actual expense is incurred.
  (b) Costs incurred as a result of taking a particular policy decision.

    (c)   The value of benefit sacrificed in favour of an alternative course of action.

    (d)   Shared costs of more than one product or service.

(a)   (b)   (c)   (d)

18.3 Arguments which support the use of absorption costing are:
    (a)   Matching – it is true and fair to set the full cost of production services to make a product against revenue from its sale.
    (b)   Stocks are not valued in accordance with SSAP 9.
    (c)   A stock build-up will not penalize the profit measured, by writing off overheads to profit and loss account during the production period.
    (d)   Relating fixed costs to production units is arbitrary and costly.

(a + b)   (a + c)   (b + c)   (c + d)

18.4 A product sells for £8 each, with variable costs of £5 each. Fixed costs are budgeted as £18,000, or £2 per unit. The break-even point is:
    (a)   Production of 9,000 units.
    (b)   Sales revenue of £48,000.
    (c)   Production of 6,000 units.
    (d)   A profit of £9,000.

(a)   (b)   (c)   (d)

18.5 With reference to the facts in 18.4, state the margin of safety:
    (a)   50 per cent.
    (b)   62.5 per cent.
    (c)   33.3 per cent.
    (d)   40 per cent.

(a)   (b)   (c)   (d)

18.6 Which of the following items does not act as a limitation of the break-even chart?
    (a)   Curvilinear relationship of cost to volume.
    (b)   Revenue set against the cost of sales rather than the cost of production.
    (c)   Requirement for constant mix in a multi-product situation.
    (d)   Difficulties encountered in identifying fixed and variable costs.

(a)   (b)   (c)   (d)

18.7 (1) Costs avoided as a result of a decision act as incremental revenue. (2) Revenues forgone as a consequence of a decision act as incremental revenue. Do you agree?
    (a) Both true.
    (b) (1) true; (2) false.
    (c) (1) false; (2) true.
    (d) Both false.

(a)   (b)   (c)   (d)

18.8 Material A was purchased for £4 per kg, and 2,800 kg are in stock. It is used regularly on a range of products, at a rate of 700 kg per week. The price fluctuates, and stands at present at £6 per kg, but when the next order is placed the price is expected to be £7 per kg. Off-cuts of material A sold for scrap are worth £1 per kg. Under opportunity cost rules what cost would be charged to a new contract which requires 200 kg of material A today?
    (a) £4.
    (b) £6.
    (c) £5.
    (d) £7.

(a)   (b)   (c)   (d)

18.9 Four products are under consideration for closure. Prima facie which one should be closed on the basis of the following results?
    (a) A loss and a negative contribution.
    (b) A loss and a positive contribution.
    (c) A profit and a positive contribution.
    (d) A contribution equal to fixed cost.

(a)   (b)   (c)   (d)

18.10 Which of the following factors are not qualitative factors in a make or buy decision?
    (a) Doubt as to the ability of the subcontractor to meet delivery dates.
    (b) Doubt as to the ability of the subcontractor to maintain quality.
    (c) The ease with which improvements can be made to the product.
    (d) The effect of redundancy on labour relations.

(a)   (b)   (c)   (d)

EXERCISES

18A   Next year's preliminary budget workings for Scrunchie, a breakfast cereal, the only product manufactured by HF Ltd, are shown below.

Budgeted revenue account for the year ended 30 September

		£
Sales (20,000 boxes, containing standard packets)		600,000
	£	
Direct materials	240,000	
Direct labour	102,000	
Variable overhead	70,000	
Fixed overhead	122,200	534,200
Profit		£65,800

Budgeted net assets as at 30 September		£
Fixed assets (net of depreciation)		310,000
Working capital:	£	
Debtors	50,000	
Stocks	65,000	
Creditors	(25,000)	90,000
Net assets employed		400,000

The existing plant and equipment is considerably under-utilized and a proposal being considered is to extend sales to supermarkets, where the product would be sold under a different brand name.

Estimated effects of this proposal are:

1. Additional annual sales, to supermarkets, 8,000 boxes at £25 per box.
2. Cost of direct materials will be reduced as a result of a 5 per cent quantity discount on all purchases.
3. Extra supervisory and clerical staff will be required at a cost of £16,000 p.a.
4. Market research has indicated that sales to existing outlets will fall by approximately 10 per cent, there will be no change in selling price to these customers.
5. Stocks and creditors will increase by £25,000 and £15,000 respectively and the credit period extended to supermarkets will be double that given to existing customers.

Required

Present data to assist in the evaluation of the proposal.

Specifically you should:

(a) Prepare a revised budgeted revenue account and statement of net assets employed incorporating the results of the proposal.

(b) Calculate the effect on profit of each of the changes resulting from the proposal and reconcile the total of these with the difference in budgeted profits.

(c) Advise management on the suitability of the proposal making any further calculations you consider necessary and adding any other comments or reservations you think relevant.

(Association of Certified Accountants)

18B Machinings Limited is engaged solely on the production of four components, P, Q, R and S, for Producers Limited of which it is a subsidiary. The budgeted production and component unit costs for the three months commencing 1 January are as follows:

	P	Q	R	S
Budgeted production	3,000	5,000	2,500	4,500
Costs:	£	£	£	£
Direct material	74	54	50	90
Direct labour	8	6	16	30
Variable overhead	5	10	5	25
Fixed overhead	7	2	4	15

The variable overhead relates exclusively to machine utilization which costs £5 per hour.

Two of the machines have been found to be defective and unsafe to use and as a result only 24,000 hours of machine time will be available for the forthcoming three-month period. However, Producers Limited requires the full quantities of components budgeted and to enable this obligation to be met, Machinings Limited has decided to buy in components to meet the shortfall in its own production. Quotations received for components of acceptable quality, subject to minimum orders of 100 are: P £95; Q £75; R £65; S £175.

You have been invited to advise Machinings Limited on the most economical way in which it can fulfil its obligations to Producers Limited, and for this purpose you are required to prepare a statement comparing the budgeted costs for the three-month period with the costs applicable to your proposal and to comment upon any matters which you consider ought to receive the attention of management.

(Association of Certified Accountants)

18C (a) Set out the basic rules which should be applied when a decision to close a business outlet is under review.

(b) Dolly's Dresses Ltd operates a small factory in the East Midlands manufacturing an attractive line of children's wear. This output is sold through four shops rented by the company within easy distance of the factory. The cost accountant has budgeted the activity of the business for the next half-year and has presented the following budgeted profit statement to the board.

Shop	Beeston		Sherwood		Mansfield		Ashfield		Total	
	£000	£000	£000	£000	£000	£000	£000	£000	£000	£000
Sales		807		1,365		834		462		3,468
Cost of goods sold	453		672		504		288		1,917	
Shop salaries	90		90		165		60		405	
Shop admin costs	165		183		243		135		726	
Factory fixed overheads	120	828	240	1,185	180	1,092	60	543	600	3,648
Profit/(Loss)		(21)		180		(258)		(81)		(180)

On the basis of this information the board of Dolly's Dresses is seriously considering the closure of the three loss-making shops.

The board believes that if the Mansfield shop is closed, customer loyalty for the product is such that 15 per cent of the Mansfield turnover would transfer to the Ashfield shop.

Required

Restate the cost data in a more suitable form and advise the management of Dolly's Dresses Ltd.

18D   Patterley Ltd manufactures four products, Paste, Quaste, Raste and Saste. The direct costs of production are estimated at:

	Paste £	Quaste £	Raste £	Saste £
Materials	36	38	42	24
Labour:				
Assembly (at £4 per hour)	8	12	16	16
Machinists (at £6 per hour)	12	24	18	36

Total fixed costs are dependent on output levels as follows:

Production (units)	Total fixed costs (£)
Up to 50,000	400,000
50,001 to 75,000	500,000
75,001 to 100,000	600,000

The sales director estimates that demand for their products in the next year will be as follows:

	Paste	Quaste	Raste	Saste
Units	18,000	30,000	27,000	15,000
Selling price per unit	£68	£90	£91	£94

The production manager states that the capacity of existing machines is 210,000 hours per annum, though this will be increased to 300,000 hours in two years time when new plant which is currently on order will be delivered. Meanwhile a local firm has offered to manufacture any of the products on a subcontract basis at the following prices:

Paste	£63
Quaste	£80
Raste	£72
Saste	£82

Required

(a) Advise the managing director to what extent the services of the subcontractor should be utilized in order to meet the expected demand for Paste, Quaste, Raste and Saste.

(b) Prepare a statement showing the profit you would expect if your advice is followed.

(c) Discuss briefly the reasoning you have applied in making your recommendation.

18E (a) 'Qualitative factors may override the quantitative answer in a make or buy decision.'

Describe the qualitative factors which are significant for a make or buy decision.

(b) A company needs 20,000 coil springs to build into its main product. It has already spent £18,000 on research and development of an appropriate coil spring, and can make the spring for £14 each. This cost comprises: materials £6, labour £3, variable overheads £2, fixed factory overheads absorbed £2 and depreciation £1. The labour cost includes overtime premium of 50p. The springs can be bought out for £12.50.

Required

Advise the management whether to make or buy.

18F Domestic political trouble in the country of an overseas supplier is causing concern in your company because it is not known when further supplies of raw material X will be received. The current stock held of this particular raw material is 17,000 kg which cost £136,000. Based on raw material X, your company makes five different products and the expected demand for each of these, for the next three months, is given below together with other relevant information:

Product code	kg of raw material X per unit of finished product	Direct labour hours per unit of finished product	Selling price per unit (£)	Expected demand over three months (units)
701	0.7	1.0	26	8,000
702	0.5	0.8	28	7,200
821	1.4	1.5	34	9,000
822	1.3	1.1	38	12,000
937	1.5	1.4	40	10,000

The direct wages rate per hour is £5 and production overhead is based on direct wages cost – the variable overhead absorption rate being 40 per cent and the fixed overhead absorption rate being 60 per cent.

Variable selling costs, including sales commission, are 15 per cent of selling price.

Budgeted fixed selling and administration costs are £300,000 per annum.

Assume that the fixed production overhead incurred will equal the absorbed figure.

You are required to

(a) Show what quantity of the raw material on hand ought to be allocated to which products in order to maximize profits for the forthcoming three months.

(b) Present a brief statement showing contribution and profit for the forthcoming three months, if your suggestion in (a) is adopted.

(c) Comment briefly on the analysis you used to aid the decision-making process in (a) and give *three* other examples of business problems where this type of analysis can be useful.

(*Chartered Institute of Management Accountants*)

18G   JB Limited is a small specialist manufacturer of electronic components and much of its output is used by the makers of aircraft for both civil and military purposes. One of the few aircraft manufacturers has offered a contract to JB Limited for the supply, over the next twelve months, of 400 identical components.

The data relating to the production of *each component* is as follows:

(i)   Material requirements.
        3 kg material M1 – see note 1 below
        2 kg material P2 – see note 2 below
        1 Part No. 678 – see note 3 below

Notes:
1.   Material M1 is in continuous use by the company: 1,000 kg are currently held in stock at a book value of £4.70 per kg but it is shown that future purchases will cost £5.50 per kg.
2.   1,200 kg of material P2 are held in stock. The original cost of this material was £4.30 per kg but as the material has not been required for the last two years it has been written down to £1.50 per kg scrap value. The only forseeable alternative use is as a substitute for material P4 (in current use) but this would involve further processing costs of £1.60 per kg. The current cost of material P4 is £3.60 per kg.
3.   It is estimated that the Part No. 678 could be bought for £50 each;

(ii)   Labour requirements:
        Each component would require five hours of skilled labour and five hours of semi-skilled. An employee possessing the necessary skills is available and is currently paid £5 per hour. A replacement would, however, have to be obtained at a rate of £4 per hour for the work which would otherwise be done by the skilled employee. The current rate for semi-skilled work is £3 per hour and an additional employee could be appointed for this work.

(iii)   Overhead:
        JB Limited absorbs overhead by a machine hour rate, currently £20 per hour of which £7 is for variable overhead and £13 for fixed overhead. If this contract is undertaken it is estimated that fixed costs will increase for the duration of the contract by £3,200. Spare machine capacity is available and each component would require four machine hours.

A price of £145 per component has been suggested by the large company which makes aircraft.

You are required to

(a) State whether or not the contract should be accepted and support your conclusion with appropriate figures for presentation to management.

(b) Comment briefly on *three* factors which management ought to consider and which may influence their decision.

(Chartered Institute of Management Accountants)

19 Management Information for Long-term Business Decisions

The long-term business decision implies that the funds of a company will be invested at the present time in a project which will operate and continue to pay off over a period of years. The term 'capital investment appraisal' is applied to decisions of this type, and is defined in the CIMA *Terminology* as 'the process of evaluating proposed investment in specific fixed assets and the benefits to be obtained from their acquisition'. A major difficulty in evaluating capital investment projects and deciding which to adopt and which to reject is that the benefits of such projects extend more than one year into the future. The year is an arbitrary accounting concept within financial accounting, which is convenient for the idea of stewardship, but with capital budgeting it is necessary to appraise the project over its full life. The appraisal must include working capital to be tied up in the project as well as the original capital investment. The activities covered by the term 'capital budgeting' are designed to ensure that scarce investment resources in a business are channelled into the most worthwhile long-term projects. The significance of ranking projects according to their potential success, and rationing out capital to them, is that the return on investment funds available to a company is optimized, and this leads to the long-term survival of the business.

Capital budgeting commences with the identification and formulation of capital investment proposals. The potential cash flows from these proposals are then estimated and evaluated so that the net cash flow received from rival projects can be compared on a common basis. Projects are ranked in order of significance according to whichever criterion is to be applied to them, and the long-term investment resources of the business are applied according to this ranking. An essential part of capital budgeting is the re-evaluation of investment proposals both during their life and after their completion. This technique audits the efficiency of the ranking and rationing procedure, and also tests the accuracy of evaluation methods. A capital project will tie up a large amount of the company's resources; will affect the profitability of the business for a long period; and may be difficult to wind up and disinvest if a wrong decision is made. It is essential that long-term assets must come 'on-stream' at the right moment to meet estimated demands. Delay may well miss the market for a new product. Decisions of this type are of necessity based on estimate and imperfect knowledge and, since they usually concern large sums of investment capital which will in turn influence the ability of the company to compete and survive, they must be taken with the utmost caution.

THE INFORMATION REQUIRED

A capital investment appraisal brings together a wide range of information which may be classified as follows.

The investment

The investment is initial cost of plant to be purchased for the project, including delivery and installation costs. These amounts may not be payable at one point in time but be spread over a period. The phasing of this expenditure is significant. The useful economic life of the machinery concerned and the scrap value to be received at the end of the project must also be estimated. Depreciation, being a formal means to spread cost over the life of the project, plays no part in capital investment appraisal.

The return

The earnings to be received from a project must also be estimated not only as an amount but in terms of the period over which they are to be received. Some projects will earn well during the early years of their life with earnings falling away in later years. Others will spread earnings evenly across the years of the life; yet others may well receive the major part of their earnings during the later years of the project life. The return profile is significant because, under present value analysis, returns earned soon after the investment is made will be more significant than funds received at a later period.

Net cash flow

Capital project appraisal should be made in terms of net cash flow. The cash generated less the cash spent in each year of the life of a project, but considered over the full life of the project, forms the basis of the appraisal decision. This means that non-cash costs such as depreciation can be ignored for the purposes of appraisal. Part of the net cash flow calculation, however, must include the incremental effect of undertaking the project. This means that such items as sunk costs, and the book value of old plant retired as a consequence of the new investment, should be ignored. Only the cash received as a result of selling such old plant can be taken into account in an appraisal. The ripple effect is important since a new project may well influence the cash flows received by other parts of the business. Clearly the effect of a project on the profitability of other parts of the firm must be considered.

Financial considerations

Most projects require working capital to service stock and debtors resulting from the project, as well as fixed capital to purchase the equipment concerned. Accordingly, working capital is a significant item in the appraisal. It is necessary to appraise the risk involved in a project and this in turn should influence the cost of capital to be tied up. A risky project will require a larger return to compensate for the risk taken. The effect of taxation, which will be an outward cash flow resulting from a project, must also be taken into account together with the fact that some capital investments may receive grants from the government paid when the project commences.

METHODS OF APPRAISAL

Capital investment appraisal can be undertaken by a number of different methods. The techniques, however, can be summarized as non-discounting methods (the payback method), return on capital employed, and discounted cash flow methods.

The payback method

The term 'payback' is defined in the CIMA *Terminology* as 'the period usually expressed in years which it takes the cash inflows from the capital investment project to equal the cash outflows'. Competing projects are ranked according to the length of time it takes to repay the capital investment, and the project with the shortest payback period is deemed to be preferable.

Example 19.1

Project A has an expected life of five years, a capital cost of £200,000 and an estimated cash flow of £50,000 per annum. This project has a payback period of four years since £50,000 per annum received over this period will repay the capital cost.

Project B has a life of eight years and a capital cost of £180,000. The cash flow per annum is £36,000, giving a payback period of six years for this project.

Therefore Project A would be selected under the payback method.

Arguments in favour of the payback method are that it is simple to operate and understand; that it concentrates investment on those projects with a short payback period, and is thus beneficial if the company is short of liquid funds; and is advantageous for projects with a high obsolescence factor since much of the cost will be paid back during the early years from projects selected by this method, thus leaving only a small amount outstanding if the life should be foreshortened by economic change.

The payback method does suffer from several serious disadvantages.

1. It fails to consider the whole life of the projects under review. It ignores the post-payback life of the projects and so fails to give appropriate consideration to profitable long-term projects, especially those which have significant cash flows late in their life. In Example 19.1 project A is preferred to project B, but £36,000 per annum flowing in from project B over an eight-year life will bring in £288,000 from that project, whereas the total cash flow for project A will be £250,000 over a five-year period.

2. The method fails to give appropriate significance to the incidence of income. It considers that cash flow received in the first year has the same significance as cash flow received in the later years of the life.

These two disadvantages reduce the validity of the payback method for capital project evaluation. This method is, however, widely used as a first-screen method, to test the liquidity rather than the profitability of projects. The fact that payback cannot differentiate properly between projects with different lives is a further serious disadvantage.

The return on capital employed

This is a rate of return method which evaluates capital projects according to the return earned on the original investment. The method certainly takes the full life of the project into account. It is considered to have limited use because it fails to account for the incidence of income received over a period, and because different methods of calculation bring a lack of consistency to the results disclosed. In Example 19.1 project A would have a gross rate of return of £250,000/£200,000 × 100/1 = 125 per cent, while project B would have £288,000/£180,000 × 100/1 = 160 per cent. This rate suggests that project B should be selected. However, if an annual rate of return is calculated, project A would earn £50,000/£200,000 × 100/1 = 25 per cent, and project B would earn £36,000/£180,000 × 100/1 = 20 per cent, and project A would therefore be selected.

Discounted cash flow

The CIMA *Terminology* described discounted cash flow (DCF) calculations as 'an evaluation of the future net cash flows generated by a capital project, by discounting them to their present day value'. The term 'present value' is defined as 'the cash equivalent now of a sum of money receivable or payable at a stated future date at a specified rate'. The DCF method evaluates capital projects by comparing the cash flow over the whole life of the project and by discounting that cash flow to its present value. Thus all projects to be compared are stated in common terms. A further advantage of this method is that the discounting procedure takes into account the incidence of income, by giving greater weight to cash flows to be received in earlier years. The time value of money is of great significance when comparing projects which have differing cash flow profiles. The DCF method can also reflect the timing of tax savings resulting from a project, thereby taking into account taxation as a significant factor in the calculation.

The present value of a future stream of cash flows is the amount which an investor would pay now for the right to receive those cash flows in due course. The value set on these future cash flows depends on the rate of return required by the investor, and this is influenced by the risk involved in the investment, a further matter for estimate. If a rate of return of 10 per cent is required, an investment of £9,091 would earn £909 in a year and thus became £10,000 in a year's time. Accordingly, £9,091 is the present value of a cash flow of £10,000 to be received in one year's time at a discount rate of 10 per cent. A similar calculation will show that £8,264 invested at the present time would grow with compound interest at 10 per cent to £10,000 in two years' time, so that £8,264 represents the present value of a cash flow of £10,000 to be received in two years' time. Calculations of this type enable projects with differing cash flow profiles to be compared on an equal basis. A cash flow received now is considered to be worth more than a cash flow of similar amount received in the future because there is less risk attached to the immediate receipt, and the funds can be reinvested to earn a return equal to the market rate for capital. The present value of £5,000 to be received in two years time at 10% is £5,000 × 0.8263 = £4,131.

There are two methods of investment appraisal which use discounting in the calculation.

Net present value method

The net present value (NPV) of a capital project is the value obtained when all cash outflows and inflows are discounted by a rate which represents the cost of capital of the company. If the result of this calculation is a negative amount, it means that the present value of cash inflows is not enough to cover the present value of cash outflows and therefore the project should not be undertaken. A project which has a positive NPV will certainly be viable, but if more than one project is competing for limited funds, the project with the greatest surplus of discounted inflow over discounted outflow will be selected.

Example 19.2

Two projects, A and B, are competing for scarce investment funds within a business. Both projects will cost £30,000 payable immediately in order to commence production. The projects both have a life of three years. Project A has estimated cash flows of £20,000 in the first year, £15,000 in the second and £5,000 in the third, a total of £40,000. The expected cash flow profile for B is the very opposite, being £5,000 in the first year, £15,000 in the second and £20,000 in the third, again totalling of £40,000. These cash flows can be discounted at the cost of capital, which is 10 per cent in this example. An actuarial table showing the present value of a pound at 10 per cent for a series of years gives £0.9091 for flows received in one year's time, £0.8263 for flows received in two years' time and £0.7513 for flows received in three years' time. For the purposes of the calculation it is assumed that all cash flows are received at the end of the year. A DCF calculation would be as follows:

Year	PV of £1 at 10%	Project A (£) Cash flow	PV	Project B (£) Cash flow	PV
1	0.9091	20,000	18,182	5,000	4,545
2	0.8263	15,000	12,394	15,000	12,394
3	0.7513	5,000	3,756	20,000	15,026
		40,000		40,000	
Present value of inflow			34,332		31,965
Present value of outflow			30,000		30,000
Net present value			3,432		1,965

Note: The PV of the outflow is £30,000, the amount to be paid out now, and is not subject to discounting for that reason.

This calculation shows that at a discount rate of 10 per cent both projects are viable, with a positive net present value. If the company had £60,000 available to invest, and no better projects present themselves, it would be wise to invest in both projects. If, however, funds are restricted then project A is to be chosen before project B. Clearly much depends on the selection of a discount rate and it is considered a disadvantage of this method that the decision as to the viability of a project rests on the selection of the rate of discount to be applied.

Some authorities suggest that the rate should reflect the cost of capital to the business to ensure that projects selected always show an adequate return on funds invested. Alternatively, it is possible to vary the discount rate when comparing projects, to take account of differences in risk attached to each project, e.g. a more risky project would be discounted at a higher rate.

The internal rate of return method

The definition of internal rate of return (IRR) given in the CIMA *Terminology* is 'a percentage discount rate used in capital investment appraisal which brings the cost of the project and its future cash inflows into equality'. The IRR earned by a project is considered to be the rate of discount which must be applied to the net cash profile of the project to bring the present value of inflows to equality with the present value of outflows

Example 19.3

Using the same figures as Example 19.2, projects A and B would be discounted as follows:

Year	PV of £1 at 15%	20%	Project A (£) Cash flow	PV at 15%	PV at 20%	Project B (£) Cash flow	PV at 15%
Now			(30,000)	(30,000)	(30,000)	(30,000)	(30,000)
1	0.8696	0.8333	20,000	17,392	16,666	5,000	4,348
2	0.7561	0.6944	15,000	11,341	10,416	15,000	11,341
3	0.6575	0.5787	5,000	3,287	2,893	20,000	13,150
Net present value				2,020	(25)		(1,161)

Project A is positive when discounted at 15 per cent, but negative when discounted at 20 per cent. Therefore the IRR, the rate of discount at which the NPV is nil, will be between these two points. It can be found by extrapolation using the formula:

$$\text{Bottom of the class } + \left[\frac{\text{Point in class}}{\text{Range in class}} \times \text{Class interval} \right]$$

$$15\% + \left[\frac{2,020}{2,020 + 25} \times 5\% \right] = 19.9\%$$

If the cash flows of project A are discounted at 19.9 per cent the PV of the inflows would equal the PV of the outflows.

Project B has a negative NPV of £1,161 when discounted at 15 per cent but we already know from Example 19.2 that it is positive £1,965 when discounted at 10 per cent. The IRR of project B is between 10 and 15 per cent, and can be located by the extrapolation formula:

$$10\% + \left[\frac{1,965}{1,965 + 1,161} \times 5\% \right] = 13.1\%$$

Clearly, this analysis suggests that if sufficient funds to invest in both projects cannot be raised, project A is to be preferred to project B.

Complications

The computations shown above are in the form of introductory exercises. In reality it is important to bring into the calculation the effects of taxation, including capital allowances.

The profit element of cash flows will generate a tax payment, usually made one year after the year in which an inflow has been experienced. At the end of a project there will be a further cash inflow from the residual value of the equipment but this too will give rise to a tax balancing charge or balancing allowance. A four-year project will therefore require a five-year computation with the capital expenditure shown as at year 0 with a discount factor of one. There may indeed be no normally recognized cash inflow from a project if it is the type of scheme where a machine is acquired to reduce costs: the cost saving acts as a positive cash flow. This cost saving will increase profits, which will in turn cause an extra amount of corporation tax (35 per cent of the cost saving) to be paid, but one year after the saving has been achieved.

Note that these complications are significant not because they influence the accounting profit or the taxable profit of the company but because they affect cash flow.

Example 19.4

The Alpha Company is considering the purchase of a large piece of machinery for £250,000. The machine will save costs of £90,000 per annum over the next four years and it is estimated will then be sold for a residual value of £50,000. Capital allowances are available on this machine at 25 per cent per annum on a reducing balance, and the corporation tax rate is 35 per cent. The company's cost of capital is 14 per cent. The first step in drafting a statement to assist management to take this decision is to find from an actuarial table the present value of a pound when discounted at 14 per cent. The next step is to calculate the capital allowances available each year as a reduction of taxable profit and to find the cash effect of this reduction by applying the corporation tax rate of 35 per cent. The cost saved of £90,000 per annum will increase profit so that 35 per cent of this amount (£31,500) will be the extra corporation tax paid as a result of this cost saving. Note that tax is paid one year after the event and must therefore be offset by one year in the computation. A net present value calculation is shown in Table 19.1.

Workings

Capital allowances	£		
Cost	250,000		
Year 1 25% allowance	62,500	× 35% reduces tax paid in year 2	£21,875
Tax written down value	187,500		
Year 2 25% allowance	46,875	× 35% reduces tax paid in year 3	£16,406
Tax written down value	140,625		
Year 3 25% allowance	35,156	× 35% reduces tax paid in year 4	£12,304
Tax written down value	105,469		
Sold year 4	50,000		
Balancing allowance year 4	55,469	× 35% reduces tax paid in year 5	£19,414

A reduction of tax paid counts as a cash inflow.

£90,000 × 35% = £31,500 corporation tax on profit increase because costs were saved.

Computation

Outflows are in brackets. Working capital of £10,000 is required to service this project, to be invested during year 1 and disinvested during year 5.

Year	Capital expenditure £	Capital allowances £	Working capital £	Costs saved £	Corp. tax at 35% £	Net cash flow £	Discount factor 14%	NPV £
0	(250,000)	–	–	–	–	(250,000)	–	(250,000)
1	–	–	(10,000)	90,000	–	80,000	0.877	70,160
2	–	21,875	–	90,000	(31,500)	80,375	0.770	61,889
3	–	16,406	–	90,000	(31,500)	74,906	0.675	50,562
4	50,000	12,304	–	90,000	(31,500)	120,804	0.592	71,516
5	–	19,414	10,000	–	(31,500)	(2,086)	0.519	(1,083)
								3,044

A positive NPV but the margin is so small that qualitative factors concerning this decision should be given greater significance.

Table 19.1   Net present value calculation for Example 19.4

CAPITAL INVESTMENT PROJECTS: CONTROL AND AUDIT

Investment appraisal is based on a series of estimates the accuracy of which will be determined only as the months and years of the life of the project pass by. Accordingly, it is important that an efficient control system should monitor the development of each project, to ensure that costs are controlled within the estimates made. A post-audit of the cash inflows and outflows will also compare actual performance with estimate and act as a useful check on the accuracy of the estimating methods. Capital projects may suffer from cost overrun, inability to meet revenue targets or delay in completion of the project. Such delays must also be reported back to the decision team, not only because the delay will affect other sub-budgets (cash, production costs and sales) but because when part of a project is not completed on time, it may effect other parts of the project which were co-ordinated at the planning stage.

A report should be made each month on the development of significant projects, disclosing the following information to management.
1. The start date and scheduled completion date, with the most recent estimate of the likely completion date, and details of penalty clauses and the effect of delay on other parts of the business.
2. Budgeted cost for the work completed to date, and the actual cost to date.
3. Reasons for over/under-expenditure so far on the project, and an estimate of any extra finance required.
4. An estimate of the cost to be incurred to complete the project with a further estimate of likely total over- or under-spend on the project.
5. The percentage completed in terms of time and cost.
6. An analysis of factors which have caused delay or increased the cost, with a comment on the quality of the work and suggestions for remedial action if necessary.

THE COST OF CAPITAL

The discount rate to be applied to calculate the net present value of a project is in practice often selected as the earning rate required by the company on its capital employed. Occasionally this rate is increased to take account of the extra risk of a certain project. In theory the discount rate should equal the cost of capital to ensure that all investment projects show a return in excess of the cost to the company of the funds used to finance the project. Projects with a return which is greater than the cost of capital will increase the value of the firm. The company, may however, recruit funds from several different sources, each of which may have a different cost by way of rate of interest. The capital structure of a business will contain share capital, reserves, and long- and short-term debt. It is usually impossible to determine which funds injected into the capital structure have been used to finance an individual project.

Accordingly, the idea of the weighted average cost of capital has developed in order to determine the discount rate which should be applied. The CIMA *Terminology* defines weighted average cost of capital as a percentage discount rate used in capital investment appraisal to calculate the net present value of the costs and future revenues of the project. It is the average cost of the combined sources of finance (equity, debentures, bank loans) weighted according to the proportion each element bears to the total pool of capital available.

To calculate such a weighted average it is necessary to examine each component of the cost of capital.

Share capital

A shareholder purchases shares on the market at a price which will give a return required for the risk involved. This is a specific after-tax return. Part of the return can be capital growth expected by the shareholder. If the company fails to earn the rate required, the shareholder will sell the shares. Clearly the risk involved in investment will influence the rate required. If the shareholder can earn, say, 8 per cent after tax by investing in a risk-free investment such as government bonds, a rate greater than 8 per cent will be required to compensate for the risk taken by purchasing ordinary shares. An investment model has been constructed to assist in the calculation of the return required by a shareholder to maintain an investment in a company:

$$K = \frac{D}{P} \times 100 + G$$

Where:
K = cost of capital
D = expected dividend
P = price of the shares
G = expected growth.
   Growth must be included in the model since not all profit is distributed to shareholders as a dividend, but is instead retained in the business to finance growth.

Example 19.5

Shares in the Alpha Company have a current market price of £2.50 each. The last dividend paid was 8.2p per share, and there is a growth factor of 10 per cent. A dividend of 8.2p per share plus growth of 0.8p equals an expected dividend of 9p per share. These figures can now be arranged according to the formula as:

$$\frac{9}{250} \times 100 + 10\% = 13.6\%$$

This figure represents the return expected by a shareholder, and if this return is not earned by the company shareholders will sell their holdings.

Retained earnings

Dividends paid are based on share capital, not the retained earnings. It is wrong to assume that retained earnings are free funds used by the company without charge. They have been retained out of profit to finance new investment in the business, and should therefore earn the same amount as the share capital because if they were distributed the shareholders could reinvest them at the same class of risk, e.g. at a return of 13.6 per cent.

Debt

Long-term and short-term lenders receive a rate of interest on their loans to the company. Since this interest is allowable for tax, the real rate of interest paid by the company is the post-tax rate. A loan of £10,000 bearing interest at 10 per cent will require an interest payment of £1,000, which is allowable for tax. Taxable profits will be reduced by £1,000 and the tax paid thereon (at 35 per cent) will be £350 less than if the interest had not been paid. The net cost of the interest is therefore £1,000 − £350 tax saved = £650. This can be expressed as the post-tax rate of interest = $10 \times (1 - 0.35)\ 0.65 = 6.5$ per cent.

It is also possible to build into the calculation the fact that when the loan was raised certain costs were paid by the company. A further formula can be used to calculate the cost of capital for long-term loans:

$$K = I(1 - t) \times \frac{\text{Nominal value of the debt}}{\text{Amount actually raised}}$$

Where I = rate of interest payable and t = the rate of tax.

Example 19.6

A company raises a debenture of £100,000 at an interest rate of 18 per cent, the cost of issuing the debentures being £5,000. The cost of this part of the capital structure of the business would be:

$$18\ (1 - 0.35) \times \frac{100,000}{95,000} = 12.3\%$$

Alternatively, this calculation can be undertaken by including the market value of the debt (the amount which the company would have to pay out today to buy back its debentures on the market) instead of the amount of funds received from the issue.

The real post-tax cost of short-term loans can be calculated in the same way. If the company borrows £80,000 on overdraft terms from its bank at a rate of 14 per cent the cost of this part of the capital structure would be $I\ (1 - t) = 14\ (1 - 0.35) = 9.1\%$.

THE WEIGHTED AVERAGE COST OF CAPITAL

The funds used to finance a business are obtained from several different sources: share capital, retained profits, long-term loans and short-term loans. These sources of funds, providing a part of the capital structure of the business, do not have the same cost of capital, and it is impossible to say which part of the capital structure has been used to finance an individual capital investment project. It is therefore necessary to calculate a weighted average cost of capital in order to find the appropriate discount rate to apply in the DCF calculation. A simple average would not be adequate to express the true cost of capital to the business, so the calculation must be weighted to give greater significance to those parts of the capital structure which have contributed greater amounts of funds.

Example 19.7

The Alpha Company has the following capital structure with costs of capital for each part of the structure, as illustrated above:
(a) £400,000 £1 ordinary shares with a market value of £1.40 per share, at 13.6 per cent;
(b) £250,000 of retained profits, at 13.6 per cent;
(c) £100,000 of 18 per cent debentures, which give a real rate of interest of 12.3 per cent;
(d) an overdraft of £80,000 at 14 per cent, which gives a real rate of interest of 9.1 per cent.

The weighted average cost of capital can be calculated by using weights based on the nominal (book) value of the items in the capital structure or on the current market value of those items, i.e. the amount required to repay them, in each case expressed as a percentage of the total value.

Nominal value calculation

	£	Weight %		Real cost	
400,000 £1 ordinary shares	400,000	48	×	13.6%	= 6.53
£250,000 retained profits	250,000	30	×	13.6%	= 4.08
£100,000 of 18% Debentures	100,000	12	×	12.3%	= 1.48
£80,000 overdraft at 14%	80,000	10	×	9.1%	= .91
Capital employed	830,000	100			
Weighted average cost of capital					13%

Market value calculation

The market value of retained profits is covered by the market price of the shares, which represents each share plus its right to a proportion of the reserves. If the market rate of interest for long-term loans is 16 per cent, an 18 per cent debenture will be worth 18/16 of nominal value.

	£	Weight %		Real cost		
400,000 £1 ordinary shares at £1.40	560,000	74	×	13.6%	=	10.06
£100,000 debentures × 18/16	112,500	15	×	12.3%	=	1.85
Overdraft – amount required to pay	80,000	11	×	9.1%	=	1.00
Capital employed	752,500	100				
Weighted average cost of capital						12.91%

In practice 13 per cent would be used for discounting purposes.

If all capital investment projects undertaken by the company earn in excess of 13 per cent, the company can assume that it will be able to service adequately the various elements in its capital structure, and hopefully attract more investment to fund future projects. These calculations are based on assumptions which could change and therefore invalidate the calculation, e.g. the risk associated with the company's shares, the share price, the dividend, the long- and short-term interest rate and the rate of corporation tax.

EXERCISES

19A   Ceder Ltd has details of two machines which could fulfil the company's future production plans. Only one of these machines will be purchased. The 'standard' model costs £50,000 and the 'deluxe' £88,000, payable immediately. Both machines would require the input of £10,000 working capital throughout their working lives, and both machines have no expected scrap value at the end of their expected working lives of four years for the standard machine, six years for the deluxe machine.

The forecast pretax operating net cash flows associated with the two machines are:

	Year 1 £	Year 2 £	Year 3 £	Year 4 £	Year 5 £	Year 6 £
Standard	20,500	22,860	24,210	23,410		
Deluxe	32,030	26,110	25,380	25,940	38,560	35,100

The deluxe machine has only recently been introduced to the market, and has not been fully tested in operating conditions. Because of the higher risk involved the appropriate discount rate for the deluxe machine is believed to be 14 per cent per year, 2 per cent higher than the rate for the standard machine. The company is proposing to finance the purchase of either machine with a long-term loan at an interest rate of 11 per cent per year.

Taxation at 35 per cent is payable on operating cash flows one year in arrear, and capital allowances are available at 25 per cent per year on a reducing balance.

Required

For both the standard and the deluxe machine calculate:
(i) payback period;
(ii) net present value.

Recommend, with reasons, which of the two machines Ceder Ltd should purchase. (Relevant calculations must be shown.)

(Adapted from Association of Certified Accountants)

19B   It is commonly accepted that a crucial factor in the financial decisions of a company, including the evaluation of capital investment proposals, is the cost of capital.

You are required to

(a) Explain in simple terms what is meant by the 'cost of equity capital' for a particular company:

(b) Calculate the cost of equity capital for X plc from the data given below, using a dividend growth model.

Current price per share on the Stock Exchange	£1.20
Current annual gross dividend per share	£0.10
Expected average annual growth rate of dividends	7%
Expected rate of return on risk-free securities	8%

(c) State the main simplifying assumptions made and express your opinion whether, in view of these assumptions, the model yields results that can be used safely in practice.

(Adapted from Chartered Institute of Management Accounts)

APPENDIX: SOLUTIONS

1 Solutions to Multiple Choice Questions

1.1	(a + b + c)	2.1	(d)	3.1	(c)	4.1	(c)
1.2	(b)	2.2	(a + b + c)	3.2	(b)	4.2	(b)
1.3	(c)	2.3	(b)	3.3	(d)	4.3	(b)
1.4	(c)	2.4	(a)	3.4	(c)	4.4	(c)
1.5	(b)	2.5	(c)	3.5	(c)	4.5	(a + b + c)
5.1	(b)	6.1	(b)	8.1	(b)	9.1	All
5.2	All	6.2	(c)	8.2	(a + c)	9.2	(c)
5.3	(a + b + c)	6.3	(c)	8.3	(d)	9.3	All
5.4	(c)	6.4	(d)	8.4	(b)	9.4	(d)
5.5	(d)	6.5	(d)	8.5	(a + d)	9.5	(c + d)
10.1	(c)	14.1	(b + c)	14.6	(c)	14.11	(b + c)
10.2	(a + b)	14.2	(c)	14.7	(b)	14.12	(c)
10.3	Neither	14.3	(d)	14.8	(a + c)		
10.4	(b)	14.4	(b)	14.9	(c)		
10.5	(a + b + c)	14.5	(d)	14.10	(b)		
16.1	(d)	16.6	(c)	18.1	(d)	18.6	(a)
16.2	(c)	16.7	(c)	18.2	(c)	18.7	(b)
16.3	(b)	16.8	(b)	18.3	(a + c)	18.8	(d)
16.4	(c)	16.9	(b)	18.4	(b or c)	18.9	(a)
16.5	(d)	16.10	(b + c)	18.5	(c)	18.10	(c)

Exercise Solutions

CHAPTER 1

1A Analysis of costs to vehicles (cost centres) and calculation of a cost per mile. Costs would be analysed as:

Running costs, e.g. fuel
Standing costs, e.g. licence/insurance/depreciation
Maintenance and repairs
Labour costs – time sheet
Operating record – idle time.

This analysis would show the relative cost and efficiency of different types of vehicle, the use made of each vehicle, the maintenance record of each vehicle and the safety record of each driver. Such data would be helpful to estimate the cost of a job when tendering for work, to decide which jobs are profitable, and which vehicles to scrap.

Excessive idle time on drivers' time sheets suggests mismanagement of the labour force.

Maintenance costs should be controlled – if they increase an independent garage might prove a cheaper alternative.

The cost of administration and selling should also be related to the level of activity and the cost for a similar period in previous years.

1B Accounting information is used by shareholders, creditors, employees, banks, the Inland Revenue and managers among others. These groups have different information needs, the managers being concerned with internal reporting and the others with external reporting. The financial accounts report to the shareholders and other external users, using the accruals concept, at the end of the financial year, and within the rules of best accounting practice. Cost accounting is required within this framework, to calculate the full cost of stocks of finished goods and work-in-progress carried forward in the accounts to the next year.

Cost accounting has the greater utility for internal reporting, where cost analysis can provide managers with control information, and data on which to base decisions and plans such as the budget. For costing it is not quasi-legal rules which dictate the quality, terms and form of the information to be provided, but the requirements of the managers, the circumstances of the company and the purpose for which the information is required. Cost information must be carefully tailored to fit the span of control and the area of responsibility of the managers concerned. While external reporting looks back to the year just finished, internal reports will forecast what is likely to occur and compare this information with actual costs.

1C (a) Operating costs: The new machinery may take some time to settle down to efficient operation, so that regular reports to management concerning power consumption/direct and indirect labour utilization/maintenance costs/waste, scrap and defective production/consumption of materials, will monitor its progress.

It will be expected that as experience of operations increases, costs will decrease – this phenomenon is often referred to as the learning curve. The frequency of reports would depend upon the circumstances. The reports to management should cover what is significant and controllable, and should attempt to compare actual cost with budgeted cost.

(b) Machine utilization: Machine time should be analysed frequently, between productive time and non-productive time (down time). The reasons for down time should be sought, e.g. breakdown, waiting for materials, maintenance, set-up time, idle time. Thus action can be taken to avoid this waste of an investment in the machinery.

Productive time should also draw a comment as to whether it is being used efficiently – compare actual production with budget.

(c) Cost information can assist with decisions concerning pricing/calculation of profit of various products to be dropped or maintained/optimum batch size calculation/alternative maintenance routines/replacement and abandonment decisions.

1D (a) **Clifton Laundry Ltd**

	Annual cost (£)	
	Coal	Oil
Fuel (120 × 60 × 12)	86,400	78,000 (156,000 × 50p)
Labour (£130 × 52)	6,760	–
(50 × £3 × 49)	7,350	–
Depreciation	–	1,560
	100,510	79,560

Depreciation is spread over the five remaining years of the life of the boiler:

	£
Staithes removed	475
Storage tank	3,500
Modification	3,825
	7,800 ÷ 5 years = £1,560 per annum

One litre of oil gives 10,000 BTUs; therefore 2.6 litres = 1,000 pounds of steam.
Therefore 10 million pounds of steam require 26,000 litres of oil.
Therefore 60 million pounds of steam require 156,000 litres of oil.

The annual cost of coal operation is £20,950 more expensive than oil. Note that only costs which are affected by the decision have been used, e.g. depreciation on the original boiler will not change so it has been ignored.

(b) Suggested price per litre $+ \dfrac{\text{Annual excess cost of coal system over oil}}{\text{Litres of oil used per annum}}$

$$50\text{p} + \frac{£20,950}{156,000} = 63.4$$

An increase of 13.4p per litre in the cost of oil will cause the oil system to break even with coal. A price increase for oil of 26.8p per cent will, if coal prices remain stable, erode the cost saving of a change to oil.

(c) (i) Expected movements in the price of coal and oil and trust in the oil representative's quote of 50p. It would be expensive to revert to coal if the cost of oil increased substantially.
(ii) Labour. It has been assumed that the boiler's attendant would be redundant. This may not be so but, if it is, what effect would the redundancy have on labour relations at the plant? Can he be redeployed? Redundancy costs must be included.
(iii) The maintenance cost of the two systems has not been brought into comparison, and the efficiency of the emergency repair service for oil installations has not been tested.
(iv) There is no ash disposal with an oil system. This may mean a cost saving or a loss of income if the ash has been sold in the past.
(v) The cost of disruption to production during the changeover. Can the change be timed for the holiday period when the plant is closed?
(vi) The cost of extra capital tied up in the oil system has been ignored.

CHAPTER 2

2A   (a) The term 'cost centre' is defined as any location, function or item of equipment in respect of which costs may be ascertained and related to cost units for control purposes. A 'cost unit' may be defined as a quantitative unit of product or service in relation to which costs are ascertained.

(b) A direct cost can be specifically related to any part of the operations of a business. An indirect cost is one which cannot be specifically tied to any cost unit but may be shared by several different activities, departments in the business or products. Indirect costs can be related to cost units only by some arbitrary method of allocation such as apportionment or the absorption of overheads.

Some costs, e.g. the salary paid to a manager of a department, may be direct so far as part of the business is concerned but indirect so far as cost units passing through the cost centre are concerned since the manager does not directly work on those units. When it comes to units of production the only real direct costs are those of the materials used to manufacture the product and the cost of direct labour paid to employees who work on the product. Indirect costs are the overhead expenses of the factory and of other activities within the business such as selling, distribution and administration.

An important factor which influences the treatment of a cost as direct or indirect will be the ease with which that cost can be traced to an individual department or cost unit. This tracing of costs depends on the situation in the business itself.

Fairness is another factor which will determine the direct/indirect decision. Overtime payments made to labour are traditionally treated as an indirect overhead expense, because it would be unfair to charge extra labour costs to certain jobs undertaken outside normal hours merely because there was not enough production time to complete the task in normal hours.

Practicality is yet another factor which infuences the direct/indirect cost classification. It may be expensive and time-consuming to trace some costs to individual cost units and the value of the information produced as a result of this effort may not be worth the cost. Cost behaviour may also make it difficult to classify direct and indirect costs. The depreciation of a machine may be fixed in the short run but it can of course be related to individual units produced by that machine.

2B   Period costs are those related to a certain costing or accounting period which should be written off against the profit of that period and not carried forward in the cost of stock or work-in-progress to be charged against a succeeding period. The opposite of a period cost is a product cost, which is related to a product and charged against revenue only when that product is sold in a subsequent cost period. Period costs include administration, selling, distribution and research overheads, and product costs include all the costs incurred in manufacturing the product, e.g. direct labour, materials and a fair proportion of the overhead expenses of the factory. The distinction between period and product costs is significant for the rules contained in SSAP 9, which states that the value of stock carried forward to a subsequent accounting period should include the direct costs of labour and materials and also a fair proportion of the overhead expenses incurred in the manufacture of that stock.

Variable costs describe costs which change in direct proportion to the volume of production. Variable cost per unit does not change but when the number of units produced is increased, so variable cost in total increases in proportion. Cost behaviour determines whether a cost is variable or fixed, but it must be stressed that as circumstances change so a cost may behave in a different manner, i.e. a cost which is fixed in one situation may become variable as conditions change. Factory rent is fixed, but if the factory closes, this cost becomes instantly variable. In the long run all costs are variable since conditions will cause them to change over a long time period.

Opportunity cost concerns the cost of forgoing the next best alternative use of resources in a business. As such the concept of opportunity cost is important in decision-making. The cost of using scarce production hours on making product A might be the profit forgone by not using those resources to make product B instead.

2C   (i) The official *Terminology* published by the CIMA defines a cost centre as a 'location, function or item of equipment in respect of which costs may be ascertained and related to cost units for control purposes'. This means that a cost centre is a point within a business to which it is convenient to group costs. The maintenance department in a factory or the power house are service cost centres, while a single machine or a complex of machines within the workshop may act as a production cost centre. Sales areas or administrative departments can also act as focal points at which costs can be gathered together for other functions of the business.

The CIMA *Terminology* defines a cost unit as 'a quantitative unit of product or service in relation to which costs are ascertained'. It is convenient to identify the product of the business and to quote costs in terms of that product whether it is cost per thousand bricks, per car produced, per hour of service given, or per tonne mile carried in a transport business. Most companies have a unit of output of some type which can be used as a comparator for the expression of cost. The relationship between a cost centre and a cost unit is that the costs of a function or activity are classified to the cost centre, e.g. an assembly department in a factory, and then as cost units pass through the cost centre the direct and indirect costs of the cost centre can be charged out to units of production by means of an absorption rate.

(ii) Suitable cost units which may be used to aid control are, for:
1. a hospital – the patient/day;
2. a road haulage business – the tonne/kilometre or ton/mile;
3. a hotel – the room/day occupied;
4. a public transport authority – the passenger/kilometre or passenger/mile.

CHAPTER 3

3A   See chart overleaf

Activity	Production dept.	Stores	Costing dept.	Buying dept.	Checking and inspection dept.	Supplier	Accounting dept.
Material required	Material requisition ⟶						
Material issued	⟵	Copy requisition ⟶					
Recorded		Bin card (reduced total)	Stock record card (credit)* Job or process (debit)				
Reorder level		Purchases requisition ⟶					
			Blue ⟵	ORDER ⟶ Green			
						White ⟶	
Order placed		Buff ⟵		Orange ⟶			Pink
Goods received						Delivery note	
Goods correct			Orange ⟵ Goods				
			Blue ⟵		received ⟶		Pink
		Buff ⟵			note		
Recorded		Bin card (increase total)	Stock record card (debit) Cost control (credit)				
Goods incorrect					Discrepancy ⟶ White		
					note ⟶		Pink
Goods invoiced						Invoice ⟶	
Invoice checked							
Recorded							Suppliers A/C (credit) Purchases (debit)
Statement received						Statement ⟶	
Check statement with ledger							
Pay						⟵	Remittance advice cheque suppliers A/C (Dr.) Cash (Cr.)
Recorded							

Solution to Exercise 3A

Legend – Documents raised shown in originating department
  – Document routed ⟶
  – Copy documents shown by extra arrows
  – Colour coding as noted
  – *in some systems the stock record card is maintained in the stores rather than the cost office.

3B   (i) Stock checkers' reconciliation form

Item	Code	Unit	Physical quantity	Checked by	Date	Stock card	Stores ledger	Unit price	Gain (Loss)
Camera prisms			560			600	600	60	(£2,400)
Flash units			385			380	380	40	£200
Shutter mechs			720			750	780	10	(£600)

(ii) Check the stock card and bin card totals – the correct physical quantity must be recorded. Write off stock losses. Investigate reasons. Debit stock losses a/c. Credit stores a/c for the material concerned.

In the case of a gain debit stores a/c for the material and credit stock gains a/c, or stock losses if no gains a/c exists, or work-in-progress if that a/c has been overcharged in the past.

(iii) Reasons for discrepancies/action.
1.   Theft from stores/no unauthorized persons in stores.
2.   Components taken for production without entry on bin card/Improve recording.
3.   Goods returned from works without paperwork/account for all movements.
4.   Clerical errors in stores ledger/internal check.
5.   Natural wastage, e.g. evaporation/reduce time in store.
6.   Stores staff misreading figures on the requisition/double-check system.

3C   (a) Relevant costs associated with stock control are ordering costs and holding costs. Ordering costs usually consist of clerical costs of preparing a purchase order and special processing and receiving costs relating to the number of orders processed. The holding costs usually consist of a desired rate of return on the investment in stock, costs of storage space, breakage, obsolescence deterioration, insurance.

Shown graphically:

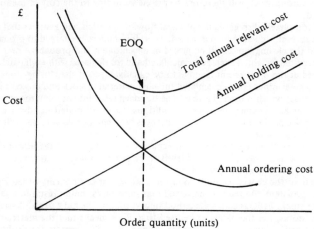

Order quantity (units)

Formula: EOQ $= \sqrt{\dfrac{2AP}{S}}$

Where:
EOQ = order size
A = annual quantity used, in units
P = cost of making an order
S = annual holding cost per unit.

(b) (i) $EOQ = \sqrt{\dfrac{2\,(14,400)(12.50)}{1.00}}$

$= \sqrt{360,000}$

$= 600$

(ii)   Orders per year $= \dfrac{14,400}{600} = 24$ orders per year.

(iii)   Cost of ordering $= 24 \times £12.50 = £300$.
Cost of holding $= 600/2 \times £1 = £300$.
Therefore total cost of ordering and holding $= £600$.

(c) The recorded balances may differ from actual physical balances due to:
1. clerical errors in the record card;
2. storekeeper's errors, clerical and physical (e.g. over-issue);
3. errors in procedure (e.g. failure to record returned material on a materials returned note);
4. unrecorded losses due to evaporation or breaking;
5. pilferage and falsification of documents.

CHAPTER 4

4A   Materials issued from the stores to production must be valued in order to calculate the cost of production and the carrying value of stock remaining for balance sheet purposes. If all purchases were made at the same price there would be little difficulty in such a calculation. However, as batches of material or components are purchased at different prices the difficulty arises as to which price to use when material is charged out. A cost flow assumption has to be made to define the accounting policy of the company and to identify which batches of material are deemed to be charged out first. An assumption concerning the flow of costs will select either FIFO, LIFO or average price pattern. Two other materials pricing methods which can be used are the standard cost and replacement price methods.

The FIFO method assumes that materials will be used in the same chronological order as their purchase. When the first batch has been exhausted the units are charged out at the cost of the second batch and so on. The closing stock will therefore be priced according to the cost of the most recent batch to be purchased.

The LIFO method completely disregards the physical flow of materials and assumes that usage will be taken from the most recent batch to be purchased. Therefore materials charged to production will be at current cost and the closing stock will be priced at an outdated and probably lower cost.

Average price: a perpetual weighted average is calculated and recalculated with each batch received. Stores issues are priced at the most recent average to be calculated, as is the closing stock.

Standard price: a predetermined cost is calculated for each material in stock and this cost is used for all issues during the period, which is usually a year. The standard takes into account the expected level of prices during the year and changes in market conditions. Costs estimated in advance may well differ from the actual price paid for the material so variances between the two amounts will be written off to the profit and loss account.

Replacement price: materials issued from store are charged to production at the price ruling in the market on the day of issue. It may be difficult to identify replacement prices so a system of indexation may be used to calculate the charge-out cost.

The methods compared: the charge to production for materials or components issued from stores should be made on a consistent and realistic basis and that same basis should result in a satisfactory balance sheet value for stock. FIFO is a logical method since it follows the most likely physical flow of materials through the stores, i.e. the oldest to be used first. This means that the material issued to production will be charged at lower, pre-inflation prices and this will overstate the profit. A LIFO assumption will charge current prices to production but the stocks remaining will be carried at low, pre-inflation prices so that the balance sheet may understate their value. Both FIFO and LIFO are difficult to administer because of the need to keep track of each separate batch of materials purchased. Both systems render cost comparison between jobs difficult because materials issued in the morning may have a different price from materials issued in the afternoon from a different batch. The average method smoothes out fluctuations in issue prices and produces a result which is between the extremes of FIFO and LIFO. It is easy to administer but a separate weighted average will need to be computed as each batch is purchased.

A standard cost for materials is easy to administer and provides a consistent charge to production since all materials are charged at the standard price. Once the difficulties of setting the standard are overcome a useful and comparable cost is derived.

Replacement cost provides a realistic current cost to charge out to production. Unfortunately this method is rejected by SSAP 9 and the Inland Revenue. To value raw material at a price in excess of the amount at which it was purchased is to take a profit before that profit has been realized by sale. Therefore FIFO or AVCO are best used for the purposes of external reporting, but replacement cost is a very useful basis of stock valuation for management decision-making purposes.

4B   (a) Mr G's yarn stock records
FIFO

Date	Purchases	£	Cost of sales	£	Stock
13/1	200 boxes at £36	7,200			200 × £36
8/2	400 boxes at £38	15,200			200 × £36 ⎱
					400 × £38 ⎰
10/2			200 boxes at £36	7,200	
			300 boxes at £38	11,400	100 × £38
11/3	600 boxes at £40	24,000			100 × £38 ⎱
					600 × £40 ⎰
12/4	400 boxes at £35	14,000			100 × £38 ⎱
					600 × £40 ⎰
					400 × £35
20/4			100 boxes at £38	3,800	
			500 boxes at £40	20,000	100 × £40 ⎱
					400 × £35 ⎰
15/6	500 boxes at £28	14,000			100 × £40 ⎱
					400 × £35 ⎰
					500 × £28
25/6			100 boxes at £40	4,000	
			300 boxes at £35	10,500	100 × £35 ⎱
					500 × £28 ⎰
			Cost of sales	£56,900	Stock loss
					100 × £35 =
					£3,500

LIFO

Date	Purchases	£	Cost of Sales	£	Stock
13/1	200 boxes at £36	7,200			200 × £36
8/2	400 boxes at £38	15,200			200 × £36 ⎱
					400 × £38 ⎰
10/2			400 boxes at £38	15,200	
			100 boxes at £36	3,600	100 × £36
11/3	600 boxes at £40	24,000			100 × £36 ⎱
					600 × £40 ⎰
12/4	400 boxes at £35	14,000			100 × £36 ⎱
					600 × £40 ⎰
					400 × £35
20/4			400 boxes at £35	14,000	
			200 boxes at £40	8,000	100 × £36 ⎱
					400 × £40 ⎰
15/6	500 boxes at £28	14,000			100 × £36 ⎱
					400 × £40 ⎰
					500 × £28
25/6			400 boxes at £28	11,200	100 × £36 ⎱
					400 × £40 ⎰
					100 × £28
					Stock loss
					100 × £28 =
			Cost of sales	£52,000	£2,800

AVCO

Date	Purchases	£	Cost of sales	£	Stock
13/1	200 boxes at £36	7,200			200 × £36
8/2	400 boxes at £38	15,200			600 × £37.33
10/2			500 boxes at £37.33	18,665	100 × £37.33
11/3	600 boxes at £40	24,000			700 × £39.62
12/4	400 boxes at £35	14,000			1,100 × £37.94
20/4			600 boxes at £37.94	22,764	500 × £37.94
15/6	500 boxes at £28	14,000			1,000 × £32.97
25/6			400 boxes at £32.97	13,188	600 × £32.97
					Stock loss
			Cost of sales	£54,617	100 × £32.97
					£3,297

Workings

$$\frac{£22,400}{600} = £37.33 \qquad \frac{£3,733 + £24,000}{700} = £39.62$$

$$\frac{£27,733 + £14,000}{1,100} = £37.94 \qquad \frac{£18,970 + £14,000}{1,000} = £32.97$$

(b) Shown below is the effect on Mr G's profit of each of the three methods of pricing material issues:

	FIFO		LIFO		Weighted average	
	£	£	£	£	£	£
Sales		67,200		67,200		67,200
Cost of yarn sold (sum of material issued)	56,900		52,000		54,617	
Stock loss	3,500		2,800		3,297	
Other expenses	2,300	62,700	2,300	57,100	2,300	60,214
Profit		£4,500		£10,100		£6,986

Prices in this case show a downward or deflationary trend. The profit measured depends on the method chosen for valuing stock sold. Under FIFO the cost of sales is based upon earlier and higher purchase prices; but the stock value is at the most recent and lowest purchase price. For LIFO, cost of sales is based mainly on the lower and more recent purchase prices, while much of the closing stock is at the highest prices ruling during the period; i.e. 4/5ths of the closing stock is valued at a cost higher than the selling price at the end of the period and this would not be considered prudent. AVCO values material issues and stocks at a point between the two other methods. The closing stock value per unit is higher than the most recent purchase price so an element of profit in the stock valuation could be said to exist. The FIFO method would be regarded in these circumstances as the most conservative as it writes off against sales all of the earlier, and higher, purchase prices.

Mr G has made a large purchase of yarn at the highest price and then held this stock during a period of falling prices. If the March purchase had been postponed until April, profits would have been greater.

The stock loss of 100 boxes of yarn has reduced profits significantly and Mr G should implement some material control procedures.

The profitability of the business is measured by return on capital employed (the profits earned as a percentage of the capital employed), i.e.

$$\frac{6 \text{ months' profits}}{\text{Initial capital employed}} \quad \frac{£4,500}{£40,000} = 11\tfrac{1}{4}\% \text{ for six months}$$

These figures exclude a charge for Mr G's services. As he is presumably spending some time running his business he is losing the opportunity of earning some remuneration elsewhere. The full £40,000 of capital is not committed to the yarn trade, and could earn interest if invested elsewhere.

CHAPTER 5

5A   (a)

Wages control account

	£		£
Cash (Note 1)	1,260	Work-in-progress a/c	912
Cash (Note 1)	355	(Note 2)	
Income tax a/c	250	Production O/H a/c	1,163
Income tax a/c	100	(Note 2)	
National insurance a/c	75		
National insurance a/c	35		
	2,075		2,075

Production overhead control account

	£
National insurance a/c	180
(employer's contribution)	
Wages control a/c	1,163
(Note 2)	

Work in progress account

	£
Wages control a/c	912
(Note 2)	

Cash and bank account

	Wages control a/c	1,260
	Wages control a/c	355

Income tax account

	£		£
		Wages control a/c (direct	
		workers)	250
		Wages control a/c (indirect	
Balance c/f	350	workers)	100
	350		350

National insurance account

	£		£
		Wages control a/c	
		(direct workers)	75
		wages control (indirect	
		workers)	35
		Production O/H a/c	
		(employer's	
Balance c/f	290	contribution)	180
	290		290

(b) (i) Employer's national insurance contributions
By its nature it is not traceable to individual batches of production. It will be debited to production overhead and charged to products along with other overheads by means of an absorption rate. An alternative treatment is to gross up the hourly wage rates to include this cost, the effect is similar to the previous method. This treatment is rarely applied.

(ii) Group bonus
There is insufficient information in the question to judge whether the bonus should be charged to either the work-in-progress account or the production overhead account. The bonus could be charged direct to batches, and through the batch costs to the work-in-progress account, if the bonus can be physically traced to individual batches and a high degree of accuracy is considered worth while. Assuming that the bonus cannot be traced to individual batches, it has been debited to the production overhead control account whence it will be charged out evenly to all products by means of the overhead absorption rate.

(iii) Overtime earnings
The actual hours of direct workers can be physically traced to a particular batch, so the basic rate element should be charged direct to that batch. The overtime premium, even if it can be traced to a particular batch, if worked to increase production generally should be regarded as a policy cost of that level of production and charged, via the overhead absorption rate, to all production. However, if overtime is worked at the request of, and is being charged to, a customer it would be legitimate to charge the premium direct to that batch or job.

By their nature earnings of indirect workers are indirect and charged to production through the absorption rate, unless there is a specific chargeable request for overtime by a customer.

Workings
Note 1:
Calculation of wages

Direct workers	£	Indirect workers	£
Attendance time		350 × £1	350
800 × £1.50	1,200	40 × £0.50	20
Overtime premium			50
100 × £0.75	75		70
Shift premium	150		
Bonus	160		
Gross wage	1,585		490
Employees' deductions:			
Income tax 250		100	
National insurance 75	325	35	135
Net wage	1,260		355

Note 2
Analysis of direct workers' gross wage

	Direct £		Indirect £
Productive time 590 × £1.50	885	210 × £1.50	315
Overtime premium 20 × £0.75	15	80 × £0.75	60
Shift premium and bonus	–		310
	900		685

Analysis of indirect workers gross wage

	Direct £		Indirect £
Attendance time 8 × £1	8	342 × £1	342
Overtime premium 8 × £0.50	4	32 × £0.50	16
Shift premium and bonus	–		120
	12		478
Total debit to work-in-progress a/c	912	Production O/H a/c	1,163

5B   (a) Moulding department

Wages control account

	£		£
Cash a/c	14,284	Work-in-progress control	
Employees deductions a/c		a/c 3,525 hrs × £3.60	12,690
(Note 1)	3,604	Production overhead	
		control a/c (Note 2)	5,198
	17,888		17,888

Note 1 Gross wages paid	Direct workers £	Indirect workers £
Ordinary time 3,600 × £3.60	12,960	
800 × £2.10		1,680
Overtime 630 × £4.80	3,024	
630 × £4.80		224
	15,984	1,904

	£
Total gross wages	17,888
Net wages paid (per question)	14,284
Employees' deductions	£3,604

Note 2 Debit to production overhead control a/c		£
Direct workers' non-productive time		
705 hours × £3.60	2,538	
Direct workers' overtime premium		
630 hours × £1.20	756	
Indirect workers' gross wages (*see above*)	1,904	5,198

(b) Effect of proposed incentive scheme on labour costs in moulding department: Compare the previous week's actual earnings of the direct operatives with that which they would have earned if the proposed scheme had been in operation.

	£	£
Existing remuneration scheme (Note 1)		15,984
Proposed scheme:		
Type 1 receiver 4,800 units × £1.90	9,120	
Type 2 receiver 1,500 units × £2,85	4,275	
Non-productive down time 2,820 hours (Note 3)		
× 20% × £2.50	1,410	14,805

The proposed incentive scheme would reduce the labour cost in the moulding department.

Assumptions
(i) That the company will pay only for the hours worked by the direct operatives; i.e. hours required for previous week's production under proposed scheme would be:

4,800 × 24/60 =	1,920	hours
1,500 × 36/60 =	900	hours
	2,820	hours
plus allowance for non-productive time		
2,820 × 20% =	564	hours
	3,384	hours
Hours available ordinary time		
(90 operatives)	3,600	hours
Ordinary time surplus to requirements	216	hours

If the surplus hours are not paid for, operatives will either work less than a basic forty-hour week, or redundancies/transfers will occur. If the ordinary time surplus of 216 hours is paid for the proposed scheme is still cheaper, but, if the volume of production falls, a point would soon be reached where the payment for surplus hours would result in the proposed scheme becoming more expensive.

(ii) That workers will respond as estimated. If targets are not achieved (a 20 per cent increase in efficiency is required) there will be more down time. If non-productive time remains at 20 per cent costs will increase and labour morale will fall.

Note 3 Calculation of allowed hours for previous week's production:

Type 1 4,800 units × 24 minutes	1,920	hours
Type 2 1,500 units × 36 minutes	900	hours
	2,820	hours

The information in the question is insufficient to assess the scheme. A solution should raise questions to identify significant points.
1. What can the company do with the surplus labour capacity? The decision is influenced by the degree of variation in the expected volume of production and whether labour can be adjusted to match this variation. This adjustment would probably be easier under the existing scheme with overtime.
2. Will there be a guaranteed minimum weekly/daily wage? Is there a guaranteed wage operating at present?
3. What payment will be made for additional non-productive time, caused by managerial inefficiency?
4. Will the scheme affect the indirect workers, or workers in other departments? The opportunity to earn higher hourly rates of pay may be a source of grievance for the workers not involved; do they participate in an incentive scheme already operating in other departments?
5. Will the quality of production be affected, or the scrap rate increase, or will extra inspection be necessary?
6. Do variable overheads vary with time worked? If so the increased efficiency of the workers will create savings on overheads.
7. Will more, or less, supervision be required? What will it cost?
8. Will the operatives find the scheme acceptable? Higher hourly rates and less hours worked may mean lower gross wages, unless a sufficient number of operatives are transferred/made redundant to maintain some overtime.

5C Mention would be made of the following points.
1. Methods of labour remuneration:
    (a) day rate (time based);
    (b) piece work (production-based);
    (c) premium bonus (day rate and bonus).
2. Importance of recording the time an employee spends on the factory premises. Employees on day rate are obviously paid for all the hours they are on the premises, but even piece workers must record their hours, if only to be correctly paid for overtime. Further use is to check punctuality. Clock cards and clock numbers are required.
3. Labour times must be recorded in detail. A labour analysis is usually undertaken showing the production and activities on which the cost was incurred. Such an analysis can be made only if every employee records in detail his or her activities and the time he or she spends on each.
4. The total employee time recorded on activities must equal the total gate time paid for, and it is necessary to insert in the costing procedure a check that ensures those two totals do in fact agree. Records are time sheets (daily or weekly) and job cards (one card per complete job or one card per operation). Total hours booked should equal total hours paid for.
5. In some cases payment is made on the basis of work completed, rather than on time taken. Piece work tickets are used.
6. The wages department is responsible for paying/calculating the employees' wages:
    (a) computation of gross wages using clock cards, piece work tickets, job cards, employee's record card;
    (b) computation of net wages, deductions being made from gross wages for PAYE, employees' national insurance, union subs etc.
7. The costing department's records need to show:
    (a) the gross amount earned by employees (separating direct from indirect) and analysing the amount to cost centres and jobs;
    (b) the analysis of earnings between normal time and overtime and bonus;
    (c) deductions from earnings which are made by the employer and paid over to third parties;
    (d) allowance made to employees and other costs associated with employment.

8. The basic data for entries into the costing records are taken from the payroll analysis.
    Double entry system can be employed. Total cash paid out for company's labour is debited to a control account and the total is analysed between direct labour charged to production (work-in-progress) and indirect labour posted to the production overhead account.

CHAPTER 6

6A (a) (i) Apportionment of overheads to production departments:

	Machine shop £	Fitting section £	Canteen £	Machine maintenance section £	Total £
Allocated overheads	27,660	19,470	16,600	26,650	90,380
Rent, rates, heat and light (by floor area)	9,000	3,500	2,500	2,000	17,000
Depreciation and insurance of equipment (by book value)	12,500	6,250	2,500	3,750	25,000
	49,160	29,220	21,600	32,400	132,380
Service department apportionment					
Canteen (by no. of employees)	10,800	8,400	(21,600)	2,400	–
Machine maintenance section (allocation)	24,360	10,440	–	(34,800)	–
	84,320	48,060			132,380

Calculation of absorption bases:

		Machine shop		Fitting section	
Product	Budgeted production	Machine hours per product	Total machine hours	Direct labour cost per product £	Total direct wages £
X	4,200 units	6	25,200	12	50,400
Y	6,900 units	3	20,700	3	20,700
Z	1,700 units	4	6,800	21	35,700
			52,700		106,800

Budgeted overhead absorption rates:

Machine shop		Fitting section	
Budgeted overheads	£84,320	Budgeted overheads	£48,060
Budgeted machine hours	52,700	Budgeted direct wages	£106,800
= £1.60 per machine hour		= 45% of direct wages	

(ii) Budgeted overhead cost of manufacturing one unit of product X

	£
Machine shop – 6 hours × £1.60 per machine hour	9.60
Fitting section – 45% of £12	5.40
	15.00

(b) The production director's suggestion avoids the problem of distortion of the results by over/under overhead absorption at the end of each period but it still produces misleading information. Problems which may result from the production director's suggestion are:
1. Seasonal fluctuations in activity and/or cost would cause the overhead cost per unit to vary from one month to the next.
2. Average cost per unit, for all products, would not accurately reflect the different use made of the two cost centres by products X, Y and Z, e.g. the budgeted average overhead cost per unit for all products is (£132,380 ÷ 12,800 units) £10.34, whilst the more accurate and specific overhead absorption rates produce overhead costs per product varying from £15.85 for product Z to £6.15 for product Y.

3. Actual overhead cost per unit would not be calculated until the end of the month, and there would be no analysis between fixed and variable overheads.
4. If selling prices are calculated as cost plus required mark-up, they may vary from month to month, the lower the activity, the higher the price.
5. The selling prices will not reflect the resources consumed and demand may well increase for the products with a low selling price caused by inequitable overhead distribution.
6. Product profitability information will be misleading, which may result in incorrect product mix decisions.

6B   (a) Main objectives of calculating overhead absorption rates are:
1. For pricing purposes. If firm is not a price taker it must calculate a price using some variant of 'cost-plus' formula. For this purpose, it must be able to estimate average unit cost.
2. For stock valuation purposes, SSAP 9 requires that stocks are valued at the lower of cost or net realizable value. By cost is meant 'full cost' incurred in getting the product into its present location and condition. Such costs include production overheads based on a normal level of activity for the year.

However, the danger is that reliance may be placed upon the resulting 'unit cost' for decision-making purposes. It has little relevance here. Decisions should be based on relevant incremental costs, and it would be beneficial if the absorption system at least allowed for the distinction between fixed and variable costs. This would also be helpful in the pricing decision, where the price has to be based on marginal cost only.

(b) (i) Calculation of budgeted overhead absorption rates:
Apportionment of overheads to production departments:

	Machinery department £	Finishing section £	Canteen £	Machine maintenance section £	Total £
Allocated O/H	31,172	25,198	12,850	11,760	80,980
Dep^n and insurance of equipment	14,000	5,250	1,750	7,000	28,000
Rent, rates, heat and light	6,000	4,000	3,000	5,000	18,000
	51,172	34,448	17,600	23,760	126,980
Service dept. apportionment canteen (basis on employees)	8,800	5,500	(17,600)	3,300	
Machine maintenance section	21,648	5,412	–	(27,060)	
	81,620	45,360	–	–	126,980

Calculation of absorption bases:

	Machinery department			Finishing section	
Product	Budgeted production (units)	Machine hours per product	Total machine hours	Direct labour cost per product £	Total direct wages £
T	3,400	2	6,800	8	27,200
C	2,800	4	11,200	6	16,800
K	1,600	8	12,800	4	6,400
			30,800		50,400

Budgeted overhead absorption rates:

Machinery department
$$\frac{\text{Budgeted overheads}}{\text{Budgeted machine hours}} = \frac{£81,620}{30,800 \text{ hrs}}$$
= £2.65 per machine hour

Finishing section
$$\frac{\text{Budgeted overheads}}{\text{Budgeted direct wages}} = \frac{45,360}{50,400}$$
= 90% of direct wages

(ii) Budgeted manufacturing overhead cost for producing one unit of product K:

	£
Machinery department – 8 hours × £2.65	21.20
Finishing section – 90% of £4	3.60
	24.80

(c) Problems associated with apportioning service department overhead costs to production departments are:
1. The difficulty encountered in determining a suitable basis for the apportionment of service department costs to production. The base selected should be one which exerts a major influence on the costs of the service department.
2. When there are several service departments working for one another as well as for the production department, the analysis can become complex. The simultaneous equation or repeated distribution methods cannot be used when complex interrelationships occur. Matrix algebra may be the only solution for complex problems.

6C (a) Kegworth Cats Ltd
Redistribute service department costs:

	Moulding £	Joinery £	Filling £	Generator £	Maintenance £
Overheads incurred	35,800	19,600	22,700	29,400	11,600
Maintenance redistributed	4,060	3,480	2,320	1,740	(11,600)
Generator redistributed	17,127	4,671	6,228	(31,140)	3,114
Maintenance redistributed	1,090	934	623	467	(3,114)
Generator redistributed	257	70	93	(467)	47
Maintenance redistributed	17	14	9	7	(47)
Generator redistributed	4	1	2	(7)	–
Overhead apportioned	58,355	28,770	31,975		

Overhead absorbed

Moulding
$$\frac{£60,000}{15,000} = £4 \times 15,730 \qquad 62,920$$

Joinery
$$\frac{£27,000}{18,000} = £1.50 \times 18,650 \qquad 27,975$$

Filling
$$\frac{£35,000}{5,000} = £7 \times 4,630 \qquad 32,410$$

Over/(under)-absorbed	4,565	(795)	435

Moulding:

Worked more hours than expected – £4 × 730	=	£2,920
Incurred less cost than expected £60,000 − £58,355	=	£1,645
	Over-absorbed	£4,565

Joinery:

Worked more hours than expected £1.50 × 650		£(975)
Incurred more cost than expected £28,770 − £27,000		£1,770
	Under-absorbed	£795

Filling:

Worked less hours than expected £7 × 370		£(2,590)
Incurred less cost than expected £35,000 − £31,975		£3,025
	Over-absorbed	£435

Note: The figures above can be expressed in T account form as follows:

Moulding

	£		£
Actual cost	58,355	WiP absorbed	62,920
P/L	4,565		
	62,920		62,920

Joinery

	£		£
Actual cost	28,770	WiP absorbed	27,975
		P/L	795
	28,770		28,770

Filling

	£		£
Actual cost	31,975	WiP absorbed	32,410
P/L	435		
	32,410		32,410

(b) Overhead absorption rates are useful for managers in that they attempt to allocate the cost of services used and other indirect costs, to cost units. The full absorbed cost per product is useful as a comparator, and enables the significance of overheads for total cost to be identified.

However if the absorption rates are based on faulty assumptions, the information which they disclose is equally unreliable. Prices calculated from inaccurate full absorbed costs, may be too high (the product is priced out of the market), or too low (price does not cover the true cost so losses are made), leading to a serious situation in either case.

Overhead absorption is a means of relating indirect costs to products, but it may be little more than a meaningless averaging operation if the overheads concerned are only remotely related to the product.

6D   (a) Overhead analysis

Cost	Basis of apportionment	Machine shop A	Machine shop B	Assembly	Canteen	Maintenance	Total
		£	£	£	£	£	£
Indirect wages	Allocation	8,586	9,190	15,674	29,650	15,460	78,560
Consumable materials	Allocation	6,400	8,700	1,200	600	-	16,900
Rent and rates							16,700
Building insurance	sq ft	5,000	6,000	7,500	3,000	1,000	2,400
Heat and light							3,400
Power	Power usage technical estimates %	4,730	3,440	258	-	172	8,600
Depreciation of machinery	Value of machinery	20,100	17,900	2,200	-	-	40,200
		44,816	45,230	26,832	33,250	16,632	166,760
Service cost centre apportionment:							
Maintenance	Machine usage hours	4,752	11,880	-	-	(16,632)	
Canteen	Direct labour hours	7,600	5,890	19,760	(33,250)	-	
		57,168	63,000	46,592	-	-	

Overhead absorption rates: Machine shop A $= \dfrac{£57,168}{7,200 \text{ machine usage hours}} = £7.94$ per hour

Machine shop B $= \dfrac{£63,000}{18,000 \text{ machine usage hours}} = £3.50$ per hour

Assembly $\quad = \dfrac{£46,592}{20,800 \text{ direct labour hours}} = £2.24$ per hour

(b) Production overhead control a/c

	£		£
Cost ledger control*	176,533	Work-in-progress	
		– overhead absorbed	
		Machine shop A	
		7,300 hrs, at £7.94	57,962
		Machine shop B	
		18,700 hrs at £3.50	65,450
		Assembly	
		21,900 hrs at £2.24	49,056
			172,468
		Under-absorbed overhead	
		– to profit and loss	4,065
	176,533		176,533

*The cost ledger control account maintains the cost ledger as a separate self-balancing system.

(c) A control account, or total account, is posted with totals or groups of individual transactions. Thus the balance on the control should agree with the total of balances in the ledger containing the detailed accounts. It is a control, because if the aggregate of the individual balances reconciles to the control account, prima facie the bookkeeping in the detailed ledger is correct: i.e. the balance of the production overhead control represents the total over- or under-absorbed overhead from all the cost centre overhead accounts.

6E   Viking Engineering Limited

Workings
Apportionment of actual overhead to the production departments from the service departments by means of the repeated distribution method of calculation:

	Machinery £	Assembly £	Maintenance £	Stores £
Actual overhead	38,500	50,000	62,500	22,500
Apportion maintenance	43,750	12,500	(62,500)	6,250
			–	28,750
Apportion stores	11,500	8,625	8,625	(28,750)
			8,625	–
Apportion maintenance	6,038	1,725	(8,625)	862
			–	862
Apportion stores	345	259	258	(862)
			258	–
Apportion maintenance	181	52	(258)	25
			–	25
Apportion stores	10	8	7	(25)
			7	–
Apportion maintenance (say)	5	2	(7)	–
	100,329	73,171	–	–

The total overheads of £173,500 are therefore apportioned above to become 'actual' overheads of the two production departments.

Absorbed overhead	Machining	Assembly
Budgeted overhead	£90,000	£75,000
Budgeted activity	3,600 mach. hours	24,000 d. lab. hours
Absorption rate	£25 per mach. hour	£3.125 per d. lab. hour
Actual activity	3,515 mach. hours	26,280 d. lab. hours
Absorbed overhead	£87,875	£82,125

(a) Machining department overhead account

	£		£
Overhead incurred	100,329	Work-in-progress a/c	87,875
		Under-absorbed	
		overhead a/c	12,454
	100,329		100,329

Assembly department overhead account

	£		£
Overhead incurred	73,171	Work-in-progress a/c	82,125
Over-absorbed			
overhead a/c	8,954		
	82,125		82,125

(b) In the machining department, the under-absorbed overhead occurred because actual expenditure was in excess of budgeted expenditure, and actual activity was below the budget of 3,600 machine hours. The excess expenditure and under-capacity should be investigated in order that the cause(s) can be identified and control action taken.

In the assembly department, the over-absorption of overhead was due to the extra capacity; the number of direct labour hours worked being greater than budget. Also, actual expenditure was below the budgeted figure of £75,000.

	Machining department hours			Assembly department hours		
Budgeted activity	3,600			24,000		
Actual activity	3,515			26,280		
Volume variance		85 (ADV)			2,280 (FAV)	
× absorption rate	£25			£3,125		

	£	£		£	£	
Volume variance		2,125 (ADV)			7,125 (FAV)	
Budgeted expenditure	90,000			75,000		
Actual expenditure	100,329			73,171		
Expenditure variance		10,329 (ADV)			1,829 (FAV)	
Total over/(under) absorption		(12,454) (ADV)			8,954 (FAV)	

6F   (a)(i) Overhead analysis sheet (figures in £000)

Cost	Total	Production Machine hours	Direct labour hours	Sales and distribution	Administration
Energy and water (area)	20		16	1.0	3.0
Electricity	14	14			
Rent (area)	180		144	9.0	27.0
Repairs – Machinery	25	25			
Buildings (area)	10		8	0.5	1.5
Maintenance of patterns	45		45		
Direct wage-related costs	115		115		
Indirect wages	83		83		
Indirect wage-related costs	10		10		
Production management salaries	133		133		
Depreciation of machinery	150	150			
Security (area)	10		8	0.5	1.5
Inspection	60		60		
Carriage out	88			88.0	
Salesforce salaries	100			100.0	
Salesforce expenses	50			50.0	
Design and estimating	75			75.0	
General management and administration	232				232.0
Advertising	40			40.0	
	1,440	189	622	364.0	265.0

(ii) The production overhead related to machinery should be absorbed on the basis of budgeted machine hours. The rate will be:

$$\frac{£189,000}{180,000 \text{ machine hours}} = £1.05.$$

The production overhead not related to the machinery should be absorbed by on the basis of direct labour hours. The rate will be:

$$\frac{£622,000}{200,000 \text{ direct labour hours}} = £3.11$$

Budgeted sales for next year are given as £4,550,000 and the absorption rate for the selling and distribution costs could be based on this figure. This gives a rate of 8% $\left(\frac{£364,000}{£4,550,000} \times 100. \right)$

Budgeted sales could also be used to absorb the administration costs at a rate of $\frac{£265,000}{£4,550,000} \times 100 = 5.82\%$.

Alternatively administration costs could be absorbed by a rate based on budgeted production cost:

	£000
Raw materials	750
Carriage on raw materials	49
Direct wages	1,040
Overhead – machinery	189
Overhead – based on direct labour hours	622
Budgeted production cost	2,650

$\frac{£265,000}{£2,650,000} \times 100 = 10\%$ on production cost.

(b)(i)   *Job 1019*

		£
Raw materials		2,888
Direct wages		3,500
Production overhead:		
300 machine hours × £1.05 =	315	
700 direct labour hours × £3.11 =	2,177	2,492
Production cost		8,880
Selling and distribution cost 8% of £12,000		960
Administration cost 10% of £8,880		888
		10,728
Quoted selling price		12,000
Expected profit		1,272
Expected profit, as percentage of selling price		10.6%

		£000
(ii) Expected profit for next year for the company:		
Sales		4,550
Less: Production costs	2,650	
Selling and distribution	364	
Administration	265	3,279
Expected profit		1,271
Expected profit, as a percentage of sales		27.93%

Job 1019 makes a profit of 10.6% of the selling price. The budget plans a percentage profit of 27.93% on sales for next year. This suggests that profits next year will be much better than for the current year, *if* the 10.6% is representative of jobs during the current year.
  Alternatively job 1019 is less profitable than the norm.

CHAPTER 7

7A   (a)   An integrated cost accounting system maintains a set of accounting records which provide financial and cost accounts using a common input of data for all accounting purposes. It is a single comprehensive accounting system. An interlocking accounting system maintains cost accounts distinct from the financial accounts. The two sets of accounts are kept continuously in agreement by the use of control accounts, or made readily reconcilable by other means. The term 'interlocking' is derived from this reconciliation achieved by the maintenance of control accounts. In the financial accounts a 'cost ledger control' and in the cost accounts a 'financial ledger control' should show balances which are equal and opposite.
  The financial ledger control account in an interlocking system enables the cost accounting system to be self-balancing. It is the repository of the 'other side' of the double entry for certain items in the cost accounts. Materials purchased (a debit) in the cost accounts would be balanced by a creditors ledger control entry to record the unpaid liability (a credit). Such an account does not form part of the cost accounts in an interlocking system, so that the debit for materials must be balanced by a credit entry in the financial ledger control account. Clearly with a large volume of transactions, individual positions cannot be made, so totals can be used to control the situation.

(b)   (i)   Reconciliation of financial and cost ledger control accounts:

Financial ledger:

	£	
Existing balance on cost ledger control account	199,800	Dr.
Less: Cost of sales	7,500	
Add: Raw materials purchased	8,000	
Less: Extension to buildings – capital expenditure	4,100	
Less: Under-absorbed overhead	11,600	*
Corrected balance on cost ledger control account	184,600	Dr.

Cost ledger:

	£
Existing balance on financial ledger control account	172,200 Cr.
Add: Depreciation	24,000
Less: Under-absorbed overhead	(11,600) *
Corrected balance on financial ledger control account	184,600 Cr.

	£
* Existing over-absorbed balance	12,400
less Depreciation charge	24,000
Under-absorbed balance	11,600

(ii)   Journal entries in the cost ledger:

	Dr. (£)	Cr. (£)
Factory overhead	24,000	
Financial ledger control		24,000
Financial ledger control	11,600	
Factory overhead		11,600

7B   (a)
1. Job costing is in operation – job ledger takes the place of a manufacturing account or work-in-progress control.
2. Full absorption costing is employed – under/over-absorbed overhead is written off the profit and loss. Selling and administration overhead is also absorbed.
3. Interlocking accounts are used – general ledger control.

Stores ledger control

		£			£
Opening balance		6,000	(ii)	Job ledger control	19,000
(i)	General ledger control	27,000	(iii)	Production overhead control	2,000
				Closing balance	12,000
		33,000			33,000

Production wages control

		£			£
(iv)	General ledger control	25,000	(v)	Job ledger control	20,000
			(vi)	Production overhead control	5,000
		25,000			25,000

Production overhead control

		£			£
(iii)	Stores ledger control	2,000	(x)	Job ledger control	30,000
(vi)	Production wages control	5,000	Profit and loss –		
(vii)	General ledger control	26,000		Under-absorbed overhead	3,000
		33,000			33,000

Job ledger control

		£			£
Opening balance		20,000	(xi)	Cost of sales	79,000
(ii)	Stores ledger control	19,000		Closing balance	10,000
(v)	Production wages control	20,000			
(x)	Production overhead control	30,000			
		89,000			89,000

Selling and administration overheads

		£			£
(viii)	General ledger control	12,000	(xii)	Cost of sales	11,000
				Profit and loss –	
				Under-absorbed overhead	1,000
		12,000			12,000

Cost of sales

		£			£
(xi)	Job ledger	79,000	Profit and loss		90,000
(xii)	Selling and administration				
	overhead	11,000			
		90,000			90,000

Sales

	£			£
Profit and loss	110,000	(ix)	General ledger control	110,000

Profit and loss a/c

	£		£
Cost of sales	90,000	(Sales	110,000
Under-absorbed overhead:			
Production	3,000		
Selling and administration	1,000		
Net profit			
(to General ledger control)	16,000		
	110,000		110,000

General ledger control

		£			£
(ix)	Sales	110,000	Opening balance		26,000
Closing balance		22,000	(i)	Stores ledger control	27,000
			(iv)	Production wages control	25,000
			(vii)	Production overhead control	26,000
			(viii)	Selling and administration	
				overhead	12,000
			Net profit		16,000
		132,000			132,000

The missing amounts were:
(iii)   £2,000 (£6,000 + 27,000 − 19,000 − 12,000)
(v)   £20,000 (£25,000 × 80%)
(vi)   £5,000 (£25,000 × 20%)
(x)   £30,000 (£20,000 + 19,000 + 20,000 + 30,000 − 10,000)
(xii)   £11,000 (£110,000 × 10%)
Profit = £16,000 (see above)
Balances carried forward:
  Stores ledger   £12,000 Dr.
  Job ledger   £10,000 Dr.
  General ledger control £22,000 Cr.

(c) (i)   Purchases of materials.
     (ii)   Direct materials allocated to jobs.
     (iii) Indirect materials (not allocable to jobs), therefore an overhead.
     (iv)   Production wages incurred.
     (v)   Direct wages allocated to jobs.
     (vi)   Indirect wages (not allocable to jobs), therefore an overhead.
     (vii) Production overhead incurred (other than materials and wages): factory expense.
     (viii) Selling and administration overhead incurred.
     (ix)   Sales value to jobs completed in ther period – D/E is debtors ledger control.
     (x)   Production overhead absorbed to jobs.
     (xi)   Production cost of jobs completed in the period.
     (xii) Selling and administration overhead absorbed to jobs completed in the period.

7C   Journal entries for Integar plc:

	£	£
2 May Stores ledger control	24,000	
Direct material price variance	1,500	
Supplies plc – credit ledger control		25,500
Charge stores with standard cost, credit supplier with actual price, W/O difference to a variance account.		
5 May Work-in-progress	16,800	
Stores ledger control		16,800
1,400 kg at £12 transferred from stores to work-in-progress.		
8 May Abnormal loss on stores	14,400	
Stores ledger control		14,400
120 kg at £12 wasted – charge to a cost account, and credit stores.		
10 May Stores ledger control	1,200	
Work-in-progress		1,200
Charge stores and credit WiP a/c with material returned from the job.		
Supplies plc	1,275	
Direct material price variance		75
Stores ledger control		1,200
Credit stores with standard cost of material returned to supplier. Write back the variance on these goods, and debit supplier with actual price, thus reducing what is owed to supplier.		
Work-in-progress	4,800	
Stores ledger control		4,800
Charge out replacement material to the work-in-progress.		

(b) Integrated accounting systems are considered to be superior to non-integrated systems since only one set of accounting records is required to provide both financial and cost accounting data. Information from a common input can be used for both accounting purposes. A non-integrated system separates the financial accounts from the cost accounts, keeping them separate and independent from each other, but reconciling the results derived from the two systems from time to time.

Advantages of an integrated accounting system:

1. If a single system is used, the necessity to reconcile financial and cost accounts is avoided.
2. Computerization of a large volume of input data enables the information to be classified in a number of different ways for cost and financial accounting purposes. There is no real need to separate the two systems and duplicate all the difficulties of entering transaction data into the system.

Limitations of an integrated system:

1. Difficulties may arise if different accounting policies are required for financial accounting and cost accounting purposes. For example, a marginal costing system producing information for managerial purposes would not relate well to the requirements for full absorption costing in financial accounts according to SSAP 9.
2. Integration means that the recording system is trying to undertake two tasks at the same time, and in a sophisticated organization with many different types of transaction the chart of accounts may produce confusion and an overload to the system.

7D   Transactions which might form part of a reconciliation between profits calculated from financial accounting records and profit derived from cost accounting records are:
1. *Items excluded from cost accounts*:
   (a)   quantity discounts and trade rebates, cash discounts;
   (b)   rents received;
   (c)   abnormal losses and gains;
   (d)   donations;
   (e)   profit or loss on sales of assets;
   (f)   Income from non-trading activities – investment income, interest on invested surplus funds;
   (g)   write-offs of goodwill and other intangible assets;
   (h)   corporation tax provided;
   (i)   transfer to reserves;
   (j)   dividends paid and proposed.
2. *Items excluded from financial accounts*:
   (a)   notional charge for rent where premises are owned;
   (b)   notional interest charged on capital employed;
   (c)   adjustments made to depreciation rates and asset lives compared with those for financial accounting purposes;
   (d)   use of different stock valuation methods;
   (e)   under/over-absorption of overhead expenses.

CHAPTER 8

8A   (a)   Each job is numbered and costs are accumulated on the job cost card. Materials are charged out by a requisition on the stores (MR). Materials return notes (MRN) record surplus or substandard materials returned to the stores.

Labour is analysed at the month-end and charged to jobs.

Overheads are charged to jobs on the bais of a preset direct labour hour rate. The use of a DLH rate may mean that overheads are related in some way to labour cost or time.

Miscellaneous expenses are identified with individual jobs.

(b)

Estimated cost:	£
Material	7,213
Labour	6,000
Overhead	3,600
Miscellaneous	1,260
	18,073
Price	20,000
Estimated profit	1,927

Actual profit £763 – shortfall of 60 per cent.

Material costs: £7,540 against estimated £7,213 – increase 4.5 per cent.
Labour costs: £6,660 against estimated £6,000 – increase 11 per cent.
Overhead costs: £3,744 against estimated £3,600 – increase 4 per cent.
Miscellaneous: £1,293 against estimated £1,260 – increase 2.6 per cent.

With overheads at £1.80 per hour and an overhead estimate of £3,600, the job is scheduled for completion in 2,000 hours. The estimated labour cost of £6,000 means a labour rate of £3 per hour. This has been paid up to 1 July, but in July an average rate of £4.5 was paid – overtime? Then, 2,080 hours of labour time were used to complete the job – 4 per cent time increase.

Delivery was one month behind schedule, and the invoice was sent out three months after delivery.

(c) Control action *after* the job is finished is ineffective, unless it contributes towards a pool of experience which will be used to prevent a repetition of mistakes on future jobs. You should investigate reasons for:
1. Delivery delay – 'stock-out' or production delays, or estimating errors?
2. Invoicing delay – why wait three months after delivery?
3. Excess hours worked and overtime paid – check supervision.
4. Excessive material costs – bad buying or careless estimating?

(d) A comparison of actual and estimated costs, with percentages and reasons, would prove a helpful addition to information shown on the job cost card.

8B (a) Advantages of job costing:
1. Reveals the cost of each job, and the profit made.
2. Costs to date can be found quickly, so that mistakes or excessive costs are shown up at an early stage.
3. Cost can be compared with estimate, again to reveal excessive costs, and to check on the estimating procedures.
4. Comparison can be made with other jobs.
5. 'Cost plus' jobs require reliable costing records.
6. Work-in-progress stock for periodic accounts easily computed.

(b)		Foundry	Assembly	Printing
Budgeted fixed overhead		£75,000	£72,250	£64,500
Budgeted machine hours		20,000	5,000	30,000
Budgeted direct labour hours		8,000	17,000	4,000
FOH: absorption: Machine hour		£3.75	–	£2.15
Direct labour hour		–	£4.25	–

Job 1473		£	£
Foundry:	Materials		4,680.00
	Labour		119.00
	Overheads		97.50
			4,896.50
Assembly:	Materials	950.00	
	Labour	531.00	
	Overheads [59 DLHs × 4 – 25]	250.75	1,731.75
Printing:	Materials	211.00	
	Labour	55.00	
	Overheads	23.65	289.65
Total cost			6,917.90

CHAPTER 9

9A (a) The distinguishing features of contract costing are:
1. The contract may continue over several years, and therefore many costing periods. This feature causes difficulties in profit measurement, since if cost is to be matched to activity, and performance measured for a certain period, assumptions must be made as to the proportion of the price earned, before the work is completed.
2. The contract relates to a specific order, and activity is site-based. Thus the contract is a cost centre, and costs can be recognized and allocated with greater facility. Contract costing has a high proportion of direct costs, derived from its form of organization.

(b)   £000
Cost of work b/d from previous year   250
Cost of work this year:
  Material (10 + 512 − 18)   504
  Stock shortage credited to contract, net of HO charge
  [4 − (0.4% of 504 − 4)]   (2)
  Labour   487
  Plant hire   96
  Expenses   74
  Overhead [(1,840 × .05% − 13]   79
                                                                              1,488
Cost to completion   215
Estimated total cost   1,703
Price   2,100
Estimated final profit   397

$$\frac{\text{Work certified}}{\text{Price}} = \frac{1,840}{2,100} \times 397 = 348 \text{ profit to be taken to date.}$$

Alternatively:

Certificate − Cost of work certified
1,840 − (1,488 − 35) = £387, therefore take £348

This figure should be treated with prudence, but since insufficient information is given in the question, greater accuracy cannot be achieved.

(c) Calculation of profit to date of £348 cannot now be made since price and completion costs are no longer as in part (a). Therefore apply formula:

$$2/3 \times \frac{\text{Cash}}{\text{Certificate}} \times £387$$

But you would need to find the cash figure, and decide if a two-thirds fraction was sufficiently prudent.

9B   (a)   Contract accounts

	Peterborough development		Nottingham development	
Balances 1 April 1987 b/f:	£	£	£	£
Cost of work not yet certified	14,000			
Plant	204,000			
Materials	6,000			
Profit in suspense		3,000		
Transactions for year:				
Materials to site	47,720		24,540	
Issues from stores	4,280		2,460	
Plant	12,000		166,000	
Wages	32,560		34,820	
Overheads	16,800		16,180	
Other expenses	4,640		4,000	
Balances at 31 March 1988:				
Cost of work not certified		16,000		6,000
Plant on site		146,000		130,000
Stock of materials		16,000		8,000
Therefore cost of work certified		161,000		104,000
	342,000	342,000	248,000	248,000

(b)   Calculation of profit on Peterborough development

Value of work certified (given)   194,000
Less cost of work certified   161,000
Profit   33,000
2/3 proportion   22,000
Reduced by retention: 22,000 × 90% = £19,800

Peterborough development

	£	£
Cost of work certified b/d	161,000	
Value of work certified		194,000
Profit for year	19,800	
Therefore profit in suspense c/f	13,200	
	194,000	194,000

Calculation of profit/loss on Nottingham development

Nottingham development

	£	£
Cost of work certified b/d	104,000	
Value of work certified		100,000
Loss on contract		4,000
	104,000	104,000

		£
Therefore overall profit to be taken =		19,800
	Less	4,000
		15,800

	£	£
(c) Balance sheet entries		
Fixed assets (WDV)	276,000	
Stock of materials	24,000	
Work-in-progress	22,000	
Reserve of profit		13,200

Contract account

	A £	B £	C £		A £	B £	C £
Work-in-progress b/f			150,000	Stock returned	500		
Plant b/f			20,000	Scrap sales	200		
Material b/f			1,000	Material stock c/f*	4,100	3,000	1,000
Material cost	40,000	25,000	9,000	Plant c/f*	12,000	4,000	4,000
Labour cost	30,000	10,000	10,000	Work-in-progress c/f*	75,433	36,500	201,381
Overhead cost	2,500	1,000	5,000	Loss to P and L		1,000	
Plant purchased	15,000						
Plant		8,000					
Accruals	1,000	500	1,000				
	88,500	44,500	196,000				
Net profit to P. and L.	3,733	–	10,381				
	92,253	44,500	206,381		92,253	44,500	206,381

Workings

Contract C	£		*Contract A*	£
Cost	196,000		Cost	88,500
Less items c/f	5,000		*Less* credits	700
	191,000			87,800
Less profit taken	5,000		*Less* items c/f	16,100
Cost to date	186,000			71,700
Plus cost to complete	4,000		*Less* not certified	3,700
Plant to complete	1,000			
Material to complete	1,000		Work certified	68,000
Contingencies	1,000		Certificate	75,000
Cost to completion	193,000		Profit to date	7,000
Price	210,000			
Expected profit	17,000			

Contract C

$$\frac{200}{210} \times \frac{190}{200} \times \text{£17,000} = \underline{15,381}$$

Less profit already taken $\underline{5,000}$

Profit now taken $\underline{10,381}$

WiP 186,000 + 15,381 = £201,381

Contract A

$$\frac{60}{75} \times \frac{2}{3} \times \text{£7,000} = \text{£3,733}$$

Wip = 71,700 + 3,733 = £75,433

Contract B	£
Cost	44,500
Less items c/f	7,000
Cost to date	37,500
Less work not certified	1,500
	36,000
Certificate	35,000
Loss	£1,000

WiP cost to date *less* loss = £36,500

(b) Balance sheet shows item marked * as assets; WiP shown net of cash received.

9D   (a) (i)

Hospital contract account

	£000		£000
Plant	240	Materials returned	47
Hire of plant	77	Plant c/d	165
Materials	662	Materials c/d	50
Direct wages	960	WiP c/d	2,625
Direct wages accrued c/f	40		
Wage-related costs	132		
Direct expenses	34		
Supervisory staff: direct (90 + 20)	110		
Regional office expenses	50		
Head office expenses	30		
Surveyors' fees	27		
Profit to P. and L. a/c	525		
	2,887		2,887
Plant b/d	165	Wages accrued b/d	40
Materials b/d	50		
WiP b/d	2,625		

Profit calculation:

*Contract price		3,000,000
Cost to date	2,100,000	
Estimated cost	300,000	2,400,000
Estimated profit		600,000

$$\frac{\text{Cost of work completed}}{\text{Total estimated cost}} \times \text{Estimated profit}$$

$$\frac{2,100,000}{2,400,000} \times 600,000 \qquad 525,000$$

(ii) Work-in-progress valuation for balance sheet:

Cost to date	2,100,000
Attributable profit	525,000
	2,625,000
Cash received	1,800,000
	825,000

(iii) A more prudent method of calculating profit to date on uncompleted contracts is:

	£000	£000
Value of work certified		2,000
Cost of work to date	2,100	
Cost of work not certified	500	1,600
Notional profit		400

Formula often used:

$$2/3 \times \frac{\text{Cash received}}{\text{Value of work certified}} \times \text{Notional profit}$$

$$2/3 \times \frac{1,800}{2,000} \times 400 = \text{£240,000}$$

(b) The Companies Act 1985 stipulates that stocks of raw materials or work-in-progress or finished goods should be shown in the accounts at the lower of cost or net realizable value. The company in the question has included profit attributable to uncompleted contracts in the work-in-progress stock figure. This treatment is in accordance with SSAP 9. Clearly the management of the company take the view that the accounts would not show a true and fair view if this profit were to be omitted and accordingly they have taken advantage of another rule in the Companies Act which allows the valuation rule under Schedule 4 of the Act to be overridden and ignored if such action leads to a true and fair view.

CHAPTER 10

10A   (a) *Workings*

	Volume basis		*Revenue basis*		*NRV basis*	
	Volume	*Joint*	*Revenue*	*Joint*	*NRV*	*Joint*
	kg	*cost*	*£*	*cost*	*£*	*cost*
Large 20,000 × 0.5 kg	10,000	£7,000	13,000	£4,225	7,000	3,539
Small 20,000 × 0.15 kg	3,000	£2,100	15,000	£4,875	11,000	5,561
	13,000	£9,100	28,000	£9,100	18,000	£9,100

Profitability statement

	Volume basis		*Revenue basis*		*NRV basis*	
	Large	*Small*	*Large*	*Small*	*Large*	*Small*
	£	*£*	*£*	*£*	*£*	*£*
Sales	13,000	15,000	13,000	15,000	13,000	15,000
Joint	(7,000)	(2,100)	(4,225)	(4,875)	(3,539)	(5,561)
Post-separation costs	(6,000)	(4,000)	(6,000)	(4,000)	(6,000)	(4,000)
Profit	–	8,900	2,775	6,125	3,461	5,439

(b) Each basis shows a different profit for the two products. It is questionable whether any of them is a reliable guide to management as to the profitability of the products, because the profit is completely dependent upon the apportionment of joint costs. To base the analysis on volume is to ignore value, and to use revenue is to divide joint costs on the basis of a factor which is not immediately relevant at the split-off point. The net realizable value basis may be more significant than the other methods since joint cost is apportioned on the basis of value at the split-off point.

It would appear that no method shows a real relationship to joint costs, so profit figures based on apportionment may be of little value to management. The best that can be said is that the two products together show a profit of £8,900. Perhaps contribution could be used to compare large and small.

	Large	*Small*
	£	*£*
Revenue	13,000	15,000
Post-separation costs	6,000	4,000
Contribution to joint costs	7,000	11,000
Contribution per unit	35p	55p

Small makes a greater contribution than large, so if the product mix could be changed in favour of small, then resources could be employed in a more profitable manner.

(c)

Incremental revenue per tile £1 − 75p		25p
Cost of second process	15p	
Transport costs	3p	
Less packaging saved	(1p)	17p
Extra profit per title		8p

On a batch of 10,000 tiles profit would increase by £800.

10B   (a) Material £83,600 and conversion costs £58,000 = a total process cost of £141,600 which, if divided by output of 40,000 kg gives a cost of £3.54 per kg.

	Product X (£/kg)	Material B (£/kg)
Raw material	3.54	3.54
Conversion costs	1.80	–
	5.34	3.54
Adjust for yield	÷0.9	
Total cost	5.93	3.54
Selling price	5.60	6.00
Profit/(loss)	(0.33)	2.46

(b) The profit or loss of product X depends on the basis of apportionment of the joint costs. Accordingly, this information is not useful in the context of decision-making. Materials A and B are joint products so any decision concerning A should be taken in the light of its effect on B. Overall the process shows a profit. Any decision to vary the quantity or output mix of the process should be taken in the light of cost behaviour when circumstances change.

(c)

	£
Sales value method	
Material A: 9,000 kg sold for (£5.60 − [£1.80 ÷ 0.9])	32,400
Material B: 30,000 kg × £6	180,000
	212,400

$$\text{Material A proportion} = \frac{32,400}{212,400} \times \text{joint cost £141,600} = £21,600$$

Profit calculation on new basis for raw material A

£21,600 ÷ 10,000 kg	£2.16
Conversion cost	£1.80
	£3.96
	÷0.9
	£4.40
Selling price	£6.60
Profit margin	£1.20

Joint costs apportioned per sales revenue ensure that if the process as a whole is profitable each joint product will show a profit. This will avoid some erroneous decisions, but is still an unreliable basis for decision-making.

10C   (a) Process I

	Materials	Processing costs	
Equivalent units (kg):			
Work completed	160,000	160,000	
Closing work-in-progress	30,000	20,000	(66% complete)
	190,000	180,000	

Total costs:	£	£
Opening work-in-progress	20,000	12,000
Period costs	75,000	96,000
	95,000	108,000

Therefore cost per equivalent unit =	95,000	108,000
	190,000 units	180,000 units
Total cost £1.10	= £0.50/kg	= £0.60/kg

Value of work completed:
160,000 kg at £1.10 per kg = £176,000

Value of closing work-in-progress:
Materials   − 30,000 kg at £0.50 per kg = £15,000
Processing costs − 20,000 kg at £0.60 per kg = £12,000
                                                £27,000

(b) Starcomp sales	£	£
240,000 kg at £2 per kg		480,000
Less costs		
Process II − Materials	120,000	
− Processing costs	120,000	
Process I − Compound	192,000*	
		432,000
Profit		£48,000

* Every kg of compound used on Starcomp costs the company £1.60 of revenue forgone by not selling the compound at once. This is its 'opportunity' cost: 120,000 kg at £1.60 = £192,000.

(c) 40,000 kg of compound remain, so 80,000 kg of Starcomp can be produced.

	£
Compound − 40,000 × £1.6 =	64,000
Process II − Material (£160,000 − £120,000)	40,000
− Labour (£140,000 − £120,000)	20,000
Cost of making 80,000 kg	124,000

Therefore £1.55 per kg.
Any price in excess of £1.55 per kg would show a positive contribution.

10D   (a) Joint products are produced by a single process which is undertaken in such a way that the products cannot be identified separately until the end of the process. The products emerge from the joint process at the split-off point, and if they are judged to have equal significance at this point (either in terms of volume or sales value etc.) they are considered to be joint products. If one product is dominant over the others, it is said to be a main product with by-products.

(b) The costs of the joint process are attributable to all the joint products produced from that process, but if those costs are apportioned to the joint products the validity of the cost per product derived from this exercise may be misleading. The methods used for this apportionment divide the joint costs on the basis of volume, sales value or net realizable value at the split-off point. This division is entirely artificial, and does not produce a reliable figure for the purposes of determining profit per product or for other managerial decision-making purposes. The only justification for the apportionment of joint costs seems to be to place a value upon unsold stock at the end of a costing period.
    Where no further processing after the split-off point is envisaged two methods of apportionment may be used.
1.   The physical unit method: the total output of the joint product is expressed in terms of weight or volume, and the joint costs are apportioned according to the relative weight or volume of each product.
2.   The sales value method: the aggregate sales value of the joint products is computed, and the joint costs are spread between the joint products on the basis of their proportion of the total sales revenue expected.
    The sales value method computes the same gross profit percentage for all the joint products, and is

used in preference to the other methods since it is less subject to distortion. The physical unit method suffers from the disadvantage that there may not be a common unit of measurement of weight or volume for the joint products, i.e. one may be a liquid and another a solid.

(c) An 'equivalent unit' is a notional quantity of completed production substituted for an actual quantity of incomplete physical units in process, when the aggregate work content of the incomplete units is deemed to be equivalent to that of the substituted quantity of completed units. The concept of the equivalent unit is applied in process costing to compute an appropriate value in terms of units for production which is incomplete at the beginning and the end of a process. This is necessary if an average cost per unit is to be derived for the process. The calculation is as follows: Total costs divided by (equivalent units to complete opening stock plus completed units entering the process and completed during the month plus equivalent units for the work undertaken on the closing stock).

(b) *Product Y*		£	
Direct materials	300 units	2,100	
Distillation costs		3,300	
		5,400	
Less: cost of X1	75 units	1,350	
	225 units	4,050	÷ 225 = £18 per unit

Product Z		£	
Direct materials	200 units	1,400	
Distillation costs		2,400	
		3,800	
Less: cost of X2	80 units	1,520	
	120 units	2,280	÷ 120 = £19 per unit

Product XXX		£	
Distillation X	400 units	4,300	
X1	75 units	1,350	
X2	80 units	1,520	
	555 units	7,170	
Blending cost		1,155	
		8,325	÷ 555 = £15 per unit

(c) Alternatively the income receivable for by-product B could be shown in the profit and loss account as miscellaneous income.

Solution 10E (a)

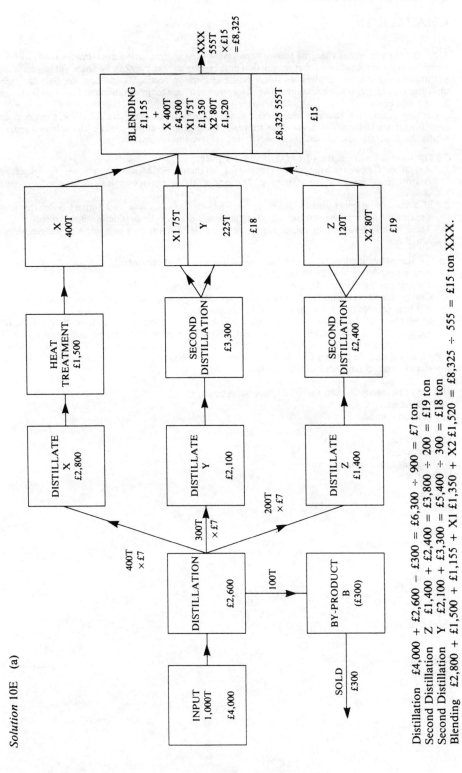

Distillation £4,000 + £2,600 − £300 = £6,300 ÷ 900 = £7 ton
Second Distillation Z £1,400 + £2,400 = £3,800 ÷ 200 = £19 ton
Second Distillation Y £2,100 + £3,300 = £5,400 ÷ 300 = £18 ton
Blending £2,800 + £1,500 + £1,155 + X1 £1,350 + X2 £1,520 = £8,325 ÷ 555 = £15 ton XXX.

Flowchart for Exercise 5E

CHAPTER 11

11A   (a) The reason for charging service department costs to production departments is to attribute manufacturing overheads to direct production cost centres so that they can be absorbed to cost units passing through the cost centres. In this way the absorption costing system can calculate the fully absorbed cost of a unit of production. The absorption rates are set in advance and based on budgeted activity and costs.

Another reason for charging out service costs is to assist in their control. Where production departments are charged for the services they use, there is an incentive to act efficiently and reduce waste. An arbitrary apportionment base will not achieve this advantage.

(b) The present system suffers from three disadvantages:
1.   Actual costs, however large, are all charged out, so there is no incentive within the power house to control costs and improve efficiency. The power house manager gains no benefit from cost control.
2.   If a user department wastes power or uses power frugally, little cost impact is felt by that department because the wastage or saving is spread over all the production departments.
3.   There is little feedback to the power house manager to assist cost control, e.g. budget versus actual cost.

(c) The alternative method proposed will lead to improved cost control.
1.   Production departments will pay for what they use.
2.   Comparison of use with budget – managerial responsibility.
3.   Charges based on normal efficiency in the power house means that the power house management will bear responsibility for operational inefficiencies.
4.   Fixed costs of the power house are governed by overall factory demand, so they should be apportioned to manufacturing departments. Apportionment of budgeted cost means that if actual costs are less than budget the power house management are credited with the cost saving.

Problems arising from the use of the new system concern the recording of power consumed, and the analysis of costs to fixed and variable classes.

11B   (a) Cost analysis form for vehicle operating costs
Type of vehicle
Registration number

	£
Labour costs:	
Drivers' wages	
National insurance contributions	
Holiday pay	
	_____
Running costs:	
Fuel	
Oil	
Tyres	
Repairs and maintenance	
	_____
Fixed costs:	
Insurance	
Road fund licence	
Depeciation	
Overheads absorbed	
	_____
Total cost	_____
Miles run	
Tonnage carried	
Cost per ton/mile	

(b) Weekly bus operating statement
For week No. ....

	Week ended		
	1	(etc.)	Total
Route operated or contract	£	£	£
Revenue – Cash			
– Concessionary fares	_____	_____	_____
	_____	_____	_____
Direct costs – variable:			
Wages			
National insurance contributions			
Holiday pay			
Fuel			
Fuel rebates	( ) (	) (	)
Oil			
Tyres			
Repairs and maintenance	_____	_____	_____
	_____	_____	_____
Direct costs – fixed:			
Insurance			
Road fund licence			
Depreciation	_____	_____	_____
	_____	_____	_____
Total direct costs	_____	_____	_____
Revenue less all direct costs			
Less: Overheads – Allocated			
– Apportioned	_____	_____	_____
Net profit	_____	_____	_____

(c) The cost of the passenger transport manager would be allocated directly to that function. This is fair unless he spends part of his time on the administration of other parts of the business. The employment cost of the accountant will be allocated to general administrative overheads together with the costs of other managers, rent, rates, security and the cost of operating the new administration office. Items such as rent, rates, light and heat would need to be apportioned between administration and direct service functions such as the maintenance department or the garage facilities. The cost of these functions would in turn need to be absorbed on a user basis to the three revenue earning segments of the business, namely heavy haulage, light vans and passenger transport.

CHAPTER 12

12A Main points to be covered by the draft memorandum:

Objectives – Plan
           – Co-ordinate
           – Communicate
           – Control
           – Motivate

Advantages:
1. Identify, emphasize, clarify responsibility.
2. Early regular consideration of basic policies.
3. Focus on contribution of each part to overall profit.
4. Co-ordination – parts geared to main plan.
5. Comparator – actual against plan – remedial action.
6. Remind managers of level of performance they have committed themselves to achieve.
7. Sales, purchases and stocks planned together so capital employed kept to a minimum – identify shortfall of funds required over funds available.

8. Decentralize responsibility yet maintain control.
9. Achieve cost-conscious organization.
10. Budget acts as an executive instruction.

2 marks would be awarded for use of a memorandum format.

12B (a) A public sector organization or local government authority receives a significant proportion of its revenue directly from the central government, and collects the rest from its local population by way of local tax. The cash limits system allocates the revenue to be received between the various requirements for funds to provide services. Planning in this situation means that managers must use the limited resources at their disposal to provide the best possible service within those limits. Expenditure on services must not exceed the funds available to pay for those services unless the local authority is able to borrow funds to finance current expenditure. There is no profit motive within this system, but this is replaced by the guiding principle of providing the best possible service with the available resources. The principle is similar to that which applies to a service department in a company.

In a business the budgetary plan attempts to maximize profits within the parameters imposed by a different set of limiting factors. The return on capital employed, or profit per pound of sales, also guides the allocation of resources within a commercial organization.

The advantages of a fixed budget system from the point of view of a local government authority are:
1. The limitation of resources by means of a fixed budget enforces careful allocation of funds to alternative needs and the use of cost/benefit analysis.
2. The cash limit determines in advance how much is available for the provision of services and enables firm plans to be established which will avoid overspending.
3. A fixed budget enforces discipline on local authority managers in that they know that no extra funds can be provided and that they must take prompt action when actual results exceed budgeted expenditure during the course of the year.
   Disadvantages:
1. If cash limits are to be imposed in the forthcoming year, managers may boost their spending budgets by building in 'slack' in order to receive adequate funds after the cuts have been made.
2. The establishment of a fixed budget may limit the flexibility of the organization to extend or improve services.
3. If, as the end of a financial year approaches, the previously authorized cash limit has not been spent, the managers of that part of an organization will spend up to their authorized amount. Such expenditure organized at a late stage may prove wasteful, whereas the reallocation of these funds would improve services in other parts of the authority.

(b) A budget manual expresses the procedures by which the budget for an organization is to be computed, and the responsibilities of individual managers for drafting, refining and finalizing the budget, including a timetable of dates by which decisions are to be made. The composition of the budget committee and the role, authority and responsibilities of the budget officer will be detailed in the budget manual. The budget manual acts as a guideline to the way in which the budget is to be produced. Students would answer in terms of one of the three items below.

In a private sector organization the budget manual might include an organization structure for the business/details of the timetable for the preparation of the budget/blanks of budget forms/the responsibilities of the budget committee with details of its members.

In a public sector organization the budget manual might include details of the main sources from which revenue is expected, and for which expenditure is required/a system whereby expenditure is authorized and controlled/a system for virement whereby expenditure within a budget can be transferred from one department to another/a timetable for the preparation of the budget/details of the forms to be used.

For a local government authority the budget manual might include a chart showing the various committees which sit to organize the services provided by the authority/the headings under which revenue might be received/standard forms to be used/a timetable for budget preparation/a list of officers responsible for preparing the budget for each department. In a local government authority there may well be a trading services department which acts as a business, operating alongside other departments which provide a service to the community, e.g. leisure services, roads, education etc.

CHAPTER 13

13A   (a) The principal budget factor is a factor which limits the activities of an undertaking. The constraint is therefore a good point at which to start the budget procedure, so that other budgets are co-ordinated to this principal limiting factor; e.g. it is usually the level of expected sales, but it can be the availability of materials, labour or finance which holds back a business from improving its potential profit.

(b) A fixed budget is designed to remain unchanged irrespective of the level of activity achieved. A flexible budget recognizes the different behaviour of fixed and variable costs when activity levels fluctuate.
   The flexed budget shows the cost of behaviour expected for the level of activity achieved, and is thus a good comparator for actual cost to measure operating efficiency, and achieve cost control.

(c)

Forecast (i)	A	B	C
Volume	22,000	40,000	6,000
Labour cost	£2	£1.50	£1
Total labour cost £110,000	£44,000	£60,000	£6,000
Labour available £135,000			

Therefore sales is principal budgeting factor.

Forecast (ii)			
Volume	30,000	50,000	7,000
Labour cost	£2	£1.50	£1
Total labour cost £142,000	£60,000	£75,000	£7,000
Labour available £135,000			

Therefore labour is principal budgeting factor.

13B   (a)(i)

	Product		
	A	B	C
Sales	12,000	15,000	10,000
Stock increase	180	200	160
Good production required	12,180	15,200	10,160
Loss of product (5/95 × 15,200)		800	
Total production	12,180	16,000	10,160

(ii)

	V	W	Material X	Y	Z
Product A					
(units of material × 12,180)	60,900	36,540	–	–	12,180
Product B					
(units of material × 16,000)	64,000	32,000	48,000	16,000	16,000
Product C					
(units of material × 10,160)	–	60,960	50,800	40,640	–
	124,900	129,500	98,800	56,640	28,180
Expected material loss					
(20/80 × 28,180)	–	–	–	–	7,045
Materials usage	124,900	129,500	98,800	56,640	35,225

(iii)

	V	W	X	Y	Z
Materials usage	124,900	129,500	98,800	56,640	35,225
10% stock reduction	2,000	3,000	1,500	500	900
Materials purchased	122,900	126,500	97,300	56,140	34,325
× unit cost	55p	50p	35p	60p	80p
Cost of purchases	£67,595	£63,250	£34,055	£33,684	£27,460

Total material purchase budget = £226,044

(b) An ideal standard expresses what can be attained under the most favourable conditions – no allowance is built into the standard for inefficiency such as spoilage or machine breakdowns. It represents perfection and is thus normally unattainable.

An attainable standard is one which can be attained by efficient produciton, with built-in allowances for expected difficulties such as normal idle time etc. Attainable standards are realistic, and thus useful for budgeting and supportive of employee morale.

Ideal standards are rarely used – variances based on them show only the improvement which could theoretically be made.

13C (a) *Workings*
(1) Loaves made this quarter: £246,000 ÷ 50p = 492,000 × 0.4kg = 196,800 kg
£180,000 ÷ 30p = 600,000 × 0.2kg = 120,000 kg

Material used   316,800 kg

316,800 kg cost £110,880; therefore dough costs 35p per kg.

(2) Standard wage rate is £2.40 per hour

Large loaf takes 30/240 × 1 hour	=	7.5 minutes to make
492,000 loaves	=	61500 hours
Small loaf takes 20/240 × 1 hour	=	5 minutes to make
600,000 loaves	=	50,000 hours
Labour time (111,500 hours × £2.40 + 10p)	=	£278,750

Standard times next quarter will be:

Small loaf: 5 minutes − 20%	=	4 minutes
Large loaf: 7.5 minutes − 20%	=	6 minutes

(3) New standard labour cost:

Small loaf 4/60 × £2.70	=	18p
Large loaf 6/60 × £2.70	=	27p

Actual cost last quarter:

Small loaf 5/60 × £2.50	=	20.8p
Large loaf 7.5/60 × £2.50	=	31.25p

(4) Variable overhead rate
Direct labour hours were 111,500
£19,800 ÷ 111,500 hours = 17.8p as DLH rate.

	Large loaf	Small loaf	Total
Materials purchases budget:			
Budgeted sales	500,000	550,000	
Standard material usage	0.4 kg	0.2 kg	
Budgeted consumption	200,000	110,000	310,000
Stock reduction			15,000
Budgeted purchases – volume			295,000
Budgeted price 35p + 5% (36.75p)			36.75p
Budgeted purchases			£108,412
Direct labour budget:			
Budgeted sales	500,000	550,000	
Standard time	6 mins	4 mins	
Total time (hours)	50,000	36,667	86,667
Standard wage rate: £2.70 per hour			
Hours available (150 × 40 × 13)			78,000
Overtime			8,667

Budgeted cost 86,667 × £2.70 =	£234,001	
8,667 × £0.675 =	£5,850	
	£239,851	

(b) Cost saving:
At this quarter's efficiency it would take 100/80 × 86,667 hours to complete next quarter's budget = 108,334 × £2.50 = £270,835

Thus the productivity agreement saves the company £36,834 in wages. Also, since direct labour hours will be reduced by 24,833* hours the variable overheads at 17.8p per hour will be saved = £4,420.

*111,500 hours − 86,667 hours

13D   (a) Production budget:

	Product		
	K	B	
Budgeted sales (units)	3,000	4,500	
Add Closing stock per budget			
(15/60 × 3,000 = 750)(20/60 × 4,500 = 1,500)	750	1,500	
	3,750	6,000	
Less Expected opening stock	1,050	1,200	
Budgeted production	2,700	4,800	

Material purchase budget:			kg
Budgeted production (units)	2,700	4,800	
Material consumption per product (kg)	6	2	
Total material consumption	16,200	9,600	25,800
Add Budgeted closing stock (10/60 × 25,800)			4,300
			30,100
Less Anticipated opening stock			3,700
			26,400

Material purchase budget = 26,400 kg × £3 per kg = £79,200.

Direct wages budget:		
Budgeted production (units)	2,700	4,800
Standard hours per product	5	3
Standard hours for budgeted production	13,500	14,400
Total time = 27,900 standard hours		
Convert to expected productive man hours 27,900 × 10/9 =		31,000
Add Budgeted down time 20% × 31,000		6,200
Total attendance required		37,200
Maximum labour time available:		
65 workers × 40 hours × 12 weeks		31,200
Therefore overtime hours		6,000

Total wage budget will be:	£
31,200 hours × £4	124,800
6,000 hours × £6 overtime rate	36,000
Total wages budget for direct workers	160,800

(b) To calculate the amount paid out in cash each week for materials and wages the following information would be required:
1. Stockholding policy and expected weekly material stock movement. This information will lead to the amount bought each week.
2. The amount of credit taken from suppliers and also cash discounts received.
3. List of materials received in previous period and due to be paid for during the budget period.
4. Ordering pattern – one large order or several small orders will influence when cash is paid out.
5. Wage payment intervals – weekly etc. – and the amount of arrears brought forward from a previous period, and earnings carried forward for payment in a subsequent period.
6. Wages earned each week during the budget period (this may be constant as production is planned to be even). Is overtime concentrated in certain weeks?
7. Employees' deductions and their payments, e.g. tax deducted weekly but paid to Inland Revenue monthly; NI deductions; pension fund.
8. Allowances to employees – dirty money or shift premium etc.

13E　(a) Cash budget

	January £	February £	March £	April £
Balance b/d	10,000	9,000	3,890	9,090
Sales	–	15,200	57,100	80,000
	10,000	24,200	60,990	89,090
Purchases	–	11,550	24,500	26,950
Wages	–	4,800	19,800	22,200
Variable overhead	–	960	4,600	7,080
Fixed overhead	1,000	3,000	3,000	3,000
	1,000	20,310	51,900	59,230
Balance c/d	9,000	3,890	9,090	29,860

Workings

Sales	Amount £	20%	Discount 5%	Net £	50% previous month	20% two months before	8% three months before	Total cash receipts
January	–	–	–	–	–	–	–	–
February	80,000	16,000	800	15,200				15,200
March	90,000	18,000	900	17,100	40,000			57,100
April	100,000	20,000	1,000	19,000	45,000	16,000		80,000
May	100,000	20,000	1,000	19,000	50,000	18,000	6,400	93,400

Production (units)	Feb Sales	Mar Sales	April Sales	May Sales	Total
January	800				
February	2,400	900			3,300
March		2,700	1,000		3,700
April			3,000	1,000	4,000
May				3,000	
	3,200	3,600	4,000	4,000	

Purchases (units)

	Production	50%		Total	Price	Amount
January	3,300 in February	1,650		1,650	× £7	= £11,550
February	3,700 in March	1,850	+ 1,650 =	3,500	× £7	= £24,500
March	4,000 in April	2,000	+ 1,850 =	3,850	× £7	= £26,950

Direct wages

			£	Paid in
January (units × cost)	800 × 6	=	4,800	February
February	3,300 × 6	=	19,800	March
March	3,700 × 6	=	22,200	April
April	4,000 × 6	=	24,000	May

Variable overhead

	Units	£	February	March	April	May
January	800 × 2 =	1,600	960	640		
February	3,300 × 2 =	6,600		3,960	2,640	
March	3,700 × 2 =	7,400			4,440	2,960
April	4,000 × 2 =	8,000				
			960	4,600	7,080	2,960

Fixed overhead (net of depreciation)

	£	January	February	March	April
January	3,000	1,000	2,000		
February	3,000		1,000	2,000	
March	3,000			1,000	2,000
April	3,000				1,000
		1,000	3,000	3,000	3,000

(b) The amount receivable from customers in May is £93,400.

CHAPTER 15

15A   *Outline*
The behavioural aspects of budgeting and standard costing are all important and appear to have been ignored or dealt with badly, by the Haskins senior management.

Production workers view with great suspicion any form of performance appraisal and it would be expected that they would react adversely to the unannounced introduction of a standard costing system. If Haskins senior management are considering introducing a standard costing system then full and frank discussions must take place with the union and production workers involved to explain the system and its objectives. Without the agreement and co-operation of the personnel involved any standard costing will be largely useless.

Senior labour standards
1.   Detailed operation and process specifications to establish standard labour times.
2.   Agreed methods of manufacture.
3.   Work study projections (union involvement?).
4.   Labour standards must specify the exact grades of labour to be used as well as the times involved.
5.   Concept of standard hour/minute is important and can be defined as 'the quantity of work achievable at standard performance, expressed in terms of a standard unit of work in a standard period of time' (CIMA *Terminology*).
6.   Forecast of wage rates (personnel department).

Types of standard
1.   Basic.
2.   Ideal.
3.   Attainable.
4.   Current.

CHAPTER 16

16A   (a)(i) Standard cost per unit = £8

	£	
Cost of sales	263,520	
Less opening stock	(120,800)	
Plus closing stock	146,080	
Standard cost of production	288,800	÷ £8 = 36,100 units.

(ii) Materials used at actual cost (£170,310) deduct adverse price variance (£2571) to calculate standard cost of materials used (£167,739). The usage variance can then be calculated as:
(Actual quantity × Standard cost) − (Standard quantity × Standard cost)
(− £167,739) − (36,100 × £4.60) £167,739 − £166,060 = £1,679 ADV.

(iii) Standard labour cost of actual production

	£
36,100 × £2.10 =	75,810
Add adverse rate variance	4,760
Less favourable efficiency variance	(3,240)
Actual direct labour cost	77,330

(iv) Actual quantity at standard cost is £167,739
Divide by standard cost per kg = £167,739 ÷ 2.30 = 72,930 kg.
Actual cost £170,310 ÷ 72, 930 = £2.335.

(b) Price variance:
1.   Estimates of future prices in error when the budget was drafted.
2.   Quantity purchased falls - discounts lost.
3.   Inefficient buying.
4.   Change in quality of materials purchased.

Usage variance:
1. Increased wastage by poor handling in the factory and a lack of care on the part of direct labour.
2. Records incorrect.
3. Standard not well set.

16B   (a)(i) Standard rate is £787,800 ÷ 202,000 hours = £3.90 per hour.
Standard time is 400,000 units ÷ 200,000 hours = 30 minutes.
Labour efficiency variance:
(Actual hours × Standard rate) − (Standard hours × Standard rate)
(202,000 × £3.90) − (420,000 × ½ hour × £3.90)
£787,000 − £819,000 = £31,200 FAV.

(ii) Overhead expenditure variance
Budgeted variable overhead is £200,000 ÷ (400,000 units × ½ hour) = £1 per hour.
(Actual expenditure) − (Fixed overhead + Variable overhead)
£620,000 − (£400,000 + 202,000 × £1) = £18,000 ADV.

(iii) Fixed overhead volume variance
£400,000 − [420,000 × (½ hour × £2)] £420,000 = £20,000 FAV.
Budgeted FOH − FOH absorbed
£400,000 − [420,000 × (½ hour × £2)] = £420,000 = £20,000 FAV.

(iv) Variable overhead efficiency variance
(Actual hours × Standard rate) − (Standard hours × Standard rate)
(202,000 × £1) − (210,000 × £1) = £8,000 FAV.

(b) Fixed overhead volume variance arises because the actual output on which the absorption is computed differs from the budgeted volume, e.g. in (a) above 20,000 units were produced in excess of budgeted production.
   The overall variance can be analysed into sub-variances to disclose the reasons for over- or under-production, e.g. capacity used or efficiency of production.

(c) Efficiency ratio

$$= \frac{\text{Standard hours for actual output}}{\text{Actual hours}} = \frac{210,000}{202,000} \times \frac{100}{1} = 104\%$$

Labour cost per unit is below standard so profit will increase. A bonus scheme would share this profit with the employees. Fixed costs are also spread over a larger volume of production so unit cost falls. The size of the profit would depend on whether the extra production could be sold at a standard profit margin.

16C   (a) A standard hour is the quantity of work achievable at standard performance, expressed in terms of a standard unit of work in a standard period of time. From this definition it can be seen that the standard hour is more a measurement of work than a measurement of time. It is a convenient means whereby the quantity of production of a department or factory can be expressed, especially if the department or factory produces a variety of products. It is therefore a common denominator between tables and chairs made in a furniture factory. Even products expressed in kilogrammes and litres can be brought into one common term if they are expressed as standard hours of work.
   A furniture manufacturer makes tables and chairs. If the standard time for manufacturing a chair is four hours and the budgeted production units of chairs are 3,000, this production can be expressed as 12,000 standard hours. If a table takes six standard hours and 4,000 are budgeted to be made, then the standard hours for this work are 24,000. Total standard hours of production in the factory for the month would be 36,000.

(b) The capacity usage ratio is calculated as:

$$\frac{\text{Actual hours worked}}{\text{Budgeted hours}} \times 100\%$$

(c) The efficiency ratio is calculated as:

$$\frac{\text{Standard hours of actual output}}{\text{Actual hours worked}} \times 100\%$$

(d) The production volume ratio (sometimes known as the activity ratio) is calculated as:

$$\frac{\text{Standard hours of actual output}}{\text{Budgeted hours}} \times 100\%$$

As in the example above let the standard hours for actual output = 36,000, the actual hours worked = 40,000 and the budgeted hours = 45,000. The ratios are then computed as:

Efficienty ratio $= \dfrac{36,000}{40,000} \times \dfrac{100}{1} = 90\%$

Capacity ratio $= \dfrac{40,000}{45,000} \times \dfrac{100}{1} = 89\%$

Production volume ratio $= \dfrac{36,000}{45,000} \times \dfrac{100}{1} = 80\%$

Efficiency × Capacity = Activity: 90% of 89% = 80%.

The work has been completed at 90 per cent of efficiency since the standard time for production achieved is 90 per cent of the time actually taken to produce the work. If management intended to work the factory for 45,000 budgeted hours and achieved only 40,000 hours, they have used only 89 per cent of the capacity they intended to use. The work produced is equivalent to 36,000 standard hours, but the management intended to produce 45,000 hours of work, therefore they have been only 80 per cent active.

16D   (a) Variance analysis

			£	
Material - Pine *price*	(AP × AQ) − (SP × AQ)			
	£11,250 − (2.80 × 4,500) £12,600		1,350	FAV
usage	(SP × AQ) − (SP × SQ)			
	(2.80 × 4,500) − (2.80 × 3,720)			
	£12,600 − £10,416		2,184	ADV
			834	ADV
- Varnish *price*	(AP × AQ) − (SP × AQ)			
	(3.50 × 290) − (3 × 290)			
	£1,015 − £870		145	ADV
usage	(SP × AQ) − (SP × SQ)			
	(3 × 290) − (3 x 310)			
	£870 − £930		60	FAV
			85	ADV
(b) Labour rate	(AR × HP) − (SR × HP)			
	£36,400 − (6 × 5,200) 31,200		5,200	ADV
Idle time	(SR × HP) − (SR × HW)			
	(6 × 5,200) − (6 × 4,800)			
	£31,200 − £28,800		2,400	ADV
Efficiency	(SR × HW) − (SR × SH)			
	(6 × 4,800) − (6 × 4,960)			
	£28,800 − £29,760		960	FAV
Total labour variance			6,640	ADV

(c) Favourable price variance - efficient buyer paid less than standard price for the timber. Adverse usage variance - inefficiency in production - too much waste and scrap - could be caused by low grade labour.

However, did the buyer purchase timber of adequate quality? - if not, he or she has saved £1,350, but has cost £2,184 through excess wastage in the factory when raw material is used and proves inadequate.

16E   Working paper for weaving shed operating statement – April

Material variances		Yarn A		Yarn B
A. Standard cost of actual output				
Economy 35,000 metres		(× 0.2kg × £3)		(× 0.2kg × £4)
		£21,000		£28,000
Super 34,000 metres		(× 0.2kg × £3)		(× 0.3kg × £4)
		£20,400		£40,800
		£41,400		£68,800
B. Standard cost of actual consumption		£39,000		£76,000
13,000 kg × £3				
19,000 kg × £4				
C. Actual cost of actual consumption		£40,500		£72,000

	Yarn A	Yarn B	Total
	£	£	£
Materials usage variance (A − B)	2,400 F	7,200 A	4,800 A
Materials price variance (B − C)	1,500 A	4,000 F	2,500 F
Materials cost variance (A − C)	900 F	3,200 A	2,300 A

Direct labour variances

A. Standard cost of actual output – Economy (35,000 × 1/5) =   7,000 std hours
                                    Super   (34,000 × 1/4) =   8,500 std hours
                                                              15,500

15,500 std hours × £2 =   £31,000
B. Standard cost of actual hours worked 15,800 hours × £2 =   £31,600
C. Actual cost of actual hours worked =   £30,500

		£
Labour efficiency variance	(A − B)	600 A
Wages rate variance	(B − C)	1,100 F
Total wage variance	(A − C)	500 F

Variable overhead variances

$$\text{Budgeted rate per hour} = \frac{£24,000}{16,000 \text{ hrs}} = £1.50$$

Standard cost of actual output 15,500 std hours × £1.50 = £23,250
Actual costs incurred   = £24,750
Variable overhead expenditure variance   £1,500 A

This can be analysed further into detailed expense variances by flexing the variable overhead budget by standard hours actually produced.

	Fixed budget	Flexed budget	Actual expense	Variance
	£	£	£	£
Power (50p/hr)	8,000	7,750	8,250	500 A
Indirect labour (60p/hr)	9,600	9,300	9,000	300 F
Maintenance (40p/hr)	6,400	6,200	7,500	1,300 A
	24,000	23,250	24,750	1,500 ADV

Fixed overhead variances

$$\text{Budgeted rate per hour} = \frac{£20,000}{16,000 \text{ hrs}} = £1.25$$

	£
A. Standard cost of actual output 15,500 × £1.25 =	19,375
B. Fixed budget	20,000
C. Actual expenditure	21,050
Fixed overhead volume variance (A − B)	625 A
Fixed overhead expenditure variance (B − C)	1,050 A
Total fixed overhead variance (A − C)	£1,675 A

The expenditure variance can be analysed into detailed expense variances as follows:

Fixed budget		Actual expenses	Variance
	£	£	£
Supervision	6,400	6,950	550 ADV
Heat and light	2,500	2,900	400 ADV
Depreciation	6,300	6,200	100 FAV
Rent and rates	4,800	5,000	200 ADV
	20,000	21,050	1,050 ADV

16F   (a) *Material price variance* - on purchases

	Powder	Chemical	Tubes
A. Standard cost of purchases:			
Quantity purchased	10,000 kg	1,200 litres	5,200 tubes
Standard price			
(Note 1)	£0.75	£2.40	£0.30
=	£7,500	£2,880	£1,560
B. Actual cost of purchases	£7,000	£2,880	£1,580
	(10,000 ×	(600 ×	(200 ×
	£0.70)	£2.30)	£0.40)
		+	+
		(600 × £2.50)	(5,000 × £0.30)
Material price variance (A − B)	£500F	NIL*	£20 A

*This could be misleading and further analysis of the possible trend in price variance for this material should be made.

Material usage variance

	Powder	Chemical	Tubes
C. Standard material	(4,500 × £1.50)	(4,500 × -0.60)	(4,500 × -0.30)
Cost of production	£6,750	£2,700	£1,350
D. Standard material			
Cost of actual	£7,350	£2,520	£1,356
issues (Note 1)	(9,800 × £0.75)	(1,050 × £2.40)	(4,520 × £0.30)
Material usage variance (C − D)	£600A	£180F	£6A

Direct wages variances:

A. Standard cost of actual production	
4,500 tubes × £1.80	£8,100
B. Actual hours worked × standard hourly	
rate 2,050 hours × £4.50	£9,225
C. Actual wages	£8,910
Direct labour efficiency variance (A − B)	£1,125 A
Direct wages rate variance (B − C)	£315 F

Note 1: Materials - calculation of standard purchase price of each ingredient.

	A	B	A ÷ B
			Standard
		Standard	purchase price
	Standard cost	quantity	of each
	per tube	per tube	ingredient
	£		£
Powder	1.50	2 kg	0.75 per kg
Chemical	0.60	¼ litre	2.40 per litre
Tube	0.30	1 tube	0.30 per tube

(b) *Materials price variance*

This variance reflects the efficiency of the purchasing department, but there are other influences on price variances, e.g.:

1. A downward trend in market prices for powder not anticipated when the standards were established. Good buyers should be able to forecast such movements.
2. For powder a purchase of lower quality material resulting in a favourable price variance might also cause an adverse usage variance for this material.

3. For chemicals, a nil variance may cover the start of a price increase trend beyond the control of the purchasing department. Alternatively the last purchase of chemicals could have been of a better quality than that specified in the standard.
4. The extra price paid for the purchase of a small quantity of tubes does appear to indicate inefficiency. Perhaps a quantity had to be obtained at short notice, at any price, to maintain production, reflecting perhaps poor storekeeping, or slow processing of material requisitions.

Materials usage variance
The production department may be using the material more, or less, efficiently than standard, but there are other possible explanations, e.g.:
1. For tubes, pilfering at the point of issue, or damage by incorrect handling in stores.
2. The favourable variance for chemicals might indicate improved quality giving a better yield, or a change in technical standard not yet incorporated into the standard cost.
3. The adverse variance for powder might reflect inferior quality purchases or incorrectly adjusted equipment, e.g. weighing scales. Alternatively, inefficiency in handling powder in transit to production, e.g. split bags, could cause the variance.
4. An error in documentation could account for part of the variances.

Direct labour efficiency variance
The adverse labour efficiency variance might be caused by lazy operatives, who are not producing enough, but there are many other possible causes, e.g.:
(a) poor quality material causing difficult handling, waste and rejects – idle time;
(b) incorrectly adjusted or badly placed equipment;
(c) poor production scheduling – idle time;
(d) introduction of new equipment – learning problems;
(e) introduction of new members into the team of workers.

16G   (a) Finishing department's productivity ratio

Product	Output	×	Standard hour allowance	=	Total standard hours produced
X	2,200 units		3 hours		6,600
Y	5,250 units		½ hour		2,625
					9,225 standard hrs

$$\text{Efficiency ratio} = \frac{\text{Standard hours for actual production}}{\text{Actual hours worked}} = \frac{9,225}{10,800} = 85.4\%$$

(b) Finishing department's variance analysis statement – direct wages

	Month 1 £	Month 2 £
A. Standard cost of actual production	36,900	37,000
B. Actual hours worked @ standard hourly rate	43,200	36,000
	(10,800 × £4)	(9,000 × £4)
C. Actual hours paid @ standard hourly rate	43,200	38,400
	(10,800 × £4)	(9,600 × £4)
D. Actual wages paid	44,800	39,600
	£	£
Direct wages efficiency variance (A − B)	6,300 A	1,000 F
Direct wages idle time variance (B − C)	Nil	2,400 A
Direct wages rate variance (C − D)	1,600 A	1,200 A

(c)   *Wages control account (month 1)*

	£		£
Cash	44,800	Work-in-progress a/c	36,900
		Direct wages efficiency variance a/c	6,300
		Direct wages rate variance a/c	1,600
	44,800		44,800

Work in progress control account (month 1)

	£		£
Wage control a/c	36,900		

An alternative method might be to transfer the wages paid to work-in-progress account and write off the variances from this account.

(d) Labour efficiency variances do not measure the net effect on profit of labour efficiency being different from that specified in the standard. Other factors are:

1. A guaranteed weekly wage means the cost of the direct workers is fixed, whether or not they are efficient. In month 1, if the workers had achieved standard efficiency (at output levels shown in the question) they would have been productively working for only 9,225 hours and standing idle for the remaining 375 hours of the basic working week (9,600 − 9,225 hours). The cost of inefficiency of £6,300 should be reduced by (375 hours × £4 per hour) £1,500 to £4,800, which is the amount of overtime payment at normal hourly rates.

2. The efficiency variance measures the cost, or benefit, of differing efficiency at standard wage rates. In month 1 presumably all of the overtime has been caused by inefficiency as the output could have been achieved in normal time. Therefore all of the rate variance, which is overtime premium, is the result of inefficiency and should increase the adverse efficiency variance.

    In month 2 the reverse situation arises. Perhaps labour has produced 9,250 standard hours in the 9,000 hours available. The company has saved 250 hours of overtime premium through labour efficiency. The company may also have saved payment of the excess (over standard) hourly rate, i.e. £4.125 − £4.000 for that 250 hours. Therefore calculating the efficiency variance at (£4 × 250 hours) £1,000 understates the extent of saving by the company.

3. Labour efficiency may affect the utilization of other resources within the organization, e.g. improved labour efficiency could result in adverse material wastage (i.e. in order to increase output, efficiency of use of materials may suffer).

4. Increased volume of production cuts fixed cost per unit.

16H   (a) Budget statement

Overhead	Fixed £	Budget variable £	Total £	Actual £	Variance Adv. £	Variance Fav. £
Management	30,000	–	30,000	30,000	–	–
Shift premium	–	3,600	3,600	4,000	400	
National insurance	6,000	7,920	13,920	15,000	1,080	
Inspection	20,000	9,000	29,000	28,000		1,000
Supplies	6,000	6,480	12,480	12,700	220	
Power	–	7,200	7,200	7,800	600	
Light and heat	4,000	–	4,000	4,200	200	
Rates	9,000	–	9,000	9,000	–	–
Repairs and maintenance	8,000	5,400	13,400	15,100	1,700	
Materials handling	10,000	10,800	20,800	21,400	600	
Depreciation	15,000	–	15,000	15,000	–	–
Administration	12,000	–	12,000	11,500		500
Idle time	–	–	–	1,600	1,600	
	120,000	50,400	170,400	175,300	6,400	1,500

Total variance (6,400 − 1,500) = 4,900 adverse.

(b) National insurance: the rates fixed for the period may have increased so this cost is beyond the control of management.

Inspection: costs are lower than expected. Investigation should take place to discover whether the standard of inspection has been reduced. Perhaps there are less inspectors than was planned or an expected salary increase has not yet been implemented.

Repairs and maintenance: the cost of planned maintenance should be forecast with reasonable accuracy but unexpected repairs not included in the budget will influence the actual cost. The monthly charge may therefore vary from the budget but over a period of time this variance should even out.

Idle time: normal idle time is included in the budget. Abnormal idle time cannot be forecast with accuracy.

(c) (i) Highlighting variances which exceed a specific figure will not be adequate for control purposes. The significance of the variances is important so any comment should be based on a statistical analysis, e.g. consideration of variances which were plus or minus say 6 per cent of the budget.
(ii) Actual costs should be analysed to show the fixed or variable elements, which should correspond to the budget. Management information should analyse variances to those which are controllable and those which are non-controllable. This analysis enables the production of a much fairer evaluation of manager performance.

(d) (i) Overhead absorbed is as follows: $36,000 \times £4.40 = £158,400$.
(ii) The amount overspent is £4,900.
(iii) The volume variance can be calculated as follows:

Allowance	170,400	
Absorbed	158,400	
	£12,000	(Adverse)

Or, as per CIMA *Terminology*:
Actual hours $\times$ standard overhead rate $-$ (Budgeted fixed overhead + [actual hours $\times$ variable overhead rate])
$36,000 \times £4.40 - £120,000 + [36,000 \times £1.40]$
$158,400 - £170,400 = £12,000$ (Adverse).

161   (a) The discussion should cover the following points:
1. Variances highlight a situation where there has been departure from the budget or intended performance. Thus the attention of management is focused on exceptions to the rule, and time is saved in the appraisal of cost information.
2. Variances stress the need for remedial action to bring activities back on to the course expressed in the budget.
3. Accountability: variance analysis accentuates the responsibility of managers for the costs of departments which they control, and promotes the need for managers to report to their superiors on remedial action. This in turn ensures the involvement of senior management in budgeting and reviewing performance in those departments which are under their overall control.
4. Variances may provide significant information to show how standards are unreal, which should influence the preparation of the budget and standards for the next accounting year.

(b) *Workings*
$£180,000 \div 15,000 = £12$ as variable overhead absorption rate.
$£270,000 \div 15,000 = £18$ as fixed overhead absorption rate.

Standard cost per unit of product P

			£
Material	3 kg	at £4.40	13.20
Labour	0.5 hours	at £5.00	2.50
Variable overhead	0.5 hours	at £12.00	6.00
Fixed overhead	0.5 hours	at £18.00	9.00
			30.70

(i) Materials
Price variance:
$\dfrac{£336,000}{£4.20} = 80,000$ kg used and purchased
Actual quantity $\times$ (Standard price $-$ Actual price)
$80,000 \times (4.40 - 4.20) = £16,000$ Fav.
Usage variance:
(Standard quantity $-$ Actual quantity) $\times$ Standard price
$(75,000 - 80,000)\ £4.40 = £22,000$ Adv.
Labour:
Rate variance:
(Standard rate $-$ Actual rate) Actual hours
$(5.00 - £5.40)\ 14,000 = £5,600$ Adv.
Efficiency variance:
(Standard hours produced $-$ Actual hours worked) $\times$ Standard rate
$(12,500 - 14,000)\ £5 = £7,500$ Adv.

Overhead
Expenditure variance:
[Fixed overhead + (Actual hours × Standard variable overhead rate)] − Actual production overhead
    incurred
[£270,000 + (14,000 × 12)] − £430,000 = £8,000 Fav.
Efficiency variance:
(Standard hours for actual production − Actual hours) × Standard overhead rate
(12,500 − 14,000) £30 = £45,000 Adv.
Volume variance:
Actual hours × Standard overhead rate − [Fixed overhead cost + (Actual hours × Variable
    overhead absorption rate)]
14,000 × £30 − (£270,000 + 14,000 × £12)
£420,000 − £438,000 = £18,000 Adv.

(ii) Operating statement

		Favourable	Adverse	£	
Standard cost of actual production				767,500	
Variances:		*Favourable*	*Adverse*		
Material:	price	16,000			
	usage		22,000		
Labour:	rate		5,600		
	efficiency		7,500		
Overhead:	expenditure	8,000			
	efficiency		45,000		
	volume		18,000	74,100	Adv
Actual cost				841,600	

16J   (a) Standard product cost sheet for one unit of product XY

		£
Direct materials	8 kg × £1.50	12.00
Direct wages	2 hrs × £4.00	8.00
Variable overhead	2 hrs × £1.00	2.00
		22.00

Workings

Direct materials	£		kg
Actual costs 150,000 kg	210,000	Actual usage	150,000
Price variance (FAV)	15,000	Usage variance (ADV)	6,000
Standard	225,000		144,000

£225,000 ÷ 150,000 kg = £1.5 per kg standard cost.

Usage variance $\dfrac{£9,000 \text{ adverse}}{£1.5}$ = 60,000 kg adverse.

$\dfrac{144,000 \text{ kg}}{18,000 \text{ units}}$ = 8 kg per unit

= 8 kg × £1.50 = £12

Direct labour:		£
Actual cost	32,000 hours	136,000
Rate variance (ADV)		8,000
Standard		128,000 ÷ 32,000 hours = £4 per hour

Efficiency variance $\dfrac{£16,000}{4}$ = 4,000 hours

$\dfrac{36,000 \text{ hours}}{18,000 \text{ units}}$ = 2 hours per unit

Overhead:		£
Actual cost	32,000 hours	38,000
Expenditure variance	(ADV)	6,000
Standard	= £1 per hour	32,000
Efficiency variance (FAV)	4,000 hours	4,000
		36,000

(b) Three types of standards can be used.

1. A basic standard is establised for use over a long period and represents the base from which the current standards have developed. This standard remains unaltered for an indefinite period and is not subject to revision when material prices or labour rates vary. This standard serves as a baseline from which to measure the extent of changes over time and is therefore of little use in comparison with actual costs for the purpose of the evaluation of managerial performance.
2. An ideal standard is one which can be attained under the most favourable conditions. Perfect efficiency is rarely attained so variances derived from ideal standards serve only as an academic exercise to show up the difference between actual performance and perfection. As such they are of little use to evaluate managerial performance since they are almost impossible to attain. If such standards are applied the morale of management may suffer.
3. An attainable standard is based on normally expected efficiency. Allowances are built into an attainable standard for levels of normally aceptable waste, or machine breakdown, or other reasons which cause acceptable idle time. This standard is of the greatest use in practice since it represents the performance expected to be achieved.

CHAPTER 17

17A   (a) The arguments supporting the use of absorption or marginal costing systems concern the different treatment of fixed overhead costs in these two systems. Absorption costing absorbs fixed costs to products and carries them forward in the stock valuation, whereas under marginal costing the fixed cost is written off against profit in the period during which it is incurred. Once fixed costs are written off in this way, the marginal costing system can report information to management in terms of contribution.

The arguments are in four areas:

1. Marginal costing does not apportion or absorb fixed costs, and thereby avoids the cost of these tasks, while at the same time it avoids the use of unreliable figures for managerial decision-making purposes.
2. The absorption costing method enables stocks to be valued on the basis of direct cost plus a proportion of overheads, so that this valuation is in line with SSAP 9. Marginal costing carries forward stocks at variable production costs.
3. Significant differences between the two systems concerning the amount of profit reported in a period are calculated if there is a difference between the volume of units produced and sold during the period. This difference is caused by the fact that if stocks are increased, under absorption costing those stocks will carry forward into the next period a proportion of the fixed costs of the current period. The marginal costing system writes off all fixed costs to the period in which they were incurred. Therefore marginal costing demonstrates in the profit figure the relationship between sales volume and profit, but under absorption costing the profit is influenced not only by the level of sales but also by the level of production.
4. A further difference between the two systems concerns the manner in which information is presented to management. Absorption costing is a total cost concept and can be seen as a guide to long-term costs and therefore to performance. Marginal costing, however, emphasizes the variable costs of different activities and their contribution to fixed costs and profit. Thus marginal costing is a short-term concept which can be used for decision-making, but in the long run contribution in total must be sufficient to recover the fixed costs of the business.

(b) *Workings*

Absorption costing	£/unit	£/unit
Selling price		3.00
Direct materials + labour	1.10	
Variable production overhead	0.20	
Fixed production overhead	0.60	1.90
Gross profit		1.10
Variable selling + administration overhead	0.10	
Fixed selling + administration overhead	0.40	0.50
Profit		0.60

Marginal costing	£/unit	£/unit
Selling price		3.00
Direct materials + labour	1.10	
Variable production overhead	0.20	
Variable selling + administration overhead	0.10	1.40
Contribution		1.60

(i)

	£
Fixed production overhead absorbed = 260,000 units × 0.60 =	156,000
Budgeted fixed production overhead	144,000
Over-absorbed fixed production overhead	12,000

(ii)

	£
Absorption profit: 230,000 units × 0.60/unit =	138,000
Add: Fixed production overhead over-absorbed	12,000
Less: Fixed selling + administration overhead under absorbed (10,000 × 0.40)	(4,000)
	146,000

Marginal profit:	
230,000 units × £1.60/unit =	368,000
Less: Fixed overheads	240,000
	128,000

(iii)

	£
Absorption profit	146,000
Less: Stock increase 30,000 units × £0.60	18,000
= Marginal profit	128,000

(iv) The profit figures determined under both absorption and marginal costing would be the same in situations where the level of production and the level of sales are the same, and where in addition there is no change in the fixed overhead absorption rate between opening and closing stocks.

17B   (a) Two products with a constant mix can be treated as one for the purposes of break-even analysis, by using average contribution per £1 of sales weighted per the mixture.
Contribution X: £1 − 45p = 55p
                    Y: £1 − 60p = 40p
Average is (X at 55p × 0.7) + (Y at 40p × 0.3) = 50.5p per £1 of sales.

$$\frac{\text{Fixed cost}}{\text{Contribution per unit}} = \text{B/E sales} \qquad \frac{£1212000}{£.505} = £2,400,000$$

(b) Revenue of £4,000,000 × P/V ratio of 0.505 = contribution £2,020,000. This less fixed costs of £1,212,000 = £808,000 profit. Changed sales mix gives a different average contribution: (X at 55p × 0.5) + (Y at 40p × 0.5) = 47.5p.

Profit = (4,000,000 × 47.5p) − £1,212,000 = £688,000.
Break-even = £1,212,000 ÷ 0.475 = £2,551,579.

The profit volume chart is shown below.

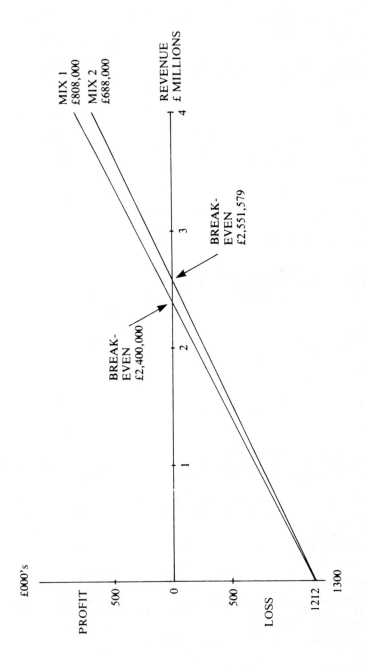

MIX 1
£808,000

MIX 2
£688,000

REVENUE
£ MILLIONS

BREAK-
EVEN
£2,551,579

BREAK-
EVEN
£2,400,000

£000's

PROFIT

500

0

500

LOSS

1212

1300

Both mixes make a loss equal to fixed cost at nil production

Both mixes make a loss equal to fixed cost at nil production

(c) Product X contribution required:

$$\frac{\text{Fixed costs £455,000 + Contribution £700,000}}{\text{Contribution per unit 55p}} \div = £2,100,000.$$

	£000	£000
17C (a) Budgeted profit statement		
Sales (£900,000) ÷ £9 × 1.5 × £8.		1,200.0
Less Variable cost of sales		
Direct materials (£200,000 × 1.5 × 0.95 × 0.98)	279.3	
Direct labour (Note 1)	204.6	
Production overhead (£50,000 × 1.5)	75.0	
Selling overhead (Note 2)	84.0	
Distribution overhead (£36,000 × 1.5)	54.0	696.9
Contribution		503.1
Less Fixed costs (Note 3)		
Production overhead	141.6	
Administration overhead	93.6	
Selling overhead	52.8	
Distribution overhead	24.0	312.0
Net profit		191.1

Contribution per unit = £503,100 ÷ 150,000 units = £3,354.

Notes

1. Direct labour = $£120,000 \times \dfrac{130,000}{100,000} \times 1.1$ £171,600

$+ £120,000 \times \dfrac{20,000}{100,000} \times 1.1 \times 1.25 = $ £33,000

£204,600

2. Variable selling overhead = $£63,000 \times \dfrac{£1,200,000}{900,000} = £84,000$

3. Fixed costs = (£38,000 + £80,000 + £78,000 + £44,000 + £20,000) × 1.2 = £312,200

(b) Break-even point – current year

$$\frac{\text{Fixed costs £260,000}}{\text{Contribution £431,000}} \times 100,000 \text{ units} = 60,325 \text{ units}$$

Break-even point – budget year

Overtime is only incurred on the final 20,000 units so it is likely that the break-even point occurs at a level of output achievable in normal time.

Thus direct labour =

$$\frac{£171,600}{130,000 \text{ units}} = £1.32 \text{ per unit}$$

rather than

$$\frac{£204,600}{150,000 \text{ units}} = £1.364 \text{ per unit}$$

Therefore adjusted contribution per unit = £3.354 + 1.364 − 1.32 = £3.398.

$$\text{B/E point} = \frac{£312.000}{£3.398/\text{unit}} = 91,800 \text{ units}$$

Although sales volume is forecast to increase by 50 per cent profit increase is only 12 per cent. This is due first to a reduction in contribution per unit of sales, and second to a rise in fixed costs. The inevitable consequence of these two changes is an increase in the break-even point.

(c) Production budget (units)

	Month 1		Month 2		Month 3	
Closing stock	19,500	$\left(\begin{array}{l}12{,}000 + \\ \frac{1}{2} \times 15{,}000\end{array}\right)$	20,500	$\left(\begin{array}{l}15{,}000 + \\ \frac{1}{2} \times 11{,}000\end{array}\right)$	17,000	$\left(\begin{array}{l}11{,}000 + \\ \frac{1}{2} \times 12{,}000\end{array}\right)$
+ Sales	10,000		12,000		15,000	
	29,500		32,500		32,000	
− Opening stock	16,000	$\left(\begin{array}{l}10{,}000 + \\ \frac{1}{2} \times 12{,}000\end{array}\right)$	19,500		20,500	
= Production	13,500		13,000		11,500	

17D (a) (i)

	£
Selling price	25.00
Variable cost	14.00
Contribution	11.00
Commission	1.40
Net contribution	9.60

Break-even = £85,056 ÷ 9.60 = 8,860 packs.

(ii)

	£
Contribution £11	
Fixed cost	85,056
Plus extra salary	14,989
Contribution required	100,045

Break-even = £100,045 ÷ 11 = 9,095 packs.

(iii) Margin of safety
 (i) 11,000 − 8,860 = 2,140

$$\frac{2{,}140}{11{,}000} \times \frac{100}{1} = 19.45\%.$$

(ii) 11,000 − 9,095 = 1,905

$$\frac{1{,}905}{11{,}000} \times \frac{100}{1} = 17.3\%.$$

(iv) Profit on budgeted sales: commission 11,000 × £9.60 − £85,056 = £20,544; salary 11,000 × £11 − £100,045 = £20,955.
   Salary alternative is to be preferred – it makes a greater profit at budgeted volume, but if budgeted volumes are not achieved, the commission basis is best since it has a lower break-even and greater MOS.

(b) Assumptions:
1.   Linearity of costs and revenues across the volume range.
2.   Sales-oriented – ignores stock changes.
3.   Unreal at extreme limits of volume range – relevant range.
4.   Cost behaviour static across volume range – stepped costs.
5.   Costs easily identifiable as fixed or variable – not so.
6.   Single product or constant mix.

17E   (a) The advantages would include the following:
1.   Avoids the necessity to allocate, apportion and absorb fixed overheads – doubtful logic of some apportionments.
2.   Contribution as a measure of performance removes doubts about the allocation of fixed overhead.
3.   Stocks are valued at direct cost and fixed costs are written off in the period during which they incurred – such costs are related to a time period. Thus the impact on profit of fluctuations in the volume of stock is reduced.
4.   Marginal costing shows more clearly the impact on profit of fluctuations in the volume of sales.

(b) Full absorption costing
Production overhead absorbed: £75,000 ÷ 20,000 = £3.75. Production costs: material £18, labour £9, variable overhead £6, and fixed overhead £3.75, totalling £36.75.

	January		February		March	
Sales (units)	20,000		22,000		20,000	
Production (units)	23,000		20,000		19,000	
	£	£	£	£	£	£
Sales		900,000		990,000		900,000
Opening stock	–		110,250		36,750	
Production cost	845,250		735,000		698,250	
	845,250		845,250		735,000	
Closing stock	110,250		36,750		–	
Cost of sales		735,000		808,500		735,000
Gross profit		165,000		181,500		165,000
Variable sales cost	45,000		49,500		45,000	
Fixed sales cost	45,000		45,000		45,000	
Fixed admin. cost	36,000	126,000	36,000	130,500	36,000	126,000
		39,000		51,000		39,000
Production overhead over-absorbed *		11,250		–		(3,750)
Net profit		50,250		51,000		35,250
* Absorbed cost 23,000 × £3-75		86,250				
		75,000				
		11,250				

Note:
Sales for January and March are the same but profit fluctuates because 3,000 extra units were produced in January, and £11,250 of over-absorbed fixed overhead was added back in January.

17F   (a) (i) Profit statement – marginal costing

		March £			April £
Sales: 1,500 at £35		52,500	3,000 × £35		105,000
Less: Variable cost of sales					
Opening stock	Nil		500 × £15	7,500	
Variable manufacturing cost 2,000 × £15	30,000		3,200 × £15	48,000	
				55,500	
Less: Closing stock 500 × £15	7,500		700 × £15	10,500	
	22,500			45,000	
Variable selling, distribution and administration 15% of sales	7,875			15,750	
Direct cost of sales		30,375			60,750
Contribution		22,125			44,250
Less: Fixed costs:					
Production	15,000			15,000	
Selling, distribution and administration	10,000	25,000		10,000	25,000
Profit/(loss)		(2,875)			19,250

(ii) Profit statement – absorption costing

		March £		April £
Sales: 1,500 at £35		52,500	3,000 × £35	105,000
Less: Cost of sales				
Opening stock	Nil		500 × £20	10,000
Production cost				
2,000 × £20	40,000		3,200 × £20	64,000
				74,000
Less: Closing stock 500 × £20				
	10,000		700 × £20	14,000
	30,000			60,000
Fixed production overhead				
under-absorbed	5,000		over-absorbed	(1,000)
Production cost of sales		35,000		59,000
Gross profit		17,500		46,000
Less: Variable selling,				
distribution and				
administration:				
15% of sales	7,875			15,750
Fixed selling, distribution				
and administration	10,000	17,875		10,000 25,750
(Loss)/Profit		(375)		20,250

(b) Reconciliation of profit statement

		March £		April £
Results using marginal	Loss	(2,875)	Profit	19,250
Fixed production overhead c/fwd				
in 500 units valued at full cost				
which included £5 fixed overhead		2,500	b/fwd	(2,500)
Fixed production overhead c/fwd				
in 700 units valued at full cost				
which included £5 fixed overhead				3,500
Results using absorption	Loss	(375)	Profit	20,250

(c) Whether to use an absorption or marginal costing system depends on the situation and accountant concerned. Management favours marginal costing in a decision-making environment, and for control purposes using contribution as an important criterion. SSAP 9 favours absorption costing when stocks are being valued for balance sheet purposes, because relevant fixed overheads should be included in valuations, and carried forward under the accrual convention.

17G   (a) The assumptions which underlie cost–volume–profit analysis are as follows:

1. That costs can be analysed into their fixed and variable elements, that there is no intermediate semi-variable classification. The analysis assumes that fixed and variable costs can be easily recognized, and that they will continue to behave as fixed or variable costs throughout the volume range.
2. That fixed costs will remain fixed whatever the volume of production achieved. This is a broad assumption that the fixed costs will be the same for a production quantity of one or, say, 50,000 units. This assumption is just not credible but if applied in the short run only or within the 'relevant range' then it may appear as feasible.
3. That selling prices will remain the same across the entire volume range. Clearly linearity cannot be assumed for selling prices because price must be reduced if extra sales are to be attracted; and even then the volume of extra sales in response to a price cut will depend upon the elasticity of demand.
4. That the analysis is for a single product or for a constant mix of products. It is difficult to analyse the cost–volume–profit relationship if the mixture of products sold changes at different parts of the volume range.

5. That conditions remain the same. C-v-p analysis assumes that prices and costs will remain constant and will not be affected by inflation whether at the same or different rates, and that there are no changes in productivity or other production economies.
6. That stocks remain the same at the beginning and end of the period. This analysis sets the cost of goods produced against sales revenue, but if stocks are built up or decreased, then the cost of goods sold would be different from the cost of goods produced.

(b) (i) Holiday home costs and income statement

Guests	Income p.a. £	Variable costs £	Fixed costs £	Total costs £	Profit (loss) £
6	18,000	7,740	16,000	23,740	(5,740)
7	21,000	9,030	16,000	25,030	(4,030)
8	24,000	10,320	16,000	24,320	(2,320)
9	27,000	11,610	16,000	27,610	(610)
10	30,000	12,900	16,000	28,900	1,100
11	33,000	14,190	22,000	36,190	(3,190)
12	36,000	15,480	22,000	37,480	(1,480)
13	39,000	16,770	22,000	38,770	230
14	42,000	18,060	22,000	40,060	1,940
15	45,000	19,350	22,000	41,350	3,650

There are two break-even points in this situation, neither for an exact number of guests. The home breaks even just after nine guests per week, for all weeks of the season. To be certain of avoiding a loss management should work to a minimum of ten guests a week. This is a tight margin since with over ten guests fixed costs rise, and occupancy must rise to thirteen per week before a profit is made.

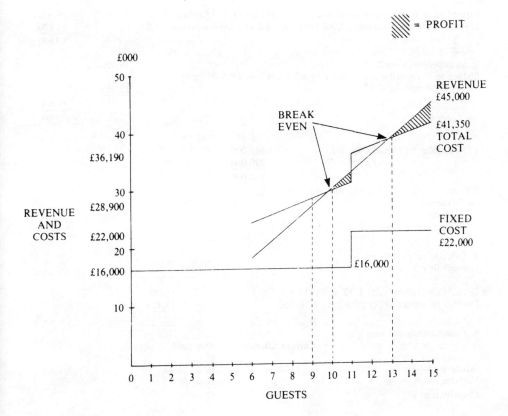

CHAPTER 18

18A   (a) Revised budget revenue account for HF Ltd, for the year ended 30 September (for workings see note 1)

	£	£
Sales (26,000) boxes)		740,000
Direct materials	296,400	
Direct labour	132,600	
Variable overhead	91,000	
Fixed overhead	138,200	658,200
Profit		81,800

Budgeted net assets employed in HF Ltd, as at 30 September

	£	£
Fixed assets (Net)		310,000
Working capital: Debtors (Note 2)	78,333	
Stocks	90,000	
	168,333	
Creditors	(40,000)	128,333
Net assets employed		438,333

(b) Difference in budgeted profit – Existing   65,800
                                    Proposed   81,800
                                                 +£16,000

Effect on profit of changes resulting from proposal:

Gains   £
Contribution earned on supermarket sales 8,000 boxes × £5 (Note 3)   40,000
Material quantity discounts 18,000 boxes × £0.6 or 20,000 boxes × £0.6   10,800
                                                                                  50,800

Losses
Extra supervisory staff   16,000
Reduction in contribution on existing sales 2,000 × £9.4 (Note 3)
(or 2,000 boxes × £10.00)   18,800

                                                                                  34,800
Net change   + 16,000

Notes
	£
1. Total sales will be 18,000 × £30	540,000
8,000 × £25	200,000
	740,000

All other variable costs multiplied by 26,000 boxes
i.e. Materials   × £11.40   (£12 minus 5%)
     Labour   ×   5.10
     Variable overhead   3.50
                        £20.00

2. Calculation of debtors
Current debtor period 1/12

	£
Debtors on existing sales 1/12 × £540,000	45,000
Debtors on supermarket sales 2/12 £200,000	33,333
	78,333

3. Contribution per unit

	Current situation	*Proposed*
	£	£ £
Selling price	30	30 or 25
Variable costs	20.60	20 or 20
Contribution	9.40	10 or 5

18B   Machine Hours Required:

P	3,000 × 1	=	3,000
Q	5,000 × 2	=	10,000
R	2,500 × 1	=	2,500
S	4,500 × 5	=	22,500
			38,000
Available			24,000
Shortfall			14,000

	Variable Cost	Buying in Price	Cost Increase if Bought	Machine hours saved per unit by buying	Cost per machine hour saved	Ranking for purchase
	£	£	£		£	
P	87	95	8	1	8	4
Q	70	75	5	2	2.5	2
R	71	65	−6	1	−6	1
S	145	175	30	5	6	3

The variable cost of R is higher than its purchase price, so it should be bought in. This strategy would save 2,500 machine hours. The cost of Q per machine hour saved is lower than that for the other two components, and thus Q should be the next component to buy in. This would save a further 10,000 hours. The remaining 1,500 machine hours should be saved by buying in 300 units of S.

	Required	Buy	Make	Machine hours	Cost	Budget Cost
					£	£
R	2,500	2,500			162,500	177,500
Q	5,000	5,000			375,000	350,000
S	4,500	300			52,500	652,500
S			4,200	21,000	609,000	
P	3,000		3,000	3,000	261,000	261,000
				24,000	1,460,000	1,441,000

Comments
1. Fixed overhead is apportioned to the components, but this cost should play no part in the decision since it will not change in total, whatever decision is taken.
2. R should be bought rather than made, even if sufficient machine time is available, because the buying price is less than the variable cost of production. Qualitative factors such as reasons of strategy might reverse this comment.
3. Actual Cost Exceeds Budget by £19,000 analysed as:

	(i)	Costs saved by buying R	2500 × £6 =	(15,000)
	(ii)	Costs increased by buying Q	5000 × £5 =	£25,000
		Costs increased by buying S	300 × £30 =	£9,000
				£19,000

18C   (a) Basic rules for closure decision – contribution is significant.
1. Cost behaviour in the context of closure – do certain costs change their classification?
2. Negative contribution – close unless improvement is foreseen.
3. Positive contribution – do not close: lose contribution to fixed costs.
4. Positive contribution – do close if can use resources to produce a greater contribution.
5. Ripple effect – effect of closure on other parts of the business.

(b) Cost statement rearranged on a contribution basis.

Shop	Beeston	Sherwood	Mansfield	Ashfield	Total
	£000	£000	£000	£000	£000
Sales	807	1,365	834	462	3,468
Cost of sales	453	672	504	288	1,917
Gross profit	354	693	330	174	1,551
Variable costs in context of closure:					
Shop salaries and admin	255	273	408	195	1,131
Contribution to factory overheads	99	420	(78)	(21)	420
Factory fixed costs					600
Profit/(loss)					(180)

Advice

If the three loss-making shops are closed a positive contribution of 99 will be lost and negative contributions of 99 will be avoided – the overall loss will remain the same.

Mansfield and Ashfield have negative contributions so if they are closed the remaining contribution is 519 and the loss is reduced to 81.

If Mansfield is closed and 15 per cent of its turnover transfers to Ashfield, the Ashfield contribution will increase by 15 per cent of Mansfield gross profit, i.e. 49.5, and Ashfield then shows a positive contribution of 28.5 so will remain open and the loss will be further reduced to 52.5. However, it is still a loss which can be avoided only if plans are made to increase turnover or cut costs.

18D   (a)

Products	P	Q	R	S
	£	£	£	£
Selling price per unti	68	90	91	94
Less: Marginal cost per unit	(56)	(74)	(76)	(76)
Contribution per unit	12	16	15	18
Contribution per limiting factor	6	4	–	3

R will be bought in because the purchase price (£72) is less than its marginal cost (£76)

Products	P	Q	R	S
Demand (units)	18,000	30,000	27,000	15,000
Machine hours/units	2	4	–	6
Total machining requirement	36,000	120,000	–	90,000
			=	246,000 hours

Current shortage of 246,000 – 210,000 = 36,000 hours; therefore firm should manufacture P, Q and S in that order.

	Production Quantity	Machine hours	Cumulative machine hours
P	18,000	36,000	36,000
Q	30,000	120,000	156,000
S	9,000	54,000	210,000
	57,000		

Leaving 6,000 units of S to be bought in at £82 per unit; therefore buy in all of product R, i.e. 27,000 units, and 6,000 units of S.

(b) *Income statement*

	Own manufacture			Bought in		Total
Product	P	Q	S	S	R	£000
	£000	£000	£000	£000	£000	
Sales	1,224	2,700	846	564	2,457	7,791
Less: Marginal cost or bought in cost	1,008	2,220	684	492	1,944	6,348
Contribution						1,443
Less: Fixed costs						(500)
Net profit						943

(c) Buy product R because its marginal cost is higher than its buy-in price.

Limiting factor – manufacture product which offers the highest contribution per limiting factor first, thereby increasing total profit.

18E   (a) *The qualitative factors influencing a make or buy decision*

If a component is made in the main factory, the producer can check to ensure that it is well made, but if it is subcontracted there is less immediate control over the standard of the output. The main manufacturer must assure itself that the components bought out maintain the desired quality, especially if the component has an exacting specification. Faulty components built into the main product can cause breakdowns after sale, thus adversely affecting the reputation of the main product, and increasing the cost of after-sales service. These costs cannot easily be quantified.

With bought-out components there is always the fear that the supplier will not meet the scheduled delivery dates. Factors outside the control of the main manufacturer such as a strike or machine breakdown at the subcontractor's factory can interrupt supplies and disrupt production schedules at the main factory. When a component is made in the main factory it is easier to improve quality control and co-ordinate production to usage, to avoid stock-outs, keep stocks to a minimum, and also utilize idle capacity.

There are strategic arguments against buying out components. If a company comes to depend on its suppliers they may be able to increase their price by negotiation for further orders; or the company could find itself cut off from supplies if a rival takes over the subcontractor, or offers more for the use of its production capacity. Production in the main factory facilitates the design and introduction of improvements to the component. Security is improved since there is no need to inform another company of plans for improvement to the product which might be passed on to rival producers.

If components are bought out, part of a skilled workforce may become redundant at the main producer's factory, and this could cause a fall in morale and perhaps even a strike. The company is more confident of its ability if it can demonstrate that it can provide components for itself; such a demonstration will keep other component suppliers 'on their toes' and may prevent them from attempting to take advantage of the main company when quoting for future orders. Management may wish to place the company in a position of self-sufficiency and growth, thus adopting a policy of not buying out components as a means to achieve this objective.

(b) The £18,000 of research and development cost is a 'sunk' cost and not relevant to the decision. The overtime premium is significant for the decision; it will be paid if the springs are made, so labour will cost £3 to make the springs and nothing if the springs are bought.

The bought-out price must be set against the variable cost. Material £6 + Labour £3 + Variable overhead £2 = £11. Therefore the company saves £1.50 on every spring it makes rather than buys.

Fixed factory overhead is not relevant to this decision since that cost will not change whichever way the decision goes.

18F   (a) Contribution per unit of key factor

	701	702	821	822	937
	£	£	£	£	£
Selling price	26.0	28.0	34.0	38.0	40.0
Less: Direct costs					
Direct materials	(5.6)	(4.0)	(11.2)	(10.4)	(12.0)
Direct wages	(5.0)	(4.0)	(7.5)	(5.5)	(7.0)
Variable production overhead	(2.0)	(1.6)	(3.0)	(2.2)	(2.8)
Variable selling overhead	(3.9)	(4.2)	(5.1)	(5.7)	(6.0)
Contribution	9.5	14.2	7.2	14.2	12.2

$\frac{\text{Contribution}}{\text{Key factor (materials)}}$	170%	355%	64%	136%	101%
Ranking	2	1	5	3	4

Allocation of materials:

Product	Units	Kg/unit	Kg	Cumulative
702	7,200	0.5	3,600	3.600
701	8,000	0.7	5,600	9,200
822	6,000	1.3	7,800*	17,000

*Balancing figure (17,000 kg − 9,200 kg = 7,800 kg: 7,800 ÷ 1.3 = 6,000 units).

(b) Contribution and profit

			£	£	£
Contribution:					
Product	702	7,200 × 14.2	102,240		
	701	8,000 × 9.5	76,000		
	822	6,000 × 14.2	85,200	263,440	
Fixed overhead:	702	7,200 × 2.4	17,280		
production	701	8,000 × 3.0	24,000		
	822	6,000 × 3.3	19,800	61,080	
				202,360	
Fixed overhead:					
selling (3 months × £300,000 p.a.)				75,000	
Net profit				127,360	

(c) The analysis employed the contribution/key factor method. Materials were the key factor, so the contribution related to the use of this scarce resource enabled products to be ranked in order of profitability. Other examples of business problems where this type of analysis can be useful include:
1. optimizing the use of labour;
2. optimizing the hours of machine time available;
3. maximizing the return from farmland when deciding which crops to grow.

18G (a) Estimated cost of contract for 400 components

		Unit cost	Total cost
	£	£	£
Materials:			
3 kg M1 at replacement cost of £5.5	16.50		6,600
2 kg P2 at replacement cost			
of P4, i.e. £3.60 =	£7.20		
Less: Further processing cost of			
currently held P2 (2 × £1.60)	£3.20	4.00	1,600
		20.50	8,200
Part no. 678 – direct cost		50.00	20,000
		70.50	28,200
Labour:			
5 hours' skilled at replacement cost of £4.00	20.00		8,000
5 hours' semi-skilled at £3.00	15.00		6,000
		35.00	14,000
Variable overhead – 4 machine hours at £7		28.00	11,200
Total variable costs		133.50	53,400
Add: Incremental fixed costs (£3,200 ÷ 400)		8.00	3,200
Total incremental costs		141.50	56,600
Profit		3.50	1,400
Suggested selling price		145.00	58,000

The contract for 400 components should be accepted. The offered price of £145 each is greater than the incremental costs of production. In no circumstances should the work be undertaken at a price of less than £141.50.

(b) Three factors which management should consider when taking this decision are:
1. The possibility of repeat orders: perhaps a successful conclusion to this contract would bring further work to JB Ltd. Will idle capacity be available to meet such extra orders in the future? Does JB wish to move into this class of work, and establish a reputation which will bring orders from other customers?
2. Behavioural considerations: if the contract is accepted it will provide considerable employment for the labour force – 4,000 hours are required. A full order book will improve morale.
3. Costs: replacement costs for materials and wages have been used in this cost estimate, but when a cost statement is drafted to account for this job traditional methods will be employed. Therefore it is to be expected that some costs will be charged against the contract at less than replacement cost, and that the eventual profit disclosed will be greater than £1,400.

CHAPTER 19

19A

Capital allowances		Standard	De-luxe
		£	£
Cost		50,000	88,000
Year 1	25%	12,500	22,000
		37,500	66,000
Year 2	25%	9,375	16,500
		28,125	49,500
Year 3	25%	7,031	12,375
Year 4	Balancing allowance	21,094	37,125
	25%		9,281
			27,844
Year 5			6,961
Year 6	Balancing allowance		20,883

Tax paid – Standard machine

Year	1	2	3	4	5
	£	£	£	£	£
Cash flow	20,500	22,860	24,210	23,410	
Less: Capital allowances	12,500	9,375	7,031	21,094	
Taxable profit	8,000	13,485	17,179	2,316	
Corporation tax at 35%	2,800	4,720	6,013	810	
Paid		2,800	4,720	6,013	810

Tax paid – De-luxe machine

Year	1	2	3	4	5	6	7
	£	£	£	£	£	£	£
Cash flow	32,030	26,110	25,380	25,940	38,560	35,100	
Less: Capital allowances	22,000	16,500	12,375	9,281	6,961	20,883	
Taxable profit	10,030	9,610	13,005	16,659	31,599	14,217	
Corporation tax at 35%	3,510	3,363	4,552	5,831	11,060	4,976	
Paid		3,510	3,363	4,552	5,831	11,060	4,976

Standard machine
NPV Calculation – outflows in brackets:

Year	Capital expenditure	Cash flow	Tax paid	Working capital	Net cash flow	Discount at 12%	
	£	£	£	£	£		£
0	(50,000)	–	–	–	(50,000)	–	(50,000)
1	–	20,500	–	(10,000)	10,500	0.892	9,366
2	–	22,860	(2,800)	–	20,060	0.797	15,988
3	–	24,210	(4,720)	–	19,490	0.712	13,877
4	–	23,410	(6,013)	–	17,397	0.636	11,064
5	–	–	(810)	10,000	9,190	0.567	5,211
NPV positive							5,506

Payback: Net cash flow up to year 3 = (£10,500 + £20,060 + £19,490) = £50,050: therefore payback in three years.

De-luxe machine
NPV Calculation – outflows in brackets

Year	Capital expenditure £	Cash flow £	Tax paid £	Working capital £	Net Cash flow £	Discount at 14%	£
0	(88,000)	–	–	–	(88,000)	–	(88,000)
1	–	32,030	–	(10,000)	22,030	0.877	19,320
2	–	26,110	(3,510)	–	22,600	0.769	17,379
3	–	25,380	(3,363)	–	22,017	0.675	14,861
4	–	25,940	(4,552)	–	21,388	0.592	12,662
5	–	38,560	(5,831)	–	32,729	0.519	16,986
6	–	35,100	(11,060)	–	24,040	0.456	10,962
7	–		(4,976)	10,000	5,024	0.400	2,010
NPV positive							6,180

Payback: Net cash flow up to year 4 (£22,030 + £22,600 + £22,017 + £21,388) = £88,035; therefore payback in four years.

Conclusion
NPV method shows the de-luxe machine as the better investment, payback prefers the standard machine. This demonstrates the disadvantages of the payback, which is biased against good long-term projects with healthy cash flows in later years. The difference is small so qualitative factors are significant.

19B (a) The cost of equity capital is the return which must be earned on that capital (whether distributed or not) in order to satisfy shareholders and maintain the price in the market of the shares. The cost of equity capital covers not only dividend income paid out to shareholders but also the growth factor derived from retained profits. The return required to maintain demand for a company's shares will depend upon general factors which affect the whole market for equities and specific factors which affect demand for the shares of a particular company. The cost of equity capital can be determined by the application of the dividend growth model to share capital. Retained profits will require a similar cost of capital to that of share capital.

(b) The dividend growth model when applied to these circumstances is

$$K = D/P \times 100 + G$$
$$= 0.10/1.20 \times 100 + 7$$
$$= 15.33\%.$$

(c) The dividend growth model assumes that:
1. The expected growth will take place, and that growth will continue into the future at that rate.
2. Dividends in future will be at the same rate as for the current year.
3. The share price in the market will increase in proportion with the growth in earnings.
   While the dividend growth model is a useful guide, these assumptions increase the uncertainty attached to the result. Capital budgeting rests on a number of estimates and the dividend growth model merely injects a further set of estimates into the calculation.

Index